The Beauty of Kinbaku

(Or everything you ever wanted to know about Japanese erotic bondage when you suddenly realized you didn't speak Japanese.)

Master "K"

**Second Edition
Completely Revised and Updated**

King Cat Ink
New York, USA

Suirensha
Tokyo, Japan

First published in 2008,
revised & updated
second edition, 2015.
Japanese language
Edtition, 2013.

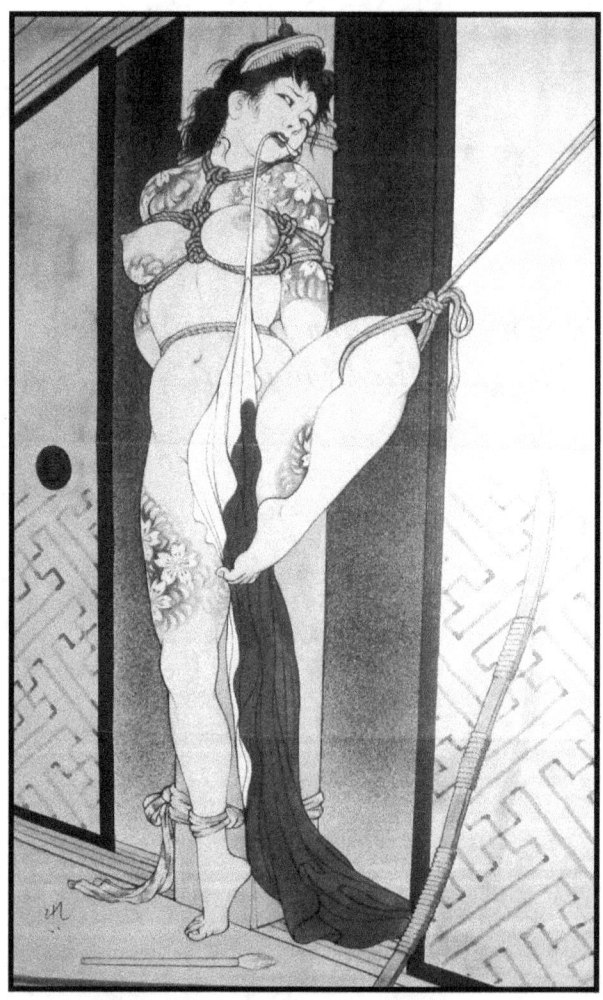

Illustration by Minomura Kou, AKA Kita Reiko
SM Kitan, December 1975

ISBN-13: 978-0692344651

Table of Contents

Acknowledgements

The author would like to thank the following for their invaluable help in the creation of this second English edition of "The Beauty of Kinbaku":

In Japan:

M. K., friend of my student years in Japan and beyond, whose remarkable generosity has added many treasures to the archive and whose passionate interest and yearly trips to Tokyo have allowed the author to always stay vicariously current on matters Kinbaku.

Alice Liddell, correspondent, friend and colleague, whose efforts and numerous kindnesses have made this book at least fifty percent better than it might have been.

U. Nonaka and R. Nakahara, directors of Fuuzoku Shiryoukan (The SM Library), Tokyo and their staff for their many kindnesses, for valuable correspondence on the subject of Kitan Club magazine and all the magazines of the "SM golden era" and for permission to reprint several illustrations from the rare historical texts held in the library's collection.

K. Taira, founder of Fuuzoku Shiryoukan, for his wise insights into Edo and Meiji Era art and artists.

Gold View Co., Ltd, film distributors, for permission to screen and reprint stills from "Bakushi" and "I am an SM writer," including the "Bakushi" poster and the portraits of Arisue Go, Yukimura Haruki and Saotome Hiromi.

The late Nureki Chimuo sensei, for his kindness in granting an interview to discuss the history of modern Kinbaku in 2007 and for his generous and flattering comments about the first edition of this book which led to an unforgetable meeting in 2010.

Miyabi Kyodo, friend and artist, for answering seemingly endless questions about his art and his teacher Minomura Kou (AKA Kita Reiko) and for permission to reprint one of his own beautiful works.

Osada Steve, for his years of friendship, advice and grammatical concerns and for permission to publish his own portrait and those of Osada Eikichi and Nureki Chimuo.

Yukimura Haruki (the author's sensei) for his friendship, his kind comments on the first edition of this book and his many insights into the history of his art which have contributed so much to this second edition.

Urado Hiroshi (the author's sensei) for his friendship, his gracious comments on the first edition of this book and for the many hours of discussion we subsequently shared about movies in general and the many famous Nikkatsu studio films he worked on in particular. Also, thanks are due him for his remarkable kindness in introducing the author to the publisher of the 2013 Japanese edition of this book.

Takahashi Masato, president of Suirensha publishing, distinguished academic publisher of the Japanese edition of "The Beauty of Kinbaku" (2013), for his many kindnesses and helpful and creative suggestions that made that edition and, by extension, this second English edition better books. Special thanks for his kind permission to use several photographs from the Japanese edition.

Yamamoto Norio, brilliant translator of the Japanese edition of this book, for his rigorous fact checking and attention to the proper spelling of Japanese names in romaji.

Matsumoto Yutaka, former president and chief executive officer of Sanwa publishing, for his friendship, his gracious support of the Japanese edition of this book, his valuable insights into the world of Japanese publishing and for the unforgettable experience of arranging a meeting with Kuroiwa Akiko, widow of the late Dan Oniroku.

In the United States:

My friend Takashi for his fine insights into Kinbaku, for facilitating communication with Miyabi Kyodo and for his numerous expert translations of material the author was too swamped to do.

Los Angeles celebrity photographer Michael Helms (www.michealhelms.com) for his tremendous generosity in granting permission to publish photographs (for which he holds the exclusive copyright) that he took at several professional engagements we both participated in during 2015.

DNE Photography for permission to publish several photos of my Kinbaku to be found in the Gallery section of this edition for which he holds the exclusive copyright.

Erotic Exposures for permission to publish several photos of my Kinbaku to be found in the Gallery section of this edition for which he holds the exclusive copyright.

Liquiderotica for permission to publish one photograph of my Kinbaku in the Gallery section of this edition for which he holds the exclusive copyright.

My student Zetsu for permission to reprint several photos of my Kinbaku in the Gallery section of this second edition for which he holds the exclusive copyright.

My student Yzen for his generous assistance in producing several photographs of my Kinbaku exclusively for this edition.

My former assistant Faviola Llervu for her translation of several source materials used in the writing of the first English edition of this book.

And finally, my sincere thanks to my numerous students for all their support and many searching questions over the years.

Introduction

If, on the publication of the first edition of this book in 2008, a friend had told me that it would go through three printings, sell thousands of copies to readers in over 60 countries all over the world, be translated into Japanese (in 2013), be embraced by the Japanese Kinbaku world as well as reviewers and general readers in Japan, go into a second printing there in less than 3 months, and that I would then be asked to introduce a second, updated, expanded and revised English edition, I'd certainly have shaken my head in wonder. It is, therefore, with a profound sense of gratitude to everyone who has found value in my work that I write these few lines of introduction to this second edition of "The Beauty of Kinbaku."

When I was in Tokyo publicizing the Japanese edition I was often asked how it came to be that a Westerner could write a book about so Japanese a topic. At first I was bewildered and even a bit embarrassed by this question. While I was flattered that my work was being appreciated in the country of Kinbaku, I was also a bit nonplussed that some readers where surprised that I would (or could) do it at all! However, I then realized that my answer to them might lie in the very objectivity of my situation.

Perhaps, like a film director working in an exciting foreign country who has the opportunity to see a different culture with an unfamiliar eye and, therefore, is able to discern certain truths and patterns about a world not his or her own, I had the same kind of objectivity (and the great desire) to study and understand the complete world of Kinbaku, what it is and where it came from, and then to write about it not just as an erotic art but also as something unique to Japanese culture and identity; a view that takes in its historical, cultural and aesthetic roots as well.

In addition, I realized that out of sheer good fortune, my interest and study of Kinbaku (which began over 40 years ago) coincided with the beginnings of and then the continuing rise in public interest in the subject and I was able to not only have access to important early published materials but also to meet and talk to many of the great early practitioners of the art; men like Nureki Chimuo, Yukimura Haruki and Urado Hirochi.

As with the first edition, this book seeks to entertain and also be useful by answering those questions, solving those riddles and addressing those mysteries that have perplexed the non Japanese speaking Western enthusiast of Kinbaku (also known as Shibari) over the years. In this the author hopes to de-mystify and clarify but not diminish this most intriguing of Japanese erotic arts.

Four years were spent rigorously researching and writing the first edition and more time has been spent updating this one. Museums have been visited and re-visited, numerous historical and modern works have been translated and respected authorities contacted in an effort to verify every statement made herein. It's been an exciting experience and even after forty years of studying Japan and Kinbaku, I'm delighted to find that there's always something new to learn. Of course, mistakes do occur and I take full responsibility for any errors and/or omissions.

Who is this volume for? Well, it's certainly not for everyone. If the thought of any sadomasochistic practice as part of a loving relationship is repellent to you then you've picked up the wrong book. Likewise, if causing pain is your thing then you'll also likely be disappointed since Shibari/Kinbaku can and should be one of the most loving and sensual of SM experiences.

However, anyone who has been struck by the beauty of a Shibari image, thrilled to the concept of binding a lover or of being bound oneself (vincilagnia) or been curious as to how such a unique, exotic, dramatic and beautiful form of bondage art could develop as part of the history and culture of Japan will, I hope, find some value here. And the book's amusing subtitle is meant only *somewhat* in jest. Japanese is one of the hardest of languages for the Westerner to learn and this can become an almost insurmountable barrier to understanding if the subject under scrutiny is unusual and complex, as is certainly the case here.

This work is divided into seven chapters: the world of Kinbaku; thirty key figures in Shibari/Kinbaku history; a gallery of photographs; a glossary of Shibari terms; a "how to tie" section; an afterword and, finally, an extensive bibliography and index.

It should be noted that all names used are presented in the traditional Japanese manner; that is the last (or family) name is given first, i.e. Smith, John. In addition, the names of famous Shibari/Kinbaku artists, their art works and techniques and other Japanese historical figures and personalities mentioned in this book use the spellings most commonly seen in the West. This is because the vagaries of romaji (the 19th century writing system that transfers the traditional pictographs of Japanese kanji into the Latin alphabet) have caused many variations in the spelling of these names over the years and I have seen even so famous a name as Itoh Seiu spelled: Ito Seiu, Itoh Seiyu and Itoh Su. My only recourse to this problem is to use the spellings that I have encountered the most in my researches, even though they come from both older and newer romaji systems.

In this book I discuss many of the famous Japanese "rope masters" of history and today. The term "rope master" can be translated as "Kinbakushi" or "nawashi" or "bakushi" or "seme-shi" and several other variants. Simply out of personal preference and convenience, I have chosen to use the term "bakushi" when referring to master rope artists.

Throughout the course of this book, usually at the end of each section, the reader will see questions printed in **bold** type followed by an answer. These are actual questions chosen from the hundreds I've been asked since the publication of my first book ("Shibari, the Art of Japanese Bondage"-Glitter/Secret Press, 2004) and they run the gamut from the very sophisticated, **"How did a Japanese martial art become an erotic art?"** to the amusing, **"Wasn't Shibari invented in 1972 by two California dudes working in the porn biz?"**

Finally, in addition to discussing the numerous historical and technical aspects of Japanese style erotic bondage; this book hopes to address two basic questions: "Is Shibari/Kinbaku an art? And "What is the beauty of Kinbaku?"

Questions:

"What is the difference between the words Shibari and Kinbaku?"

The terms Shibari and Kinbaku are virtually synonymous and both have been used in Japan for many years. However, Shibari (the older term) generally means "to bind" or "to tie" whereas Kinbaku (a more modern word coined in the early 1950s) means to "bind tightly" or to "bind in a sexual context." The word "Kinbaku" also carries the added meaning of being the art of traditional Japanese erotic bondage. That is, Shibari done in the traditional or historical manner for an aesthetic and/or erotic effect. (Author's note: In this book these words will be used interchangeably.)

"Wasn't Shibari invented in 1972 by two California dudes working in the porn biz?"

No.

The World of Kinbaku
Spirituality, History and Commerce

What is Shibari/Kinbaku? Briefly put, it is the technique of safe, sensual, dramatic and erotic bondage that's been raised to an art form in Japan. As a Shibari/Kinbaku teacher and practitioner for over forty years, I've been amazed at the recent surge in popularity in the West for this most Japanese of subjects. Certainly, the current popularity for all things Japanese in the United States and on the Internet are two of the main causes for this as Shibari images now routinely pass through the ether and all across the globe. This is both a positive thing, in that most cultural exchanges are positive, and also something of a dilemma since, as might be expected with a subject grounded in a language so foreign to most English speakers as Japanese, many confusions and misunderstandings occur and the context for these images is often missing.

When a Westerner first encounters a Shibari/Kinbaku image they usually note with surprise its erotic power and the complexity of the rope design. They might be stimulated or disturbed but they're usually not bored. This is certainly understandable due to the dramatic nature of these pictures and especially true of an art that most Westerners see solely in terms of European or American sadomasochistic (SM) practices. There it is an interest that can be viewed, despite the increasing tolerance in the West for divergent sexual orientations and the fact that upwards of 15% of the population professes some interest in SM, as strange and unusual. However, this reaction is also rather unfortunate because it is so limiting. How limiting? Well, it might surprise the reader to learn that the historical origins and uses of Shibari/Kinbaku run the gamut from centuries old martial arts to modern manga (Japanese comics), from 18th century judicial punishments to 19th century theatrical presentations and from sophisticated love making techniques, dating back 1500 years, to famous works of Ukiyo-e (woodblock print) art, modern advertising and pornography; a very wide range of activities, indeed.

How did this occur and why did it happen in Japan? These questions might seem difficult to answer but the truth has always been out there in that country's fading manuscripts, oral histories, yellowing photographs and modern works that record the fascinating history, both worldly and spiritual, of its people. One simply has to learn to look in the right places.

Tying the knot, the practical and sacred bonds of Japan

A Japanese friend of mine recently said to me that, "Tying for the Japanese people comes almost as naturally as breathing." By this he meant that the Japanese have a special affinity for an activity that is grounded so deeply in their culture and everyday lives. For instance, most Westerners appreciate how beautiful and intricate the wrappings of Japanese gift packages are and how lovely the kimono is, with its obi tied gracefully across the wearer's middle and how dramatic samurai armor appears, every protective element of which is tied on to the warrior's body. Remarkable to Western eyes, these sights are fairly common for the Japanese; as is another interesting and artful tradition, the practice of ceremonial tying called **Mizuhiki.**

Mizuhiki is actually the name for strong thin twine that is used to

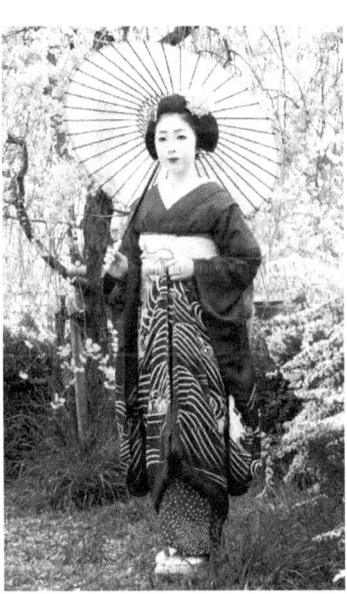
Kimono with obi

decorate envelopes made of **washi**, traditional Japanese paper. In Japanese society these envelopes are presented to friends, acquaintances and business associates to convey good wishes and/or to express thanks, gratitude and condolence. The knots used to tie the envelopes carry such evocative names as the chrysanthemum flower tie or the plum tie and look every bit as beautiful as the names imply.

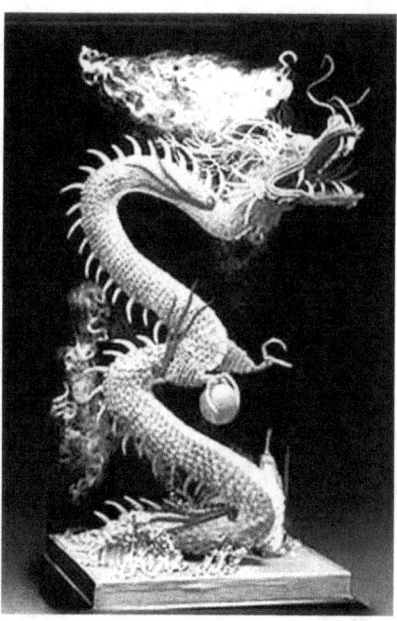

Mizuhiki dragon

The history of Mizuhiki dates back to the Heian Era of Japan (794-1185) when ladies of the court learned intricate knot tying to decorate gifts and letters. Specific knots communicated the identity of the sender and even expressed the sender's feelings much in the same way that the "language of flowers" did in Europe's Middle Ages; the tradition that gave us such symbolism as the red rose conveying the idea of "passionate" love. During the Edo Era (1603-1868) this twine was used to tie up the hair of samurai into their fashionable and distinctive "top knot," an identifying symbol of status for that fiercely proud warrior class. Today Mizuhiki art is often seen at wedding ceremonies where the table decorations and other ornaments, kimonos, the wedding dress and even the bride's hair clip, are either adorned by or created with it. Most spectacularly, Mizuhiki is used by fine artists to create delicate, celebratory sculptures of paper in the form of "auspicious" animals such as the crane, turtle or the mythical dragon.

However, such well known examples as these are just the tip of the iceberg for a culture where tying and the use of rope for significant, even religious, activities has been an integral part of life for centuries. This is the first important reason why Shibari/Kinbaku must be looked at quite differently than Western bondage. It is part of an artistic aesthetic that has many deep historical, religious and cultural resonances rather than just a means of restraint and while it isn't the intent of this book to be a sociological or anthropological study, a few more examples of these close connections between tying and the Japanese culture might be useful.

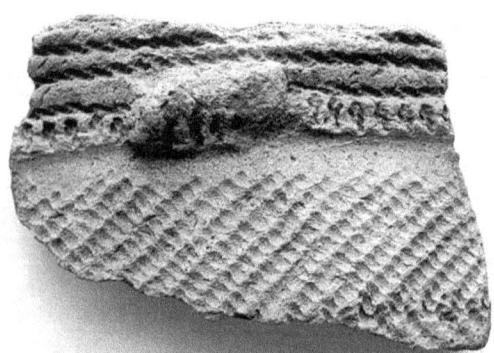

Jomon pottery with twisted cord design, circa 5000 BC

Where does the oldest pottery in the world come from? It comes from Japan and is a product of the Jomon culture, Japan's oldest known historical era dating back, at least, 13,000 years. Of interest to us is the fact that Jomon means "twisted cord" and this is the distinguishing decorative characteristic of its ancient pottery. The Jomon people were hunter-gatherers but they used twisted cords to decorate their day to day pottery and, more significantly, their religious vessels.

Around 300 BC rice cultivation began in Japan, probably imported through China or Korea. As is well known, rice is Japan's most important crop and has been cultivated by the Japanese for over 2000 years. Its fundamental importance to the country and its culture is reflected in the facts that rice was once used as a currency and that the Japanese word for cooked rice (**gohan**) has also the general meaning of "a meal." In short, rice is essential to life and sacred to the Japanese.

To give thanks for the successful harvest of so important a crop as rice would be a natural expression of the people growing it. This is a fundamental aspect of Japan's oldest religion Shinto and artful tying has a place here, too.

Shinto, literally "The Way of the Gods," is Japan's indigenous folk religion and can be traced back to, at least, the end of the Jomon period (300 BC). It is a pantheistic, ancestor and nature worshipping belief system. Shin, also known as Kami, is the generic term for the gods, goddesses, divine spirits, and various demonic and semi-benevolent nature spirits that are worshiped, prayed to, celebrated and/or feared in Shinto. The second character, To, means road, path or way. Over 109 million Japanese currently practice some form of Shintoism.

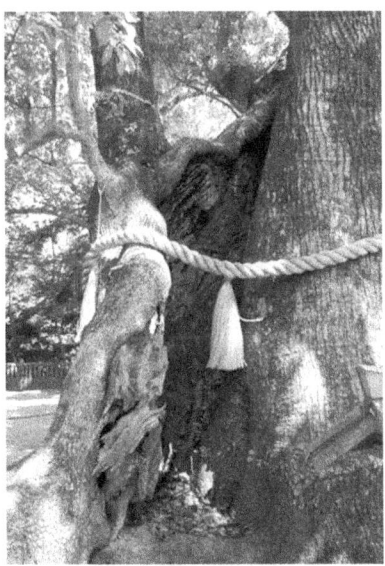

Shimenawa denoting a sacred space

Kami inhabit the water, rocks, trees, grass and other natural objects and places. These various objects and places are not symbols of the gods and spirits; rather they are the abodes in which they reside and are venerated as such by the Shinto worshiper. Of importance to us is that the abode of the Kami is considered sacred and is usually encircled with a **shimenawa** (a rope festooned with sacred white papers) that creates a sacred space that is itself venerated. It should also be noted that while these days most people use cotton, nylon or hemp cord, originally rope in ancient Japan was made from rice straw, thus making the reason for giving thanks even more obvious and the worship even more pointed. Shimenawa are most commonly found on the **torii** (the ceremonial gateways) of Shinto shrines and also on other sacred objects, such as trees, rocks and other revered structures.

Other important connections between the Shinto religion, its shrines and sacred rope or tying include the **chino-wa**, a rope ring used for cleansing ceremonies in spring, autumn and at the New Year, **kadomatsu**, a specially tied stand of bamboo or pine placed near the entrance of the home to welcome the New Year and **hinawa**, a thin cord lit at a shrine and then brought back to the home so that all who live there might continue to enjoy a good harvest and prosperity the whole year round.

Japan's famous **Sumo wrestling** began as a Shinto ritual to pray for a bountiful harvest. Introduced into ceremonies of the Imperial Court sometime in the Nara Era (eighth century), Sumo wrestling, the national sport of Japan, is mentioned in one of the country's first written histories, the Kojiki, which dates from A.D. 712. Most modern-day Sumo traditions were developed under the patronage of the court and in the Edo Era (1603-1868) professional Sumo groups were organized to entertain the rapidly expanding merchant class. Simply put, it is one of Japan's most idiosyncratic and important sports.

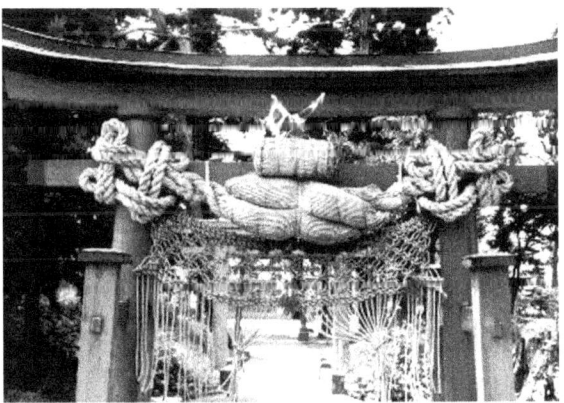

Shimenawa marking the gate (torii) of a Shinto shrine

Of interest to us is that the Sumo wrestler's ceremonial belt or loincloth (the **mawashi**) is decorated with rope to look identical to the shimenawa that creates the sacred spaces of Shinto. Wearing this belt the Sumo wrestler performs **shiko** (stomping on the floor of the wrestling space with first the right and then the left leg) to purge any bad

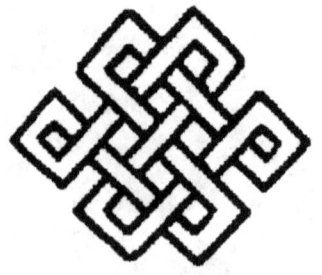

Endless knot

spirits hidden underground and to encourage positive Kami to appear.

Japan's second great religion, Buddhism, arrived in Japan in AD 538 from Korea and today is practiced by over 96 million people. Called Bukkyō in Japanese, Buddhism is a philosophical system of rigorous mental and physical practice that attempts to end all suffering by adherence to strict ethical and spiritual guidelines. It offers a moral code based on compassion and non-violence and, through meditation, a way to achieve spiritual insight. It was founded in northeastern India 2500 years ago and is based on the teachings of Siddhartha Gautama, who is known as the Buddha.

Many Japanese practice Shintoism and Buddhism concurrently. The explanation for this duality is characteristic of the Japanese people's tolerant attitudes toward religion where having a mix of various religions in one's daily life is common. Consequently, Shintoism and Buddhism have flourished together (sharing deities and sacred grounds) for most of Japan's recorded history.

While Shintoism has many sacred uses of rope, Buddhism, originally from India, has fewer. However, those it does have are significant. For instance, there is the "endless knot" of Buddhism.

This intriguing design is one of the eight auspicious symbols of Buddhism and symbolizes the intertwining of wisdom and compassion, the perfection of knowledge.

There are many divinities worshipped in Japanese Buddhism, almost all originating in India and often represented in its spiritual artworks. One is **Fudō Myō-Ō**, the central deity of the Myō-Ō (Kings of Light), of the esoteric *Shingon* sect of Japanese Buddhism. Esoteric Buddhism emphasizes the use of magic to control supernatural forces in order to reach spiritual enlightenment. In art, Fudō Myō-Ō is usually depicted with a devil-subduing sword in his right hand (representing wisdom cutting through ignorance) and a rope in his left hand (to catch and bind up demons and/or the opponents of Buddhism). He often has a third eye in his forehead (all-seeing) and is usually pictured seated or standing on a rock (because Fudo is "immovable" in his faith).

Then there is Jizō, one of the most loved of all Japanese Buddhist divinities. Usually depicted as a monk, he is traditionally seen as the guardian of children and the protective deity of travelers and firefighters. Roadside statues of Jizō are a common sight all over Japan. Of special interest is the famous "Bound Jizō" dating from the Edo era.

This particular statue became known as the "Bound Jizō" because of a remarkable criminal case. As the story goes, the famous judge Ōoka Tadasuke was called upon to discover the thief of a cartload of cloth stolen from a kimono maker who had fallen asleep next to the statue. Amazingly, Ōoka ordered the statue to be arrested, bound and brought

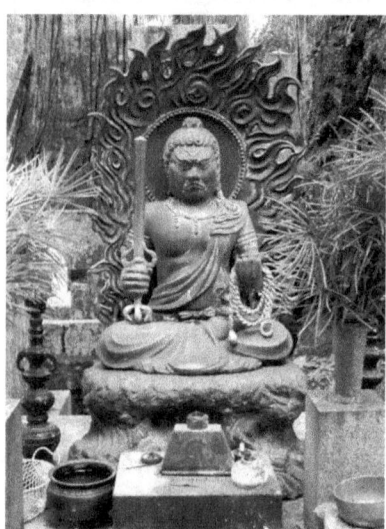

Fudō Myō-Ō

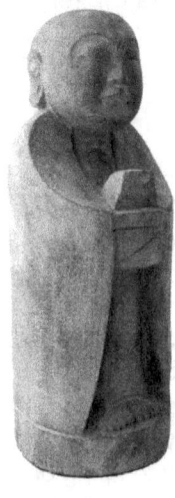

Jizō

to court for dereliction of its custodial duty to travelers! When the local population heard this they came from all over to see this odd form of jurisprudence and when the tied statue arrived in court the spectators burst into laughter. Appalled by this breach of court etiquette, Ōoka sternly ordered each spectator to be punished with a token fine-a small swatch of cloth. When they all paid their fines, the robbed kimono maker identified a piece of cloth from one spectator as identical to that stolen in the crime. That spectator, who was the actual thief, was then arrested, and Ōoka ordered the Jizō statue released as having discharged his duty. Ōoka was a clever judge.

In 1925, the statue was removed from downtown Tokyo to the little Narihira Santosen Temple on its outskirts where it still stands. There, tradition dictates that petitioners for aid (including victims of theft) visiting this Jizō tie a rope (sold by the temple for 100 Yen) around the statue. When their wish is granted, the petitioner unties the rope. So popular is this practice that the statue is worn almost smooth because of over 200 years of binding.

Along with the transmission of Buddhism, the famous Sanskrit sexual text, the Kama sutra, was also introduced from India into Japan in the sixth century AD.

The version of the Kama Sutra traditionally practiced in Japan is usually referred to as the "Forty-eight sexual positions" (**Shijuhatte**). The origin of this famous manual of love making can easily be traced back to Hindu India where the Kama Sutra was compiled around 300 AD. The Forty-eight sexual positions in the Shijuhatte seem to have derived from the Chinese interpretations of the Kama Sutra and not directly from the original Indian text. In the process of transferring from one country to another some positions in the Kama Sutra may have been dropped and replaced by those more specifically Japanese.

Of special interest to the student of Shibari/Kinbaku is that four techniques from the Shijuhatte specifically utilize rope (or the cords from the kimono) in their realization. These are the **Rihishirazu, Kubihiki Renbo, Yabusame** and **Daruma Kaeshi** positions. These couplings appear unique to the Japanese version of the Kama Sutra and freely incorporate elements of bondage in sexual play between consenting adults. The Daruma Kaeshi especially, where one partner's ankles and thighs are tied together, bears a striking resemblance to a common Kinbaku technique for binding the legs (**Futomomo shibari**).

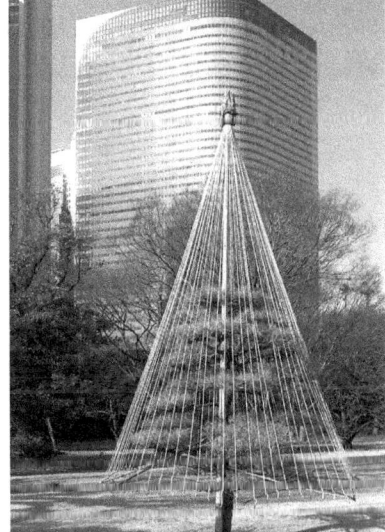

Other examples from history and daily life that show the close connection between artful tying and the Japanese are numerous and various. For instance, the elegant way some trees are bound in order to protect them in winter (**yukitsuri**) or even the way barrels of sake are wrapped for shipping. A visit to my favorite Japanese restaurant recently revealed three casks used as decoration. Each cask was beautifully wrapped and tied in such complex and distinctive patterns that they would even stand comparison with Buddhism's "endless knot." There are many more examples. However, I think the diversity of the above makes the point.

Yukitsuri-protecting trees for winter

And if the Western reader is surprised by how sexual tying (bondage), an activity that can sometimes carry a regrettable negative connotation in the West, and spirituality have been combined and accommodated by the Japanese, it should be remembered that the Japanese culture is very different in sexual orientation from any Western society based on Judeo-Christian beliefs. To quote the Kinsey Institute's four volume "International Encyclopedia of Sexuality" (1997-2001), Robert Francoeur Ph.D.

and Raymond J. Noonan Ph.D., general editors: "The Shinto religion recognizes neither good nor evil, so the concept of sin and personal guilt so commonly associated with sex in Western cultures does not exist in the Japanese tradition. . . . Nor does Shinto or the many forms of Japanese Buddhism have the notion of original sin. Neither religion has a single Deity who acts as Law-Giver and Eternal Judge of human wrongdoing. Japan lacks—and has lacked throughout its history—an organized, hierarchical, and centralized church for which sexuality is thought to be a sure path to damnation. In many ways, modern Japan retains—and *aestheticisizes* (italics mine)—an open 'peasant frankness about things sexual.' This is not to say that Japan is a peasant society—it is nothing of the sort. Instead, Japan is the only major industrialized nation that has *not* demonized sexuality under the rubrics of sin, danger, and pollution."

Now, does this mean that the Japanese bakushi (rope artist) or SM stage performer is thinking about or is even aware of these spiritual and cultural connections when they strive to entertain their audiences of jaded "salary men" or create their erotic imagery? It almost certainly does not. However, the distant resonances are there and it is surprising how often many of the greatest Shibari/Kinbaku artists and performers over the years, people like the late, legendary Akechi Denki sensei and the still active Yukimura Haruki and Arisue Go refer to a "spiritual connection" when they talk about their partners and their art. Arisue Go was particularly eloquent on this subject in a 1997 essay in his book "Jissen Kinbaku: Shibari kata Kyoshitsu" where he called Kinbaku a uniquely Japanese form of "aesthetic eroticism."

And for those of us not using Shibari in a commercial way but who only strive to give pleasure and express gratitude and affection to a beloved partner through the techniques of Kinbaku, is the adjective "spiritual" really that inappropriate? Frankly, as a definition for the private areas where such love, art and mutual trust are contained and expressed, the phrase "sacred space" seems more than fitting.

History and the origins of Kinbaku

When a Westerner looks at authentic Shibari/Kinbaku for the first time, their first question is often, "How did such a complicated style of tying come into being?" Put another way, how did so erotic a method of sexual bondage, where a hemp/jute rope molds and sculpts the human body so exquisitely so as to create art and, ideally, give such pleasure to the participants ever evolve? Is it a product of the unfathomable, enchanted East with its supposedly mysterious and ancient sexual secrets or . . . is it more mundane and understandable than this?

The simple answer is that the history of Shibari/Kinbaku is a reflection of the history and culture of Japan. Its centuries of isolation from the rest of the world, its often violent feudal past as well as its artistic sophistication all played a part. In the previous section we've explored some of the connections between Japanese society, religion and various unusual and meaningful styles of tying. We've looked at the different types of symbolism that rope can convey as well as some of the intricate patterns it can make. It's now time to explore the brutal realities of history in two further precursors to modern Shibari/Kinbaku, hojojutsu and the "official punishments."

Hojojutsu, the capturing and tying martial art

The early history of Japan is, as with many countries, a history of warfare. Towards the end of the 15th century, after years of intermittent struggle between powerful families, conflicts between clans erupted into civil war. These hundred years of conflict, spanning the Onin war (1467-1477) and the "Sengoku jidai" or "warring states period" (1492-1560) are noted for their brutality as various factions vied with one another to control Japan. At such a time the martial arts flourish and it is here that we begin to see a distinctive Japanese approach to the capture and restraint of prisoners, the evolution of hojojutsu.

Hojōjutsu (sometimes called **Nawajutsu**) is the traditional Japanese martial art of restraining an opponent using cord or rope. It is thought that hojojutsu was once one of the 18 vital fighting skills taught to Japanese warriors. In combat it was not uncommon for a samurai to carry a rope for attack, defense, for use as a tool or as a restraint for prisoners of war. Originally encompassing many different materials, techniques and methods from the earliest martial arts schools (ryu), hojojutsu is a quintessentially Japanese combat art and a unique product of Japanese history and culture.

Shimuza Takaji demonstrating a hojojutsu tie from the famed Ittatsu-ryu, circa 1960

Although Japan's often violent history has made the study of feudal armor and weapons such as the bow and the samurai sword (along with the techniques for their use) fairly straightforward, the exact origins of the formal, studied, use of rope for restraint and as a fighting technique remain somewhat obscure. Itatsu Yasuhiko's fascinating chapter on hojojutsu in his excellent 1992 book, *Yoryoku/Doshin Jutte Hojo* ("The Constable's Arts"), suggests that hojojutsu might have been included in the teachings of the Takenouchi-ryu of martial arts, founded in 1532. This school, one of the oldest in Japan and still in operation, once taught 630 different fighting techniques, about 150 of which are still practiced today. Regardless of its exact origins, what is clear is that hojojutsu was and is a very effective means of capture and binding and understanding its basic techniques is vital to an understanding of how modern Shibari/Kinbaku evolved.

All of the historical hojojutsu ties that we know of today display a shrewd understanding of human anatomy and succeed through several recurrent themes of applied restraint. These include leverage-removal (tying limbs in various positions that decrease the power they can generate), rope-placement (to discourage struggling or to make it ineffective and/or dangerous, i.e., by placing one or more loops of rope around the neck) and creating constriction around sensitive nerve points on the upper arms, wrists or other areas (where determined struggle puts pressure on blood vessels and nerves thus numbing these extremities).

In 1603, at the battle of Sekigahara, Tokugawa Ieyasu finally overcame all resistance and at last unified Japan. He forged a rigid social structure (with the samurai class on top), created an effective administrative bureaucracy and built a capitol city. The years 1603-1868 were those of the Tokugawa shogunate and are called the "Edo era" today. Edo, modern day Tokyo, was the shogun's capital and so became the cultural, governmental and economic center of Japan.

During 250 years of Tokugawa rule, Japan remained free from civil war and, most importantly, existed in almost complete isolation from the West. This did not end until United States Commodore Matthew Perry opened American trade with Japan in 1854, the Tokugawa shogunate dissolved under internal pressure and the Emperor Meiji assumed power in 1868, thus beginning a rush to modernization and militarism that would culminate in World War II.

Of the many keys to understanding the origins of Shibari/Kinbaku, the centuries of near isolation Japan experienced until 1854 is central. During this time, free from outside influence and the advancements of metal technology (that produced easily available handcuffs, chains, etc.), hojojutsu became a prominent law enforcement technique and rapidly developed in sophistication and symbolism. Low ranking samurai (**doshin**), no longer needed for warfare, assumed administrative posts as police and dealt with the day to day crime fighting problems of both major cities and outlying provinces; crimes as diverse as brawling, arson, treason and murder. These duties often involved the taking of criminals and so the combat techniques of warfare became the vital policing techniques of peacetime.

Generally speaking, Hojojutsu in the Edo era can be divided into two broad categories: **Hayanawa** and **Honnawa**.

The first, Hayanawa, is the capture of prisoners done with a strong, thin cord (usually 3-4 millimeters in width) called a hayanawa or "fast rope." This cord was carried by constables in a small bundle (on their wrists, belts or in their kimono sleeves) that fed cord from one end as needed. This **torinawa** ("capture-rope") was coiled so that the cord would pay out smoothly as it was passed around the prisoner's body, neck and arms as he or she was tied. This was usually accomplished by one constable in the course of performing an arrest and while the prisoner was actively resisting, so it had to be accomplished quickly.

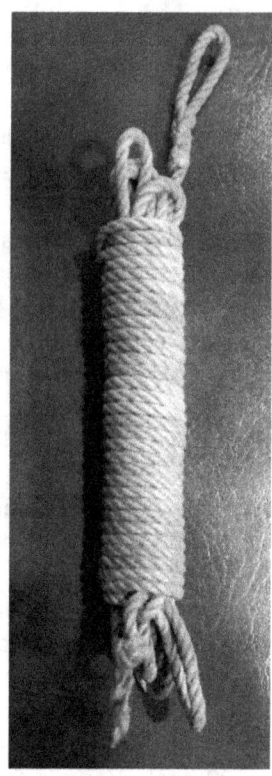
Torinawa

The second category, Honnawa (meaning "main" or "official" rope), were ties effected with one or more cords which like the torinawa could be of several different lengths but was a proper hemp/jute rope, possibly 6 or more millimeters in diameter and used to provide a more secure, long-term binding than was possible with the torinawa. This method of tying was used for transportation of prisoners to a place of incarceration and examination, restraint at legal proceedings and, in the case of particularly severe crimes, for the public display of the prisoner prior to execution.

Honnawa ties were usually applied by a group of constables, two to four in number, whose presence allowed the creation of more intricate, time consuming and ornate patterns than was the case with the torinawa. This was also the method used for tying prisoners who had to be transported across provincial borders or to distant territories since the officials of different jurisdictions jealously guarded their own methods of tying and several guards surrounding a prisoner allowed for a measure of secrecy. Again, according to Itatsu in his book, "Yoryoku/Doshin Jutte Hojo," the accepted rules for this type of tying were:

1. It must be impossible to escape from, even if the prisoner dislocates his joints.
2. The prisoner must not be able to understand the process of the tie.
3. The tie must not deliberately cut off circulation to any part of the body or cause nerve damage.
4. The tie must be beautiful.

What is of particular interest and importance to modern Shibari/Kinbaku is that both forms of tying, hayanawa and especially honnawa, combined effective restraint with a distinct visual aesthetic. This aesthetic consideration is, in some ways, the most fascinating and remarkable aspect of hojojutsu.

The ability of the Japanese to ritualize and beautify daily objects and activities, from the tea ceremony to flower arranging (**ikebana**) to package wrapping, has long been noted. Incredibly, the same was true for hojojutsu as different ties were used for the different classes of society with the distinctive and often beautiful patterns showing clearly on the prisoner's backs. This aesthetic aspect to the tying patterns is, after tie construction, the second most important inheritance that hojojutsu has bequeathed to modern erotic Shibari/Kinbaku. This is true even though the most complex elements of the hojojutsu patterns were displayed on the "canvas" of the bound prisoner's back whereas Shibari/Kinbaku patterns are usually created on and for the front of the torso. It should also be noted that some of the names of specific hojojutsu bindings have been transferred, in whole or in part, across the centuries to Kinbaku.

For instance, noble samurai were often bound with the **nijyuuhishi nawa** or "double diamond" tie or the **shin kikkou**, a tie that creates an ornate, hexagonal, pattern. By contrast, peasants might be bound using the **juumonji nawa**, a rather simple cross tie. There were different and specific ties for priests (different styles each for Shinto, Buddhist, or mountain ascetic), women and children. Prisoners who tried to escape were bound with the **sarashinawa** that cut off circulation in the fingers, while prisoners to be exiled to penal islands were bound with the **tasukenawa** so that they could better balance themselves on shipboard. Most terrible of all, condemned prisoners were tied using the **kirinawa** with its distinctive small diamond/chain pattern and obvious neck restraint. The remarkable result of all this differentiation of ties is that a passing spectator could often tell just from the type of bondage being used the social class of the prisoner as well as their crime and perhaps even their punishment.

The reason for this clear differentiation in bindings is due to the fact that in Japan being bound was one of the most shameful fates that could befall a person, signifying complete disgrace and ostracism from society. Since the Edo era had a very rigid social structure with the samurai class at the top and, in descending order, the farmers, artisans and at the bottom the merchants, keeping one's place in society, even as a prisoner, was paramount. This shame in being bound, of being an outlaw outcast, has carried a fearful fascination for the Japanese for centuries and is an important psychological aspect of their SM play. Recently, in correspondence, a quite famous Kinbaku model confessed to me that she'd rather have her aged parents see her having sex than see her being tied. Such was/ is the psychological frisson of being bound.

Sometimes this concern with "binding protocol" had, from the safety of historical perspective, a somewhat amusing side. In the capitol city Edo, where many high ranking nobles (**daimyo**) lived or visited, the poor police constables had a problem. What if, during an arrest, a noble was taken who later was proven innocent? The officer could face censure, disgrace and even worse. The solution? A unique feature of Edo style hayanawa is that there are often no real knots

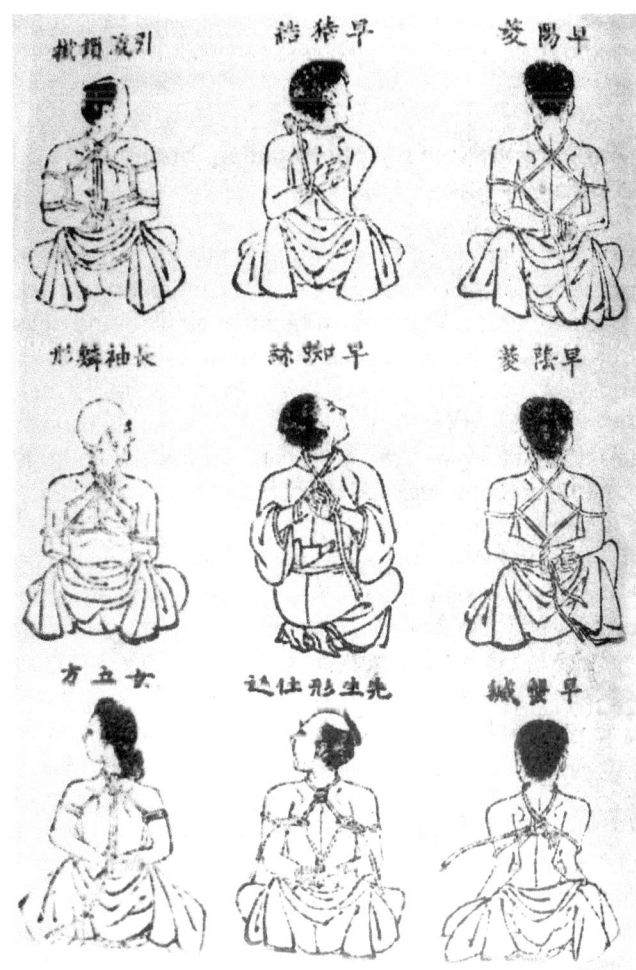

Feudal era scroll (Mori clan) showing various hojo-jutsu tying techniques, some based on class

in the bindings. Instead, the rope is intricately wrapped to bind the prisoner. This lack of knots gave the arresting officer a degree of deniability if, in court, he was ever accused of impropriety. After all, the prisoner wasn't really "tied," just wrapped! This was only true in Edo, the capital of the shogun and of protocol. In the provinces true knots were always used. Interestingly enough, in modern Kinbaku there is a style of tying that also just uses wraps with few or no knots.

During the years of war and conflict all warriors studied hojojutsu but after 1603, during the Edo era, only those involved in law enforcement specialized in this martial art. There were many different ryu's (schools) during that time that taught some form of hojojutsu to the police and to some of the increasingly underemployed samurai class. These schools had various styles, from those of the Sasai-ryu that taught only hayanawa (quick binding arrest techniques) and allowed for a more rushed and slapdash look, to the Ishii-ryu, unique among the different sects of hojojutsu in that it taught bindings used only for torture and interrogation.

It is interesting to note that different ryu often taught different styles of ties for similar purposes and, in other instances, different schools taught the same tie but called them by different names. This explains some of today's confusions over the naming of certain Shibari/Kinbaku patterns inherited from hojojutsu. For instance, the famous Ittasu-ryu (founded in the 17th century) taught a beautiful tie called the Shin-kikkou (true kikkou) which was six sided and named after the hexagonal pattern found on the back of the Japanese tortoise. However, the Taisho-ryu taught a diamond (hishi) shaped tie that they *also* called the kikkou. Both names are correct and both beautiful patterns have found their way into modern Kinbaku art.

(Author's note: in the photo gallery of this book several of the more distinctive hojojutsu ties are shown.)

Of course, not all of these varied binding techniques were used. Different Edo era constabularies or police forces employed different ties and even used different colored ropes to make their arrests. For instance, officers from the Kitamachi bugyou (the division responsible for law enforcement in the north of Edo) as well as the Hitsuketouzoku-aratame (the arson squad), vital in a city built of wood, used white ropes, wide and thin respectively, to make their arrests. Conversely, those officers patrolling the south of Edo (and also prison guards) used dark purple ropes. The Kanjyo bugyou officers (loosely translated as the "tax police") and those working for the Jishya bugyou (the constabulary that regulated religious groups) also had their own distinctive ropes and ties.

In general, the average Edomachi Bugyou (Edo police constable), and presumably his relative in the provinces, was said to use ties from as many as three different hojojutsu ryu in his duties and, understandably, to modify them for his own use in various situations. An intriguing piece of evidence I discovered in the preparation of this book gives credence to this claim.

The oldest photographic example of hojojutsu that I have in my collection dates from 1870. It was probably taken by Shimooka Renjo who is generally regarded as the "father of Japanese photography" and was certainly one of the first professional photographers in Japan. The picture in question is a recreated studio shot of a tied prisoner kneeling before a daimyo (feudal lord) or magistrate with a constable in attendance. The photo was almost certainly made for the "tourist trade" in the early days of the Meiji era when the first European and American visitors to Japan craved souvenirs depicting the quickly disappearing sites, ceremonies and occupations of the shogun's feudal times. To my surprise, this historical image, created at a time when these feudal policing procedures were still well known, shows a tie pattern that isn't duplicated in any of the numerous reference works containing the hundreds of recorded hojojutsu patterns that I've consulted. It is unique, practical and attractive and is just the sort of tie a hard working officer would use.

As the Meiji era progressed in its headlong rush to modernism, most vestiges of the Tokugawa years quickly disappeared and even the samurai class faded from the scene. Such was also the case with hojojutsu. Police officers continued to use the technique during the **Meiji (1868-1912) and Taisho (1912-1926)** eras but the teaching of it even to them was greatly reduced with the introduction of handcuffs, legs irons and other more "modern" instruments of police procedure. During World War II many documents and scrolls describing hojojutsu's techniques were destroyed in the numerous fires that engulfed Japan and most of the traditional martial arts were then suppressed by occupying United States forces. Today, hojojutsu is taught in only a few martial arts academies and, while we have images that show what many historical ties looked like, the secrets of such schools as the Kiraku-ryu and the Hida-ryu have been lost forever. This is a pity since hojojutsu is certainly a unique Japanese martial art and should be preserved.

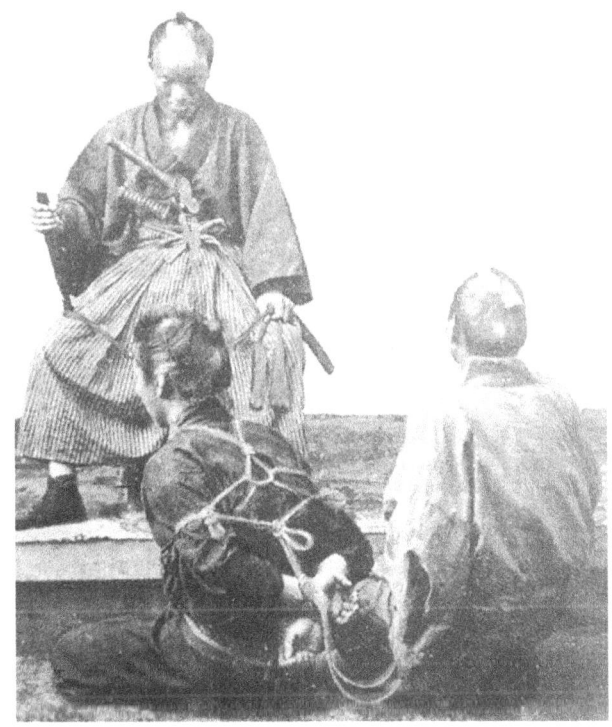

Hojojutsu, circa 1870. Photo by Shimooka (?)

Still, the Tokyo police continue to be taught a form of hojojutsu based on the Ittatsu-ryu techniques and some teachers of traditional martial arts in Japan as well as educational institutions work to preserve and maintain vestiges of the art form. Most of the information in this section comes from the Edo Keiji Hakubutsu Hozonkai (the Edo Crime and Punishment Museum of Meiji University in Tokyo) which holds records for over 500 different types of hojojutsu patterns and also maintains the Nawa Yumio archives and collections of historical policing equipment.

Nawa Yumio, a revered figure in Japan (someone we will encounter again in the history of Shibari/Kinbaku), was the soke (head of and heir to the style of) Masaki-ryu Bujutsu, a school of martial arts. He wrote several books on the subject of Edo era policing, was the historical consultant on several films and television shows and worked as a historical advisor on various matters dealing with law-enforcement. There are also several texts on hojojutsu that still survive in print. Mizukoshi Hiro's recently reprinted book, *Torinawajutsu*, offers historical background followed by practical instruction in more than 25 traditional ties including some recreated from rare and very old texts. And then there is the long out-of-print book by the late and legendary martial artist Fujita Seiko. This monumental work, *Zukai Hojojutsu*, could be considered the bible of the art, showing hundreds of ties from many different schools. It's authenticity is beyond question being drawn from the records of Fujita's own father, a Meiji era police inspector and expert on hojojutsu who retired in 1912. Unfortunately for Western practitioners, neither of these authors has any work in English.

The history of the martial art of hojojutsu is certainly a fascinating one and its role as one of the ancestors to modern erotic Shibari/Kinbaku is beyond question.

Questions:

"How has hojojutsu influenced modern erotic Shibari/Kinbaku?"

It's done so in two important ways. First, this most complex and sophisticated of tying techniques demonstrates all of the pitfalls and dangers that can be caused by rope binding, from nerve compression to strangulation. The early samurai practitioners of hojojutsu usually did not care if their prisoners, taken in combat, were injured but, as we shall see, these dangerous techniques have been studied, modified and reengineered to make modern erotic Shibari, when properly executed, safe and enjoyable. Second, the concern with formal beauty in the creation of hojojutsu ties and patterns continues to be an important aesthetic inspiration.

"When the samurai class was dissolved at the end of the Tokugawa era, what happened to all the hojojutsu teachers and practitioners?"

In the Meiji government's rush to modernize, the samurai class was dissolved. Those samurai able to find work in law enforcement did so and thereby displaced many non samurai police officials. The result was that many of the lower class officers proficient in hojojutsu, as well as many martial arts instructors, found themselves out of work with their tying skills no longer needed. Most turned to other occupations but some were still able to put their expertise to work by making straw sandals, creating decorative knots for temples and by doing ship rigging.

Official and unofficial punishments, the imagery of power

The second practical inspiration for modern day Shibari/Kinbaku (and indeed for much of modern Japanese SM) is to be found in some of the dramatic and unusual ways that "criminals" were dealt with throughout Japan's feudal history.

Like many other aspects of its culture, Japan's earliest legal precepts were imported from and heavily influenced by China. Recent excavations there have shown that such practices as public executions, tattooing of criminals and various other public chastisements and gruesome disfigurements were all part of the legal system of the Ch'in dynasty, the first to unify China in 221 BC. These punishments correspond quite closely to what Sasama Yoshihiko and Kashiwa Shobou in their book *Zusetsu: Nihon no Gōmon Keibatsu-shi* ("The History of Torture and Punishment in Japan") as well as various other scholars such as, Nawa, Ono, Inoue, Hara, Osatake, Shigematsu and Botsman (see bibliography), describe as typical penalties employed during Japan's earliest periods; from the Yamato dynasty (approximately 538-710 AD) and Nara era (710-794 AD) through to the particularly brutal Sengoku ("Warring States") period of 1492-1560. This is further supported by evidence that several well known Japanese weapons and law enforcement tools such as the samurai's sword and the Edo era police constable's **jutte** (iron truncheon) and **sodegarami** or "sleeve entangler" (a pole like weapon used to entangle a fleeing criminal's clothing), probably had their origins in ancient China.

Until the Edo era, such diverse and barbaric punishments as disfigurement, being flayed alive or stoned, tied in straw mats and drowned, thrown off cliffs, pulled apart by oxen, etc., were handed out by whatever lord, clan or power was in charge of whatever area, busy or backwater, in which "the offence" occurred. And regardless of the authority, the intent of these public punishments was to demonstrate the sovereignty of the power over the people and to hold up the convicted as a potent example to dissuade others from pursuing similarly "illegal," "immoral" or "traitorous" behavior. In this we see an important social and psychological aspect of the Japanese character that will be a fundamental part of that country's SM practices up until the present day, the concept of shame.

Unlike Western Judeo-Christian cultures where a sense of personal guilt for transgressions against God and man has been emphasized, in Japan it has long been the individual's honorable relationship to the group that is paramount. Or, to put it another way, the West is a guilt-based culture while that of Japan is based on shame, with the chief distinction being that the former is an internalized emotion while the latter depends on the presence of a group. This explains why the "theater of public disgrace" is so often a part of Japanese criminal punishment history. In the West the "perp walk," with the offender paraded in handcuffs before the media, is a regular, if very brief, part of the labeling of a criminal. In Japan such parading is and always was a major component of the punishment.

It was during the Edo era that the first codified set of legal statutes was introduced to regulate judicial punishments for the Tokugawa shogunate. In 1742, under the eighth Shogun, Yoshimune, the so-called "One Hundred Articles" (**Kujikata Osadamegaki**) became the primary source that Edo officials turned to when determining punishments; in effect Japan's first penal code. Many of the more inhuman penalties from the past were prohibited but the list of crimes and their sanctioned punishments was still a long one and included such sentences as: death by crucifixion, sword and, for the crime of arson, burning at the stake as well as "lesser punishments" such as slavery, banishment, forced labor, confiscation of property, public beatings and/or being displayed while bound and **irezumi** (tattooing), to indicate types of felonies committed and to identify repeat offenders.

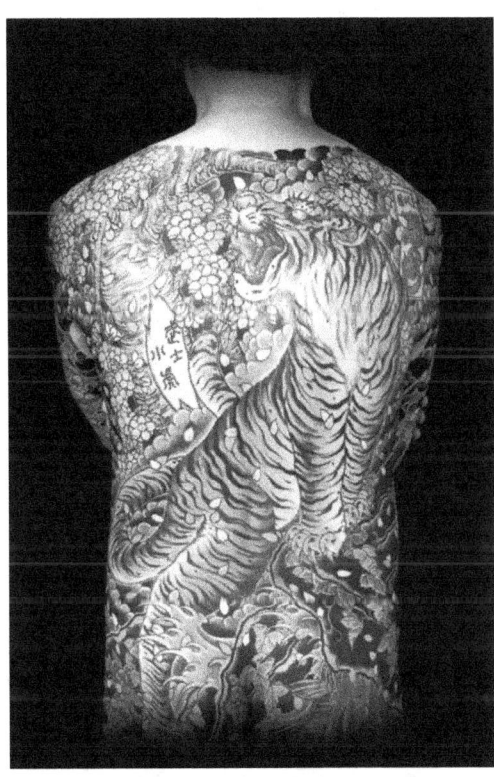

Modern irezumi art

The most common tattoo was two one inch bands on the upper left arm although the practice of tattooing the words "evil" or "dog" on the criminal's forehead was also known. Men, women and even children as young as nine years old were tattooed for crimes and this punishment was no slight affair as a criminal tattoo excluded a person from nearly all aspects of normal society. Before being tattooed a prisoner was often publicly bound and beaten using thin bamboo strips rolled into a bundle. Fifty strokes was the norm.

One of the more interesting consequences of this tattooing of criminals was that it spawned the practice of offenders trying to cover up the criminal "label" by incorporating it into a larger tattoo design; thus the legendary art of Japanese tattooing was furthered. As with Shibari/Kinbaku, this is another example of a uniquely Japanese art and aesthetic being inspired by a completely unlikely and surprising source.

The most horrendous punishments of crucifixion (also known as "stringing up") or beheading by sword were reserved for crimes of murder, blackmail, treason and several other serious capital offences A samurai might be allowed to perform ritual suicide, or **seppuku**, to preserve his honor but a commoner convicted of a capital crime had no such recourse to so awful a punishment.

According to Harvard scholar Daniel V. Botsman in his excellent book, *"Punishment and Power in the Making of Modern Japan,"* the first European traders and missionaries thought the practice of crucifixion was introduced into Japan with Christianity in the 16th century. However, this was not the case since, "the practice of stringing people up on wooden frames before executing them can be traced back to at least the twelfth century in Japan."

Before the "stringing up" the condemned prisoner would be bound (sometimes with the kirinawa hojojutsu pattern) and paraded around town on horseback followed by upwards of 30 armed men. The route would always take the parade through the commoner's sections of Edo so the maximum number of people could take note of

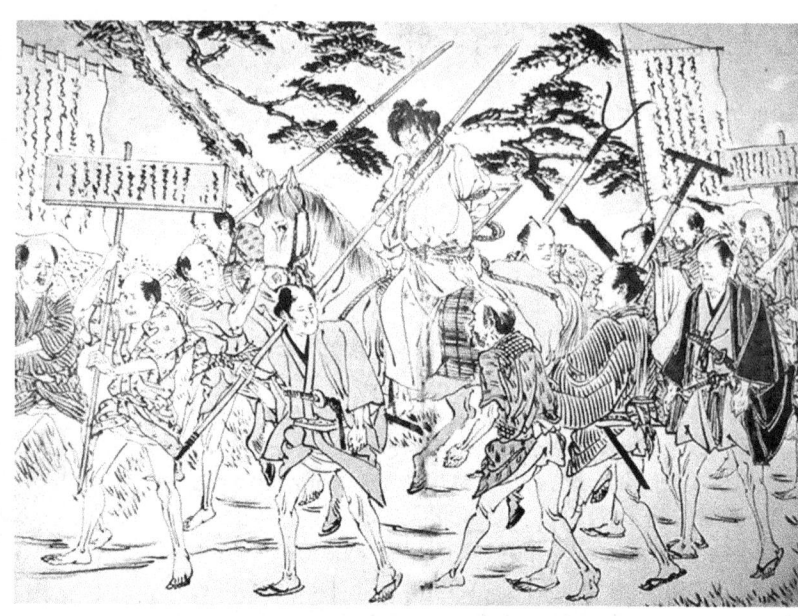

Criminal procession—from Tokugawa bakufu keiji zufu by Fujita Shintaro, 1893

crime's consequences before the execution grounds were reached. There the criminal (male or female) would be bound to a cross before being executed by spear. After death the body would be taken down, its head cut off and then this most grisly "trophy" would be placed on top of a specially constructed stand for public display.

Even the locations of Edo's two execution grounds played their part in this theater of punishment. One was located to the south of Edo on the famous Tokaido road and the other to the north near a confluence of other highways that entered the capitol. Thus, again to quote Botsman, "When furnished with signs of shogunal justice, the execution grounds were unforgettable markers of the approach to his capitol."

Such "bodies as signs" imagery of Tokugawa power was not limited to executions. More minor offences were also punished by public displays, either by being bound and/or flogged, with a sign posted nearby announcing one's crimes, or by a disgraced parade through town. Nearly 1000 men were publicly flogged in Edo between 1862-1865 and during that same time fifty execution parades per year, nearly one per week, were recorded as having been held in the capitol. One was even photographed by the visiting European photographer Felice Beato. It seems the average citizen of Edo could hardly escape the sight of official punishments in everyday life. Is it any wonder then that the dramatic spectacles of bondage and punishment should become so important a part of Japanese drama and art, both "straight" and SM tinged?

The practice of public chastisement even affected non-criminal areas. For instance, the prostitutes of Edo's famous Yoshiwara (or "pleasure quarter") that transgressed against their masters by attempting to run away were often punished by being bound for the night outside of their establishments. This also occurred in the provinces and was reported as happening as late as 1869 by the famous British diplomat and Japanophile A. B. Mitford, one of the first Europeans to live and work in Japan at the dawn of the Meiji restoration. On a trip to Edo from Yokohama he reported in his journal that, "At one of these high-road pleasure-houses, . . . I once saw a very melancholy sight: an unhappy girl had contrived to make her escape, . . . she was caught and brought back, and to punish her, having been beaten and ill-used, she was bound hand and foot, and exposed in that condition in front of the house, as a warning to those of her mates who might attempt to follow her example."

It is a sad truth that throughout human existence torture has been used for many ignoble reasons. Japan has certainly not been immune to this and there are numerous references to the practice throughout its historical records. Even during the relatively cultured Heian period (794-1185) beatings were allowed in order to punish wrongdoers or to extract confessions to crimes. In the Edo era it was officially sanctioned in order to extract such confessions. This was vital to the workings of Tokugawa justice because official proceedings, from which sentences would be given out, were almost never conducted unless there was every reason to believe the suspect would confess publicly at them—usually because the confession had already been obtained, written out, and sealed before the official trial began. Failure to obtain such a public confession was thought to bring the government into disrepute. Naturally, the professed ideal was to obtain the confession without the use of torture by questioning alone, skill at which was a point of pride; but there's no real way of knowing how often this standard was even aimed at, much less met. If it wasn't, then torture was the only way to get the required confession and that was its major purpose.

Even today, in comparison to other countries in the developed world, Japan has a unique prosecutorial system. Ninety-nine percent of criminal defendants are convicted in Japan and almost all are convicted following their own confessions. Prosecutors tend to bring charges only when they have a signed confession from the accused and such confessions often occur after long questioning by police. Although defendants have a right to counsel, it is generally not possible for them to obtain counsel between their arrest and indictment. This makes it difficult to judge the true extent of criminal activity in Japan, since many possible criminals refuse to confess and are thus never indicted.

Naturally, torture is no longer allowed but it was a basis of Tokugawa law and, as was the case with hojojutsu, we are fortunate that our knowledge of this remote and arcane area of Japan's judicial past is so well documented and detailed. This is thanks in part to two major historical texts: *Tokugawa bakufu keiji zufu* ("The Pictorial Book on Penal Affairs of the Tokugawa Government") edited and drawn by **Fujita Shintaro** in 1893 and *Gōmon Jikki* ("Actual Record of Torture") by **Sakuma Osahiro**, also written in 1893.

The first is a pictorial book published to support the Meiji cause for the rapid modernization of Japan after the downfall of the Tokugawa shogunate. In it the artist Fujita Shintaro illustrated the harsh punishments meted out by the Tokugawa to their people in order to propagandize the supposedly more enlightened Meiji government then taking over. The second document, by Sukuma, was a personal narrative of experience.

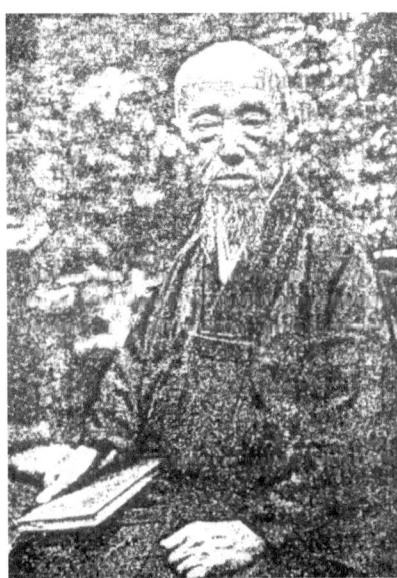

Sakuma Osahiro was born in 1839 into a family that served in the Edo constabulary. From age 11 he started learning the constabulary arts and went on to work within that branch of law enforcement. After the Meiji Restoration he worked as a city court judge and died in 1923 at the age of 84. He wrote *Gōmon Jikki* in 1893 because he was getting older and, since there were few people left alive with firsthand knowledge of torture during the late Edo period, he wanted to leave an accurate historical record. Both sources tell the same detailed story and have been the foundation for much of the useful research done on this subject.

Judge Sakuma Osahiro, circa late 19th Cetury

According to both documents, during the Edo Period there were four levels of legal torture: flogging; pressing with stones; the shrimp/prawn (or ebi) tie; and rope suspensions (or tsuri). Naturally, these last two are of most significance to the history of Shibari/Kinbaku. Although ranked and usually administered in this fashion, they were sometimes used in combination, going back and forth until a confession from the suspect was obtained. Each level could be pursued up to a named point—a certain period of time or a certain number of strokes. If this failed to obtain results, either the same technique would be tried again after a given interval (often two days) or a different one would be tried. Most official tortures were conducted in private in small torture chambers designated for this purpose. Usually the room had a pillar in the center and was located in out buildings attached to official government offices, constabulary posts or jails. Any and all of these tortures were used on women as well as men.

Flogging. This was done with the suspect kneeling and bound around his/her upper arms. Two stout ropes were also sometimes held taut by a pair of assistants on either side or in front and back of the suspect. A special scourge was used, called a **shimoto** or **muchi** (the latter is the generic word for any type of whip), and beatings were administered to the back. This was the mildest form of torture used to elicit a confession.

Pressing with stones. This torture, literally "embracing the stones," was carried out with the suspect kneeling. Often the prisoner was forced to kneel on a corrugated wooden or iron surface looking something like an exaggerated washboard with pointed ridges. His/her arms were tied behind the back, sometimes to the post of the room, and then large square slabs of stone, about one inch thick, were laid one after another on the tops of the suspect's thighs. This simple but excruciating torture was said to be nearly foolproof in obtaining a confession and most prisoners confessed during either the beating or stone tortures, so it was very rare for a prisoner to proceed to the ebi-zeme, but there are records of it occurring.

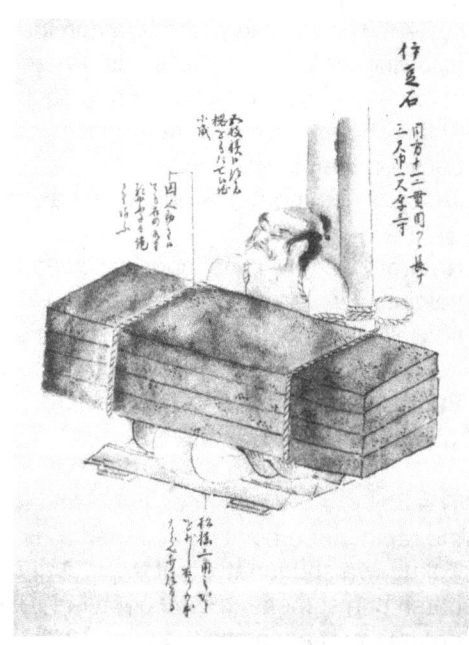

Pressing with stones

Ebi-zeme or the shrimp/prawn tie. If the prisoner didn't confess under the stone torture, then the ebi-zeme was administered next. Amazingly, we can actually trace the origin of this exotic form of rope torture back more than 300 years. It is believed that the ebi-zeme was developed around 1681-1683 by a town constabulary arson and theft investigator named Nakayama Kageyu. The brutality of this torture is due to the seriousness of the crime being investigated—arson. As has been well documented, fires in the Edo era of Japan killed hundreds of thousands.

In creating the ebi, first the suspect's hands were tied behind the back, the forearms placed on top of each other, the wrists bound together with a rope going around the upper arms. Next he/she was forced to sit cross-legged. The ankles were then bound together with the two ends of the rope then brought up and over the shoulders where they were looped through the rope binding the arms. Then the torturer would use his foot to press down on the suspect's back, forcing the chest down toward his/her crossed calves, at the same time pulling up on the ropes and thus raising the suspect's feet off the ground. When the suspect was doubled over as far as physically possible, and a little farther, the second rope was tied off on the first. Then they waited.

This tie had several punishing aspects: one physical, as the diaphragm was forced upwards toward the chest making breathing difficult and the other psychological, with the prisoner forced into a bowing, submissive, posture.

There have been two explanations given for the name ebi ("shrimp"/"prawn"). One was that the suspect was bent over like a curled shrimp. The other was that after a short time in this position the person turned red like a cooked prawn. In fact, there was a sequence of colors when the torture lasted for several hours: first red, then purple, then violet, then pale blue. The latter stage was the signal for the torture to end if the pain had not already produced a confession. Continuing once the pale blue stage was reached resulted in death.

Suspension (tsuri-zeme). This was regarded as the last resort in attempting to extract a confession. It was carried out by tying the suspect's arms behind the back and then suspending him/her by the wrists. The author Inoue Kazuo in his book *Zankoku no Nihon-shi* ("Cruel Japanese History") states, "As recorded in the document *Koujigata osademegaki,* 'Tsurushi-zeme' (tsuri-zeme) was one of the official tortures of the Edo period. In illustrations in *Tokurin genbi-roku* and other sources, the prisoner's hands were pulled behind his/her back and bound with the '*Nawagake*' (a thin straw covering placed over the wrists and used to prevent the suspension rope from cutting into the skin) and then they

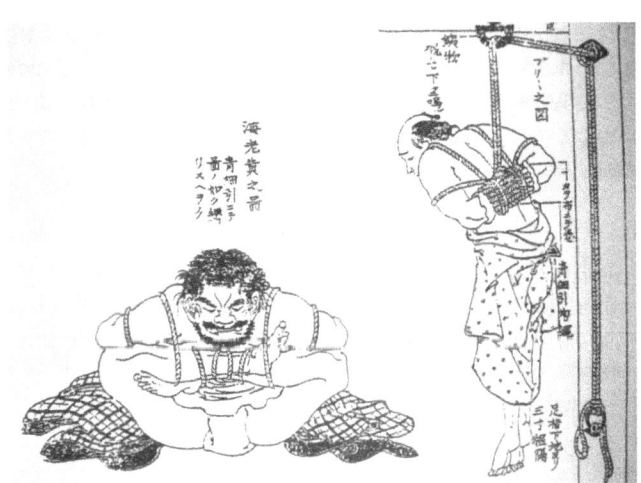

Ebi-zeme and tsuri-zeme

were suspended from the rope around their arms. Clothing was removed from the parts of the body touched by the rope. The pain of the torture came from the pressure imposed on the wrists and chest from the weight of the prisoner's own body. The prisoner was lowered to the ground from time to time and allowed to rest, with the suspension time gradually increased. The prisoner was often tormented in suspension, as guards poked him/her with sticks, pulled on the rope or swung or twirled the prisoner in suspension. For an especially reluctant suspect a large stone weight might be laid on the shoulders. As with the previous two tortures, suspension might be accompanied by flogging." It is also believed that there were various forms of suspensions. For instance, one variation was to suspend the suspect upside down by the ankles; but the wrists were more usual.

All four of these approved tortures were administered under the eyes of clerks who made an official record of the proceedings and all were confined within certain limits to make absolutely sure permanent damage or death did not result. Naturally, most interrogations never got as far as the ebi-zeme or tsuri-zemi since most prisoners were likely to confess under the first stage of torture, or at least the second. But a few really stubborn individuals went through the whole sequence.

For instance, there's a famous story about a woman named Fukui Kane who was arrested in 1871 on suspicion of murdering her patron, a government official named Hirosawa Sareomi. As was the custom then, she was tortured to obtain a confession. Amazingly, this went on for almost three years with no success! Her tolerance for torture leading some to suggest that she might actually be enjoying the process! Her jailers were bewildered. Eventually, she was released and the murder, for which Fukui was the sole suspect, went officially unsolved. Perhaps Ms. Fukui had *several* secrets?

This failure to obtain a confession in some cases is one of the reasons that, in the waning years of the shogunate, the ebi-zeme and tsuri-zeme were not applied as often as they had been in the past. Failure was embarrassing and some officials felt these tortures were more valuable as psychological weapons of possible things to come rather than as practical tools.

In addition to these "official" tortures prescribed for the capitol, Edo, other variations were used in the provinces. It is said that in outlying districts farmers accused of being tax cheats were sometimes suspended upside down from bridges by pulleys. Their heads were then lowered into the water for minutes at a time in an attempt to convince them to pay up. Another form of suspension torture called the **Surugadoi** or **Surugōmon** (Suruga "inquiry" or Suruga "torture") was developed by a local constable named Hikosaka Kyubei in the Suruga province (an area that is part of the Shizuoka prefecture in the center of Japan) in the early years of the Keicho period (1596-1614). In this torture the prisoner's arms and feet were brought up and tied closely together behind his/her back, a stone was usually tied to the waist and he/she was suspended face down with the hands and feet up. For added inducement to confess the prisoner was sometimes spun around like a top! Fortunately, this torture was rarely used.

Much more common were unofficial tortures done outside the strict letter of the law by regional lords (daimyo) or by powerful owners of brothels or properties employing many workers. These penalties could sometimes be downright bizarre such as the **hebi-zeme** or "snake torture" where the victim was exposed to poisonous snakes. While this punishment is actually reported to have happened in the Maeda daimyo household in the Ishikawa Prefecture it has become famous due to its recreation in several historical films.

Not the stuff of fantasy were the cruel tortures inflicted on prostitutes. According to the sixth scroll of an Edo-era report called the *Yōgoto Kenbunroku*, prostitutes were subject to harsh punishment and even torture for infractions against their owners. These included deprivation of food, privy cleaning, humiliations, beatings and suspensions. One torture involving rope was to bind them in asanawa (hemp/ jute rope) and then to throw water on them, causing torment when the cords dried and constricted. Another punishing binding was called the **buriburi** or **tsuritsuri** where the hands and feet are bound together and then the person is suspended by all four limbs like a game animal after a hunt.

The cruel ingenuity of these punishments seems awful and fantastic today but such was the history of feudal Japan. And this historical legacy even extended into the era of World War II. During that conflict Japan's dreaded military secret police, the Kempeitai, were accused of committing atrocities using some of these same techniques to ellicit information from captured prisoners of war.

In 1879 the official use of torture to extract confessions was finally prohibited by the Meiji government and this paved the way for the promulgation in 1880 of Japan's first Western-style penal code. Centuries of brutality came to an end but not without leaving its mark on the memories and consciousness of its people. And it is in this "sphere of the imagination" that we must next look for the origins of Kinbaku; an amazing transformation from historical brutality to erotic art and performance and one of the most fascinating aspects of Shibari/Kinbaku history.

Questions:

"How has Japan's feudal punishments and tortures influenced modern erotic Shibari/Kinbaku?"

The influence on Japanese SM is obvious with the historical symbolism of public punishments and the psychological concept of shame being most apparent today. Practically, several specific ties from the feudal era, the ebi and the buriburi (now called the tanuki), carefully re-engineered for safety, are still practiced in modern erotic Shibari/Kinbaku. Most importantly, tsuri-zeme (suspensions) have been completely transformed and turned into acrobatic display and a mainstay of Shibari/Kinbaku play and stage performance. Far from "torture," this carefully executed descendent of feudal brutality is capable of safely "flying" the receptive participant into ecstasy.

Art from brutality, the birth of erotic seme-e

Given all of the cultural and historical links, it is not surprising that such unique forms of arrest and punishment as hojojutsu and the One Hundred Articles should become elements used in Japanese literature, the graphic arts and drama. Just as the "Old West" of America became the stuff of legend, spawning thousands of works of 19th, 20th and 21st century "cowboy art," so too did Japan's feudal past inspire its artists. However, when did this begin? When did these often shocking realities begin to become aestheticized?

Certainly, the custom of punishing in public drew the man in the street's attention and often created quite a stir. As with public executions in early modern Europe, revulsion at the sight was often tinged with fascination. A letter from 1832 survives that suggests this quite clearly. Written by a prostitute living near one of the execution grounds to the friend of an important daimyo, Matsura Seizan, who recorded its contents, it extends the following invitation, ". . . blossoms are in bloom, there has been a crucifixion, people have come out, and things are lively. You must pop over for awhile."

This morbid interest in Tokugawa crime and punishment certainly led both to being incorporated into various forms of popular culture. In 1823 the well known playwright Tsuruya Nanboku IV (1755-1829) used the execution ground at Suzugamori for scenes in a kabuki play involving the legendary outlaw Banzuin Chobei. An execution is never shown but the foreshadowing is clear and so effective was this device that the play quickly became known simply as "Suzugamori." Other famous criminals were similarly celebrated by even earlier balladeers, woodblock print makers, writers and others in much the same way that Jesse James was (and still is) lionized in the United States. However, this is simple history and legend as art. The process of the eroticization of this material is more difficult to chart.

Erotic sadism and masochism (SM) have always existed in mankind (various studies have estimated that somewhere between 10% and 15% of the world's population has some predilection) but the turning of this interest into a pleasurable or aesthetic activity requires, at least, four very specific things:

1. Leisure time.
2. A relatively safe environment for the work to be produced.
3. A motivating, imaginative context.
4. An interested public, no matter how small in number.

Due in large measure to the many years of relative peace that the Tokugawa shogunate provided its people, as well as a rise in the wealth and status of the merchant class and the nearly unlimited leisure time that the underemployed samurai enjoyed, many of the above conditions appear to have been in place in the mid to late 18th and early 19th centuries. From the stability of the late Edo era, safely distanced from the brutal realities of war and rebellion, the titillating concepts (for some) of shame and punishment combined with the always prevalent interest in **shunga** (Japanese erotic prints) and theater (**kabuki** and **"new"**) to produce the first publicly distributed artistic images with a more or less overtly SM context.

Kabuki and "new" theater. The history of kabuki (one of the great traditional forms of Japanese theater) begins in 1603 during the Edo era when **Okuni**, a miko (a young woman in service to a Shinto shrine), began performing a new style of dance drama in Kyoto, a city that most scholars consider Japan's historical center for learning and the arts. In this new type of drama female performers played both men and women in short comic plays about ordinary life. The style was instantly popular with the public and Okuni was even asked to perform before the Imperial Court.

In the wake of this success rival troupes quickly formed and kabuki was born as an ensemble dance drama performed by women, a form very different from its modern incarnation. Much of its appeal then was due to the ribald, earthy and erotically suggestive performances put on by many troupes and this appeal was further augmented by the fact that the performers were often also available for prostitution! Even the word "kabuki" has its erotic associations. Originally indicating behavior that was scandalous or "offbeat," it came to be written with the formal Chinese characters for "song" (ka), "dance" (bu) and "prostitute" (ki), the latter changing only in the later Meiji period to the character for "skill."

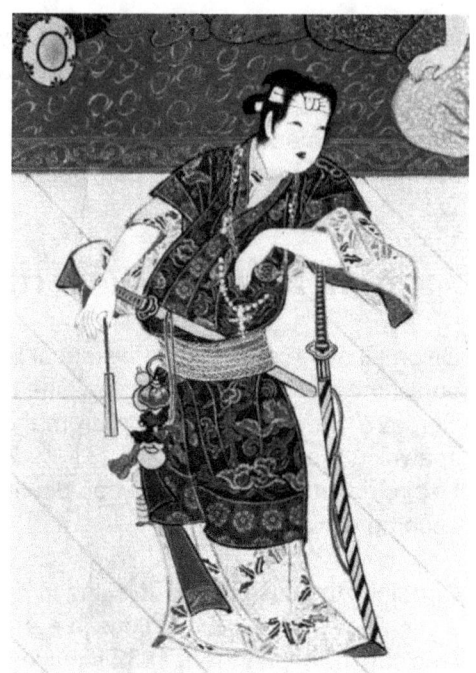

Kabuki founder Okuni, in performance

Eventually, as a result of this threat to public morality, women were banned from performing by the Tokugawa shogunate and replaced by young males. Ironically, the young male actors who took over kabuki also engaged in prostitution and audience disturbances continued to break out. In 1652 the shogunate again clamped down and troupes composed only of older male actors were required to perform more formalized and strictly theatrical dramas. Male actors who specialized in playing women's roles, called **onnagata**, emerged and families of onnagate specialists developed.

This final style of kabuki grew out of opposition to **Noh** drama, an older surviving Japanese theatrical form (with origins in the 14th century), and along with **bunraku** (puppet theater) with whom it often shared stories and playwrights, became one of the most popular entertainments of the Edo era. Kabuki theater wanted to shock its audience with more lively and timely stories than Noh drama offered and its plays generally depicted thinly disguised historical events, ghost stories or famous legends emphasizing moral conflicts, tragedies between star-crossed lovers or, like the example mentioned earlier, exciting tales of famous outlaws, samurai, action, revenge and loyalty. The point is that this form of theater was wildly popular with an emerging middle class, that it had its titillating aspects (as with today's movie stars, famous kabuki actors were highly paid, much admired and dreamed about) and told exciting and melodramatic stories, sometimes taken from daily life. In short, kabuki theater was the perfect setting for narratives of violence using arrest, capture and punishment for dramatic effect.

As with modern film, kabuki, almost from its beginnings, used violence and cruelty as key elements of dramatic construction. From such violent scenes kabuki's famous concept of an "aesthetic of cruelty" (**zankoku no bi**) evolved. To quote the authoritative four volume "Kabuki Plays on Stage" series, edited by James R. Brandon and Samuel L. Leiter, zankoku no bi refers to the "quality of beauty arising in scenes of torture or death that are performed in a stylized, musical fashion." In such stylization appears the first theatrical impulse to aestheticize SM.

A perfect example of this occurs in the 1757 play *Kinkakuji* ("The Golden Pavilion") when Princess Yuki is bound to a cherry tree on the orders of the evil Lord Daizen, then draws images of mice with her toes in the fallen cherry blossoms at her feet. The mice magically appear and free her. Another example is the tale of Princess Chujo (AKA Chujo Hime) who was bound and left in falling snow by her tormentors; a famous story that's been turned into several kabuki dramas over the centuries.

Certainly, most of these plays could never be called *overtly* sadomasochistic. However, elements of bondage and torment did begin to appear and it is here that Japanese theater's influence on the creation of Shibari/Kinbaku as an art and dramatic spectacle can first be recognized.

Similar to zankoku no bi, kabuki scenes of **semeba**, more commonly known today as **seme-e** (a mid 20th century word usually translated as scenes or situations of *realistic* torture, "torment," "persecution," or "domination"), also started to become a recurring aspect of kabuki theatricals and began to be noticed by audiences. These scenes usually involved the arrest, capture or punishment of a leading character, often the samurai hero or the virtuous maiden, two traditional stock types of kabuki theater.

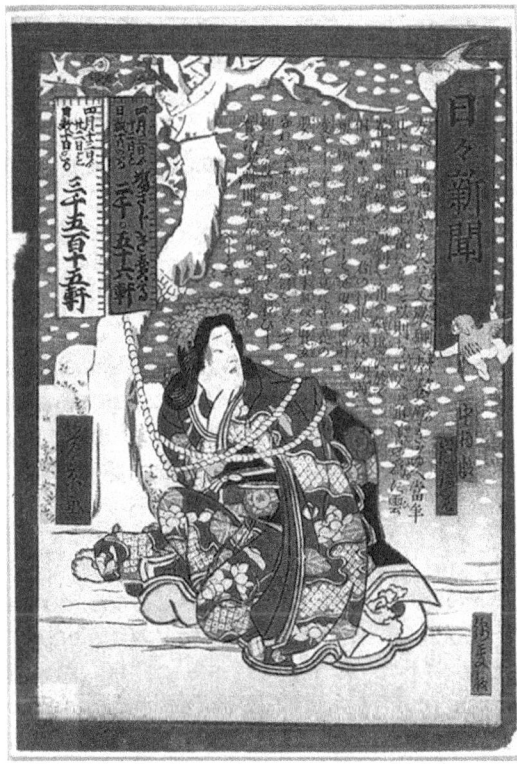

Kabuki print featuring actor Arashi Rikan IV as Princess Chujo bound in snow, circa late 19th century

This trend continued during the early Meiji period in so called "**new theater**" productions where even more contemporary subjects were treated in plays modeled on Western theater standards and featuring more naturalistic settings and acting. It is during this time frame, specifically in 1896, that a 14 year old boy named Itoh Hajime walked into the Haruki Theater in Tokyo and saw one of these melodramas. Thus would begin a lifelong fascination with seme (*the act of domination*) and seme-e (*art that depicts a scene of domination or punishment*) that would change the course of erotic art in Japan. Hajime grew up to be **Itoh Seiu** (1882-1961), one of Japan's most famous (or notorious, depending on your point of view) artists and generally recognized as the father of modern Shibari/Kinbaku.

The 1995 book, *Nihon ero shashin-shi* ("The History of Japanese Erotic Photography") by Shimokawa Koushi gives a concise description of this fateful performance in its chapter, "The Appearance of SM Photos," and it's worth quoting in some detail:

"As is clear to anyone, SM play is a big part of modern sexual culture. You can't talk about modern sexual culture without talking about SM. But SM is not something that started in modern times. In an earlier period, specifically at the time of the Sino-Japanese war, there was something of an SM boom.

"In Meiji 29 (1896), in June, in the Haruki Theater in Tokyo a play about the Sino-Japanese War, *Nisshin Sensou: Youchi no Katakitan*, opened. The story is about three military nurses who fall into enemy hands. They are tortured, but being loyal and patriotic, they refuse to talk. After the war, these three nurses meet up again with the soldiers who tortured them, but in a display of Japanese humanity, they forgive their tormenters.

"This play was very popular since the system for nurses had just been set up and people were very interested in their experiences at war. This story about female nurses, and their patriotism, greatly appealed to the public of that time.

"There was something else about the play that had a big affect. There was scene after scene in which the nurses were tied and tortured with their hair becoming disheveled and their thighs and breasts subject to attack. At that time, there were no female actors yet and the parts of the three nurses were played by onnagata (male actors who specialized in female roles). That was said to be very erotic and became quite a source of talk.

"The great seme-e artist Itoh Seiu saw this play when he was still a boy and stated, 'My chest clutched at the scenes where the nurse's hair became disheveled.' . . . After this, many other plays opened with similar themes and there was something of an SM boom. As Seiu said, 'It is certain that the theater at that time fanned public interest in Shibari.'"

We will return to Itoh Seiu, one of the most important figures in the creation of modern Shibari/Kinbaku art, and also to his love for bondage and disheveled hair several times in the course of this book, particularly in the biographies section, but here we can conclude by saying that kabuki and "new" theater productions that included seme-e material had a profound effect on him and on the general development of an SM consciousness in Japan. In later years Itoh would write several books about seme-e including *Seme no Hanashi* ("About Domination" or "Thoughts on Domination") in 1929 (reprinted in 1952) and *Kuronawa ki zen* ("The Complete Black Rope Diary") in 1951. In both of these works he devotes pages to listing the many kabuki and "new" theater productions, playwrights, actors and graphic artists that specialized or excelled in seme-e material.

One interesting practical effect that such seme-e scenes had involved the aesthetics and techniques of tying as used in these plays, techniques that would later affect modern Shibari/Kinbaku. As previously noted, hojojutsu patterns were always placed on the backs of prisoners and were generally tied using thin cord or hemp rope. Obviously, such techniques weren't suitable for the stage where actor's faces had to be seen at all times and where the ropes doing the binding of the heroes, heroines and villains had to be large and colorful enough to be noticed from the back of the theater. In addition, since male onnagata played all the female roles, tying with rope became both a challenge and an ideal way to accentuate the female form, certainly a potent source of eroticism. Each of these aspects of theatrical tying had its effect on modern Shibari/Kinbaku as early practitioners experimented with larger size ropes (before most returned to the approximately 6 mm diameter of true hojojutsu cord) and the fashion of creating intricate patterns on the front of the body, to say nothing of emphasizing the beauty of the female form with artful turns of nawa (rope), became established.

As the Edo era faded and Japan entered and progressed into the 20th century, theatrical performances that included seme-e material evolved into performances that concentrated on seme-e and this in turn inspired the SM stage shows of the legendary **Osada Eikichi** (1925-2001) in the 1960s which were, in turn, the precursors of today's modern SM club shows. At the same time dramatic films concentrating on SM themes became big business in Japan . . . but that's another story still to come. What cannot be denied is that the aestheticization and eroticization of bondage and "domination" began in the Edo and early Meiji theatrical and artistic worlds.

The graphic arts. Concurrent with the theater, the graphic arts also contributed to keeping the imagery of Edo era tying and punishments in the public's consciousness and helped turn them into the stuff of drama and erotic fantasy. While not a major theme for Japanese artists, the subject did crop up quite often in various forms of Edo era printmaking and painting.

Ukiyo-e, "pictures of the floating world," is the well known genre of Japanese woodblock prints and paintings produced between the 17th and early 20th centuries and featuring motifs of: landscape, the theater, tales from history, sumo wrestlers, folk tales and the supposedly exotic world of the courtesan. The art form rose to great popularity in the metropolitan culture of Edo during the second half of the 17th century.

Ukiyo-e prints were mass-produced and were meant mainly for townsmen and the burgeoning merchant classes who, though generally not wealthy enough to afford an original painting, did want to partake of luxury-type goods. The greatest artists of the age produced ukiyo-e, including: Hiroshige, Hokusai, Kunisada, Kuniyoshi, Utamaro and Yoshitoshi. Of the numerous subjects dealt with by these artists, so called "actor's prints" were one of the most popular.

As with today's movie and TV stars, Edo era Kabuki actors were famous, much admired and their likenesses were often reproduced in all sorts of ways: as prints, posters, post cards and even as decorative designs for fans. It was a most profitable genre for the printers. Scenes from popular plays then on stage would often be reproduced and, occasionally, the imagery of

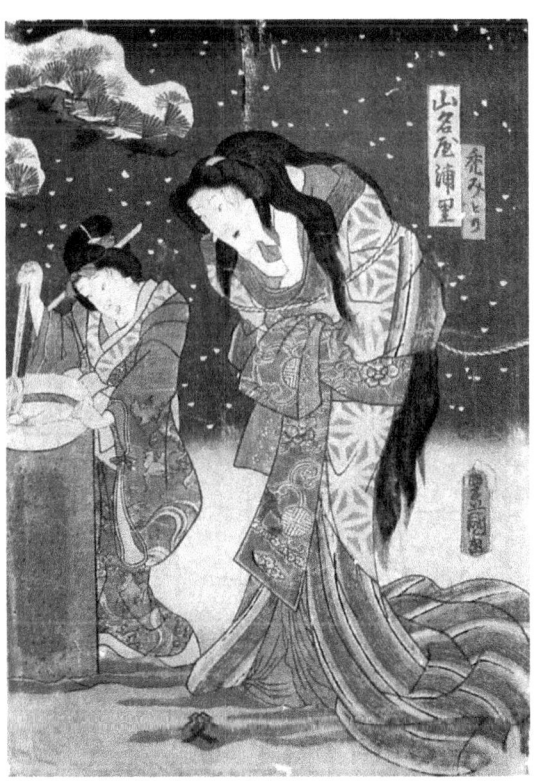

Bound onnagata in a kabuki print by Kunisada, circa 1850

hojojutsu, capture and punishment would appear, as in this print by **Kunisada Utagawa** (1786-1865).

Kunisada was one of the most prominent and prolific ukiyo-e artists specializing in actor and kabuki prints during the mid-19th century. The accompanying scene is clearly from a play and most probably shows the actor Bando Shuka, the foremost onnagata of his day, in a dramatic seme-e moment (note the hojojutsu rope). The reason we can't be positive about the actor's identity is that this print dates from the mid 19th century during the "Teppo reforms" when the Tokugawa government's off again, on again, censorship of kabuki prohibited artists from putting the actor's names and the names of the plays they appeared in on the prints they sold. This had not been the custom in the past and the names would be allowed again after this censorship eased in 1862. That said, Bando is the likely subject since the date is right (he died in 1855) and the likeness and dramatic setting is similar to several prints Kunisada did that are named.

Sometimes even the posters advertising a kabuki or "new" theater production carried explicit references to scenes of seme-e. Itoh Seiu, in his 1929 book *Seme no Hanashi*, discusses a sign painter in Yokohama named Gyohan who did promotional posters for theaters. The artist took such delight in advertising the seme-e scenes that his paintings were judged crueler than necessary and the police made the theaters take them down!

Yoshitoshi Tsukioka (1839-1892), also known as Yoshitoshi Taiso, was an even more influential artist for modern Shibari/Kinbaku. Generally regarded as the last great ukiyo-e master whose career spanned the late Tokogawa and early Meiji eras and so the great rush to modernization in Japan, Yoshitoshi brought a brilliant imagination and remarkable technical skills, including a Western sense of perspective, to his work creating images of great psychological depth and dramatic power. For this reason he is now

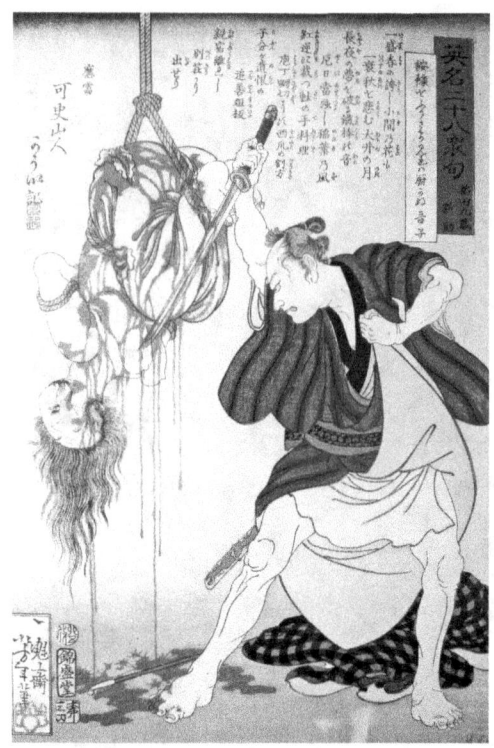

Ukiyo-e from the series "28 Famous murders with verse" by Yoshitoshi Taiso, 1867

almost universally recognized as the finest Japanese print artist of his era.

We will talk more about Yoshitoshi in the biography chapter so for now it's only necessary to note that he is the one indisputably great ukiyo-e artist who returned to scenes of a seme-e nature over and over again in his career both as a print maker and as a newspaper illustrator. His skill at creating images of violence and the supernatural have caused some critics to label his work as "bizarre" or "perverse" but this is only because the shock value of a few of these pictures overshadowed and drew attention away from the majority of Yoshitoshi's output. It also needs to be remembered that, in a way, he was somewhat similar to today's modern horror film directors who strive to create bloody effects simply in order to give their audiences a pleasurable but safe chill. In this he certainly succeeded but he wasn't alone.

During the early 19th century, stories of horror and cruelty, reflecting the brutal realities of both the day and times past, were expressed often through plays, books, and woodblock prints and artists such as Hokusai, Issen, Kunisada and Kuniyoshi (Yoshitoshi's teacher) designed many of these images. Violent or not, these types of pictures were what the customers and publishers wanted and Yoshitoshi was a product of his time. Certainly, while studying under Kuniyoshi, he developed the skills for creating horrifyingly graphic designs. One of his earliest series of prints, "*Twenty-eight famous murders with verse*" (1866-1867), based loosely on famous real-life murder cases depicted in kabuki plays and done in collaboration with the artist Yoshiiku, is particularly shocking but it made his reputation. A particularly grizzly plate from the series is presented here. It also demonstrates a remarkable eye for the technical aspects of hojojutsu and tsuri zeme (suspensions).

In later years, Yoshitoshi would combine this eye for detail with a talent for depicting psychology and subtle eroticism and produce several of the most remarkable "bondage" images of the 19th century. These images would, in turn, have a lasting effect on later seme-e and Shibari/Kinbaku masters such as Itoh Seiu.

A second type of ukiyo-e print called **shunga** carried even more explicit erotic content.

The term shunga means "*picture of spring*" with "spring" being a common Japanese euphemism for sexual activity. Edo era shunga sought to express the sexual mores of the merchant class in the widest variety of forms possible and therefore depicted heterosexual and homosexual love, the old and young and a wide range of fetishes. Such variety was due to the fact that the perception of sexuality in Tokugawa Japan differed markedly from that of the modern Western world. Sex in general was considered a normal and healthy activity and people were less likely to associate with one particular sexual preference. For this reason the many sexual pairings depicted in shunga were a matter of providing as much variety as possible. It was remarkably popular and was enjoyed by rich and poor men and women of all classes. And despite on occasion being out of favor with the shogunate censors it carried very little stigma. Almost all ukiyo-e artists made shunga at some point in their careers without it affecting their prestige as artists.

Several of the more famous shunga prints could be said to carry a hint of seme (domination) including the famous 1814 erotic masterpiece by **Hokusai Katsushika** (1760-1849), "The Dream of a Fisherman's Wife."

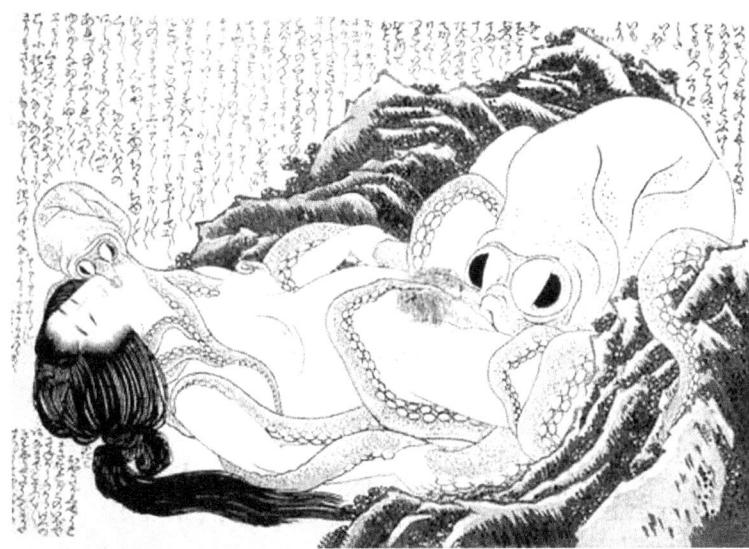

Few ukiyo-e painters remained aloof from the genre and some experienced artists even found it to their advantage to concentrate on its production. It is said that producing a piece of shunga for a high-ranking private client brought an artist enough money to live on for about six months. For the less affluent it

"The Dream of a Fisherman's Wife" by Hokusai Katsushika, 1814

was traditional to buy newly married couples less expensive shunga prints or books (called enpon) and women could obtain it themselves from lending libraries, which only speaks again to the genres ubiquity.

Naturally, most shunga depicted scenes of standard heterosexual coupling but sexual seme-e would appear on occasion. Kunisada Utagawa included a graphic shunga image of bondage and forced sex in what most art critics consider his most beautiful erotic book, the three volume *Shiki no Nagane* ("Scenes of the Four Seasons") published in 1827 and **Koryusai Isoda** (1735-1790) did an evocative print (probably a book illustration) of what is perhaps a brothel keeper punishing a bound courtesan, circa 1770.

Following the Meiji Restoration in 1868 ukiyo-e prints began to be supplanted by photography and went out of fashion in Japan during the bunmei-kaika, Japan's Westernization movement. Ironically, at about the same time ukiyo-e were introduced into Europe and became an important source of inspiration for European Cubist, Impressionist and Post-Impressionist artists such as Vincent Van Gogh, Claude Monet, Edgar Degas and Mary Cassatt, resulting in a style called Japonism.

As for shunga, it also succumbed to the introduction of photography, of the erotic variety. It too gradually declined beginning at the start of the Meiji era but its influence is still felt today in the sexually explicit **hentai anime** and **manga** cartoons and comics produced by Japan's huge adult media industry.

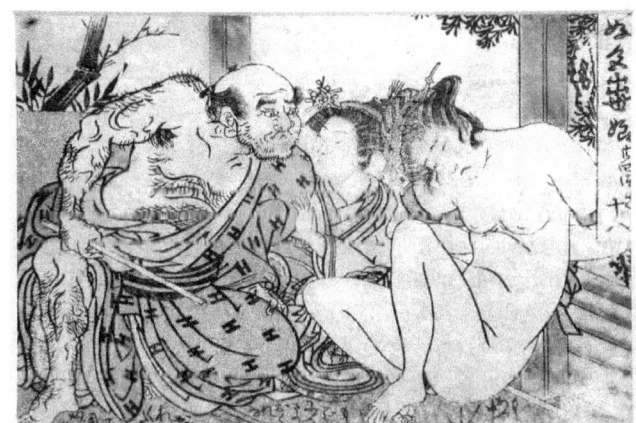

However, for artists such as Itoh Seiu with a predilection for SM the influence of Yoshitoshi and the seme-e of the 19th century remained profound and never died. It would be a key component in what would be the emergence of an overt SM culture in Japan and of the development and exploitation of modern erotic

Book illustration by Koryusai Isoda, circa 1770

Shibari/Kinbaku in art, publishing, photography and film during the next century.

Publishing and photography: Itoh and the evolution of SM

As the 20th century dawned, images of 19th century seme-e remained simmering in the public's consciousness but Japan's drive to create a modern and powerful nation kept all such reactionary and obsolete trappings of a feudal past decidedly out of fashion. Late 19th and early 20th century wars against the Chinese (1894-1895) and Russians (1904-1905) brought Japan unexpected (to the West) victories and propelled it into the forefront of modern nations where the rush to modernism and militarism preoccupied its rulers.

However, the past is not so easily forgotten and nostalgia for times lost affected some of Japan's better authors and artists, if not its militarist politicians. Such was the case with Itoh Seiu, the boy so fascinated by seme-e, who grew up to train as an artist and then to specialize in depicting everyday scenes from the history and customs of old Edo. This might surprise those who know Itoh only as Japan's most famous SM artist but the truth is that he tried a number of jobs in his early career including creating painted backdrops for kabuki theater and working as an illustrator for the Yomiuri Shimbun, still one of Tokyo's major daily newspapers, to make his living. As for the "preoccupation" that would ultimately make him famous, it had to be kept decidedly underground. This is another aspect of the formation of the famous Japanese "SM scene" that needs a fuller explanation.

To the Westerner, today's Japan often seems a very liberal place, especially as far as sexuality is concerned. Certainly it is true that Japan's accepting attitudes towards many religions and healthy, nonjudgmental approach to most sexual matters over the years have created a greater tolerance in that country for these all too often contentious areas of human activity. However, this was not always the case. The Shogun Tokugawa Ieyasu's persecution of Christians in the early 1600s as well as general shogunate repression of any political dissention or comment, even to the extent of prohibiting the mention of the Tokugawa name in books or of family images in ukiyo-e prints, certainly shows that there were many areas of censorship in feudal Japan. As with kabuki theater, various other arts and activities were also subject to intermittent government censorship that ebbed and flowed over the years. For instance, from 1790 on a formal system of censorship requiring government seals of approval was mandated for all ukiyo-e prints and most shunga was published privately. During the Meiji era censorship was still enforced and even an artist as famous as Yoshitoshi had several of his designs suppressed.

For the most part, this was still the climate when Itoh began his explorations into what today we would call SM art. Of course, in his day, at the beginning of the 20th century, there was neither much understanding nor use of that term. "Seme-e" covered all artistic presentations of any scene of "torment" and "hentai seiyoku" ("abnormal sexual appetite") was the usual phrase that covered all nontraditional sexual activities. Such was the state of affairs until after WWII. This is why when Itoh began to publish his studies of seme-e, hojojutsu and the beginnings of Kinbaku, he did it privately.

The emergence of Itoh Seiu. In the late 1920s and early 1930s Itoh, then in his 40's, began to gain some recognition as an artist by having several books of his illustrations of old Edo brought out by the publisher Castle North Studies. Privately, he also began to publish his studies of seme and seme-e. Among the first of his self published books were 1928's *Seme no Kenkyu* ("Domination Research") and 1929's *Seme no Hanashi* ("Domination Conversation or Discussion"), works which could be billed as the first true bondage/SM photography, commentary, and art collections ever published in Japan.

In them Itoh presented, for the first time in Japanese art, images that were fundamentally erotic in conception and *obviously* sadomasochistic in orientation. Of the numerous characteristics that define Itoh's style and would make this artist a near legendary figure, several stand out.

First, he was a superb draughtsman and colorist capable of depicting subtle variations in psychology and mood, as this lovely image of a bound woman in snow with her black hair in disarray amply demonstrates.

Second, his use of nude or nearly nude models in bondage was remarkable, provocative and certainly intended as sexual. It must be remembered that it had only been since 1871 that professional nude modeling was known in Japan, an event considered so unusual that we still know the name of the first model! **Miyazaki Kiku** was hired by a painter who came from France to pose nude for one month. This is the first recorded instance of a professional nude model in Japan. In 1896 Tokyo Geijutsu Geidai (The Tokyo School of Fine Arts) started a Western painting program and scouted for nude models. Many of the first were male laborers but Miyazaki signed up for a monthly salary.

Third, his inspiration was clearly the Edo era punishments, both official and private. Itoh's technique was to photograph his models after binding and tormenting them in various ways and then to use the photos as inspiration for his paintings.

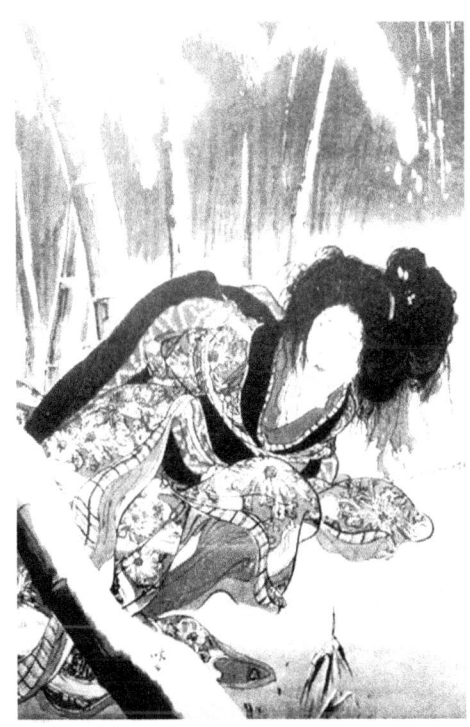

"Bound Woman in Snow" by Itoh Seiu

Photo after photo from his work books depict all the punishments of the Tokugawa era (various suspensions, pressing with stones, the ebi, etc.), including private punishments such as the *mokuba* (wooden horse), used almost exclusively on woman. In this torture the prisoner was stripped from the waist down, her hands bound behind her back and she was placed straddled atop a fairly sharp angled board!

Fourth, as is clear from the above, Itoh was definitely a sadist. That said, his masochistic partners were willing participants and there is no way of knowing how far Itoh usually went in approximating real tortures. From his writings it's quite clear that he tried to take care not to injure his partners by creating safer techniques to approximate the dramatic scenes of seme that he wished to paint. This obvious and intelligent approach had a major influence on artists attempting similar material in the decades to come. However, on at least one occasion, during the creation of one of his most famous works, "Woman Suffering in Snow," inspired by his fascination with the Princess Chujo legend and other tales, he clearly went too far. Again, to quote from *Nihon ero shashin-shi* ("The History of Japanese Erotic Photography") by Shimokawa Kōshi:

"The shooting for Itoh Seiu's seminal work, *Yukizeme* ("Woman Suffering in Snow"), was done in 1923, in February. Seiu always liked snow and found a play in which a woman is subjected to suffering in snow, *Akegarasu Yume no Awayuki*, particularly erotic. At that time he had a disciple (deshi) named Sakamoto who rented an old farmhouse in the Tokyo suburb of Takaido for use as an atelier. Behind the house was a bamboo grove and across from it were vast plum fields called Yoshida-en. Seiu knew about this and had always wanted to tie a woman there. The day finally arrived.

"Accompanying him was Seiu's second wife, his model Kiseko, a photographer named Suzuki and a helper named Takahashi. Seiu's first wife was completely uninterested in physical intimacy and SM and that union dissolved after ten years. But Kiseko had been an art model and was strongly submissive and she quietly submitted to whatever demands Seiu made of her."

In "Itoh Seiu: a biography," Fumiko Saito continues the story based on writings actually left by Seiu and Sakamoto:

"We tied up (the nearly nude) Kiseko and disheveled her hair, and led her deep into the garden and made her walk around for 30 minutes '. . . Seiu pushed her down into a snowdrift, and for about seven minutes she was half buried in snow as her suffering facial expression was captured by the lens.'

"That was the first shot. Then they moved on to the second. Seiu broke the ice on the pond and made to force Kiseko in. Sakamoto tried desperately to make him stop, arguing that the mud in the pond was deep and that it was known as the bottomless swamp. But Seiu said, 'It'll probably be ok if we stay near the edge.' And he told her to get in. It took her ten minutes to actually get in, and as she stood in the blowing snow, she was shivering so hard that she couldn't get her teeth together, but even so, she silently obeyed his order.

"Kiseko's lower body was in the frigid water, and we left her there like that for a while. We waited until her expression changed. When it was clear she was really suffering …., we took the picture, focusing on her expression under ice torture. She could no longer get out of the pond by herself, so Takahashi and Suzuki helped her out.

"That still wasn't enough. Takahashi washed the mud and dirt from her body and Seiu suspended her from bamboo trees. As part of Seiu's seme research, he had learned from an old man a hojojutsu technique of using bamboo poles in binding and was quite accomplished in Shibari, but this business of forcing her into snow, and a frozen lake, and then even pouring water on her, had the others very worried about Kiseko's physical safely. Itoh kept pushing her on, in the end getting five shots.

"As can be seen by examining the details of this photo shoot, there was an SM boom in progress and even compared to today's hard SM photo shoots, this was quite a hard shoot. Kiseko recovered and talked about the experience and it became quite a topic of discussion. As the renter of the house, Sakamoto was attacked by doubts and became practically unable to paint."

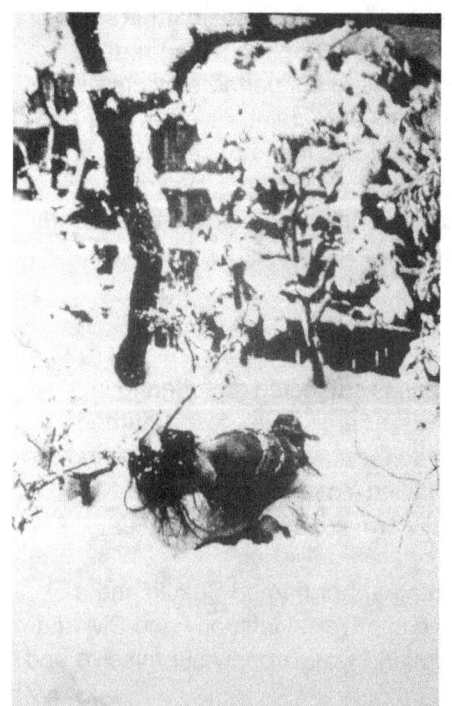

"Yukizeme" by Itoh Seiu, circa1923

Based on the above description, it is very easy to dismiss Itoh as a dangerous crank for so wantonly flaunting common sense. The "scene" might have been relatively "consensual" but it certainly broke the borders of "safe and sane." After all, when Van Gogh cut off his ear at least he didn't maim anyone else!

And yet . . . talented artists are sometimes driven, cruel, egotistical and unreasonable. Think again of Van Gogh . . . and William Blake and Picasso and many more. And regardless of his questionable common sense and overt sadism, it can't be denied that Itoh was an extremely gifted artist. Perhaps it's best that we think of him as an early type of obsessed "performance artist," one of those outrageous individuals who sometimes create remarkable things. One could also argue that Itoh's uniqueness as a painter came first from his great visual skill and taste but also from his stubborn determination to capture what he called, "beauty in suffering." That is, those emotions of real desire and real drama caught on the razor's edge between pain and pleasure during the experience of consensual sadomasochism.

In an article entitled, "Recollections on the Making of Maidens Suffering in Snow," Itoh recalled his great joy and satisfaction in realizing, after 19 years of dreaming, his "wildest artistic fantasy" and that, "On the night I finished shooting, I got drunk and made love to my wife like I had never done before!" In relief one presumes the beleaguered Mrs. Itoh had fully recovered.

A further consequence of this sensationalistic work was a growing reputation as a rebel in avant guard art circles. His book *Seme no Kenkyu* might be suppressed by the authorities and he might even be briefly arrested in 1930 for doing prints that were viewed as a satire of Confucianism, but an issue of Sunday Mainichi magazine, a very "normal" publication, featured a visit to his studio. He was becoming famous or, at the very least, infamous.

It should be pointed out that Itoh Seiu wasn't the only artist exploring the nascent connections between art and SM at this time. There were others. For instance, admired "pulp" authors such as Shimozawa Kan and Nakauchi Chouji and illustrators such as Kanamori Kan'you and Natori Shunsen were writing and drawing for various general audience magazines in the 1930s and frequently slipping in SM and seme-e type material. In addition, the late 1920s and early 1930s was also the time of the avant guard *Ero-Guro* movement in Japanese literature and the arts.

The name Ero-Guro (or *Eroguronansensu*, in full) is an anagram of sorts made from the English words "erotic grotesque nonsense" and describes early 20th century Japanese art and writings that depict violence and the bizarre in a somewhat erotic manner. These words were used because they had an air of the new and modern for the Japanese artistic intelligentsia of the 1920s. Roughly contemporaneous with the excesses of Weimar art and culture in Germany, the erotic, grotesque, nonsense, movement was a fringe group of artists but they did influence the various media of photography, graphic design, painting, poetry and detective fiction. Well known Japanese literary figures such as the mystery novelist **Edogawa Rampo** (real name Taro Hirai—the pseudonym "Edogawa Rampo" is actually a Japanese rendering of Edgar Allan Poe) and pioneering sexologist **Umehara Homumei** were major figures. Although Itoh was not a part of this movement per se, it is significant that both he and the Ero-Guro occupied the same time frame in the early 20th century and both involved themselves with what, at the time, was controversial writings and art.

Nor was Itoh the only photographer doing hojojutsu inspired "bondage" studies. It's likely that a man named Itoh Keijiro (no relation to Itoh Seiu), who more commonly went by the name **Itoh Chikusui**, also arranged seme-e photographic sessions in pre and post World War II Japan. These photos by various photographers were later sold by Chikusui to early SM magazines and appeared as the work of a seme-shi ("domination artist/master") named Kanai Yukio, a fictitious name created by the magazine's editors.

However, Itoh Seiu was the lightning rod for most of this type of material and as, despite increasing 1930s censorship, he published book after book (six on seme between 1928 and 1932) and paintings, scrolls and sketches, he began to draw other like-minded individuals into his circle.

Throughout his over 50 year career, Itoh would often hold sessions in his atelier or at other locations where a model or models would be tied (sometimes in elegant costumes and using elaborate sets) and photographs, sketches and paintings done. Participants in these daring events encompassed a wide cross section of artistic types including the above mentioned Itoh Chikusui, an onnagata named Sendai Baiko (who became a disciple of Itoh Seiu's) and **Ueda Seishiro**, a fledgling publisher. Not surprisingly, quite a few of these talents would emerge later in the century and be active in the rise of post war SM publications. And while Itoh couldn't be said to be consciously developing the techniques of what would become modern Kinbaku, his need to create safe versions of hojojutsu ties and seme for his models was leading him and his followers in that direction. It only needed time and a degree of public interest and acceptance for this historically based erotic art to evolve further.

Unfortunately, all such explorations were postponed by the devastation that was World War II. As is well known, between 1939 and 1945 Japan, like much of the rest of the world, was decimated by this conflict which left the country in ruins. What is often forgotten by the student of hojojutsu and seme-e art is that many of the most valuable and important historical pieces concerning these subjects were destroyed in this conflict. Itoh Seiu himself is said to have lost everything, all his early artworks, in the American bombings of Tokyo in the summer of 1945. As a friend living in Japan recently told me, "People couldn't save treasures, let alone themselves, their children, their old parents. It was bad."

With the end of the war life began to return to a semblance of normality and, in the flurry of reconstruction and the calm of peace, conditions were suddenly right for the re-emergence of SM oriented art, including the emerging techniques of Kinbaku, this time in spectacular fashion.

Kasutori—("bootleg sake") and the "golden age" of SM magazines

The tale of how the first truly SM oriented magazines began publishing in Japan can be somewhat garbled depending on who's telling the story but the basic outlines are fairly consistent. After the war there appeared a number of what we in the West would call "pulp magazines" catering to various interests. These were wryly called "kasutori" ("bootleg sake" or "low grade liquor") because of the cheap paper on which they were printed and because of their often vaguely salacious and erotic content.

The most famous of these pulps was the now legendary Kitan Club Magazine, its name taken from the abbreviation of the word "*ibunkitan*" meaning "strange stories" or "curious tales." This tabloid journal combining sensationalist fiction with vaguely erotic content was launched in 1947 and intended for the general reader. It quickly gained a loyal following including two readers from Osaka who were to have a decided impact on the future of Kinbaku.

Suma Toshiyuki was hired by Kitan Club's publisher, Yoshida Minoru, as an editor early in the magazine's formative years and **Tsujimura Takashi** was a reader who, one day in 1948 while bored at his post war job of counter duty at the local hardware store, decided to submit a short story to the magazine figuring he couldn't do any worse than the writers he was reading. To his delight it was accepted and this started him on a 25 year association with the magazine.

Suma Toshiyuki in time would become the author, editor, publisher and bakushi (rope artist) known as **Minomura Kou** and, taking the name of **Kita Reiko** (his wife's maiden name), one of the greatest Shibari/Kinbaku artists ever to put paint to paper, a legend in Japanese SM. Tsujimura would become one of the most famous early bakushi and a writer whose column, "Camera Hunt," would be one of the magazine's most popular features, one that profoundly influenced the course of Japanese Shibari/ Kinbaku. For his column Tsujimura would carefully tie amateur enthusiasts and professional models in a variety of creative ways using safe *tsuri* (suspension) and *newaza* (floor) techniques and then give his readers a record of this play in words and pictures. For many this was their first introduction to the concept of Shibari/Kinbaku as an affectionate, mature and consensual erotic activity.

Minomura had been a member of Itoh Seiu's circle and Tsujimura had been interested in Shibari since childhood so they were perfectly placed and ready to step in when publisher Yoshida began casting around for some new ideas to help increase circulation. Stories with a vague seme-e (SM) style and content were decided upon and began to appear. In 1950 the first illustration by Kita Reiko was published and in 1951 a novel by Tsujimura made its debut.

At this time it's interesting to note how literary these "pulps" really were. In large part these were magazines of stories: historical, comic, thrilling and erotic and in all genres, even mystery and science fiction. Photographs were expensive to publish and didn't reproduce well on cheap paper and illustrations were time consuming to do, so the written word was paramount. This meant the audience for these "low grade" magazines was actually quite literate, a significant plus, generally speaking, for consumer appreciation of erotic fantasy and imaginative material of all kinds. As an old Japanese saying goes, "Anything is permissible … in the mind." Or to put it another way, to safely appreciate fantasy, erotic or otherwise, it's best to have some intelligence, common sense and imagination.

It was in 1952, in the July issue to be exact, that a true commercial breakthrough occurred when the magazine published Kita Reiko's famous illustration, "Ten Positions of a Naked Tied Woman." This simple but elegant line drawing of 10 "bondage" images caused a sensation in the buying public and increased sales significantly. This so pleased publisher Yoshida that he set the future course of Kitan Club firmly in the direction of erotic SM.

In their comprehensive study, *Nihon Kinbaku Shashin Shi* ("The History of Bondage Photos in Japan"), co-authors Nureki Chimuo and Masami Akita state that "*Ten Positions of a Naked Tied Woman* was the trigger that set the magazine on a specialized course of bondage, . . . and is without doubt Japan's first (publicly printed) modern illustration of blatantly sexual seme-e, . . . that quite clearly targeted its appeal to bondage enthusiasts." They go on to state that, "In (sexual) seme-e, Kita Reiko had in fact renewed what was largely a kabuki passion of master Itoh Seiu."

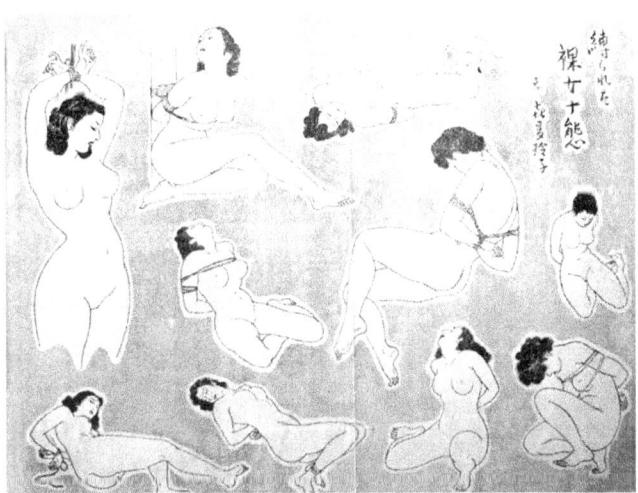

"Ten Positions of a Naked Tied Woman"
By Kita Reiko—Kitan Club, 1952

After this there was no holding back and story after story, drawing after drawing featured bondage used in a generally erotic way. Kita Reiko even produced at least three different versions of his famous illustration (with ever more tied women included) for various Kitan Club issues and stories of male domination were also created and also proved quite popular.

A second milestone was reached that same summer (1952) when editor Minomura, after getting permission from the publisher, asked Tsujimura to tie the model **Kawabata Tanako** for the first Kitan Club nude bondage photo. Photographs of nude models had appeared in other magazines before this but this was the first nude in bondage done expressly for a commercially published, SM oriented, monthly magazine offered for general sale (as opposed to Itoh's often banned private publications). This event also marked, as Tsujimura stated in an autobiographical article published years later (SM King, July 1973), the first use of the words "Kinbaku" and "Kinbaku model" in print. As startling as this anecdote seems, my inclination is to believe it. In my research I have found no earlier use of this unusual word in any document involving seme-e, bondage art, Japanese history or hojojutsu In addition, there is other circumstantial evidence that suggests the truth of this claim. Prior to 1952, Itoh Seiu in his many books and writings always used the words "Shibari" and "seme," among other terms, when discussing his work. However, after 1952 and the rise in popularity of Kitan Club he started to use the word "Kinbaku" to describe sophisticated, Japanese style, rope bondage.

In my archive I'm fortunate to have complete runs of Kitan Club and its equally famous competitor Uramado and it's fascinating to watch the evolution of both publications and the emergence of the art of Kinbaku during these early years. It's especially startling to note that these were truly specialized erotic magazines that appealed to a very selective, interested and sophisticated (in terms of rope bondage and related SM subjects) audience. For instance, after this watershed year of 1952, elegant Shibari illustrations by Itoh and many other gifted artists routinely appear in every issue and the techniques of safe tying are often addressed alongside the usual pulp stories and erotica. Photos become more numerous, including many taken over the years by Itoh and his circle and, in a more scholarly vein, several articles by respected experts are published on the history of seme in Japan and on the Tokugawa punishments of 1742 (i.e., by Nawa Yumio in six installments in Uramado).

Taking an issue at random; in June 1954 Kitan Club published a remarkable double page spread of photographs reproducing several classic hojojutsu ties (front, side and back) on a nude model and in the same issue there is a ten page article (illustrated with nine photographs) by Tsujimura discussing a "Kinbaku session" and the tying techniques employed. Various other fetishes are discussed in the issue as are the "aesthetics" of erotic photography and there's a reader's column where customers get to voice their interests and criticisms. There's even a story concerning seppuku, the age old tradition of ritual suicide for disgraced samurai!

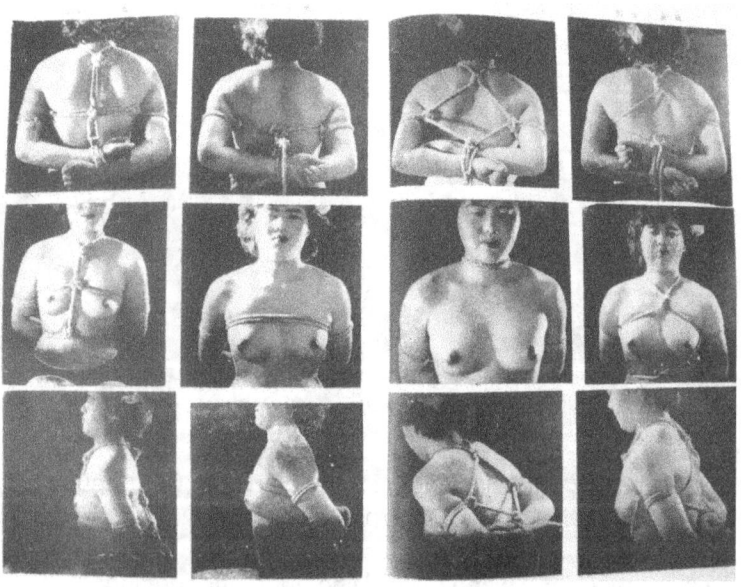

Authentic hojojutsu ties reproduced in Kitan Club—June, 1954

According to Minomura, there was a passionate interest in the types of ties used in the pictures and illustrations of those early days and new techniques were avidly commented upon. Because of this a controversy erupted over certain Kinbaku photos then being produced.

Nude "bondage" images were becoming much more common and various photographers strove to create striking patterns and bold designs. However, in some photos the Kinbaku became secondary as ropes were loosely "draped" over the obviously posing models. In fact, there was a veritable outburst of this, so called, "rope fixing nude art" during the early years of the first SM magazines and this infuriated people like Itoh Seiu and his followers who considered it to be a "despicable imitation of true bondage art." As is obvious from looking at his work (and that of people like Minomura Kou), bondage was something more than just the mechanical fastening of ropes around a subject's body. To Itoh such fake techniques led to insincerity, commercialism and pornography. True passion and emotion as well as skilled craft had to be demonstrated if the Kinbaku was to be called art. Some say it was Itoh Seiu's revulsion against these "fake" works of bondage art that led him to devote his energies toward the creation of a distinct bondage "school" and this school in time became the mainstream form of rope tying as an art form in Japan. In consequence, Itoh's status as one of the founding fathers of Kinbaku as an artistic means of expression seems secure.

By 1956 Minomura Kou had left Kitan Club to start his own magazine, the aforementioned Uramado or "Back Window" magazine, which quickly rivaled Kitan Club in popularity. One of its greatest calling cards was the illustrations it published featuring, of course, the beautiful work of Kita Reiko (AKA Minomura Kou). So devastating a loss was this defection to Kitan Club that they hired noted artist Shibatani Saijiro and gave him the name **Taki Reiko** in the hopes that Kita Reiko might not be too badly missed!

The use of these pennames for authors and contributors to the magazines became quite common at this time, as it had for the "pulps" in the United States in the 1930s. The reasons were a desire for anonymity when writing and drawing erotica and to make the magazines appear to have more columnists than they actually did. Suma Toshiyuki (AKA Minomura Kou/Kita Reiko) used at least 9 different names when writing his articles, short stories, criticism, novels and creating his illustrations and a young man named Iida Toyokazu, who Minomura hired as an editor on Uramado, used at least a dozen! This young man would continue in the business as both a prolific author and an admired bakushi, first as Toyo Kanichiro and then under the legendary name **Nureki Chimuo**. Until his passing in 2013, Nureki was for decades generally regarded as the greatest living Kinbaku master. He also wrote many books on the subject he knew best, including the above mentioned *Nihon Kinbaku Shashin Shi* ("The History of Bondage Photos in Japan").

In addition to running interesting articles and locally produced Kinbaku photos and art, these early SM magazines also printed illustrations from the early Western "bondage" publications of John Willie and Irving Klaw, including cartoons by famous "fetish" artists such as: Willie, Stanton, Jim, Mario and Eneg. These were obtained for the magazines by Morishita Takashige of the company Phoenix who had many contacts in the US and it's interesting to speculate how much Willie (real name: John Alexander Scott Coutts, 1902-1962), who is generally regarded as one of the finest Western bondage and "fetish" artists ever to have published, might have been influenced by the Japanese and vice versa. Evidence suggests that he, and by extension the course of "Western bondage," was strongly influenced.

According to various sources, including the authoritative second edition of "The Adventures of Sweet Gwendoline" by John Willie (Belier Press, 1999), the artist was quite aware that his art and photos were being published in Japan because he was being sent copies and/or excerpts of Kitan Club (and possibly Uramado) by an American correspondent known as "Doc," a US military officer stationed in Japan in the 1950s. The images of Kinbaku he saw apparently inspired him and he, "extracted a few ideas for use in his own photographs."

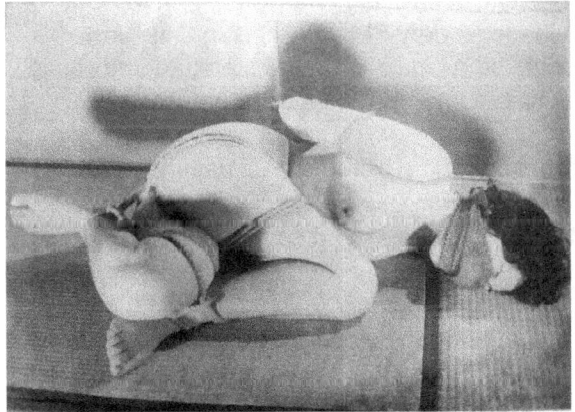
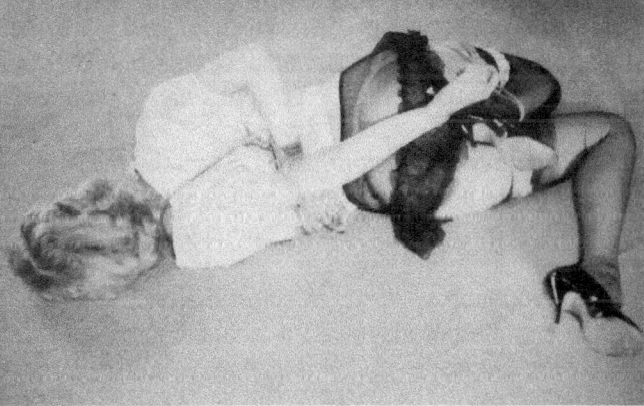

Imo mushi shibari by Minomura Kou, 1953   *John Willie, Hollywood, CA, circa 1957-1961*

Fortunately, a lot of John Willie's photos and art have been published over the years and it's clear by comparing the dates when the photos were taken that more than "a few" ideas from Kinbaku were borrowed. In his early photos, done between 1937 and 1944, the bondage is quite simple and there is almost no Japanese influence or inspiration. However, in the 1950s, especially during his "Hollywood period" of 1957-1961, it's clear that he was often copying Japanese ties that first illustrated the early Japanese SM magazines of 1953-1956.We know Willie was the one being influenced because many of the Japanese ties pictured in Kitan Club, etc. were, of course, based on the hojojutsu patterns and Edo Era punishments of centuries past. This is particularly obvious in Willie's photos because he does so many positions that clearly mimic such classical Kinbaku ties as the *ebi Shibari*, the *agura Shibari* and the *imo mushi Shibari* and because he does so many pictures using short bamboo sticks (*takezao Shibari*) and the *hashira*, the ubiquitous standing pole of Japanese architecture that is a fairly rare detail in Western buildings. This only goes to show that even at this early date there was cross cultural communication and influence.

In fact, in many ways Kitan Club and Uramado were both quite similar to John Willie's legendary magazine "Bizarre" which also tried to provide a forum for "alternative" sexual interests in the late 1940s and early 1950s in America. The Japanese might have been more successful than Klaw and Willie, whose publications and companies soon perished under US censorship, but it wasn't easy.

In 1955 Kitan Club ceased publication for over a year due to governmental pressure and only came back in a reduced format in 1956. It's shocking to see the difference between the issues of those years. Gone are the pages of daring photos and art and even the creative and beautifully colored covers have been reduced to stark black and white. The magazine wouldn't really recover until 1960.

Much of the material in the above section comes from well known author and Kinbaku model **Saotome Hiromi** whose 2003 book, *Kitan Kurabu no Hitobito* ("Kitan Club People"), written in collaboration with Kitahara Domu, is a mine of fascinating information. It's clear from her timeline that, as opposed to what Westerners often think, it was a long fight to gain the freedom of action Japanese publishers of erotica currently enjoy.

1962: The March issue of Kitan Club is labeled as harmful material (*yūgai toshō*) by panels in Kanagawa and Hiroshima prefectures because of the color photos. In response, the editors start some self-censorship—cutting the so-called "gravia" photos (big color photos). On May 4, they are formally told by a publishing association to self-regulate.

The famous novel, ***Hana to Hebi*** ("Flower and Snake") begins to serialize in Kitan Club from the Oct-Sept issue. Written by Kuroiwa Yukihiko (better known as the legendary SM author, **Dan Oniroku)** under the early penname Hanamaki Kyotaro, this novel would be a landmark in SM literature and would be republished under the Dan Oniroku name in various formats numerous times over the years.

1964: Kanagawa prefecture again slams the magazine, this time for the pictures in its January issue. In response, the number of shops refusing to take the February issue increases rapidly. The censors also put the brakes on *Hana to Hebi* and start cutting certain words from stories and serialized novels.

1965: A youth protection committee sharply criticizes the February issue. In the March issue no photos at all are printed. Kanagawa Prefecture complains that it doesn't see any evidence of self-censorship in the November issue.

1969: On the February cover, the word "for adults" appears for the first time. Tsujimura complains that Kitan Club is being singled out for censorship, "Why are they only strict with Kitan Club?"

1972: "Gravia" photos are back from the January issue.

1973: Increased censorship, including erasing parts of pictures and the use of stamps to cover objectionable images, begins.

1975: After nearly 20 years Kitan Club, now a shadow of its former self, ceases publication with the March issue.

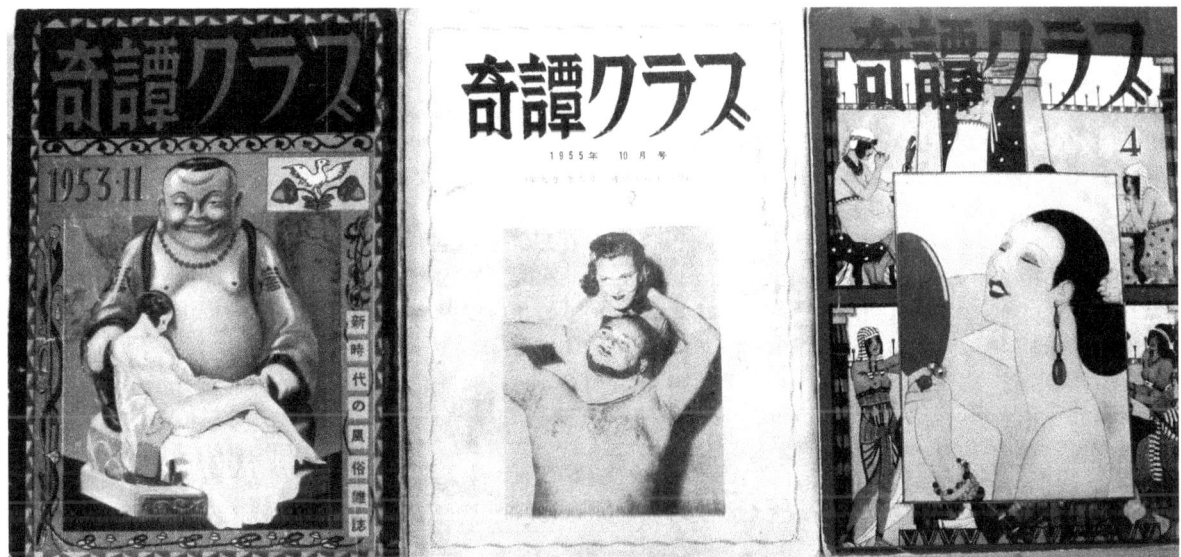

Kitan Club covers—note effects of censorship on the middle issue

In truth, by the middle of the 1960s, due to increasing pressure from the authorities, the first "golden age" of SM magazines was to all creative intents and purposes over. Uramado had also ceased publication, after nine years, in 1965 transforming itself into the far safer, more ordinary and much less controversial, Suspense Magazine.

While this is to be lamented, what is remarkable is that these early SM magazines were published at all and that they contained so much quality material. Regardless of one's thoughts on the morality and effect of "erotica" on society, these publications contained numerous examples of superb art by talents as diverse as the mysterious **Ishizuka**, the classically trained religious artist **Kobinata**, the *bijin* ("beautiful woman") specialist from the ukiyo-e tradition **Kitoh Akira** and the noted surrealist **Nakagawa Ayako** (AKA Fujino Kazutomo). As was the case during the time of shunga, many remarkably fine artists turned their hands to Kinbaku and SM art in these years, even if they did it using a nom de plume.

As for the evolution of the art of Kinbaku, these were truly the formative years. Beginning with fairly rudimentary techniques heavily influenced by hojojutsu, Kinbaku began to evolve because of the need to tie for photo sets and as a result of the interest in SM "play." Rope patterns that once appeared on the backs of prisoners switched to the fronts of beautiful models. The challenge was to make these effective historical ties safe, beautiful to look at and, if possible, erotic; for the most part the same qualities required of the honnawa ties of hojojutsu. Only the eroticism was added but this was a seismic shift in intent as the punishments of hojojutsu and seme became the art and eroticism of Kinbaku.

This is also the time when the naming of various ties and positions began in earnest, again influenced by hojojutsu and seme traditions. Minomura Kou and Tsujimura Takashi (and, of course, Itoh) were at the forefront of this creating many of the classical Kinbaku patterns we use today and some remarkable advances in "rope technique" occurred just before the first "golden age" magazines crashed. However, as was the case with the censorship of kabuki art in the 19th century, this latest freeze was also not to last and there would soon be a second flowing of "low grade sake" in the 1970s, distilled by many of these same creative people.

The emergence of "modern" SM and the second wave of magazines

What we would recognize today as familiar Kinbaku art and modern SM really began in the second wave of SM publications beginning in the early 1970s. At this time, censorship was relaxed (save for the scapegoat Kitan Club) and numerous specialty SM/Kinbaku magazines found their way into publication. Arriving sometime in the decade between the early 1970s and the early 1980s were such titles as: SM Collector, SM Select, SM Kitan (first published as Abu Hunter before changing its name), SM Mania, SM Fan, SM Sniper, SM Spirit and SM King.

What prompted this explosion was the emergence, in the late 1960s, of SM as a legitimate erotic activity in the mainstream consciousness of the Japanese public. Itoh's secret obsession was suddenly "hip" and as long as the practice of it didn't disturb the *wa* ("harmony") of society by being too overt or too offensive it began to be tolerated. Generally speaking, this is the same attitude that prevails today. Society's understanding of sadomasochism had changed and become more open in part because of the success of several films and the late night television program "11 pm," which frequently addressed the subject of SM and other formally risqué subjects. Tsujimura Takashi even appeared as a fairly frequent guest on the program after he provided expert advice and did the bondage for several historical films directed by Ishii Teruo and produced by the Toei Company, a very mainstream studio. And he was not alone as other SM "players" soon followed. In short, the term "SM" became generally known and came out of the closet; a major shift after being a hidden culture for years.

In many ways, this second wave of SM magazines picked right up where the first had ebbed. The differences being that the magazines were now more overtly sexual and the printing technology had improved. In consequence, the quality in the reproduction of both photographs and art had vastly increased. Color had also become the norm, for at least some of the magazines' pages, and this allowed for vivid reproductions of an artist's work.

Minomura Kou was again influential in this era as "adviser," artist, author, bakushi and critic for both SM Collector and SM Kitan as well as a contributor to many of the other publications. The magazines he worked for became known for their fiction, commentaries, cartoons, Kinbaku tutorials (offered by Nureki Chimuo under his first bakushi name Toyo Kanichiro) and outstanding color art inserted into every issue.

In addition to the always unique work of Kita Reiko, several of the older artists continued to be represented, such as Kobinata and Kitoh Akira. Added to these talents were newer names that began to receive favorable notice such as the remarkable pencil sketch master **Muku Youji**, the bijin painter **Kasuga Akira** and **Ozuma Kaname** whose trademark would become the astonishing and brilliantly colorful irezumi (tattoos) with which he regularly adorned the intricately bound Edo era maidens in his paintings. In the early years of the SM resurgence magazines competed for these fine artists.

Illustrated short stories continued to dominate the pages of the magazines and authors like Nureki (under his numerous pennames) and Minomura Kou wrote reams of copy. Another greatly admired and prolific writer was **Chigusa Tadao**. A very private individual and a man of great talent who never revealed his true identity, Chigusa was said to be a high school teacher in Kanazawa. He first wrote for Kitan Club and Uramado and then throughout the SM resurgence of the 1970s, ultimately publishing over 420 works of fiction. Today his much sought after erotic novels often fetch hundreds of dollars apiece when they appear on auction.

Women authors also made their mark at this time with the talented **Matsui Raiko** working for several magazines at once and penning her own SM novels. And these novels were not just serialized pulp magazine versions. Several publishers (Uramado, Amatoria-sha, etc.) put out series of high quality, hard cover volumes that usually included numerous color and/or black and white illustrations by name artists and written by the best talents in the field.

The most famous SM writer in these years continued to be Dan Oniroku (of "Flower and Snake" notoriety) who began his own magazine in 1972 called SM King. This "kasutori-shi" really tried to be a cut above the others and got a lot of early buzz as a magazine edited, "only by female editors." It was quite an ambitious publication as every issue featured: illustrated fiction (involving Kinbaku and other fetishes), portfolios of color art by the best talents, numerous Kinbaku photo sets and tutorials, early SM manga (comics), interviews with notable SM people, historical articles, reader's columns and occasional film criticism. Dan even hired Tsujimura Takashi as **Kinbaku shidou** ("Kinbaku teacher") for SM King to supervise some of the tying shown in his magazine and to continue his always popular "Camera Hunt" column. So popular did this feature once again prove with readers that Minomura Kou countered with his own column, "Rope Hunt," for his own magazines!

One notable difference between the first group of SM magazines in the 1950s and 1960s and this second batch is the slightly greater reliance on photographs as the years went by. Most magazines featured at least two well produced Kinbaku photo sets per issue with models tied in ever more interesting and stylish ways. Males in bondage and domination were also featured and Western "bondage photos" were still being imported from the United States. Looking at these Western images it's hard not to notice their crudeness and more pointed misogyny in comparison with the better Japanese efforts. Partly this is due to the higher quality Japanese photography by such masters as **Sugiura Norio** whose use of strong, dramatic, "single source" lighting in SM Select and SM Fan would become his trademark. That said, it's also true that in most ways the Japanese "take" on this kind of material was more aesthetically complex and sophisticated.

True fans (called "maniacs") could even tell the subtle differences between Kinbaku styles in the various magazines. Minomura Kou, for instance, when he worked as a bakushi, favored elegantly simple and traditional floor ties and patterns that were carefully constructed to cause models the least amount of physical stress and instead created situations of shūchi ("shyness" or "shame"). The younger Toyo Kanichiro (Nureki Chimuo) favored a more forceful style of tying using many ropes and complex patterns and Tsujimura Takashi, always creative, began to experiment with safely creating tsuri (suspensions) for his willing partners.

It's difficult to know exactly how popular these monthlies were at the time but some conclusions can be drawn from the sales figures of one of the most successful publications, SM Select. In Dan Oniroku's autobiographical writings published in 1999, Hana wa Kurenai ("Flowers are Crimson"), he states that SM Select boasted 100,000 copies sold per month at its zenith, much more than SM magazines had in the past which he further suggests usually sold no more than 50,000 copies. Regardless of the exact figures, if even remotely accurate, this is a remarkably healthy circulation for such a specialty magazine. Even so, these monthlies were usually bought by the already interested "maniacs." The general public became aware of Kinbaku and SM because of TV and the movies. The filmic side of all of this is a fascinating story and worth a slight detour.

SM in the movies and the remarkable case of Nikkatsu studios

The complex history of Japanese erotic films is worthy of a book of its own and luckily there is such a volume and it's in English! Thomas and Yuko Mihara Weisser's excellent "Japanese Cinema Encyclopedia-The Sex Films" (1998, Vital Books Inc.) is a well written and entertaining source of information on all aspects of the Japanese erotic film industry: its history, censorship, films, stars, producers and directors. Fortunately, as far as the SM side of this business is concerned, the history is fairly straightforward.

By the early 1970s, about the same time as the second SM magazine boom began, the Japanese film industry was in serious trouble. Audiences were deserting the theaters in droves for television and the glory days of post war Japanese Cinema, the years when directors such as Ozu Yasujiro, Mizoguchi Kenji and Kurosawa Akira had astonished the West with such masterpieces as "Tokyo Story," "Ugetsu Monogatari" and "The Seven Samurai," were long over. Both Ozu and Mizoguchi had passed away by this time and Kurosawa had even tragically attempted suicide after the failure of his independently produced 1970 film "Dodesukaden." Fortunately for movie lovers the world over, Kurosawa would recover and, with financing from *outside* Japan and the help of such admirers and fellow directors as

George Lucas ("Star Wars") and Francis Ford Coppola ("The Godfather"), go on to create several more cinema masterpieces in the 1980s and 1990s.

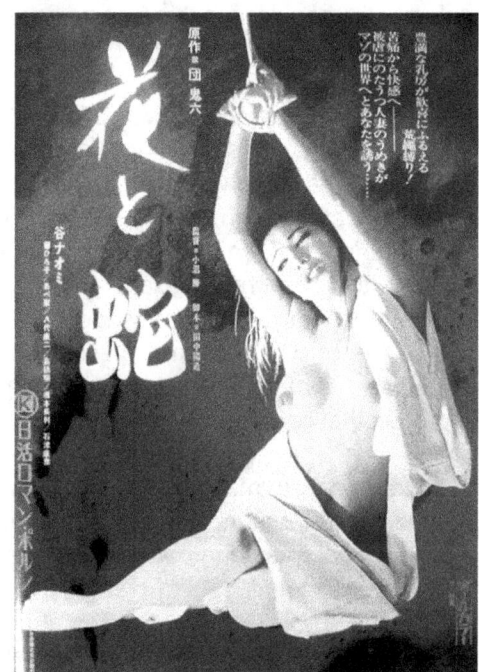

Nikkatsu studios, created in 1912, was one of the major Japanese production companies then feeling the strain. On the verge of bankruptcy they came up with the novel idea of throwing their dwindling resources into **pinku eiga** (erotic/sex films) which until 1971 had only been the province of second and third rate companies. To get an idea of how momentous a decision this was, imagine the reaction in the United States if MGM had dropped the musicals and gone into pornography!

As shocking as this seems, the move proved relatively successful and in 1974 the company's board decided to try a new line of pinku eiga, which they had re-named **roman-porno** ("romantic pornography"), this time incorporating SM themes. On June 22, 1974 the first film version of Dan Oniroku's famous novel *Hana to Hebi* ("Flower and Snake") was released and was quickly followed by *Ikeniie Fujin* ("Wife to be Sacrificed"). Both films were directed by **Konuma Masaru** and starred the remarkable actress **Tani Naomi**.

Poster for "Flower and Snake" starring Tani Naomi—© Nikkatsu Studios, 1974

Whether this was sheer commercial desperation or a shrewd understanding of the zeitgeist of the moment can't be known but the results were spectacular. "Flower and Snake" was very successful but "Wife to be Sacrificed" turned out to be a blockbuster, becoming not only Nikkatsu's biggest hit of the year but also one of the studio's five top grossing films *of all time*! Further SM oriented films quickly followed.

Although remarkable, perhaps we shouldn't be too surprised by this success given Japan's general tolerance for sexual material in the past. Films with erotic overtones had been accepted and admired for quite a few years with director Suzuki Seijin's 1964 classic "Gate of Flesh," a story of turmoil and passion among prostitutes at the close of WW2, generally being considered the first mainstream Japanese film to contain nudity. Still, to produce quality films concentrating on SM themes was a bold move.

The stories for Nikkatsu's SM product were a mixed bag ranging from the frankly tasteless and misogynistic to the artful and psychologically complex. The intense "Wife to be Sacrificed" tells the story of a deranged divorced man who kidnaps his ex-wife in order to try to reconcile and "Flower and Snake" explores the intertwined lives of a younger man trying to overcome an early sexual trauma and the young wife of a rich older man who learns she's attracted to SM. Clearly, such relative psychological and narrative complexity takes these stories out of the realm of pornography and, while it's true that in most Western countries these films would never qualify as "politically correct," the argument can be made for artistic merit. That said, perhaps the West is becoming more tolerant. "Wife to be Sacrificed" had its US premier 24 years after its initial release when it opened in San Francisco in 1998 to good reviews.

Tani Naomi in a recent interview reflecting on the success of her Nikkatsu films said, "I believe these films offer *quality* consisting of, 1.) a highly dramatic plot, 2.) an entertaining aura, coupled with, 3.) a distinctly Japanese ambience." The quality she speaks of was the other important factor that allowed the best of these tightly scripted films (each running no more than 70 minutes in length) to do well at the box office. Nikkatsu had the resources to give them first rate production values and better than average acting. Although not expensive to make (most cost no more than about 1.8 million yen, about $180,000), they did draw on the expertise of fine studio craftsman, attractive stars and solid writers and directors.

In Matsushima Toshiyuki's book, *Nikkatsu Roman Porno Zenshi* ("The Complete History of Nikkatsu Roman Porno"), Konuma Masaru, director of "Wife to be Sacrificed" and "Flower and Snake," talks about how the studio allowed the directors great control over the content of their films, only requiring that a sex scene be included every ten minutes! Handling these scenes was a major challenge since full nudity was strictly prohibited by the censors. In truth, a great deal of creativity had to be shown in order to stay within the bounds of what was permitted but these limitations often provoked remarkably interesting ideas and visuals. Obviously, this meant that the more intelligent the filmmaker the more interesting the result. Certainly Konuma was one of these unique talents as attested to in a recent documentary by one of his more famous younger assistants, Nakata Hideo; a young man he also mentored and the director of the 1998 horror hit "The Ring."

As far as the Shibari/Kinbaku in these films is concerned, that posed a special challenge. It was one thing to tie for still photos but to bind actors in the classical style and not fake the techniques while still allowing them to act was quite a feat. It certainly required more skill than loosely tying the heroine to the railroad tracks! As mentioned previously, Tsujimura Takashi had pulled this off for several very violent historical films for Toei studios: *Tokugawa Onna Keibatsu-shi* (1968), *Zankoku-Ijou-Gyakutai Monogatari: Genroku Onna Keizu* (1968) and *Tokugawa Irezumi-shi Seme Jigoku (*1969). For "Wife to be Sacrificed" and "Flower and Snake" the job fell to an extremely talented, creative and literate bakushi named **Urado Hiroshi**.

In a 1977 issue of "Sun and Moon" magazine Urado talked about his experience of being the "Kinbaku shidou" for these famous films. He describes how director Konuma asked him for his creative suggestions on what types of Kinbaku to tie for each scene and then, surprisingly, let him do pretty much what he wanted. He also mentioned that he liked Konuma because he was a "romanticist" like himself. The result of this creative freedom and similar take on the material was a remarkably inventive series of Kinbaku ties that beautifully complimented the narrative. Urado used all sorts of classical and modern techniques and, working in some very difficult conditions of wind and rain, produced artistically interesting ties that challenged and, like a fine costume, enhanced the beautiful Tani Naomi. In *Kifujin Shibari Tsubo* ("Nobel Lady: Bound Vase") from 1977 Urado even had to tie Tani naked to her lover, back to back, and riding bareback on a galloping horse! This was a very dangerous stunt to do and, even using a hidden belly strap for the horse and creative camera angles, required a lot of skill.

Quite a few of the more spectacular scenes in these films involved doing tsuri (suspensions) with actors, not just stunt people, pulled high into the air and it was at this time that intelligent bakushi like Tsujimura and Urado, building on the experience of doing the magazine still shoots, worked out safe methods for recreating what were after all serious torture techniques. These dazzling circus type stunts even became the stuff of stage shows as the pioneering SM maestro Osada Eikichi took up these safer techniques and began his legendary performances in Tokyo, attracting huge crowds. As mentioned earlier, his shows become the forerunners of today's SM club acts, most of which involve exciting Kinbaku aerials.

Dan Oniroku continued his collaboration with Nikkatsu and Tani Naomi until her retirement in 1978. Together they turned out 15 slickly produced SM films, a remarkable total for only six years. In addition to the films already mentioned, here are a few of the more interesting Nikkatsu SM titles featuring stories by Dan, the lovely Ms. Tani and/or artful Kinbaku in various combinations: *Ori No Naka No Yōsei* ("Fairy in a Cage"), *Dan Oniroku Shoujo Shibari Ezu* ("Image of a Bound Girl"), *Dan Oniroku Nawa To Hada* ("Rope and Skin") and *Hakkinbon Bijin* ("Beauty's Exotic Dance – Torture!"). *Hakkinbon Bijin* is loosely based on the autobiographical writings of Itoh Seiu and *Dan Oniroku Nawa To Hada* is Tani Naomi's last film. I offer these titles because several of them are available on DVD with English subtitles.

By the time Nikkatsu's Roman Pornos began to run out of steam at the beginning of the 1980s, the studio had produced more than 1100 titles, many of them SM themed, and although even Nikkatsu used the term pornography to describe their "pink" films, these movies should not be confused with "porn" as we know it today. More accurately and in fairness, *pinku eiga* should be called erotica. For while it's true that the genre indulges in some strong and perverse storylines—pink movies have forever been attacked by church groups and moral guardians worldwide—all the Nikkatsu films are soft core and in Japan, at least, were seen as viable escapist entertainment.

Shibari/Kinbaku, 1980-today: art, pornography or personal passion?

It is remarkable to the author how much has changed in the world of Kinbaku in the few years since the first edition of this book appeared. Economics have a great deal to do with it to say nothing of the world wide effects of the Internet and social media. Great figures have passed from the scene and new ones have risen to prominence and the art of Kinbaku has crossed the borders of Japan and has now become quite popular, at least in terms of counter culture interest, all over the world. This chapter will try to put this all in a historical context as well as detail some of the more significant developments.

Since 1980, SM and Shibari/Kinbaku have become accepted parts of the Japanese erotic and even cultural landscape. No longer the "flavor of the month," they have become an almost commonplace element in the huge Japanese erotic industry that arose in the 1980s. Itoh would be amazed. SM images and "performances" appear more openly than ever before on stage, in magazines, manga (comics) and on film and TV. In addition, Kinbaku performances and "how to tie" clips regularly feature on YouTube and other web sites and, of course, it is its own category of pornography. As might be expected, all this has both its pluses and minuses.

On the plus side, the very popularity of this type of material has led to more commercial opportunities for talented rope artists. For instance, since the late 1970s some very skilled practitioners have appeared on the scene and lifted the art of Shibari/Kinbaku to new heights. Talented bakushi of the older generation like **Yukimura Haruki**, **Arisue Go**, the late and brilliant **Nureki Chimuo** and **Akechi Denki** each contributed their considerable skills to different types of media exploitation and helped raise the bar for creative, dramatic and beautiful Shibari everywhere they appeared. In the 1980s and 1990s Akechi Denki, wearing his trademark dark sunglasses, seemed to especially represent the art of Japanese

Kinbaku to the rest of the world.

On the minus side, as the practice of Shibari/Kinbaku and SM became more commercialized and the province of big business, it lost much of its novelty and not a little of its artistry. Like your favorite small restaurant that, due to popularity, decides to expand and in so doing loses many of the qualities that made it your favorite, the consequences of blatant commercialism are often mixed.

In addition, the rise of the Internet and social media has meant that anyone with a computer can offer lessons, performances or Kinbaku products on line, regardless of their expertise or quality, thus creating a true "buyer beware" situation for an often vulnerable and impressionable public.

In the post 1980 publishing world for instance, many of the better second wave SM magazines (SM Kitan, SM Collector) were out of business by the mid-1980s, casualties of competition and various censorship pressures. Dan Oniroku's SM King folded in 1975 and the remarkable Minomura Kou suffered a stroke sidelining him from most of the creative activities he once dominated. In their place the so-called "modern" SM

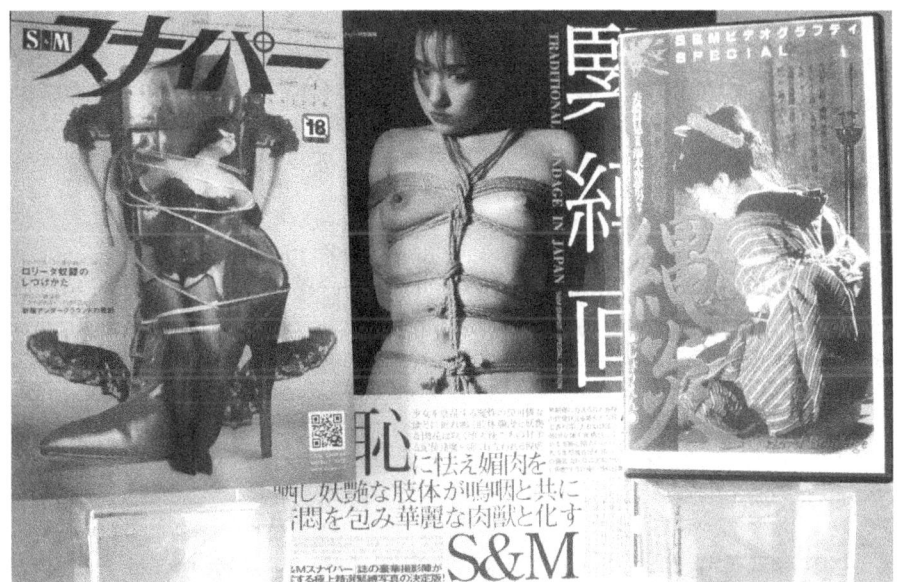

Modern "adult" SM magazines, model books and video/DVDs

magazines, such as SM Sniper, began to monopolize the marketplace and others were created, such as Mania Club from Sanwa Publishing. These periodicals placed a premium on still photographs and so-called "sensational" material for younger readers. Out went much of the art and almost all of the fiction and in came pages of glossy photos and "photo features" on scatology, cutting, orgies and other controversial, "edgy" subjects.

Taking up issues of SM Sniper and Mania Club from 2007 is instructive. Once past Sniper's eye-catching cover, in this case a photo *copying* an inventive 1940s cover illustration for John Willie's "Bizarre" magazine, we find a periodical that's almost one third advertisements. These ads for sex clubs, various dominatrix and sex performance aids are garish in the extreme. There are very few articles of any sort and almost no art in the magazine, the bulk of its pages being filled with "reports" from various "sexual events" whose amateurish pictures, though liberally catering to different erotic interests, seem to compete for "shock value." There are several professional photo sets, one that's quite well produced from the well known veteran photographer Tanaka Kinichi, but here again the interest is in viewing the hapless model from all angles while the Kinbaku is perfunctory and uninteresting. The issue of Mania Club shares many of these same qualities, though it does have the occasional article of historical interest. The single quality Shibari/Kinbaku photo set in it is by Sugiura Norio. He, at least, doesn't seem to have forgotten how to take a dramatic and interesting picture.

Comparing these commercial products to the "golden age" magazines is to realize with a shock how much art and sophistication has been lost for if one phrase characterizes most of Japan's later day SM media, it is "lack of imagination." That almost surprising literary quality of years past intended for the relatively educated and sophisticated reader seems virtually gone. This is why, when the winds of change first began to blow, Tsujimura Takashi decided to end his "Camera Hunt" column. He felt it was no longer as relevant as it once was when people had few sources of information about SM and he felt he simply couldn't keep up with the new reader's expectations for SM play with enemas and vibrators. Kinbaku legend Nureki Chimuo agreed, often decrying in interviews the lack of creativity shown in an "everything is permissible" environment and referring to himself as "a Shibari robot;" one who ties but seldom with the necessary emotional commitment for art.

Of course, as the old joke goes, "One man's pornography is another man's erotica" or, to put it another way, each age gets the entertainments it deserves. Mr. Matsumoto Yutaka, president and editor in chief at Sanwa Erotica, one of Japan's major publishers of SM and other sexually oriented magazines, said in an interview, "Us here, who are in the SM publishing industry, we are actually providing cutting-edge entertainment, . . . By catering to the fantasies of our readers we are constantly pushing the envelope, breaking taboos, opening new possibilities for sexual quality time. And as such we are making an important contribution to society."

Why did this change in Magazine content occur? There are many reasons but one is simple economics. Where once there were many magazines relating to SM and Kinbaku on Japanese newsstands, today there are almost none. The rise of the Internet has dealt a death blow to most fringe type publications and, as of this writing, there are less than a handful that remain, many publishing irregularly. In such a climate, Sanwa publications and the editors at Mania Club should be complimented for having the courage to continue despite fewer readers and having to cater to what a few years ago would have been called "the lowest common denominator" in its audience but in today's more "politically correct" world would be called "courting diversity."

Be that as it may, there is still the question of taste and there seems no question that in comparison to the early years of Minomura Kou, Dan Oniroku and the others, of the post 1980's magazines that deal with some type of SM and/or Shibari/Kinbaku more than a few lacked a decided, . . . elegance. Of course, not every one was devoid of interest. In fact, for years (until it ceased publication in 2008 to become a web only offering) SM Sniper had, since its founding, contained one feature that was simply remarkable.

One of the most famous and internationally respected Japanese photographers is **Araki Nobuyoshi**. He has published numerous highly regarded photography books, appeared in gallery exhibitions all over the world and photographed the cover of the "Spring Fashion Supplement" for the New York Times. Also, since 1979 his photo essay "Kinbaku Sha Rosen" appeared each month in SM Sniper. This alone says volumes about the tolerance for sexual individuality in Japan for I can think of few other countries where such a daring act by so famous a figure wouldn't at least raise an eyebrow.

Each month he created an elegant bondage photo set featuring an amateur or professional model. Apparently these women (and sometimes men) flocked to him from all over the country, asking to pose in Kinbaku and then be photographed by this world famous artist. Former Sniper editor Konishi Yōhei was the individual who got Araki started in this venture and it's interesting to hear how it all began.

Konishi relates that he approached Araki out of the blue in 1979 and proposed that he do SM photos for the magazine. As the editor tells it, "The SM magazines that existed at that time were 'mania magazines' geared to doctors, lawyers, school teachers—in other words, *real readers* (author's italics). Hoping to make something just a little more commercial, I looked to Araki for his assistance." Araki agreed and after the first shoot found he thoroughly enjoyed it. He commented, "On a shoot I always tell the model, I'm not going to tie your heart. Just let me tie your body. However, in truth, the moment I tie them their expression changes . . . they show me who they truly are."

Araki's Shibari photos are like no one else's. Beautifully composed and featuring interesting backgrounds and settings, his models always come across as real people living their lives but revealing intimate moments. As artful as the photography is, one wishes the Kinbaku was more often a bit more skilled since the same relatively simple techniques and positions are repeated ad infinitum. However, the tying was often done by various SM Sniper editors and the quality varied over time.

So popular have his bondage studies become that Araki has had numerous books of these pictures released, three being quite unusual. In 2008 a book of his Shibari photos combined with classical Japanese woodcuts was published under the title "Araki meets Hokusai" and in 2006 he created, in the manner of Itoh Seiu, a scroll of black and white stills brilliantly hand accented with brightly colored paints. Finally, in 2012 came the monumental (and monumentally expensive at $1000) "Bondage/ Kinbaku" published by the wonderful Taschen Company. This three volume set featured what the artist considered the best "bondage" photographs from his entire career and quite a bit of the Kinbaku in them was done by the talented bakushi and photographer Watanabe Yasuji, the last editor in chief of the print version of SM Sniper magazine.

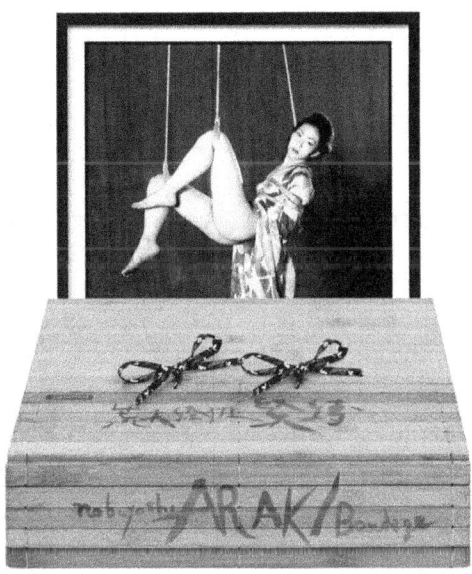

"Bondage/Kinbaku" by Araki Nobuyoshi, 2012

These three efforts, the scroll and the Taschen set having been released in numbered and limited editions, are Kinbaku photography as fine art. Without question, Araki's challenging images have gone a long way towards introducing and legitimizing the art of Kinbaku to the modern Western art scene.

Unfortunately, the demise of so many Kinbaku and SM publications in the early 21st century has meant a significant loss of economic opportunity for photographers and rope artists alike, to say nothing of the loss felt by the many fans who eagerly awaited each month's new releases.

In film, by the end of the 1980s, with the advent of cheaply produced adult videos (AV's) and stiffer government intervention, the theatrical pinku eiga market began to wane. The old methods of studio film production simply could not compete with videos shot for a fraction of the cost. In the face of such competition from the Godzilla that is the Japanese adult media industry, Nikkatsu closed its production facilities in 1988. Along with the demise of the theatrical film went much of the need for interesting plots, good acting and better than average photography. Censorship was still in place so some restrictions on what could be shown and what had to be digitally obscured still applied but the era of the porn video was at hand.

In the booming "adult" video market from 1980 through the early 2000s SM became a profitable specialty item and several companies began to prosper by releasing large numbers of books, magazines and videos. These included: Taiyo, Art Video, Sanwa and Cinemagic. The Taiyo group is probably the largest company in the field having far flung publishing interests outside of erotica. Cinemagic, begun by Yokobatake Kunihiko (the former publisher of the short lived but excellent SM Grafitti magazine) and concentrating more on video production, is perhaps the best known in the West since a fair number of their titles were imported overseas, either legitimately or in bootlegged versions, beginning in the 1990s.

Japan's adult industry is remarkable for the variety of "product" it turns out. In fact, it's safe to say that there's an adult DVD, web site, magazine, book or computer game for every niche and fringe interest no matter how odd, obscure or politically incorrect. Their freedom is extraordinary even as their content and its related moral questions complicate our perceptions and muddle our understanding. This is certainly true of the "adult" SM market and its use of Shibari/Kinbaku.

As Itoh had feared when "rope draping" had so offended him, the art of Shibari/Kinbaku usually comes in second when used in pornography. In one sense, this is a natural evolution from the time Dan Oniroku first wrote "Flower and Snake" and first combined seme with sex. However, as in all such matters, it's a question of degree and the taste and artistic skill (or lack thereof) of the people involved. As pornography became more explicit, often verging on the tasteless, violent and definitely misogynistic, Kinbaku began to seem the natural partner of this type of material instead of an art that had been usurped. Regrettably, it's when Westerners see these sorts of web sites, videos or still images that their impressions of Shibari/Kinbaku, without any historical or cultural context, are formed and this often leads to a complete misunderstanding of what the art truly is or, at least, could be. At its worst this results in the owners of Western Internet "torture" porn sites using ineptly done Shibari to dress up their sordid offerings, a move made all the more callous and objectionable by the porous nature of the Internet which allows children to be but a mere mouse click away from such material.

Interestingly enough, the Japanese have long understood this dichotomy and, even in the world of adult publishing, have to some degree attempted to address it. The truth is there are two types of Shibari/Kinbaku adult media. One type is fictional and accommodates the wildest flights of fancy running the gamut from the relatively innocent to the perverse. It includes most of the true pornography that's produced. The other presents Kinbaku as an art form and as an activity to be enjoyed by consenting adults. These two distinct types of media both utilize Shibari/Kinbaku but depend on the maturity and intelligence of the consumer to distinguish between them. Minomura Kou, perhaps the most talented artist and editor ever to work in the SM field, addressed this issue in a column he wrote for the magazine SM Collector in 1981 toward the end of his career but at the beginning of the AV era. Talking about the types of images created for pornography and film he wrote, "There are many interesting things that seem like they would be simple and interesting to do that should be left to the world of fiction. One should not be taken in by that irresponsible, romantic, world."

Since this book is about the *art* of Shibari/Kinbaku, I'll leave the irresponsible to themselves and concentrate on a few of the more exceptional examples from the current scene.

It should be obvious that the most important aspect of the art and practice of Kinbaku is when it's used in a personal way, as part of a consensual and loving relationship. Fortunately, for those more interested in doing than watching, for over 30 years there has been a slow but steady stream of "self help" instructional books and, more recently, videos, DVDs and web content produced concentrating on practical SM and Kinbaku techniques. These items were and are aimed at a general audience and supplanted the more specialist information once contained in the "golden age" SM magazines. While not always perfect, these releases do attempt to address what's clearly more than a puerile interest in the public and should be appreciated for helping to create a better, more mature, understanding of the art.

The first of these efforts dates from the early 1970s or from about the time when SM was beginning to be perceived as a legitimate erotic activity by the wider Japanese public. As such, these "how to" books suggest a very healthy and accepting trend and a concern for safety. The first useful guide to understanding and carefully practicing SM and Shibari/Kinbaku that I've seen is from 1972 and was authored by Urado Hiroshi, the talented bakushi responsible for the fine Kinbaku in the Nikkatsu/Dan Oniroku films "Wife to be Sacrificed," "Flower and Snake," etc. Its title, translated on the cover into English (!) is "SM Play: You Can Play SM." Like the title, the contents are simple and direct and offer general advice and photos on how to create straightforward but attractive Kinbaku ties and enjoy various "scenes." It was an auspicious beginning for this genre.

Since 1990 a number of famous bakushi have offered up information on their art and craft. Some of the more notable examples are: The "Rope World" series of videos from Cinemagic and Nureki Chimuo, the "How to Play SM" book and videos by Nagaike Takeshi (over the years one of Dan Oniroku's more frequent collaborators) and Arisue Go's 2 volume set, "The Book of Five Rings for Rope Arts" published by Sanwa. In addition, Haruki Yukimura, one of the most artistic and respected of bakushi, published a very intelligent beginner's guide to Kinbaku on DVD in 2007 entitled "A petite rope lecture of Haruki Yukimura". To these must be added the beautiful, four DVD set of tutorials by the gifted Miura Takumi. And, of course, one must not fail to mention the numerous books and instructional DVDs that **Randa Mai,** once the young Turk of Shibari/Kinbaku and famous for his AV productions and stage performances, released over the years.

Speaking of stage performances, these too have had their artistic moments. Ever since the late Osada Eikichi virtually invented the form in the 1960s, bakushi have taken to the stages of clubs, theaters and SM bars to entertain their fans. Competition from all the other SM venues using Kinbaku may have reduced the numbers of paying customers since Eikichi's day when hundreds of eager fans might spend as much as $1000 for a ticket to see such a show, but some quality still rises to the top. Randa Mai, when performing in the 1990s, did an act that would rival many a Las Vegas casino show with its glitz and fireworks. On a more restrained level, the German born **Osada Steve**, whose friend and mentor was the great Osada Eikichi, did an elegant suspension dominated performance with his beautiful aerialist partner **Asagi Ageha**. And women didn't only function on the bottom half of these bills. Female bakushi such as **Sayaka** and **Kanou Chiaki** have also performed on stage and some talented woman, such as author and model Saotome Hiromi, even dispense with the male member of the team altogether and do solo "performance art" style acts featuring all manner of self suspensions and dance.

Unfortunately, here too, the economics of the early 21st century has brought difficulties to the indigenous Japanese club performers. To put it simply, there simply isn't the money in performing in Japan that there was even as recently as the 1980s and 1990s. There are fewer venues that present live SM/Kinbaku stage acts and those bakushi that seek to make a living in that format (and there seem to be new ones popping up every week that try), all have had to struggle some to do so. Luckily, the increased interest in Kinbaku in the West has allowed some of these performers to travel, perform and teach and, while some of these talents might not be the most experienced, interesting or skillful, it is a wonderful way for those Westerners interested in Kinbaku to see at least the performance version of the art up close and live on stage.

In film, beginning in the early 1990s and after the fall of Nikkatsu, some independent producers and directors emerged dedicated to continuing the pinku eiga tradition and some of these films met with quite decent success despite the domination of the AV market. In the SM field, the venerable Nawa Yumio contributed the scripts to two historically accurate, if graphic, costume dramas involving the Edo Era, *Onna Hankacho I & II (1994, King Records)*. Directed by Tsushima Masaru, they each tell the story of a government agent on a secret mission from the emperor to ferret out injustice in the shogun's

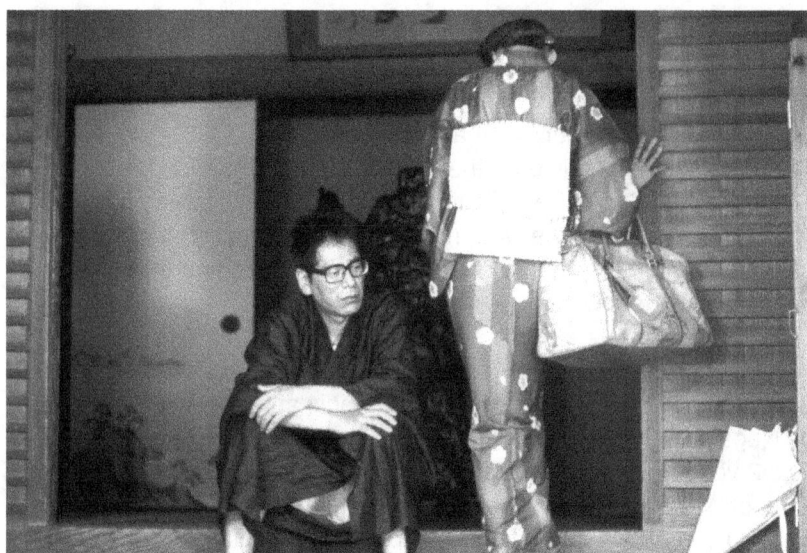

Still from "I am an SM writer," directed by Hiroki Ryuichi and starring Osugi Ren

capitol. Various cases, supposedly drawn from history, are investigated.

In 2000 came the truly delightful "I am an SM writer," directed by the very talented **Hiroki Ryuichi** and based on another novel by the venerable and prolific Dan Oniroku. Director Hiroki cut his teeth in the pinku eiga world and he brings that insider's knowledge to what is basically a bittersweet romantic comedy chronicling the trials and tribulations of an SM novelist.

The marvelous Osugi Ren plays the eponymous narrator of the piece, a successful SM author who recounts the details of why his wife left him some 20 years before due to his preoccupation with the more intellectual side of the sexual act as opposed to the physical. Immersed in his own fantasies, he feverishly documents staged SM scenarios (featuring Kinbaku by Yukimura Haruki) acted out in his living room by his young assistant and "rope expert." Oblivious to his wife's own burgeoning sexuality, he fails to notice her increasing interest in her tennis partner, a brash young American hunk, until the obvious is pointed out to him by the assistant. His reaction? After the initial rage he scribbles down the details of their imagined liaison for use in his work. Eventually, bored with the lack of emotional depth in the relationship with the American and now fascinated by SM, the wife moves on to the assistant as a last ditch attempt to provoke some degree of interest from her husband, a man who is more prone to SM ideas than the more carnal reality behind them.

What's marvelous about the film is that, in much the same manner as the indie US film "Secretary" from the same year, the SM material, despite some strong scenes, hardly exists for the sake of exploitation in its own right but rather as a light-hearted comic drama set against this backdrop; a post-modern pinku, if you will. The bondage scenes are sparse and not staged for the sake of titillation and for the most part the film charts the emotional trajectories of Osugi's and his wife's characters. Within this context there is true validity to the whimsical portrayal of what would be considered a strict sexual and filmic no-go area in other countries. What Hiroki and his talented cast get exactly right is that the key point of the SM power play, as is so often forgotten, is that both partners *consent* to acting out their fantasies—the "victim" in those scenes is a paid model who laughs as she helps tie up her own knots and addresses the writer as "sensei" (teacher/master) while it's the SM writer who truly suffers.

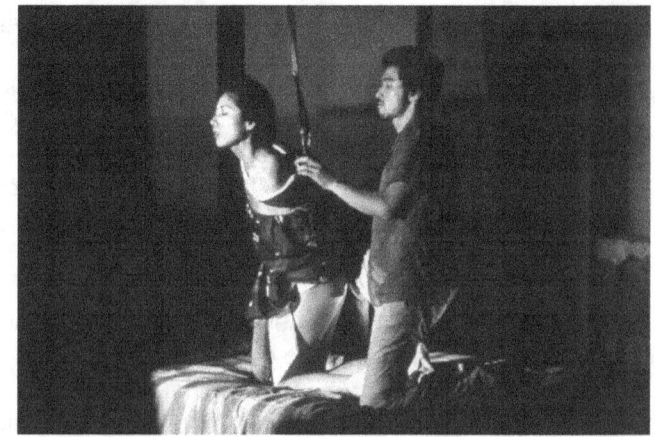

Still from "I am an SM writer" with Shibari by Yukimura Haruki—© Goldview, 2000

Making an even bigger impact was the box office success of 2004's major SM release "Flower and Snake" and its follow-up, 2005's "Flower and Snake 2-Paris." Once again, Dan Oniroku's famous story of a young wife and a disturbed youth has been re-worked, this time for a big budget version. The production values of these two films are completely first rate, surpassing even the Nikkatsu standards. In truth, the original "Flower and Snake" film from 1974 looks more than a little creaky today, despite the presence of the always radiant and convincing Tani Naomi, but these skillfully executed remakes take the story firmly and slickly into the 21st century. The director and writer of both is the very interesting talent **Ishii Takashi**; a veteran of the later Nikkatsu years and an acclaimed manga and screenplay writer. As a young man Ishii contributed haunting illustrations to such "golden age" SM magazines as SM King and SM Select and it was this visual skill that allowed him an entry into film.

Both pictures star the lovely Aya Sugimoto as the wife that ventures too far into the film's operatic world of SM. Her performances are quite remarkable, although the Japanese fans had a hard time forgiving any actress that would dare try to take the place of their beloved "goddess," Tani Naomi. There is a great deal of Kinbaku in these movies, some even as challenging to execute as in the Nikkatsu years, and that's done in fine style by bakushi Arisue Go. Although the first film was the bigger success, resulting in part 2, it's the second film, "Flower and Snake 2-Paris," that's artistically more satisfying. This is due to the fact that the intriguing plot, involving the creation of some beautiful SM art with Ms. Sugimoto as the conflicted model, is based on the extraordinary work of the quite brilliant **Miyabi Kyodo**, one of the most gifted seme-e masters working today.

The result of these two significant box office successes has been even more film versions of Dan Oniroku's venerable original, including "Flower and Snake 3" (2010) and "Flower and Snake-Zero" (2014) both with Kinbaku by the busy and reliable Arisue Go.

And then there is the excellent 2007 documentary "Bakushi," again from director Hiroki Ryuichi. This time the goal is to examine the lives and work of several world class bakushi, those rope artists who ply their trade as teachers, producers and "riggers" for video, books and magazines. The men selected are Yukimura Haruki and Arisue Go and the late Nureki Chimuo and they are joined by their favorite models: Saotome Hiromi, Sumire and Uzuki Taeko. Each rope artist is presented in a working situation or session and then reflects on his career. Each of the models the men work with also gives their thoughts.

All of the nawashi are very articulate and are shown to quite good advantage, especially Arisue Go who has the most visually interesting section; a beautiful private session with his model in an elegant tatami suite. Another plus is being backstage at a photo session with Nureki in collaboration with master photographer Sugiura Norio as they tie Saotome Hiromi. This was a request of Saotome who had worked with both men many times over the years and who wanted to get the three friends together again, "one last time." Given Nureki's passing in 2013 this is indeed a most poignant scene.

The pluses include the chance to hear each of these masters candidly discuss their craft and philosophy (w/English subtitles!) and to view some marvelous Kinbaku. The minus is that the models do not come off as well as they should. Interviewed just after being tied they appear somewhat befuddled unless one is familiar with the condition of "sub space," the typical emotionally spent state of the submissive Shibari/ Kinbaku partner just after being bound. This could be especially off putting to an inexperienced Western viewer who would like to hear the model's interesting, positive and articulate take on their experiences. Without question these intelligent woman, two of whom are well known published authors, should have been given the same opportunity to reflect as had the men. That said, one must give the film high marks for its attempt to reveal this often mysterious world. A particularly touching moment comes at the end when Nureki in response to the question of why he keeps tying despite being nearly 80 responds by saying, "I keep hoping to meet my dream girl."

Even in the generally artistically fallow AV video field there were post 1980 flashes of quality. Cinemagic is a company that's been very successful, usually releasing SM pornography. However, they have also done several series of greater interest. One such presents Kinbaku only sessions (i.e. without graphic or violent sexual content) featuring the best of the modern practitioners: Nureki, Yukimura and the late Akechi Denki, each working with attractive professional models. Another series, whose title loosely translates to "It's only Bondage," continues the themes of the old Tsujimura "Camera Hunt" column. In these videos supposed "amateurs" and "ordinary people" volunteer to experience Kinbaku done by skilled bakushi and talk about their feelings and fantasies while a camera records the experience. Of even more interest, Cinemagic released in the 1990s several historically themed videos showing Edo era techniques and, more poignantly, a "testimonial" tape honoring Minomura Kou done shortly after he had suffered his stroke. In this quite wonderful program, directed by Yukimura Haruki, many of the major SM figures of yesterday and today (Dan Oniroku, Arisue Go, Nureki Chimuo, etc., etc.) come together to talk about the artist and celebrate his art.

On occasion, individual bakushi were able to release their own Kinbaku performance tapes allowing the viewer to better study their techniques. However, here a word of caution must be raised since, unlike true "how to" programs, these "performance" tapes often hide as many techniques as they reveal. The legendary Akechi Denki did these sorts of videos for several years utilizing impressive sessions he'd done out of his well known "Studio Phantom" in Tokyo and Yukimura Haruki, perhaps the most prolific video producer of them all, has released hundreds of such tapes through his own company, Sunset Color, and also through the Taiyo group.

Even when a bakushi works for a major pornography producer it's possible for worthwhile material to occasionally appear. The very talented Kinbaku master **Naka Akira**, the one true disciple of the great Nureki Chimuo, worked for many years for Art Video, one of the more determined and graphic porn producers. In the early 2000s he was given the chance to produce his own series of soft core Kinbaku centered DVDs called the *Nawa-Etsu* or "Rope Rejoicing" series. These are beautifully lit and photographed Kinbaku performances with more than a whiff of old Edo that attractively present his impressive skills.

However, even in the world of "adult" media the winds of change that blew in with the Internet have caused major upheavals. Adult videos that once cost $100 US to buy in 1990 can now be had for a fraction of that price as streaming Internet content or bought used for a few Yen or dollars. And as in the US, in Japan both the DVD markets and pay websites for pornography have seen their customers deserting them for all the free content now available 24/7 on the net. Depending on your point of view this can be good or bad but the end result is that another income source once prized by the professional rope artist is less than once it was, sometimes much less.

As was the case with scenes of seme-e in the late Edo era of the 19th century, some of the most interesting and startling examples of today's artful tying come to us in the books of art, both graphic and photographic, that daring publishers have created. Over the last few decades almost every year has brought at least one real treasure that transcends the commerciality of the "adult" industry.

In photography some particularly impressive examples would include **Ishigaki Akira's** "Strange Fruit" (1982/1993, Shibari by **Roppongi Kaoru**), the Nureki Chimuo/**Fuji Akio** collaboration "Bind" (the small book/catalogue that records Fuji's impressive photo show at the Mole Gallery) and "Shibari 1, 2, 3" (1998-photos by Oka Katumi, Higure Keisuke and Watanabe Tatsumi, respectively). Interestingly, these last two exquisite art photography books are in the small format used for the ukiyo-e books (nishiki -e) that were printed as souvenirs for travelers to Edo in earlier times. This continuing preference for less than pocket sized books comes from Japan's history of making small, easy to carry volumes since until the modern era just about everyone, except noble lords, were walking when they traveled. The rest had to go in cramped palanquins and pay for their luggage to be carried, so smaller was better.

It might surprise the reader to learn that in Japan light bondage often makes an appearance in attractive, coffee table sized collections of erotic art photographs of beautiful female celebrities. The Kinbaku can be a major theme or hardly there and several photographers and bakushi specialize in this type of publication. For example, Arisue Go, with his somewhat gentler style, is particularly well suited to this format and has done the bondage for several very attractive soft core erotic photo books featuring such famous actresses as: Toyota Maho, Akiyoshi Kumiko and Oginome Keiko. He once even tied a female professional wrestler for a similar photo collection. His most impressive effort is probably "Pleasure in the Fall," a lovely book of photos by Kawai Takao with the former Nikkatsu actress Ogawa Minako. He also contributed to the two "tie-in" photo books that accompanied the release of the last two "Flower and Snake" films in 2010 and 2014.

More experimental in style is fashion/fine Art photographer Gomi Akira's "Yellow's the Revenge-Kinbaku Shashin" from 1993 which digitally revisits the world of Itoh Seiu. Using video captures and other modern photographic techniques he lends a new look to classical Kinbaku and seme-e themes.

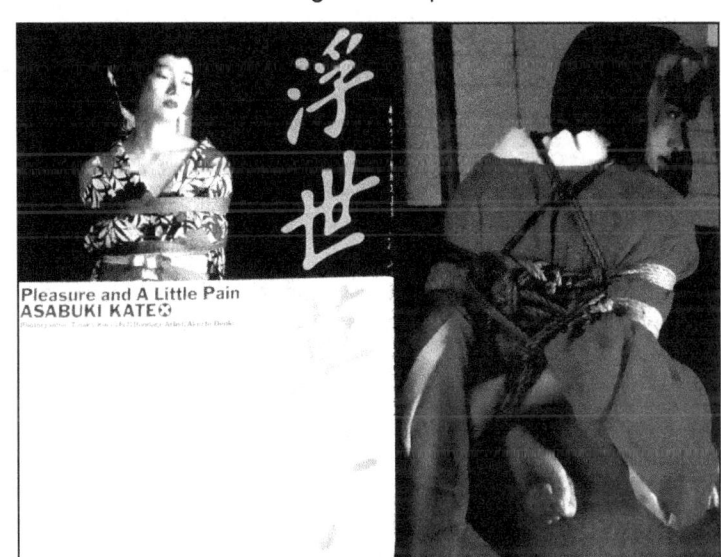

Akechi Denki masterwork, 1995

However, as attractive as these volumes are, they pale in comparison to what is probably the most beautiful of all of these types of books, "Pleasure and a Little Pain" from 1995. This quite stunning volume features the actress and model Asabuki Kate with photography by Tanaka Kinichi and Shibari/Kinbaku by Akechi Denki. What separates this effort from all the others is that every element, the lighting, settings, classic costumes, Ms. Asabuki's expressions and Akechi Denki's sometimes simple, sometimes complex but always beautiful rope work, combine to enhance one another and produce magical images of mystery, eroticism and dramatic power. If sophisticated and beautiful Kinbaku photography interests you, this truly is the gold standard.

Perhaps the most familiar Japanese "bondage" books for the Western consumer are the ubiquitous adult "rope books" that have appeared consistently since the 1950s. Most are simple paperbacks offering page after page of more or, often, less expert Shibari/Kinbaku applied to a wide variety of models in various situations. Minor porn publishers and major publishing houses have produced and exported these items over the years in large numbers. The format never seems to go out of style even as its tedious similarities blur any distinctions between the books or their publishers.

Without question, the earliest examples of this type of volume are the most unique and important with the honor of being the first commercial publication completely dedicated to Shibari/Kinbaku photography going to a special summer edition of Yomikiri Romance magazine, published on July 2, 1952 and edited by Ueda Seishiro, one of Itoh Seiu's collaborators. Basically a large pamphlet, it cannot be said to be a true book and it featured relatively simple Shibari. Still, it was a groundbreaking event in SM publishing.

A far more considerable achievement appeared on July 1, 1953 in a limited edition of 500 copies that sold for 500 Yen each (quite expensive for any Japanese book at that time). Each volume was a handmade, high quality album featuring elegant photographs of nude models in Kinbaku, each photograph carefully glued onto an individual backing and preceded by a delicate page of rice paper containing an impressionistic description of the tie and/or the photo. This lovely book was put together by Kayama Shigeru, soon to become a close associate of Dan Oniroku and a noted SM personage in Japan. The title is loosely translated as, "Beautifully Bound-The Only Album of Bound Women." The Kinbaku is by the master Minomura Kou.

The Shibari/Kinbaku presented in this beautiful album is of great interest because it depicts ties that are halfway between the older hojojutsu schools and more modern Shibari/Kinbaku. As such this book is a missing link of sorts for martial arts and Shibari researchers. In amongst the older honnawa patterns are the *takate-kote*, the *ganji garame*, the historical *ebi*, various tsuri's and even more exotic ties such as the *imu mushi Shibari* or "green caterpillar tie" (for descriptions of all these

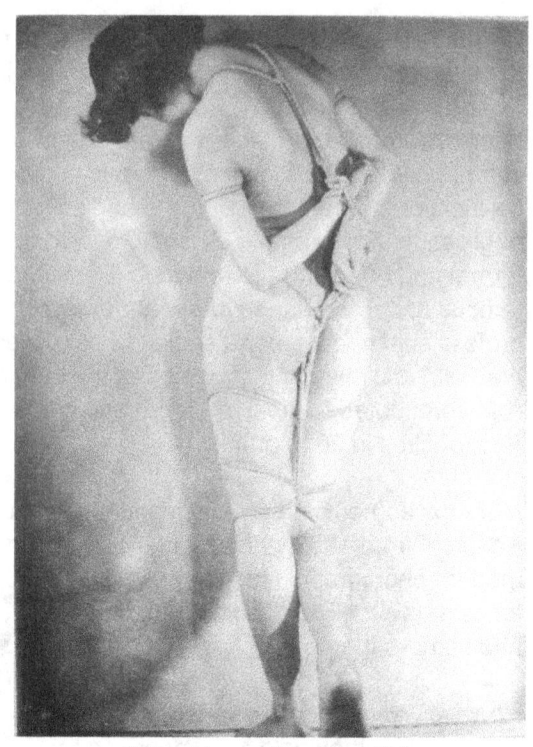

"The Alcove Ornament" by Minomura Kou, 1953

Kinbaku patterns please see the Glossary). Offered here is an elegant photograph from this album labeled only as "The Alcove Ornament." Note the obvious hojojutsu details of the neck and arm ropes.

"Beautifully Bound" was a tremendous success and spawned a sequel only a few months later, this time with Kinbaku by Tsujimura Takashi. And so the deluge began; if only the quality could have been maintained!

Over the years thousands of these types of books have been published. Some fairly interesting examples from the 1970's and 80's include several quality series created by the Haga Shoten Company in collaboration with Dan Oniroku (*Kinbaku Shashin, Fuzoku Jidai Kinbaku, etc.*), various "Special Photo Editions" from several "golden age" SM magazines (SM Collector, SM Select), the *Kinbaku Photo Shu* series edited by Nureki Chimuo (under the name, Fujimi Iku) and, more recently, any number of books published by the Sanwa company featuring the beautiful Kinbaku of Yukimura Haruki.

Some of the best of these modern versions are the work of famed photographer Sugiura Norio and feature Shibari by various rope artists, including his long time collaborator Nureki Chimuo as well as younger bakushi such as the very talented **Marai Masato**. As striking as the photography is in these current "rope books," the reader should be advised that the material is sometimes quite graphic and, though inventive, potentially disturbing.

Of course, over the years there has been less serious work released. The author remembers with a smile a "3-D" book from the 1970s where you had to wear colored glasses to have the tied models pop out at you. There have also been numerous books of manga and other cartoons and even, on occasion, toys. As some readers might know, Japan is also the land of beautiful dolls and toy models. Everything from miniature replicas of samurai, recent pop stars, "Star Wars" characters, creatures from current TV shows, manga and gorgeous kimono clad dolls have been and are being produced for avid collectors.

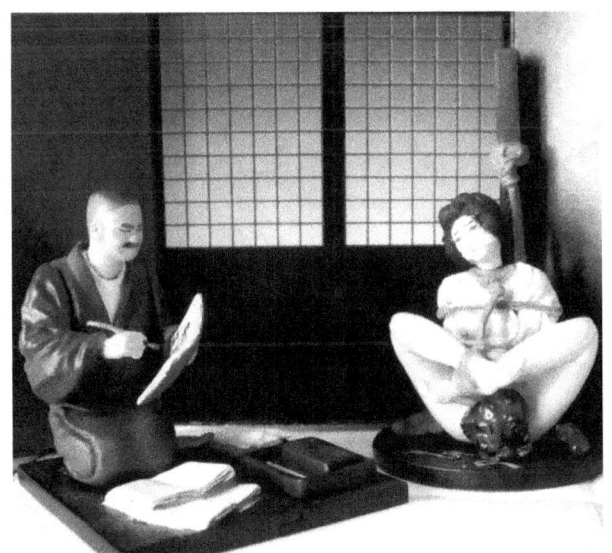

Itoh and model—toy figures by Ero-Pon

The same is true of Shibari/Kinbaku figures! A few years ago the Ero-Pon company began to release beautifully executed Kinbaku art models. So far there have been 3 editions. The first depicts well known scenes from Itoh Seiu's paintings and illustrations, including a little Itoh figure shown drawing a bound model! The second reproduces more modern Shibari ties from recent books and magazines and the third replicates some of the very detailed drawings of the master pencil sketch artist Muku Youji. While it was possible to get them in boxed sets, I'm told most were sold in vending machines! Only in Japan.

Finally, there are what could be called, for lack of a better term, the collections of Shibari/Kinbaku fine art. Itoh started this tradition with his publication of seme-e paintings and sketches in the 1920s and it has continued up to the present day. In 1952 the classically trained artist Shibatani Saijiro published a beautiful limited edition of seme-e/Kinbaku art based on historical and legendary incidents and Itoh Seiu did something similar with his lovely "12 Months of Strange Punishments" album in 1953. Each of these elegant books features colorful prints separated by rice paper upon which the incident or tale depicted is described. Today Itoh is himself considered a legendary artistic figure in Japan so it is perhaps fitting that two of the more recent and lavish seme-e/Kinbaku art books contain many of his most beautiful designs. *Itoh Seiu Gashu* ("Collected Pictures of Itoh Seiu") published by Shinchosha in 1997 and "The Secret Notebooks of Itoh Seiu," published in 2002 by Futami, collect many of his most dramatic and distinctive paintings, sketches, photographs and commentaries.

During the "golden age" of the SM magazines some quite wonderful art was created. Unfortunately, very few publishers at the time realized the potential goldmine this art represented so only two or three small compilations of this material were ever released. The best is probably *Nawa to Onna* from 1970 which catalogues a good number of black and white images from illustrators such as Kobinata, Kitoh Akira, Yamada, Oki and Ishizuka. A second worthwhile book is *Tanbi no Hakken* released as an "art supplement" to a series of novels published by SM Bugaku. This modest little volume includes a few images each from such major talents as Minomura Kou (Kita Reiko), Sogabe Yasushi and Kasuga Akira.

In the last few years more publishers have realized the value of this early magazine art so several portfolios and collections featuring work by postwar seme-e masters have appeared; for instance, two from My Way Publishers in 2008 and 2011. Unfortunately, it's been a hit or miss proposition and such acknowledged geniuses as Minomura Kou (Kita Reiko) and Kobinata Ichimu have almost no collections of their seme-e work while several considerably lesser lights do. Still, such major figures as Fujino Kazutomo, the noted surrealist painter who did his SM art under the name Nakagawa Ayako and Akiyoshi Ran, the fantasy/fabulist painter who did many of the "golden age" SM magazine covers both have deluxe editions of their work available. On a lesser scale the same goes for the elegant Kasuga Akira, who became such a favorite of Dan Oniroku's that he did the covers for several of that author's more famous novels. Perhaps the two most fortunate artists from the "golden age" are the late Muku Youji and Ozuma Kaname. Each of these superb craftsmen has had multiple books of their seme-e art published in recent years and Ozuma's tattoo filled Kinbaku paintings and prints command high prices whenever they come up for sale.

Several prominent younger artists have turned to SM or Shibari/Kinbaku for their themes and inspiration, and not just in Japan. The Englishman **Trevor Brown** created quite a stir with his beautiful "Japabon" series of colored pencil drawings inspired by visits to several of Nureki Chimuo's Kinbaku sessions. Domestically, the highly regarded **Amano Yoshitaka**, master of fantasy, animation and manga, collaborated with Dan Oniroku on a book of watercolor washes and finished paintings to celebrate the release of the "Flower and Snake" films. In a quieter vein, Editions Treville has published a deluxe three volume set of the internationally known artist **Yamamoto Takato's** Ukiyo-e inspired, erotically charged studies of delicately featured youths.

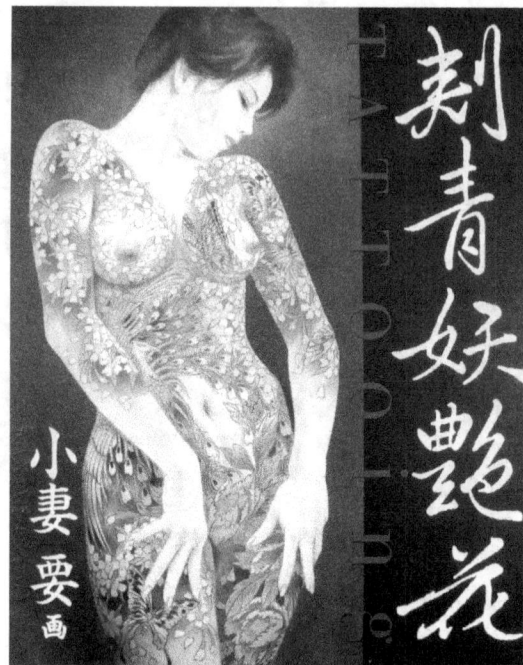

Deluxe portfolio of art by Ozuma Kaname

Perhaps most interesting of all, from a historical perspective, is the hyper-realist artist Miyabi Kyodo who certainly must be considered a significant figure in Kinbaku art. Miyabi worked as an editor on SM magazines in the early 1980s and developed a friendship with the aging Minomura Kou with whom he'd discuss his work. As such, he claims to be Kita Reiko's (Minomura's) "last student." If so, it's a deserved title for Miyabi's quite graphic and powerful imagery certainly does carry on the potent legacy of that remarkable master.

It seems a long journey from the Jomon pottery and Shinto shimenawa of ancient Japan to today's modern Kinbaku art in books, films, magazines, DVDs and the Internet but perhaps it's not so far as all that. In correspondence with the artist Miyabi Kyodo I asked him what Shibari meant to him. Here is his reply:

*"Shibari is not something you can learn in school. It is part of the basic Japanese culture conveyed from parents to children. In Japan, the nation of Shintoism, tying with nawa is a sacred act. You can see this in such examples as the 'shimenawa' used at Shinto shrines. For anything holy in which the Japanese feel 'Kami' (god, sacredness) they tie or surround it with nawa. By tying, a Japanese shows his respect. What is **behind** the nawa is sacred and so tying **with** nawa connects the 'Kami' with the human. Therefore, Shibari is neither truly art nor performance but actually a sacred act. Only those who believe in Shintoism make things sacred by tying. By the way, I am a follower of Shintoism."*

And so it sometimes is in the world of Shibari/Kinbaku, that sacred and profane art from the land the author and musician Masami Akita calls, "the sadomasochistic kingdom of the world."

Questions:

"What are the origins of Kinbaku?"

After 40 years of study, I have come to the conclusion that there are actually several, distinct, historical and artistic antecedents for modern Shibari/Kinbaku. In no particular order these are: the martial art of hojojutsu, the 1742 Tokugawa law and punishment decrees know as the "One Hundred Articles," the rise of ukiyo-e (woodblock print) art and the popularity of kabuki theater in Edo era Japan. While such pairings of brutality, justice and art might seem discordant, each of these is like a stream that, combined with the other three, form the river of Japanese SM whose images and techniques so fascinate the world.

"If Shibari/Kinbaku has some of its origins in hojojutso, how come we can't trace specific Shibari/Kinbaku masters to the heads of the various, historical, martial arts schools?"

Well, actually, we can … in a way. With the Meiji restoration in 1868 and the rush to modernize, the samurai class was abolished and with it most of the hojojutsu schools that trained them. By the early 20th century almost all vestiges of that feudal world were gone. However, when Itoh Seiu began his explorations of seme we know from the various testimonies of his colleagues and the many study photos and sketches he produced and left behind that he had learned hojojutsu skills from an original practitioner and applied those to his researches. Itoh, in turn, passed on many of these techniques and designs to others, including Minomura Kou (Kita Reiko) who was a member of Itoh's circle. Minomura, in turn, influenced Nureki Chimuo and Dan Oniroku and they have influenced many, many, more. And so it goes.

"How did a Japanese martial art become an erotic art?"

As I hope the preceding pages have shown, it was a slow process involving many artists, incidents and cultural factors. Shibari/Kinbaku has evolved because of Japan's tolerant religions and their attitudes towards sexuality, its history and martial arts, its 250 years of self-imposed isolation from the West, its love of beauty, art, form and pattern and the mysterious alchemy that connects all of these.

Thirty Key Figures in Shibari/Kinbaku History

This list of artists from various disciplines was by no means easy to compile. There were and are many creative people who have either influenced or contributed to the history and art of shibari/kinbaku over the years. That said, the names on *this* list all fit at least one of two criteria. They are either unknown or unjustly neglected in the West or they are significant figures in the *evolution* of shibari/kinbaku and have produced important works that are, in some form, available for study and appreciation *outside* of Japan.

In this group of short biographies you will find: writers, painters, producers, film directors, models, actors, magazine illustrators, martial artists, historians, publishers and, of course, rope masters (*bakushi*)—in short, a wide variety of professions and artists, from the totally commercial to the rebel outsider. Both types are listed here in a generally historical order, that is, from the earliest to the most recent.

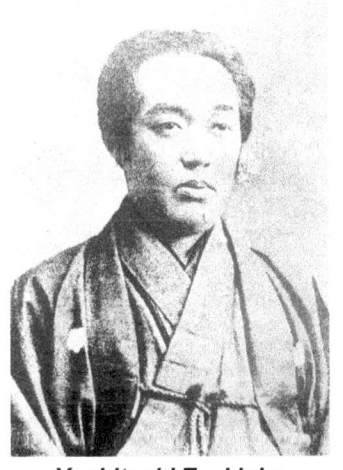

Yoshitoshi Tsukioka
(1839-1892)

Yoshitoshi Tsukioka—ukiyo-e master

At the tender age of 11 Yoshitoshi was apprenticed to the ukiyo-e (Japanese woodblock print) master Kuniyoshi and at 14 published his first full color print. By age 20 he was fully independent and listed 10th in a ranking of leading ukiyo-e artists of his day. The print series "Twenty-eight famous murders with verse" (see main text) completed in 1866 made him famous. Although known today for such images of violence, these pictures comprise only a fraction of Yoshitoshi's output and are on a par with much of the art of the era. At the time of the fall of the shogunate (in 1868), horror and cruelty were common themes in Japanese popular culture and people who were not involved in the political upheaval could experience the turbulence vicariously through Yoshitoshi's and other artist's violent prints. In those days there was even a tradition of performing Kabuki plays with horrifying subjects in the heat of the summer to produce shivers of fear!

In 1875 he became a newspaper illustrator bringing his skills to a much wider and more diverse public when his prints were sold as supplements or souvenirs. These prints also broke new ground by showing specific events in contemporary people's everyday lives. He also began to teach and was known as being a loyal, devoted, conscientious and generous master. As modernization proceeded, Yoshitoshi (and other traditional print artists) fell upon hard times. He was often ill and at one point was even forced to rip up the flooring of his own home for heating fuel. Through it all Yoshitoshi persevered and, as he aged, moved away from the bloody prints of his youth to do work with poetic undertones and great psychological depth, such as the magnificent "One Hundred Aspects of the Moon" series begun in 1886.

Widely recognized today as the last great ukiyo-e master, he is also regarded as one of the form's greatest innovators. In a career that spanned two eras, including the last years of the Tokugawa and the first years of the Meiji, he remained interested in the modern (he used Western-style visual perspective brilliantly) but became increasingly concerned with the loss of many worthwhile things from Japan's cultural history. And in a country that was turning away from its own past, he almost single-handedly managed to push the traditional Japanese woodblock print to new creative heights before the form effectively died with him.

His influence on the art of kinbaku comes not from his admitted genius for depicting violence but rather because of his ability to aestheticize and eroticize images of seme (domination). The best known picture of this sort might be from the bloody "28 murders" series but of the five remarkable "bondage" images Yoshitoshi created during his career, four depict far more sex than violence. Consider this newspaper print from 1887.

This provocative young woman is Lady Muraoka (1786-1873), a political opponent of the shogun's who was tortured numerous times in 1858, along with her kinsmen, for disloyalty. This print was done by Yoshitoshi for the Yamato Shimbun newspaper in 1887 as part of a series devoted to people who helped shape modern Japan. With her hojojutsu tie, her beautiful kimono and the wisp of hair in her mouth (a typical sign of sexual arousal in Japanese art), the artist has created, to quote distinguished Yoshitoshi scholar Segi Shinichi, an image that, "borders on sadomasochistic fantasy: she looks quite seductive in her ropes, and far younger than the seventy-some-years she would have been at the time (of her arrest)." Obviously, Yoshitoshi reduced his subject's age to heighten her erotic appeal.

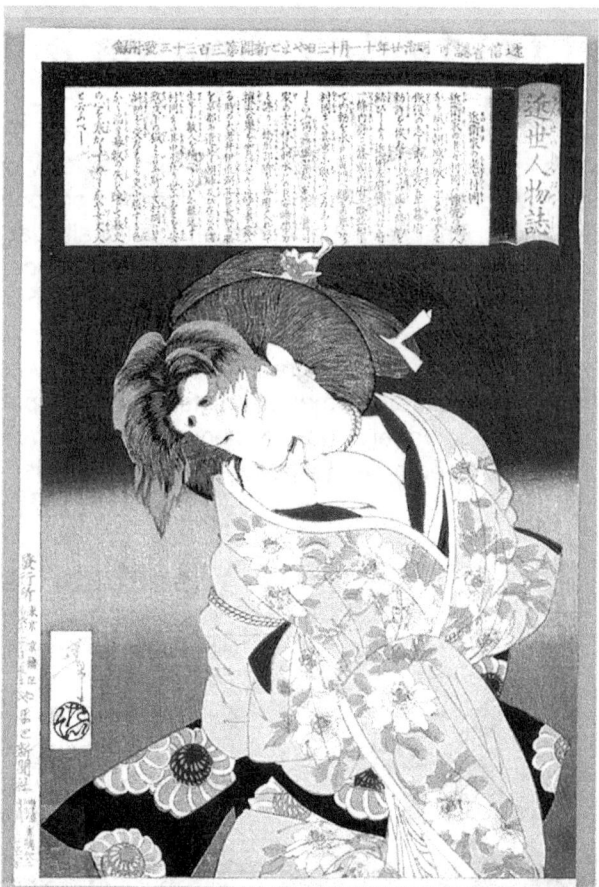

Lady Muraoka of the Konoe Clan, 1887, from the series "Lives of Modern People." Published by Yamato Shimbun Newspaper

Other compositions reveal the same qualities. There is another newspaper illustration from about the same time that shows a bound girl swooning into the arms of the rescuer that has saved her from drowning and an elegant image of a young woman suspended from a pine tree, her toes curled in sexual ecstasy, from the "Picturebook of a Journey to the West," published in 1883.

Finally, there is this stunning image.

"The Lonely House on Adachi Moor" has been confounding critics ever since its creation in 1885. Generally regarded as Yoshitoshi's most provocative image, it recreates the Noh drama/horror fable of a vampire-type hag who waylays travelers. This print is in the vertical diptych format that Yoshitoshi used for what many critics consider his finest works and

"The Lonely House on Adachi Moor," 1885

the artist brilliantly exploits the vertical space. Of course, it's the subject matter of the pregnant girl suspended in a sakasa zuri, smoke curling past her hair in a stunning visual while the brutal hag sharpens her knife that has horrified and fascinated viewers for years. This composition was considered so intensely disturbing that, although printed, it was one of only two Yoshitoshi designs ever suppressed by the Meiji government. The subtle eroticism as well as the overt brutality have fascinated Japanese SM artists for years and it's an image that continues to be provocative. In 2007 the San Francisco Asian Art Museum mounted a magnificent two-part retrospective of Yoshitoshi's Art. This was the only major piece not to be exhibited.

Itoh Seiu—artist, the father of modern kinbaku

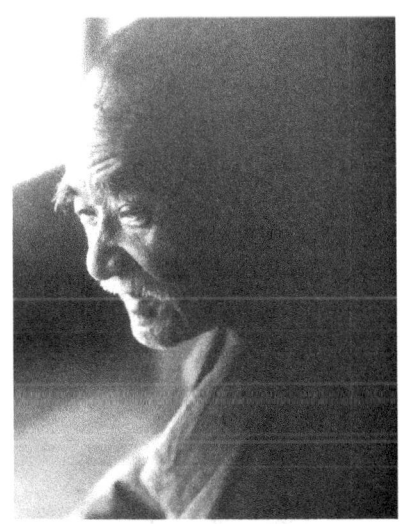

Itoh Seiu (1882-1961)

Itoh Seiu (1882-1961), real name Itoh Hajime, controversial seme scholar, seme-e master and legendary artist, is arguably one of the most important figures in the history of Japanese shibari/kinbaku and SM. Born during the last days of the Meiji Restoration, Itoh, a painter, wood block print master, photographer and writer, provides the link between the feudal and the modern in Japan's fascination with sadomasochistic practices. As an artist, he was extraordinary. As an inspiration to several generations of Japan's greatest shibari/kinbaku masters and SM artists, he was unique.

Itoh was apparently born with a sadomasochistic streak and, according to his own writings, could remember being fascinated at the age of ten by Japanese folk tales of captive princesses told to him by his mother and grandmother. His life-long fascination, truly a fetish, for black, disheveled, woman's hair also began at this time because of pictures in a storybook by Ryutei Tanehiko (1783-1842) that his grandmother read to him.

At 18 he decided to become a seme-e (or torment/domination scene) painter and never wavered from that path for the rest of his life despite taking jobs as a kabuki scene painter and a newspaper and book illustrator to support himself. Inspired by such ukiyo-e (wood block print) masters as Yoshitoshi and Kunisada, both of whom dabbled in seme-type subjects, Itoh became a seme-e master of tremendous imagination, variety and skill.

It was during the Taisho period (1912-1926) that Itoh began taking photographs, a novel hobby in early 20th century Japan. In 1923 he created his most famous work, the previously discussed, "Woman Suffering in Snow." He was forty-one. Apparently he was inspired by the folk tale *Chujo Hime* as well as an early textbook on torture techniques entitled *Semekata Kokore-gaki* and a play he found particularly erotic in which a woman is subjected to suffering in snow, *Akegarasu Yume no Awayuki*. Having learned hojojutsu techniques from an elderly practitioner and using his camera to record his work, he copied various examples of shibari and tsurizeme (suspension with rope) and took many photographs of his bound model in a winter landscape.

His use of his own shibari photographs as studies for his paintings and sketches became his standard technique. As notorious as his escapade in the snow, he once copied Yoshitoshi's famous and disturbing ukiyo-e masterpiece, "The Lonely House on Adachi Moor," with its startling depiction of a bound and suspended pregnant girl, using his own pregnant wife as his model! He had carefully worked out the safety precautions using pulleys and numerous assistants and was delighted by the results, though he admitted years later that even thinking about the risks he took attempting such a stunt gave him chills. Such reckless behavior caused him to become a most controversial figure. In fact, so famous had Itoh become that the June 1924 issue of Sunday Mainichi magazine, a very "normal" publication of large circulation, featured a visit to his studio.

Over the years, Itoh published many photos as well as paintings, drawings and commentaries in several books of seme-e and in volumes on other topics which created quite a stir in artistic circles. He is especially noted for his fine illustrations of Edo era customs and manners including pictures of feudal signs, toys, circus acts, street peddlers, religious figures, lamps, foods; in short, all manner of unique people and things soon to pass out of existence in the Meiji era's rush to westernize Japan.

His major publications include:
Six volumes on the history and customs of feudal Edo/Tokyo—published from 1927 to 1932.
Seme no Kenkyu (1929)—"The first bondage photography collection in Japan"—banned by the censors.
Seme no Hanashi (1929).
Rongo Tsukai (1930)—Itoh's first seme-e art collection—banned by the censors.
Gaka Seikatsu Uchimaku-Hanashi—an artist talks about his life (1930).
Onna Sanjyu-roku Kii (1930).
Binjin Ranmai (1932).
Edo no Sakariba (1947).
Makura (1948).
Kuronawa-ki zen (1951).
The Twelve Months of Strange Punishments (1953)—an art portfolio.

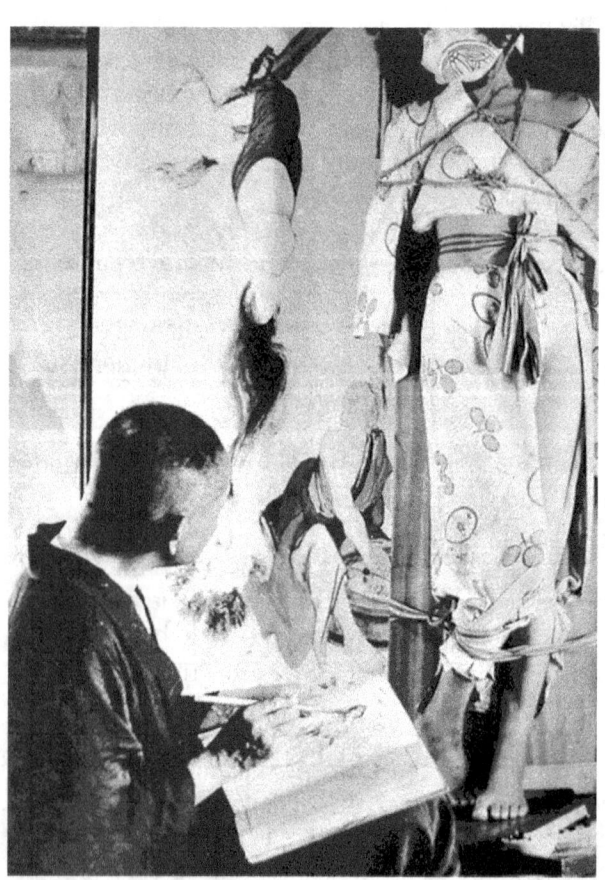

Itoh working

Despite his fame, Itoh was not always held in such high regard. In fact, he was often rebuked and he often despaired of having wasted his talents on seme-e. After a lifetime of work he confessed to Amatoria magazine in 1951 that, "The only recognition I ever received, as a person who has studied bondage since 1908, was the 'pervert' tag." Today Itoh's perversion is considered a respected "mania" and on occasion an art form, as well as being part of big business, and he is responsible for at least part of this change. He is especially credited for inspiring a distinct bondage "school" which in time became the mainstream style of erotic rope bondage known as kinbaku and an art form in Japan.

Because of his artistry in several fields, by the mid-20th century, he had begun to influence a whole new generation of shibari/kinbaku masters, editors, and graphic artists, all talented people interested in the erotic and artistic power of kinbaku and SM. Figures such as the brilliant painter and editor Kita Reiko (AKA, Minomura Kou), the legendary shibari master Nureki Chimuo and such latter-day figures as shibari master Osada Eikichi, author Dan Oniroku and master photographers Fuji Akio and Gomi Akira all credit his influence on some of their work. In his own right, Itoh's paintings, sketches and photographic studies continue to be published and as late as 1982 a beautiful book on the history of crime and punishment in Edo era Japan (Nihon keibatsu fuzoku toshi), written in collaboration with Fujisawa Morihiko and originally published between 1946 and 1952 in three volumes, was reproduced combining the earlier books into one volume and featuring only the illustrations of Itoh Seiu.

Although Itoh was not the only early 20th century artist or researcher interested in seme and seme-e, he is the most famous. There are five biographies of Itoh (and one about his first model, Oyou), several high-quality art books dedicated to his work and he has been depicted in a variety of films, sometimes as a demented egocentric and sometimes as an artistic genius.

Itoh's strength as an artist came from his great visual skill and taste and determination to capture what he called "Beauty in Suffering", that is those emotions of real desire and real drama caught on the razor's edge between pain and pleasure during the experience of sadomasochism. Like his great western contemporary John Willie (John Alexander Scott Coutts, 1902-1962), he brought artistic genius to his passion and in our own age when so much Internet "bondage" and especially torture imagery is only crude misogynist pornography masquerading as fetish art, his delicate and sensitive studies of beautiful maidens "suffering" with pleasure and desire still have the power to impress and inspire.

Minomura Kou—artist, author, publisher, bakushi, genius

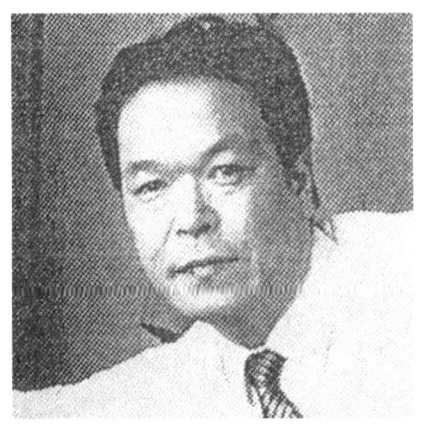

Minomura Kou (1920-1992)

Minomura Kou (1920-1992), real name Suma Toshiyuki, principal artist's name Kita Reiko (taken from his wife's maiden name), was quite simply one of the most multi-talented and accomplished persons ever to work in the SM field in Japan. Famous as one of the first editors of the legendary Kitan Club magazine and then as the creator of Uramado magazine in the first "golden age" of SM publishing in the 1950s, he was also a novelist, short-story writer, film critic, essayist, columnist, bakushi, photographer, painter, book jacket illustrator, magazine illustrator, "adviser" to SM Kitan (formerly Abu Hunter), SM Select and SM Collector magazines in the "second wave" of SM publications in the 1970s and a member of Itoh Seiu's artistic inner circle in post war Japan.

Born in Kyoto, Minomura was a precocious and imaginative child which made his remarkable introduction to shibari and SM all the more important for his future life and artistic career.

According to legend, Minomura's father had died when he was quite young, making his mother a widow at the age of 29. She was apparently a very temperamental woman and quite demanding. She would often punish young Minomura by locking him in the storage warehouse his grandfather owned. On one of these occasions, when he was seven years old, he discovered a stash of "seme-e" literature in the storehouse. He didn't yet know that's what such illustrations were called but he was transfixed by the images of princesses and lords and damsels in distress tied to trees. He has said that finding these pictures was the moment Minomura Kou was born and, after that, he didn't mind being locked in the storehouse. He later learned the collection of illustrations belonged to his grandfather, and he believed he'd inherited his grandfather's sadistic tendencies. Considering that the artist remembered these images in detail well into adulthood, a more classic case of what today psychologists would call "imprinting" could hardly be found.

Then came a fateful day when he went into the warehouse as usual, planning to look at the pictures again. As he climbed to the second floor he heard a sound and peering through the flickering sunlight and dust he saw a naked woman tied to a pillar. At first he thought it was one of the women in the illustrations magically come to life. He couldn't believe it was his mother. However, it was. His mother was stripped naked and tied with rags and kimono sashes. Her hands were bound behind her back and the end of the rag rope was tied to the warehouse pillar (hashira) supporting the roof. She was sitting, helpless, on the floor.

He later learned that his mother had squandered much of what his father had left them by playing around with actors. In fact, she had gotten involved with a younger kabuki actor and was planning to abandon the family and run away with him. Somehow her brother-in-law, Minomura's uncle, had got wind of this and was punishing her. She had obviously been left there to ponder her offense, unable to meet the actor who was waiting for her somewhere in town.

The boy was terribly shocked, and began to cry. His mother, as soon as she was aware of him, screamed at him to go away, no doubt preferring to be helpless over having her own child see her like this. He tried to untie her but she screamed that he mustn't or his uncle would get mad at him. So he embraced her, enthralled by her white skin and lovely curves and for the first time felt something like sensual, erotic, excitement. Three years later, in Showa 3 (1928), he saw this vision again in an illustration in a magazine. The illustration was of a woman in exactly the same predicament, and her name was even the same as his mother's.

He once told a famous psychologist named Takahashi Tetsu about finding his mother tied up in the storehouse. The psychologist concluded that Minomura Kou harbored hostility against his mother, and that is why he liked to "mistreat" women by tying them up. Minomura said he thought this diagnosis was "completely ridiculous." What he thought when he saw his mother was how "beautiful she was." He then wrote, "While Takahashi might be a good psychologist, he doesn't understand a thing about 'abnormal' sexuality!"

This tale is worth the retelling not just because it's a remarkable glimpse into a formative experience in the life of a major kinbaku talent but also because of how this incident would continue to resonate throughout Minomura's artistic career. Though the story might seem to be apocryphal, at least some elements of it are probably true. Minomura repeated it many times over the years (the version presented above comes from a column he wrote for the May 1975 edition of SM Collector) but more than this the truth of the story is reinforced by the evidence of countless elegant drawings and photos. Over and over again the artist Kita Reiko and the bakushi Minomura Kou would return to the subject of a beautiful woman bound to a hashira.

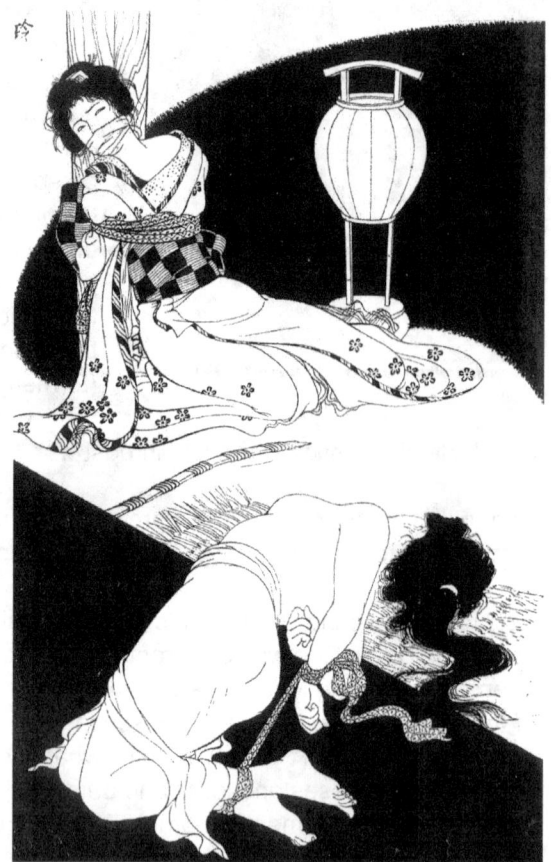

Minomura Kou/Kita Reiko magazine illustration, circa 1970

Minomura served in the Navy during the Second World War where he claimed to have learned a number of quick release ties and other rope techniques that he used in his SM work. After the war he befriended Tsujimura Takashi, Dan Oniroku, Nureki Chimuo and many others and influenced most of their careers as he quickly became one of the dominant talents and one of the most famous and respected names in SM publishing. He was the shibari master for one of the first commercial "rope book/albums" ever published in Japan and the popular success of his sketch, "Ten Positions of a Naked Tied Woman," in Kitan Club in 1952 is often cited as one of the principal reasons that magazine turned to SM for its general content and so began the tradition of SM publications that continues today. He suffered a stroke in the early 1980s which greatly reduced his prodigious creative output and he died in 1992 in Tokyo.

As a bakushi Minomura is said to have had a singular style. He preferred to use only five ropes for his ties and to create positions intended to cause shuuchi (shyness or embarrassment) in his partners. Clearly he was more interested in the subtle psychological side of SM play than in the flash of performance. Perhaps this is another echo of his experience with his mother at age seven? A student of shibari history, he discovered and named quite a few of the kinbaku ties still in use today. He used hemp rope for his photographic studies but often switched to very soft cotton in order not to discomfort particularly sensitive models. He apparently disliked tsuri (suspensions) intensely and never drew them. This the author can confirm. After an exhaustive search through all known sources, there seem to be only three depictions of suspensions in his entire output. From his interviews and articles Minomura comes across as plain speaking with a good sense of humor and a healthy attitude towards sex. He was loyal and generous to his friends. He also appears to have had great common sense as regards the difference between fantasy and reality in SM play and to hold his kinbaku partners and models in high regard.

Regrettably, the art of seme-e master Kita Reiko (Minomura) has never been collected in book form save for two modest, limited edition albums now long out of print. A memorial video tape, directed by Yukimura Haruki, was released by Cinemagic shortly before his death but many of his magnificent illustrations now exist only in the fading "golden age" magazines and novels prized by avid collectors who often pay *hundreds* of times their original cover prices to possess them. To put it simply, without the artistry, energy and genius of Minomura Kou there would be no Japanese SM as we know it today.

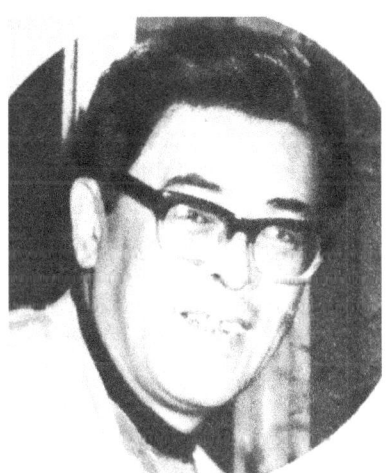

Tsujimura Takashi (1921-1987?)

Tsujimura Takashi—the romantic bakushi

Of all the major figures from the early days of SM publishing and the evolution of modern shibari/kinbaku, Tsujimura Takashi (1921-1987?) is the least remembered today. This is more than a shame because Tsujimura was one of the most influential bakushi of his day, a talented writer and a man largely responsible for developing many kinbaku styles and attitudes about SM that still have relevance today.

Tsujimura Takashi was born in 1921 in Sakai City near Osaka, Japan. He traced his interest in SM to his third or fourth year of elementary school when, in a festival on the grounds of a Shinto shrine, he saw a seme-e theater attraction, billed as a "zankoku" (cruel) show, that portrayed various acts of domination, including bondage, much in the manner of the Grand Guignol theater troupes in France. It was this show, he said, that made him fall in love with rope.

At 14, he lost his virginity to the daughter of a relative, who later became the first woman to allow him to tie her and eventually his wife. When he graduated from high school he was to go to Manchuria to work. The day before he left he tied this girl for the first time. He considered it a romantic parting. He was soon drafted, served in the armed forces during WWII, survived the conflict and, when the war was over, returned to Japan and settled in Nara Prefecture where he ran a hardware store.

Tsujimura had plenty of time to read magazines while he watched the shop and one of the magazines he came across was Kitan Club. Thinking to himself that he could certainly write at least as well as the stories he was reading, he sent a manuscript off which was accepted in consideration for a small fee. That story, published in the summer of 1948, was the start of a 25-year connection with Kitan Club. He wrote for Kitan Club under three different pen names: for comedy he used the name Shinto; for historical fiction he used the name Midori Takehiko; and for essays and stories set in modern times he used the name Tsujimura Takashi. He also contributed to other SM magazines.

In 1948 or 1949, while visiting Kitan Club's editor, Yoshida Minoru, Tsujimura met Minomura Kou for the first time. The magazine was still a general tabloid then but when it was decided to turn it into an SM magazine Tsujimura was asked to contribute a story. In the September 1951 issue of Kitan Club the name Tsujimura Takashi appeared for the first time.

At that time nude photographs of women had started appearing in various magazines, including Kitan Club. However, up to that date there had been few photographs of women in bondage. Kitan Club decided to try this. In the May-June issue in 1952, at the request of Minomura and using a model named Kawabata Tanako, Tsujimura did the bondage and so became the first magazine bakushi. According to Tsujimura, that issue also included the first use of the word "kinbaku" in a magazine and also the first use of the term "kinbaku model." In 1964 Tsujimura launched his column "Camera Hunt," which ran until 1973 and was one of the most popular features in the history of Kitan Club. In it Tsujimura worked with submissive women, professional models and amateurs, and gave readers a record of his SM play in text and photographs. In the mid-1970s he continued the column on the pages of SM King.

By reading the "Camera Hunt" columns one can feel how kind a man Tsujimura was. Although he was dominant he was never violent, and was in fact a true romantic who cared deeply about his model's comfort, happiness and safety. This is why submissive women were able to trust him. And that is surely the reason this feature was so successful with readers and continued for so long.

In 1968, upon the recommendation of his friend Dan Oniroku for whom he later worked on the magazine SM King, he was invited by Toei film company to be the "kinbaku shidou" (kinbaku adviser/teacher/leader) for a movie directed by Ishii Teruo entitled Tokugawa Onna Keibatsu-shi. He then did the rope work for two other Toei films directed by Ishii: Zankoku-Ijou-Gyakutai Monogatari: Genroku Onna Keizu (1968) and Tokugawa Irezumi-shi Semu Jigoku (1969). Also in 1968, Tsujimura was invited as a guest on the late-night television program "11 PM" which was a "coming out" of sorts because his family and friends saw him live on the show talking about SM for the first time. He appeared on the program several times after that as an expert bakushi. He also performed in his own productions of the "zankoku" (cruel) show that had so excited him as a boy.

By the early 1970s, society's attitudes towards SM had changed and become somewhat more open, in part because of the success of director Ishii Teruo's movies, the SM magazines and "11 PM," which frequently addressed the subject of SM and other formally taboo topics. The word "SM" became well known and the practice shifted from being a hidden culture to one that was generally understood. Observing this, Tsujimura decided to end his "Camera Hunt" column. He felt it was no longer as relevant as when people had few sources for information about SM and he also felt that he could no longer keep up with the "new reader's" expectations for more outrageous or violent SM play. When SM King ceased publication in 1975 Tsujimura basically retired and slowly slipped from view.

Tsujimura Takashi's importance is based on his technical achievements and on the attitude he brought to his kinbaku/SM play. Technically, he was an innovator who used the older hojojutsu forms in the development of his own "quick tying" style of kinbaku. On meeting him for the first time in Osaka in 1967, Dan Oniroku was amazed by his speed. He was also instrumental in creating the techniques for doing safe tsuri (suspensions) with his models. His direct kinbaku descendents, Osada Eikichi, Nureki Chimuo, Akechi Denki (who once trained with Tsujimura), Shima Shikou and others who popularized and further refined this type of flashy "flying," all owe a debt to Tsujimura sensei.

However, it's probably the attitude of affection and appreciation for his partners, that he clearly expressed through his very popular magazine columns, which will have the longest impact on the history of modern erotic shibari/kinbaku. This is SM as loving, consensual play and is a fitting legacy for this most romantic of bakushi.

I once asked the former SM magazine editor and artist Miyabi Kyodo for his opinion of Tsujimura Takashi and he responded, poetically, as follows:

"Master K:

Mr. Tsujimura Takashi was a shining giant star in the world of kinbaku in Japan. But today, nobody talks about him any longer and his shibari techniques have been all but lost. His shibari was first rate . . . .like. water fits into any bowl . . . so magically flexible . . . kaleidoscopic. I have the greatest respect for his work ... He undoubtedly occupies the highest seat in the Japanese kinbaku scene."

Nawa Yumio—author, historian, Edo era martial arts expert

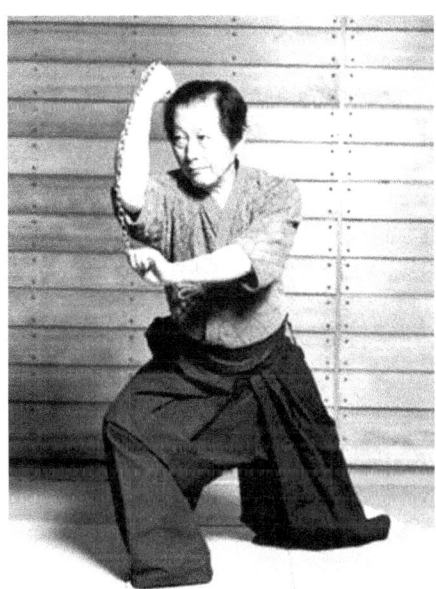

Nawa Yumio (1912-2006) was one of Japan's foremost authorities on the history and methods of hojojutsu (rope capture and restraint), law enforcement and interrogation in Edo Era Japan. He was born January 3, 1912 into a family that had been retainers to a samurai clan in the old province of Mino. He began training in martial arts at an early age, proved very talented and eventually became the head of both the Masaki-ryu of kobujutsu (school of ancient martial arts) and the Edo Machikata Jitte-jutsu (school of Edo constabulary truncheon arts). He spent over 70 years collecting and researching traditional weapons and techniques used in the capture of fugitives and his personal collection is now housed at Meiji University in Tokyo as part of their famous criminology collection.

Nawa Yumio (1912-2006)

Nawa Yumio authored numerous well-respected books including: Gōmon Keibatsu shi ("The History of Torture and Punishment") and Ninjutsu no Kenkyū ("The Study of Ninja Arts"). His most recent book, published in 1996 by Yuzankaku Shuppan, is Jitte HojōJitten: Edo Machi Bugyou no Soubi to Taihō-jutsu ("The Encyclopedia of Rope and Truncheon Capture: the Art and Equipment of the Edo era Constabulary").

Nawa Yumio also advised television and movie producers on historical accuracy and authored a popular tome, *Machigai Darake no Jikaigeki* ("Historical Shows are Full of Errors"), that criticized the way the Edo era is portrayed in television shows. He contributed his skills to the 1964 film *Nihon Gōmon Keibatsu-shi* ("The History of Torture and Punishment in Japan") released by Shintoho. He also wrote the scripts for a more recent two-part historical film depicting similar Edo-era themes, *Onna Hankacho I (1994) & II (1995), King Records.*

Nawa Yumio was influential in the Japanese martial arts community as well as in the SM and shibari/kinbaku world for almost a century. During the early years of the first "golden age" of SM magazines he contributed 11 articles on hojojutsu, Edo era tortures and related topics to *Uramado*, the SM magazine started by Suma Toshiyuki (Minomura Kou), and was largely responsible for opening up this historical world to its readers. Over the years he also contributed authoritative articles to Suspense Magazine and SM Fan. His importance to the evolution of shibari/kinbaku from the martial art of hojojutsu is central and obvious for it was his historical scholarship, understanding and expertise that allowed both public and professionals alike to adapt this ancient martial art to the modern era. He is prominently profiled in Saotome Hiromi's 1998 book *Sei no Shigoto Shitachi* ("Masters of the Underground Erotic/Sex Trade").

Muku Youji—master of the pencil sketch

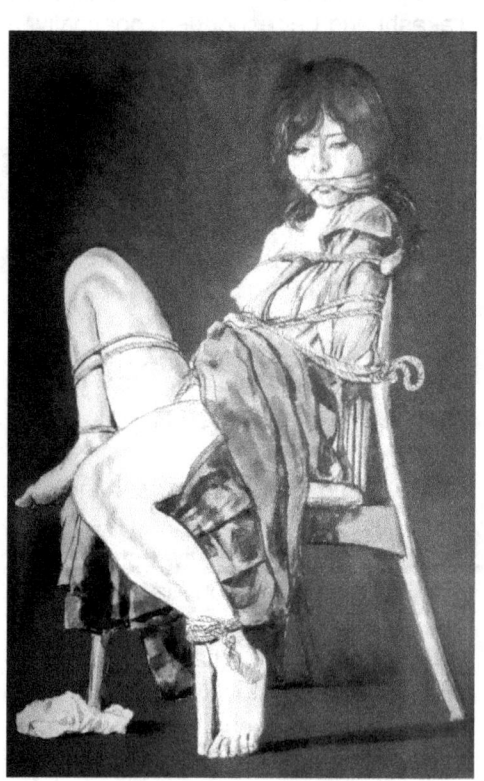

*Illustration by Muku Youji-
SM Collector-February, 1977*

During the "golden age" of SM magazine publishing in Japan readers were blessed by the talents of numerous illustrators who helped bring the fiction to life and who created early manga cartoons or comics. These artists also created beautiful, eye catching covers and even portfolios of shibari/kinbaku/SM art that were inserted into the magazines. In the earliest days, when photographic reproduction was poor, these drawings helped create erotic worlds of imagination and often, as in the case of Kita Reiko, the illustrators became as popular and important to sales as the story's authors. One of the most admired and hard working of these was Muku Youji (1928-2001) who seemed to contribute to all of the magazines at one time or another and probably produced more illustrations than any other artist of the time.

Muku Youji was born in Osaka on Nov. 11, 1928. After a fairly uneventful childhood living with his parents who were farmers, he spent most of the war years in the relative safety of the countryside. Immediately after WW II he returned to the city and worked in various minor jobs, including stints at a hotel tea room and a pachinko parlor (authors note: pachinko is a Japanese mechanical game played for amusement and prizes and related to the American pinball machine). According to several revealing autobiographical articles he wrote for the short lived magazine SM Graffiti in 1980, it was at about this time that he had his first experiences with shibari/kinbaku, taking photographs of his tied partners.

Eventually he moved to Tokyo to become a fine arts student and there joined an advertising agency while continuing his extracurricular explorations of kinbaku. Finally, in the mid-1960s, after submitting a sketch to Minomura Kou's Uramado magazine, he joined its editorial staff. He first used the penname Ochiai Ryuji before settling on Muku Youji for his illustrations which began appearing regularly on the magazine's pages and masthead. He also wrote novels using the name Toyonaka Yumeo. Something of an all around talent, he also learned professional photographic techniques and became a jack-of-all-trades around the magazine.

After five years of constant work he decided to become an independent artist and began freelancing for most of the SM magazines then being published in the early 1970s. He also did skillful manga and book illustrations and even published a volume of shibari/kinbaku photographs, *Kinbaku no Hada* ("Bondage Skin"), in 1971.

Three features distinguish Muku Youji from most of his colleagues. First, he was a tremendous representational artist. Using no more than a # 2 pencil, Muku could create figures that almost breathed with life they were so realistic. Second, he was a connoisseur of sophisticated kinbaku. The bindings he chose to represent were meticulously drawn down to the last detail. Using his own photographs as inspiration (much in the manner of Itoh Seiu), as well as carefully studying the techniques of such rope masters as Nureki Chimuo, Muku could reproduce the most detailed ties and expressions with complete fidelity. Finally, the artist had both a great sense of drama and a good sense of humor. There's always a story and life lingering around the edges of his illustrations, even those not tied to an actual narrative, and his cartoons and manga, for which he became famous, can be truly amusing.

From the early 1980s Sun Publishing began reprinting the manga he did for the early SM magazines and in the 1990s he did illustrations for SM Shosetsu and SM Mania, both from My Way Publishing. Muku Youji was one of the luckier artists of the "golden era" and found himself constantly in demand by publishers and "rediscovered" by SM fans in the 1990s. This resulted in further reprinting of his comic work and even a deluxe limited edition of his more erotic material, published in 2000. In addition, hundreds of his images have been transmitted over the Internet making much of his work available to fans.

He died on July 30, 2001 at the age of 73, one of the most famous and respected of SM illustrators.

Osada Eikichi—Father of the SM stage show

One of the true innovators in the world of SM and shibari/kinbaku is the legendary Osada Eikichi (1925-2001), the man responsible for creating the modern SM club show. Born in Tochigi prefecture in 1925 he became interested in the writings of the Marquis de Sade in his 20s when that controversial author's works were first translated into Japanese in 1947. In 1952 Osada discovered Kitan Club and soon thereafter Uramado magazine, the "Camera Hunt" columns of Tsujimura Takashi, the illustrations of Kita Reiko and the bondage photographs of Itoh Seiu, all of which convinced the young man that he wanted to follow in these artist's footsteps.

Unfortunately, the 1950s were a puritanical time in Japan and Osada had no idea how to enter this world. Instead, he found himself making a living running a printing business which prospered in the Japanese economic boom of the 1960s but still

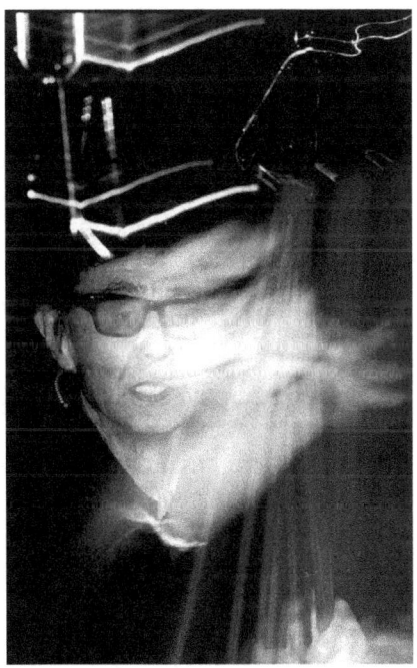
Osada Eikichi (1925-2001)

left him feeling discontented. A chance opportunity to see a modest seme-e style show finally opened the door to a new creative life. Produced, directed and acted by a man named Kazuya Mukai, this show featured a modest scene of bondage. Impressed, Osada Eikichi came to the show as often as he could and eventually found himself working for Kazuya and handling all the tying duties.

Still, Osada chaffed under the restrictions of this modest entertainment and longed for the day when he could let his imagination run free and create his own performances. That day finally came when a chance conversation with a movie producer client, for whom Eikichi was printing a poster, produced a submissive model and a tip from another friend yielded a former ballet school space for use as a theater.

Osada Eikichi's first production in his own style was held at the former Ars Nova ballet studio in Tokyo in 1965. Osada hoped for 20 spectators at most and was astonished when over a hundred packed the small space. Excited and tense, the performer and his first model, Rumi Sasamori, put on a show featuring flying ropes, whips and reckless abandon. The audience was stunned and only after Osada exited the stage did they erupt into applause and give the performers a standing ovation.

After this first performance Osada Eikichi began to be known and respected in SM circles throughout Japan. He put on shows, held private, "members only," gatherings and taught classes. As his fame grew, the uniqueness of his act allowed ticket prices to soar to 100,000 Yen (approximately $1000 at today's exchange rate) as Osada played to enthusiastic audiences at various venues, including strip clubs. He did this for almost 35 years. Of course, as the years went by and other SM attractions and acts appeared, Osada Eikichi's fortunes and health waxed and waned but he never lost his enthusiasm. Late in his career he once commented, "I feel better, both physically and mentally, whenever I get a chance to manipulate ropes."

Often, when we comment on or critique stage performances, it's from memory and memories are sometimes faulty. The stage show is an ephemeral experience and, like our memories of youth, sometimes gets better as we age. How great *was* that high school football game? Was your date *that* pretty? Did you really run *that* fast? Fortunately, in the author's collection are two video documents of Osada Eikichi in action. One is a performance tape from the 1980s and the other is a video showing him preparing his act. Both are amazing.

The author can honestly say he's never seen an SM or shibari/kinbaku act or demonstration that had half the impact of Osada Eikichi's. He really was the "flying rope man." To watch him perform on stage, racing from model to model, ropes constantly in motion is to witness the antic imp of SM come to life. In performance Osada Eikichi would suspend a model horizontally in seconds then leap on her back and together they would swing far out over his audience's heads! He was energy incarnate with a true performer's instinct for drama. The documentary tape shows some of his secrets, the use of quick release ties, an instinct for the acrobatic and a respect for innovation, but no one could rehearse such energy!

In addition to creating the modern SM stage show, Osada Eikichi is also important as one of the bakushi that helped create techniques to safely do suspensions and so liberate them from the shadows of the Tokugawa torturers. For instance, the famous back riding stunt was done by the bakushi actually holding himself up by the suspension lines in order to save the model's spine. He is also notable for his influence on the model and author Saotome Hiromi, who performed with him for several years, and on the bakushi Osada Steve, who followed in his footsteps.

Edgy, "performance Art," acts might seem rather ordinary to us today but it took tremendous courage to put on an SM show of the sort Osada Eikichi did in the 1960s. Osada's activities and techniques were, for his day and age, on the cutting edge of trends that would later become accepted practice within the Japanese SM community and every performer who has ever followed him on stage stands in his shadow and is in his debt.

Dan Oniroku—novelist, publisher, producer

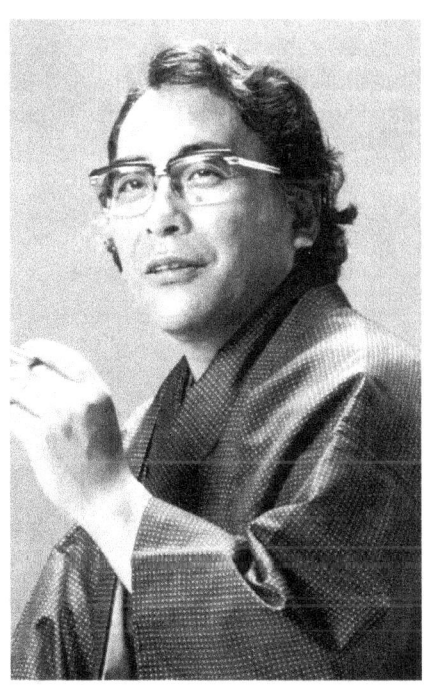

Dan Oniroku (1931-2011)

Dan Oniroku is the pen name of arguably Japan's most famous SM/fetish writer, born in 1931 in Saga Prefecture as Kuroiwa Yoshihiko. He himself said his penname could be read either as Dan Oniroku or Dan Kiroku, but the former is the name by which he is most commonly known. He graduated from Kansei Gakuin (Kansei Academy) with a degree in law, but in 1957 he won a newcomers literary prize for a short story and began his career as a professional writer. After he contributed the story Hana to Hebi ("Flower and Snake") to the SM magazine Kitan Club, he became famous as an erotic novelist which became his métier. During his lengthy literary career he penned, edited or published over 159 literary works.

He began writing Hana to Hebi under the penname Hamamaki Kyotaro in 1962, but lost all interest in it after only three chapters. He then met Minomura Kou and Tsujimura Takashi (famous bakushi and writers and editors for the legendary Japanese BDSM magazine Kitan Club). With renewed interest he finished the story which was then published to great acclaim in Kitan Club in 1964. The novel's depiction of the psychology of SM was a startling literary departure for its day and became one of Dan's major themes as a novelist. To date "Flower and Snake" has been serialized and/ or republished numerous times and at least five successful motion pictures have been adapted from it. It remains Dan's most famous literary work.

In 1969 he started his own production company Oni Pro and a year later affiliated with publisher Haga Shoten and, in collaboration with photographers and bakushi Totsuka Eisaku and Kayama Shigeru, began to publish high quality shibari/kinbaku photo collections on various themes. In 1971 he directed his own film entitled Nikujigoku and in 1972 began his successful collaboration with Nikkatsu studios on their "roman porno" series of erotic films. Many of his scripts starred the legendary actress Tani Naomi and their collaboration continued until her retirement in 1978 after the production of fifteen films.

Also in 1972 Dan launched his own "golden age" magazine, SM King. A quality publication employing the best writers and artists of the time, it got a lot of attention on its launch as a magazine employing, "only female editors." In 1973 Tsujimura Takashi was appointed as "kinbaku shidou" (rope master/ teacher) for SM King and also wrote his famous "Camera Hunt" column.

In 1989 Dan Oniroku announced that he was retiring from writing and devoted himself to the publication of the short lived chess magazine Shogi Journal (Author's note: Dan was an accomplished amateur player of shogi—Japanese chess). However, in 1995 he returned to writing and published the mainstream novel Shinkenshi Koike Jūmei. His other major works include: Ashura, Nikuno Kaoyaku, Yūgao Fujin, and Ori no naka no Yōsei as well as a fictional work based on the life of Itoh Seiyu. In 2000 his witty and wise semi-autobiographical novella Bishonen was successfully brought to the screen by director Hiroki Ryuichi under the title "I am an SM writer." Both the novella and the film are available in

English and with English subtitles, respectively.

Dan Oniroku was honored many times over the years for his creative output and in 1999 his autobiography Hana wa Kurenai ("Flowers are Crimson") was published. Ironically, Dan would have preferred to have been remembered as a serious writer and not one known mostly for his fetish work. However, his influence on the evolution and practice of modern Japanese SM and shibari/kinbaku is indisputable. He passed away in 2011 with his fame as the most important, influential and talented Japanese writer of BDSM material still unchallenged.

Urado (Urato) Hiroshi—master of kinbaku in the cinema

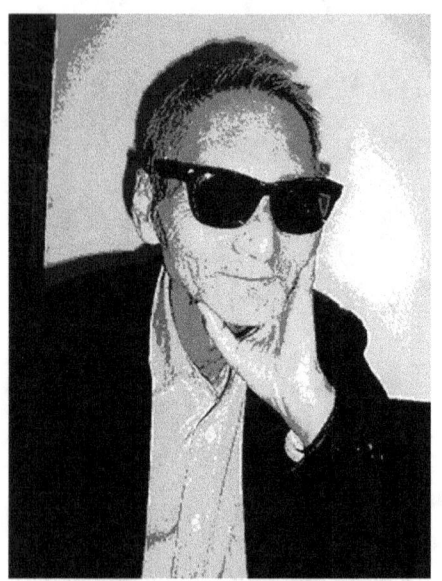

Urado Hiroshi, Tokyo, 2010.

The man who was to become Urado Hiroshi was born in 1933 in Kochi Prefecture on Shikoku. His professional name is fictitious, of course, and he himself spells it Urado (because of an association with a place name near his home town), although he's also known by the more common Urato and is happy to be called by either.

The first time he came to Tokyo was at the end of high school for a university entrance exam. The only reason he made the trip was because he wanted to see the big city; he never thought he'd pass the exam. To his surprise he was offered a place at a "reasonably prestigious university" and started his studies in the Sociology Department. As far as Urado was concerned, the main advantage to being a student in Tokyo was the right to flash his ID card at movie theaters and get in on the cheap student discounts. Significantly, his earliest ambition was to become a film director and he still tries to see 100 new films each year.

After graduation, he worked on the editorial staff of a noted children's book publisher until, in 1961, he went for an interview at Kubo Shoten Publishing. At the time, Kubo Shoten was putting out various magazines, including the Japanese version of the American pulp "Manhunt." They had also started a little magazine called "Uramado" with an SM theme and were looking for someone to help out with that. Up until then Urado professes he had no interest whatsoever in SM . . . but admits there might have been something in his unconscious.

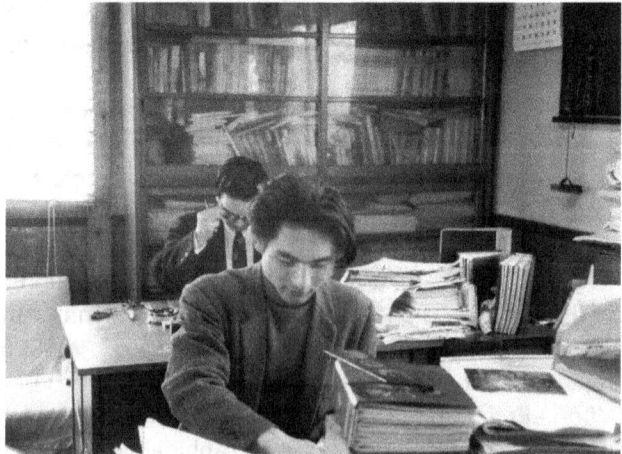

Urado Hiroshi at Uramado, circa 1962.

The editor of Uramado was, of course, Suma Toshiyuki (AKA Kita Reiko, AKA Minomura Kou), perhaps the most talented man ever to work in Japanese SM. He looked Urado's resume over carefully and said, "You can start tomorrow, if you like . . . but we don't pay well." In fact, the offer Urado got from Suma was significantly lower than he'd hoped for but the Uramado office was within walking distance from where he lived and the hours were extremely loose, so he took the job.

About a month after Urado joined the company, Suma invited him to go visit "Kyotaro-san," one of their authors who wrote under the penname Hamamaki Kyotaro. This was how Urado met the man who later became the most famous SM writer in Japan, Dan Oniroku.

In 1969, Dan organized a company (some suggest it was more a loose circle of collaborators) and called it Oni Pro. He planned some bondage photography shoots for a series of books he intended to publish and he hired Kayama Shigeru, a well known photographer, SM player, part time rope master and a close associate of Minomura Kou's to do them. Unfortunately, Kayama was expensive so Dan quietly suggested to Urado that he watch Kayama and learn how to do the bondage himself, thus saving them money.

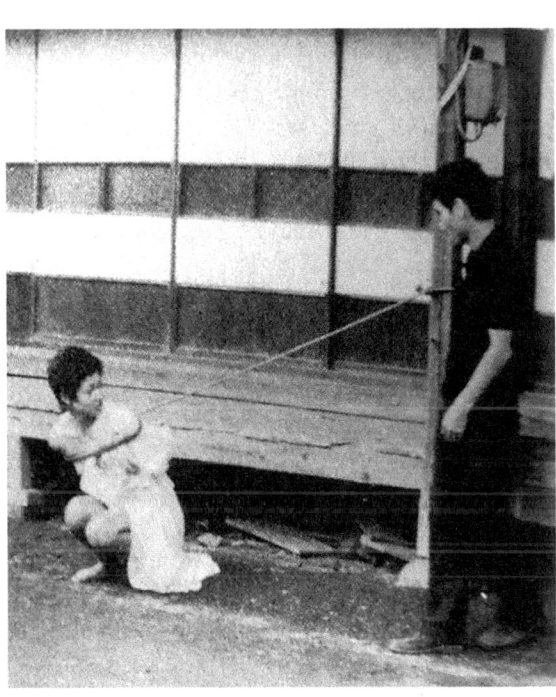

Urado tying for Dan Oniroku, circa 1970.

Urado taught himself carefully, through trial and error, and by looking at Suma Toshiyuki/Minomura Kou's bondage, both photographs of his ties and the many drawings the great artist made under his legendary nom de plume Kita Reiko. In typical Japanese apprentice style Suma never gave Urado any direct kinbaku instruction. "Suma was the kind of person who thought you should learn by yourself," Urado told us, but he says his own bondage originated with and was completely inspired by Minomura Kou, his greatest influence.

While doing various kinbaku book projects for Dan, Urado met the beautiful Tani Naomi, a model who was just gaining a name as an actress in "pink movies" but who hadn't yet started working for the bigger, more established studios like Nikkatsu. The young bakushi and model worked together successfully on several occasions, gaining trust and appreciation for each other's professionalism and skill.

It turned out to be a most fateful encounter when, in 1974, Tani Naomi's manager, having worked with Urado on the photo books, introduced him to Nikkatsu studios as that company was just beginning to discuss the possibility of doing a revolutionary project—a "kinbaku movie," of all things, that would give Tani her first starring role and which was to be based on the scandalous SM novel by Dan Oniroku, "Hana to Hebi" (AKA "Flower and Snake").

"Flower and Snake" was released in 1974 and a second SM oriented film, "Wife to be Sacrificed," also featuring kinbaku by Urado Hiroshi, quickly followed. Due to their success, Urado was hired to create the kinbaku for a large majority of the most famous Nikkatsu SM oriented films.

What characterizes Urado's kinbaku in these films is its boldness. He is often doing unusual suspensions or other difficult and potentially dangerous riggings and, it must be remembered, he was tying movie actors, not just interested SM players! The shibari had to look good, appear serious (a requirement for the fans) but still allow Naomi Tani and numerous others to act! This was no mean challenge.

It goes without saying that, when tying a movie actor, the most important thing is safety; their safety as human beings, of course, but also their safety as key figures in an expensive commercial project. As Urado put it, "Imagine if your leading lady suffered a dislocation in the middle of a shoot!" He went out of his way to put the actress at ease and assure her that her safety was paramount. He would explain the tie and work with her to make sure she felt comfortable, both emotionally and physically. There was never a single accident on his watch, and had there been one, he said, he would no longer have been able to claim himself as a professional.

As an example, he described a scene in the Nikkatsu film, "Kurobara Fujin" (Black Rose Lady), in which the actress Tajima Haruka is suspended upside down in a Sakasa zuri. He put three men on holding the end of the rope lifting her, and showed her this so she could be convinced that this was sufficient to bear her weight, and he tested with her various ways of binding her ankles so she could provide input on what felt right. He also bore her entire body weight over his own shoulder until the moment she was actually suspended.

In an interview in Sun and Moon magazine (April, 1978), Tajima describes how Urado and the film's director each wrapped one of her ankles with a mame-shibori tenugui cloth to pad them before the rope went on. Urado's wrap was perfect. It fit closely but was neither too loose nor too tight. But the director was probably worried about making it too tight, and his was too loose. She continued, "I was worried … so without reservation I asked that the director's wrap be done again more tightly. What made me place my trust in the specialist Mr. Urado was the difference in the way those two tied the cloth around my ankles."

In truth, Urado Hiroshi was as much a "kinbaku designer" or "director" as he was a bakushi. He often suggested and created the bondage for each kinbaku scene being filmed, advised on stage business and even costumes and on occasion even wrote scenes himself. For instance, it was Urado who suggested that Naomi Tani wear a bridal costume in the famous suspension scene in "Wife to be Sacrificed," an extraordinarily bold idea which added greatly to the scene's symbolism and dramatic power.

Like the kabuki theater productions of the 19th century that so influenced the father of modern kinbaku Itoh Seiu, Urado, for his Nikkatsu projects, needed to make sure the ropes could be clearly seen by the audience and that his actresses always felt and looked their most attractive. For this reason he often used slightly softer ropes dyed in vivid colors. "The rope should be like clothing," he has said, "soft and comforting and gentle on the skin. It should be part of the costume, enhancing the model and the mood."

However, this didn't mean his actors had it easy! Another example of his creative kinbaku is the famous horse scene in "Kijujin Shibari no Tsubo" (Noble Lady, Bound Vase) where Naomi Tani's character and her lover are bound back to back, riding bareback, on a galloping horse!

Urado provided a great deal of creative input for this scene, deciding that the couple in the story should be publicly shamed before being crucified, and that they should be tied back-to-back for more drama. He knew how to ride a horse because his grandfather had been a horseman but neither of the actors had ever ridden before! The staff was very worried about the actors falling off, so he tied the actors "just for show," leaving their hands free, and then tied a rope around the horse's belly to which they could hold on to, only doing the real bondage before each "take." It was a difficult scene for everyone, but Tani, being a real pro, never once complained. And all this before the age of computer effects!

The director of "Black Rose Lady," Nishimura Shougorou, expressed his admiration for Urado in an interview he gave to Sun and Moon magazine in April, 1978:

"In the course of five or six years, I had made probably 30 erotic films for Nikkatsu, but this was my first about SM. When I complained to the producer that I didn't know the first thing about SM, he said he'd introduce me to someone who knew all about it, Mr. U. Mr. Urado had already worked as shibari shidou on several SM films and seemed to be on friendly terms with the producer. I told Mr. U that I knew nothing about SM, and tried posing some questions. For example, I asked him, "Why does one tie a woman?" He replied that shibari is another form of love between a man and a woman. He really understood my questions. In the course of the conversation, I came to understand that Mr. U was a very scholarly person . . . So for all the SM scenes I put my complete trust in Mr. U, and used every one of his ideas just as they were. Perhaps you think that makes me an irresponsible director, but I recognized that his ability to express his ideas was exceptional . . . and once we started shooting, we worked together extremely well."

Urado Hiroshi worked for Nikkatsu studios from 1974 until 1988, and did about 50 films for the company. Shooting each movie would take at least two to three weeks, during which time he was on the set every day. He was paid only 50,000 yen per film in the beginning, and up to 250,000 yen per film towards the end. It wasn't enough to live on so he continued to do freelance editing as production schedules allowed throughout his time working for Nikkatsu.

Had Urado Hiroshi only done the bondage rigging for the Nikkatsu films of the 1970s and 80s he would deserve a place in Japanese kinbaku/SM history simply by virtue of the millions of fans who have seen these films over the decades. They have remained ever popular and, in fact, are attracting even more admirers today thanks to their recent re-release on DVD in Japan and in the West. "Flower and Snake" (1974) and "Wife to be Sacrificed" (1974) have both been re-mastered and distributed in English subtitled versions.

However, Urado was much more than just a creative "rigger." He was/is also a literary man of merit, a writer and scholar who early in his career wrote stories for Uramado and later scripts for Nikkatsu. In addition, Urado even once set up his own publishing company to produce books about the Meiji Restoration and other subjects.

In the SM field, he created a very profitable series of novels on SM themes for the Haga Shoten company—the SM Tanbi Bungaku series and it's two supplements, SM Tanbi Bungaku Bekkan 1 & 2; the second of these being one of the earliest kinbaku tutorial books ever published. For this effort Urado developed the concept, edited and convinced Dan Oniroku to write for the series and Muku Youji, the brilliant SM artist, to illustrate for it. In addition, Urado has edited several elegant SM magazines over the years.

Of course he also served as rope master for various book projects including several for Dan's Oni Pro organization: the three volume "Fuzoku Jidai Kinbaku" series, Yakuza Tenshi (vol. 3) and the elegant Kinbaku Taizen with photography by the talented Shinoyama Kishin. This lovely book is of special interest because it includes an early piece on Edo era tying. In 1970 Urado also did one volume of Nawa to Onna, an attractive two volume set of bondage photography published by Misaki Shobo. Hopefully, Urado's memoirs of his days at Nikkatsu will also be published one day.

However, it will be Urado Hiroshi's excellent work for Nikkatsu that will most be remembered. Like Itoh Sieu and Minomura Kou, Urado occupies a unique place in kinbaku history due to the unprecedented number of spectators, both those interested in SM and those not, who have seen the films he worked on and been influenced by his efforts.

(Author's note: In 2010 I had the great good fortune to meet and begin to take lessons from Urado sensei as well as to get to know him personally. Over the years we have become close and I will always owe him a profound debt of gratitude for his gracious introduction to Takahashi Masato, president of Suirensha publishing, my Japanese publisher.)

Tani Naomi—movie star

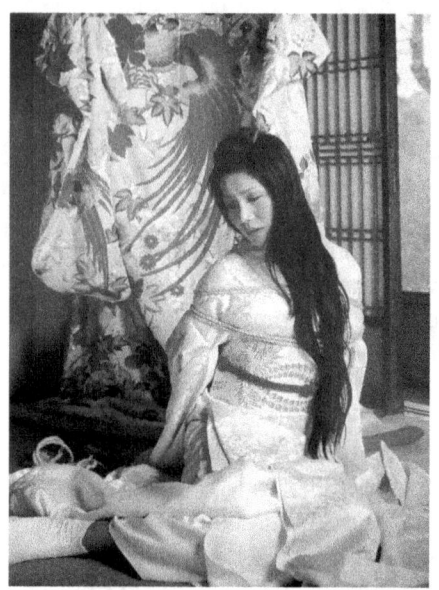

Tani Naomi

The one authentic star to emerge from the Nikkatsu studios pinku eiga era is the beautiful and talented actress Tani Naomi. For her millions of fans she is "The Queen of SM Films" in Japan.

Born in 1948 in Hakata, she moved to Tokyo at age 18 to work in the big city. With her striking good looks she was soon modeling and then was quickly offered a pinku eiga role by one of the smaller production companies. At first she was shocked by the idea of appearing in a sexually themed film but she went to the theater to take a closer look. Deciding that with a good plot and good production values these films could have merit, she took a chance.

Beginning in 1966-1967, Tani appeared in over 200 films before she began to work for Nikkatsu studios in their 1972 release, *Shinayakana Kemonotachi* ("Sensuous Beasts"). In this negligible offering she played a small part but it caused her to be noticed by the producers. Nikkatsu tried to sign her as one of their run of the mill "starlet" contract players but she turned them down, unless they would agree to make and star her in a film based on the novel "Flower and Snake" by Dan Oniroku.

The reason for this startling suggestion was that Ms. Tani believed that, "there was something special I was cut out to do. SM was to be my destiny." She thought this because in conversation with her friend Dan she realized that she was perfectly suited to portray his type of heroine. His almost humorous qualifications were:

1.) She must look good in a kimono.
2.) She must have long jet black hair.
3.) She must have a certain amount of body fat, so the bondage ropes make a clear impression on her skin.
4.) She has to be graceful under duress with strong facial expressions.

It should also be added that Ms. Tani also brought to her roles serious acting talent that lifted her performances well above even the hint of sexploitation.

The first of her Dan Oniroku films was *Hana to Hebi* ("Flower and Snake"), released in 1974. It was very successful and was soon followed by *Ikenie Fujin* ("Wife to Be Sacrificed"), also made in 1974 but not from a script by Dan. This film was a box office phenomenon, becoming Nikkatsu's fifth highest grossing film of all time and paving the way for the studio to rely more on the SM genre for their future releases. In short order, Tani Naomi became the top star of the company's "Roman Porno" SM series.

Tani Naomi was notable for taking her roles very seriously and for her complete professionalism, often performing dangerous stunts without the use of a double. In those pre-digital effects days this often meant taking significant risks. She was also smart about maintaining her appearance, even going to the extreme of never getting a sun tan during her entire 12-year movie career for fear of compromising her lovely white skin. It was this concern for her appearance and reputation for quality that caused her to retire from film at age 31, after 15 successful collaborations with Dan Oniroku, the last of which being *Nawa to Hada* ("Rope and Skin") in 1979. She simply wanted her fans to remember her at her best so she went out on top.

Since retiring Ms. Tani has lived in Kumamoto, in southern Japan, and has involved herself in various businesses and even a club named, appropriately enough, "Otani." She also enjoys going to the beach, playing golf, and I have it on good authority that she likes to go to Las Vegas to see the shows. However, she is still a famous personality in Japan and an artfully done book detailing and commemorating all of her Nikkatsu films was published in 2004.

Regardless of the passage of time, her striking image on screen remains evergreen and her remarkable, brave and committed performances for Nikkatsu helped lift at least some of their SM films beyond erotica and into the realm of art and even romance. As Tani Naomi once said of her commitment to SM films, "We can never forget there are many ways of making love."

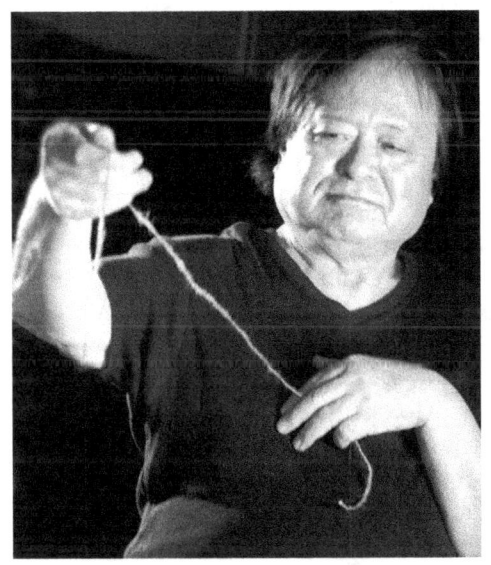

Nureki Chimuo (1930-2013)

Nureki Chimuo—legendary bakushi

Nureki Chimuo (real name Iida Toyokazu), was born in Tokyo in1930 and for the years spanning the late 1970s until his death in 2013 was generally considered Japan's greatest living shibari/kinbaku master as well as a respected author and authority on various SM related topics. It's said that the signs of his future career appeared shortly after his birth when it was noticed that he had a piece of hemp thread grasped in his tiny hand!

As a young man he often wrote stories for Kitan Club in its early days and enjoyed an extremely close relationship with its president and publisher, Yoshida Minoru. At this time he was also befriended by Minomura Kou and worked as an editor for his legendary magazine Uramado. He also prominently contributed to the "golden era" publications: Fuzoku Kitan, Abumento, Suspense Magazine, SM Select, SM Kitan and SM Collector.

A prolific writer, Nureki penned at least 30 novels or works of nonfiction in his lifetime, edited books of photographs and illustrations (using the name Fujimi Iku) and, using over 20 different pennames, contributed more than 2000 articles and stories to more than 30 different magazines. His more well known works, all excellent, include: *Nihon Kinbaku Shashin-shi* (with Masami Akita and Fuji Akio), "The History of Japanese Bondage Photography" (1996), *Kinbaku no Bi, Kinbaku no Etsuraku*, "The Pleasure of Kinbaku" (1999), *Jitsuroku: Shibari to Seme*, "True Account: Shibari to Seme" (2001), *Kitan Kurabu no Eishitachi*, "The Artists of Kitan Club" (2004), *Kitan Kurabu to Sono Shuhen*, "Kitan Club and its Milieu" (2006) and *Kinbaku: Inochi aru kagiri*, "Kinbaku: for as long as I live" (2008).

His fine literary accomplishments aside, he was best known in the West as a rope master (bakushi, kinbakushi, nawashi). This art had interested him from youth but he began to be seriously noticed professionally when he started to take over the binding duties from Minomura Kou for photo sets used in three of the 1970s second wave of "golden age" magazines, SM Kitan, SM Select and SM Collector. He did this work under his first professional bakushi name, Toyo Kanichiro. In the late 1970s Nureki started his famous "how-to" tie series with SM Kitan, and then moved the feature over to SM Collector when SM Kitan ceased publication.

Nureki's kinbaku style is complex, featuring more ropes and patterns than that of his mentor Minomura Kou. It is also more forceful and favors *kuzushi nawa*—a term sometimes applied to the art of Japanese calligraphy but one that can also be used to describe a kinbaku style whose rope design is "calculatedly unstudied" or where the pattern is uneven, beautifully textured and apparently random but is actually carefully contrived. Nureki was also one of the bakushi (along with Tsujimura Takashi, Osada Eikichi and several others) who should be credited for creating techniques to more safely incorporate tsuri (suspensions) into SM and shibari/kinbaku play and performance.

In 1985, in collaboration with the talented photographer Fuji Akio, Nureki formed the *Kinbakubi Kenkyu Kai* or *Kinbiken* society ("Society for Researching Beauty in Bondage Art"). This group sought to avoid the "crass commercialism that masquerades as bondage art" and "produce art that is more than just an extension of ordinary (bondage) photography." One of the distinctive features of the group was that all of the models were volunteers. Nureki once commented that, "One of the main reasons I started the circle was to provide a facility for masochistic woman who are often misunderstood." Before it ceased operations in 1996 it produced more than 300 videos of Nureki's techniques as well as its own magazine and other publications.

Nureki Chimuo once calculated he had tied over 4500 partners in his long career, an extraordinary number by any standard. Even into his 80s he continued to write and work as a bakushi for numerous films, videos, books and magazines. He was profiled in the 2007 documentary "Bakushi" with fellow rope masters Yukimura Haruki and Arisue Go. In this last significant screen appearance he was still critical of the commercialism of the modern SM publishing industry. Asked why he continued to tie at his age he replied, "I keep hoping to meet my dream girl." Nureki Chimuo sensei was a living legend in the SM world of Japan.

(Author's note: I had the great honor of being invited by Nureki sensei to observe a photo shoot he was commissioned to do for Sanwa Publications in 2010. Watching him work up close was a mesmerizing experience. At age 80 and over the course of several hours he quickly did many Kinbaku ties, exhibiting seemingly endless energy and enthusiasm. Not only was his work beautiful to look at as well as perfectly complimentary to his model's look and figure, but his rope tensions, the key to any model's safety, were always perfect. As an accompanying friend said to me as we left the shoot, "I could practice for 50 years and NEVER be that good." I felt exactly the same.

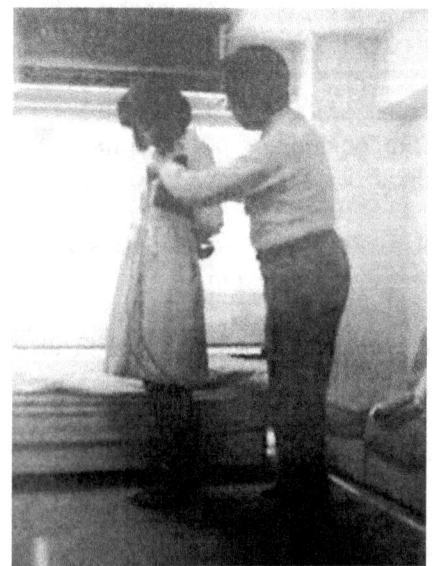

The only known portrait of the elusive bakushi Roppongi Kaoru

Roppongi Kaoru—the accidental bakushi

One of the greatest pleasures of writing this chapter of profiles of famous Japanese artists is the opportunity it affords me to introduce to Western readers names that even the most dedicated fan might not be familiar with. The history of kinbaku is filled with these interesting and creative personalities and for every Nureki Chimuo or Akechi Denki whose fame has traveled to our shores there is a Tsujimura Takashi who deserves greater recognition.

This is certainly true of the remarkable and remarkably mysterious Roppongi Kaoru (1935?-?), a talented bakushi who began his career in the mid-1970s and who had a hand in arguably three of the most significant kinbaku related events of his era: the first kinbaku art photos ever published in Western mainstream magazines, the retirement photo album of the legendary film actress Tani Naomi and the first book length memoir ever written by a working rope master. In addition, Roppongi Kaoru represents an ideal transitional figure in kinbaku history in that his complex, idiosyncratic ties encompass both older shibari styles that obviously reflect hojojutsu's early influence and the more recognizable modern techniques.

His amusing pseudonym, "Roppongi Kaoru," translates as "Sweet (or Fragrant) Roppongi" and was taken from the well known Tokyo neighborhood famous (or infamous) for its nightclubs, strip joints and hostess bars still popular with young Japanese and Western tourists, expatriates and off-duty US military personnel. In the 1970s this area featured prominently in the mercurial rise of the Japanese SM scene of clubs and publishing ventures and it was here that Roppongi Kaoru was hired to work with the talented young photographer Ishigaki Akira, a meeting that would result in an influential photo book, "Strange Fruit" (the title taken from the classic Billie Holiday song) and a little bit of kinbaku history.

Ishigaki Akira was still in his 20s and a rising photographic star when his publishers commissioned his second photo book and asked him to include some images of kinbaku carefully executed by Roppongi Kaoru. Shot quickly in 1982 at various locations outside of Tokyo (beaches, woods, an old inn), the album is a remarkable piece of work.

Haunting, evocative, colorful and beautifully lit, its images take kinbaku photography, up until then almost exclusively the province of SM and "adult" magazines, to a different level of artistry, one that would pave the way for other large format kinbaku art books (featuring the work of Nureki Chimuo and Akechi Denki, among others) that would appear in the 1990s.

"Strange Fruit" was released in a limited, "deluxe" edition in 1982 to only modest success in Japan. However, it did get Ishigaki (and by extension the kinbaku of Roppongi) an exhibition in 1983 at the East Bridge Gallery in New York City. The young photographer hoped this would be the start of an international career but little did he realize the reception his artful "bondage" studies would receive.

Scandal erupted! Visitors protested, neighborhood associations sent written complaints and feminists even defaced the gallery building! It seems that the New York of the disco 1980s was still not ready to accept kinbaku as art. To his credit, the gallery's owner (an Afro-American) refused to be bullied or intimidated and allowed the exhibition to continue and, eventually, it began to attract more appreciative audiences. One of these was an editor from the prestigious French photography magazine

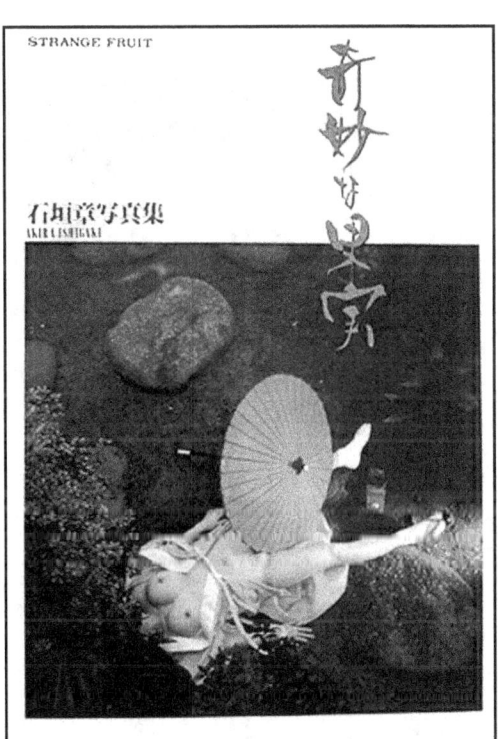

Cover of the 1993 revised edition of "Strange Fruit," photography by Ishigaki Akira with kinbaku by Roppongi Kaoru

"Photo" which resulted in a small selection of Ishigaki's kinbaku images being printed in their March, 1984 issue. A request for pictures also came from "Penthouse" in the US which also printed some photos but suffered the consequences when the issue containing them was banned outright from any sales in Canada.

It seems that, despite the compelling images, Ishigaki's combination of bondage and sensuality was too much to take for many North Americans. Still, the controversy helped motivate the publication of a revised edition of the book in 1993. More significantly, because of the courage of the gallery owner and the magazine's editors, the work of bakushi Roppongi Kaoru became some of the first true Japanese kinbaku ever presented in general audience magazines in the West.

Roppongi Kaoru's second claim to kinbaku history is due to his involvement with the legendary actress Tani Naomi, the radiant star of Nikkatsu studios' famous line of artistic and provocative SM films (see her profile above).

In 1979, after 12 years in film, Naomi decided to retire at the height of her fame and an album of kinbaku art photos was commissioned to commemorate the event. Its title was "Sayonara Naomi Tani" and the bakushi commissioned to do the tying was Roppongi Kaoru.

This book has become a coveted collector's item today due to the public's continued fascination with the star and also because Roppongi's kinbaku is quite interesting for the time. Roppongi wrote about his experiences binding the star in an article for the February 1980 issue of "Sun and Moon" magazine. In it he describes Naomi as remarkably professional, easy to work with and very brave. For example, she even insisted Roppongi complete a potentially dangerous sakasa zuri (upside down suspension) despite working in the pouring rain!

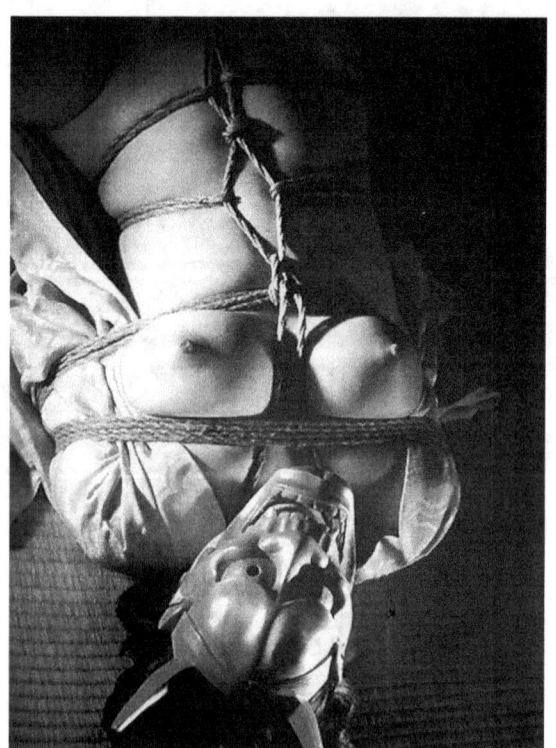

Kinbaku by Rappongi Kaoru—Photo Magazine, 1984

Like many of the most famous bakushi of his era (Nureki, Tsujimura, Minomura Kou), Roppongi Kaoru wrote a great many articles about kinbaku for numerous publications. However, unlike the above mentioned literate rope masters who wrote almost exclusively for the most commercial SM magazines of the 1970s and 80s (SM Select, SM Collector, Fuzoku Kitan, etc.), Roppongi's writings were often featured in magazines intended for true kinbaku and SM participants; in other words magazines dealing with the reality of actually doing bondage/SM and not just the fantasy of it.

Often these small circulation magazines carried such titles as "Sun and Moon," "Nichigetsu Club," "Legend SM" and the wonderfully odd sounding "Iki Iki" and were the product of one man, Arakawa Yasushi who usually went by the nom de plume "Seda." Arakawa was quite a force in the SM publishing scene of his day and Roppongi credits "Seda" with giving him his first chance to become a professional bakushi. This is why in this book he's billed as the "accidental bakushi."

As the story goes, one day publisher Arakawa/Seda got tired of doing the tying and offered his latest magazine gig to Roppongi who eagerly accepted. The neophyte rope master had observed shoots and had, of course, tied privately but this was his first paying job. Not only did the shoot go well but Roppongi won the high praise of the models for his consideration and speed. Thus he became a "pro."

In his articles, Roppongi comes across as modest, down to earth and eager to explain in common sense terms the mysteries of doing kinbaku art in all its manifestations: actual tying, magazine work, even dealing with superstar actors. However, Roppongi's crowning achievement in writing is certainly his book "Reflections of a Nawashi (rope master)" published by "Seda" in 1986. This was the first book length autobiography ever written by a working bakushi/nawashi and contains much fascinating information on Roppongi's times, adventures and techniques.

Roppongi's kinbaku is as interesting as his writings since in his rope work we see a connection between the feudal arresting styles of the shogun's police and what has become modern erotic kinbaku. Like the great Tsujimura Takashi's tying, Roppongi's shibari is something of a "missing link" in that it contains many aspects of the martial art hojojutsu, revealed in his intricate combination of elegant geometric patterns and single strands of rope, and the safety innovations developed by Itoh, Minomura Kou and others.

Roppongi Kaoru remained fairly active in the public world of kinbaku until the early 1990s and then, as his friend and patron "Seda" began to retire from publishing, this most mysterious and artful bakushi slowly faded from the SM/kinbaku scene.

Ishizuka, Kobinata, Kasuga, Maeda, Ozuma and Sorayama—six master artists

Of the many ways that kinbaku can be incorporated into artistic endeavors the graphic arts are one of the most obvious. Paintings, drawings, prints and etchings have all been created that powerfully demonstrate how the beauty of kinbaku can be an inspiration to gifted visualists.

And while many brilliant talents contributed to the "golden age" SM publications of the 1950s through the 1980s, this is especially true of the many illustrators who created the images that accompanied the stories as well as the magazine covers, the SM manga (comics), and the remarkable portfolios of SM art that would often be included in the magazines as a further inducement to buyers and subscribers. In this we see an echo of the Meiji era newspaper's practice of including free ukiyo-e prints with the morning or evening paper.

Following in the traditions of ukiyo-e, the most distinguished of these SM magazine illustrators were all very well trained and each brought a unique sensibility to their work. In truth, it would have been easy to pick well over two dozen talented artists from different eras to profile in this chapter but that would have been prohibitive. Instead, here are six of the very best, each working in a completely different style and often in different mediums and each an individual in artistic vision and dramatic expression.

Of the many reasons I'm delighted that a second edition of this book has been produced is that it allows me to present research that was unavailable for the first edition. Nowhere is this more applicable than in the case of one of the most mysterious, maddening to research and talented artists of the "golden age" of kinbaku/SM magazine illustration, the brilliant **Ishizuka Yoshiyuki**.

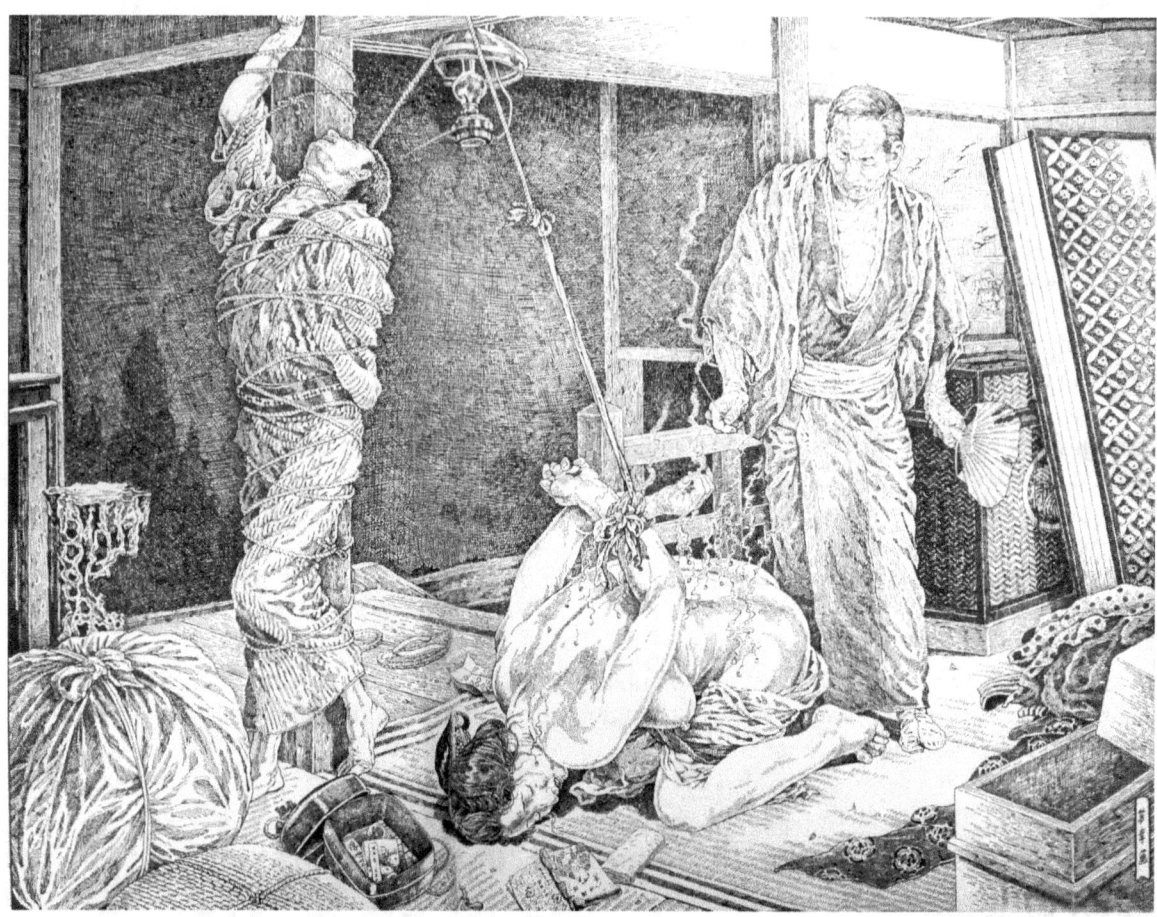

Illustration from Uramado magazine by Ishizuka Yoshiyuki, circa 1961

As should be obvious from the above illustration, Ishizuka was a remarkable artist with a distinctive style and I knew from the first planning stages of this book that I wanted to include him in this biographies chapter. The problem was I couldn't find anything about him! Zero! Zip! Nada! Even hours of research at the SM library and museums in Tokyo turned up nothing about this mysterious and talented man (other than more extraordinary illustrations). Therefore and with great regret, I resigned myself to leaving him out of the first edition and feared he would always remain for me the "mystery man" of kinbaku art.

Fortunately, in 2010 a happy accidental meeting with Nureki Chimuo at the library brought the first glimmer of light into Ishizuka's past. This was thanks to the fact that Nureki, in his youth, had worked at Uramado magazine where Ishizuka first published his extraordinary illustrations. Here is the story Nureki told.

Ishizuka was already an elderly man when he contributed to Uramado in the 1960s, and later to SM Select in the 1970s. He was a skilled metal craftsman who worked in the Asakusa area and made netsuke (Author's note: netsuke are carved button-like ornaments, especially of ivory or wood, often worn from the sash of a kimono). He, like many other fine artists, came to Uramado and offered his work because of Minomura Kou (the brilliant publisher and chief editor of Uramado magazine). He only drew two or three pictures a year, and just brought them in when he was finished. "You can understand that it took him a long time to complete those pictures—look at the detail." They were entirely his own creations, and not done to order. Uramado just bought whatever he brought in and when Minomura started SM Select, Ishizuka went with him.

As tantalizing as this information was, it still didn't fill in enough blanks. Fortunately, a conversation later in 2010 with the great movie rigger Urado Hiroshi, who also worked at Uramado at the same time as Nureki, filled in more details and added one key fact.

Urado-san confirmed what Nureki said about Ishizuka being a metal artisan in Asakusa but clarified what that means—that Ishizuka was an engraver for metal printing plates. In 1971 Urado edited Nawa to Onna (an SM art collection) and used several of Ishizuka's pictures. He pointed to the fine lines on the pages we looked at and said they showed a high level of skill. He also said he didn't think Ishizuka was the sort of man who would use a penname!

This last deduction proved the breakthrough. Thanks to the invaluable help of the librarian in charge of the manga (comic) collection at Meiji University in Tokyo, it was discovered that there was a noted illustrator named Ishizuka Yoshiyuki that was known for doing comic book illustrations for children's magazines in the early 1950s who had at one time studied under the well know artist Itoh Hikozo (no relation to Itoh Seiu).

Looking at the Ishizuka illustrations in such children's manga as "Adventure King for Boys and Girls," "Manga King" and "Thrilling Adventures," it became clear that it was the same artist. Urado-san agreed. He also felt everything about the comic pages were consistent with what he observed in Ishizuka the SM artist—a high sense of imagination and drama in setting the scene ("like a movie director"), the mood of the words he chose for his manga and kinbaku illustration's titles, etc. The final confirmation came when the same wonder librarian continued his researches until he found the artist's connection, independently, to Uramado magazine. In the June 1961 issue of Uramado he found a small reference to illustrator Ishizuka in which it was written that the artist lived in "Kojima in Asakusa" and that he had some time previously studied under none other than Itoh Hikozo!

It might amaze some to think that a 1950s era children's magazine artist would also do wonderful work for decidedly adult SM magazines. And yet, is this really so odd? It's happened before. For instance, in the United States there's the case of famed Superman co-creator Joe Shuster who, late in his career and needing money, did illustrations for the 1950s BDSM oriented, adult comic "Nights of Horror." However, Shuster did this work anonymously. Ishizuka was content to be publically credited. I can think of few better examples to illustrate the difference in attitudes about erotica between the US and Japan.

Ishizuka contributed approximately 20 beautifully executed, highly complex and original pieces of art to Uramado and SM Select magazines in the 1960s and 70s under the gentle patronage of Minomura Kou. When that genius fell ill and left publishing Ishizuka's unique SM art was seen no more. Fortunately, some superb examples were preserved in the 1971 book Nawa to Onna ("Rope and Woman") thanks to Urado Hiroshi.

Kobinata Ichimu (real name Kimuta Kiyoshi) was a particularly Japanese

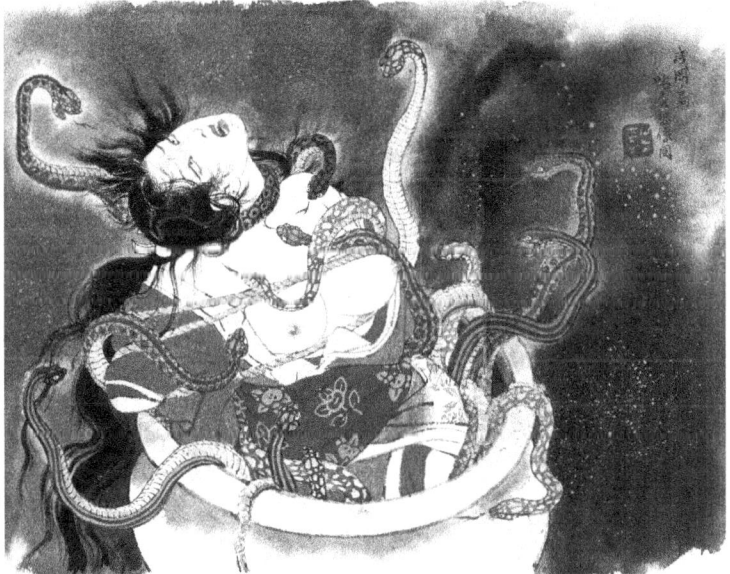

"Hebi-zeme" by Kobinata Ichimu, circa 1970

artist in that his work most closely approximates the best traditions of ukiyo-e. Although he brilliantly utilized Western techniques of perspective in his often startling and dramatic compositions, his sense of form and design was very traditional; note the interesting composition, costume and the almost kabuki-like expression depicted in the accompanying masterpiece, illustrating the infamous (and supposedly true) story of the *hebi-zeme* ("snake torture") taken from the history of the Maeda household of the Saga Prefecture. This skillful depiction of a figure in traditional Japanese costuming combined with a dramatic seme-e incident is typical of this artist.

It's perhaps not surprising that Kobinata was so classically inclined since he actually trained as a religious painter of Buddhist subjects. And it is interesting to note that he practiced and was employed at this type of religious art at the same time as he illustrated SM magazines; another remarkable example of the Japanese tolerance for the sacred co-existing with the profane.

Kobinata began illustrating for Minomura Kou's Uramado magazine in 1960, for which he continued to draw regularly until 1964. In the 1970s he worked for many publications including, Suspense Magazine, SM King, SM Collector, Abu hunter, Bessatsu SM Fan, and SM Select. He also created striking art for several of the better quality SM novels published during that era and, under his real name of Kimuta Kiyoshi, illustrated numerous mainstream books on a wide variety of subjects including young people's stories and historical novels.

He seems to have all but stopped working at about the time when the second wave of SM magazines crashed in the mid-1970s. On their return in the 1980s photography had all but eliminated most artists' jobs and Kobinata faded from the SM scene.

Unfortunately, except for a few plates in the long out of print art compilations Nawa to Onna and Tanbi no Hakken, very little of Kobinata's large output has ever been collected and published. This is doubly regrettable since Kobinata, as one of the most imaginative older artists, originated many of the techniques used in modern SM illustration while still working in the traditions of classical ukiyo-e.

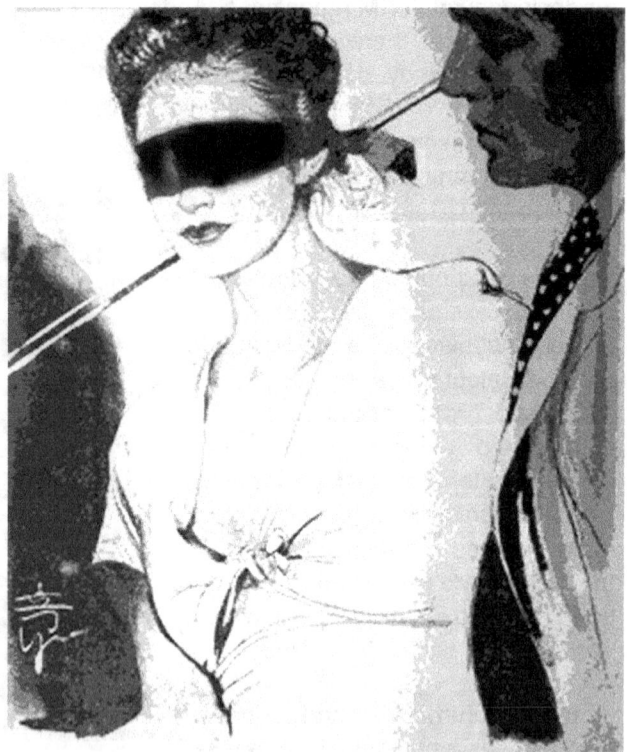

The younger artist **Kasuga Akira** (real name Dōmae Shōichi) was something of a protégé of Dan Oniroku when he came to prominence in the "golden age" of SM magazines. Dan employed him constantly during this period, illustrating numerous stories for his SM King magazine of the 1970s as well as several of his later novels. Soon this fine craftsman was working for most of the major SM publications of the time.

Kasuga was a master illustrator in the *bijin-ga* tradition. *Bijin-ga* (literally "pictures of beautiful women") was from the inception of ukiyo-e a principal genre for Japanese printmakers. In Edo era Japan these pictures depicted the fashionable and enticing women of the geisha trade, illustrated ideas of feminine beauty and/or were used to display gorgeous fabrics and fashions. Such prints were then used by the

Kasuga Akira—SM Collector, September 1979

vendors of fabrics and kimonos to advertise their wares. Kasuga Akira was a serious student of this specialty and studied under the renowned modern bijin-ga master Iwata Sentaro, an artist who today is much sought after by collectors.

In Kasuga's skilled hands this tradition of depicting feminine beauty became an erotic examination of SM sensuousness, usually depicted from the woman's point of view and as pure pleasure. Seldom is violence depicted in his work, even when such a scene could be justified by the story he was illustrating. Instead, his lovely impressionistic sketches usually convey the languid sexual contentment of his beautiful, romantically bound women.

In the 1970s and 1980s Kasuga Akira illustrated several of the better quality SM novels of the time and in the 1990s he was featured in a book of Dan Oniroku's favorite SM images published by the Alligator magazine corporation. He also illustrated several modern erotic SM novels published by Green Door Bunko. This resulted in a small but elegant album of his beautiful shibari/kinbaku/SM artwork being published in

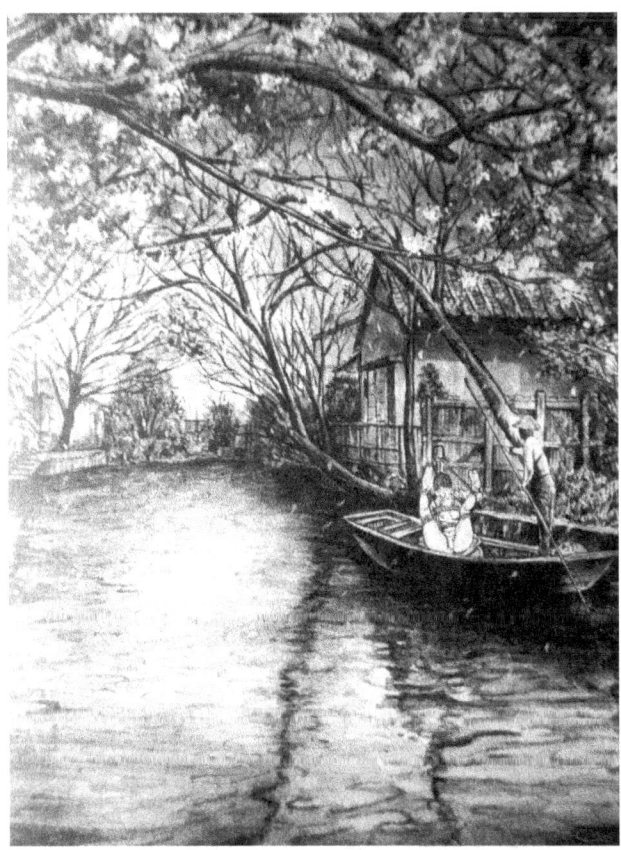

Juan Maeda—SM Collector, February, 1984

1993, also by Green Door. Shortly after this Kasuga Akira retired from SM illustration.

Another prime example of the magazine illustrator as fine artist is **Maeda Juan**. Born in Hokkaido in 1939, Maeda began his art career by becoming an apprentice to noted Gekiga (comic strip with a dramatic story) artist Oka Tomohiko in 1957. As the boom in SM magazines began in the early 1970s Maeda began regularly contributing to many of them and soon became much in demand.

His style can best be described as "lyrical" but also shocking as his beautifully drawn (in a soft pen and ink wash reminiscent of the watercolor medium) female figures are often depicted in the most strenuous of kinbaku predicaments. In addition, his signature presentation is usually a black and white image with one point (or wash) of crimson; be it a drop of blood, a distant red lantern or a decorative bit of costuming, to startle the viewer.

Another trait that sets him apart from all other kinbaku/SM illustrators is his penchant for doing beautiful and detailed landscapes in winter, summer, spring or fall where the viewer has to search out the scene of kinbaku in a corner of the frame (as in the above illustration). In this he follows in the classical traditions of Japanese art, such as in the work of Utagawa Hiroshige (1797–1858), where the Japanese landscape and the beauty of the four seasons are time honored subjects.

With the demise of most of the SM magazines, Maeda has been luckier than many of his colleagues in that he's been able to continue to earn a living and exercise his considerable talents by doing illustrations for mainstream magazines and even sports periodicals. He has also had his SM art included in two nicely done SM art compilation books released by MYWAY MOOK in 2008 and 2011 respectively

90

and in 2000 a beautiful volume of only his art entitled "Juan Maeda Art Works" was published by Ioz Japan.

Perhaps the most fortunate of all the "classical" illustrators was the extremely talented and prolific **Ozuma Kaname** (1939-2011). Over the years he has had more collections of his work published than any other artist of the "golden age" SM era. This is perhaps not so surprising since, in Ozuma's art, three different specialties come together in one beautiful image: the sensuous seme-e scene, the bijin-ga and the *irezumi* (tattoo) masterpiece.

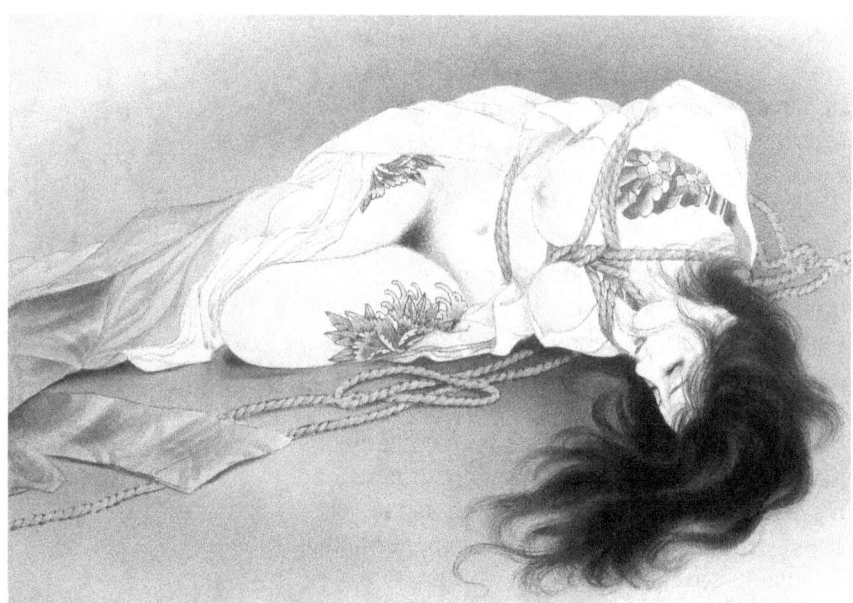

Ozuma Kaname—shibari with irezumi, circa 2000

Born in 1938 in Niigata prefecture on the Sea of Japan, Ozuma Kaname attended Art College but had to leave prior to graduation. Because of this he was forced to accept any assignment in order to make ends meet and so began illustrating for SM magazines in the early 1970s. He soon became a regular contributor to most of the era's publications and was particularly favored by SM Select, SM Collector and SM King.

Early in his career Ozuma experimented with many different styles and often aped more famous artists such as Kita Reiko. However, as he grew more proficient in his art, his creativity and dramatic imagination began to attract a large following. It was in the late 1970s that he began to combine his skills with seme-e and irezumi and started to produce his signature style of picture; Edo era maidens with flowing black hair, covered in glorious, colorful irezumi and bound with thick hemp rope in sensuous poses of rapture, shame or torment.

At the end of his life Ozuma Kaname was every bit as famous a designer of tattoos as he was an SM artist and was acknowledged as standing in direct descent from Kuniyoshi Utagawa, the early 19th century ukiyo-e master who first popularized the art of irezumi with his print series "Popular Tales of the Marsh: One Hundred and Eight Portraits of Heros." Admired throughout the world by tattoo aficionados for his magnificent creations, Ozuma was flooded with requests from tattoo artists and hopeful clients.

Collections of his SM work began appearing early in his career and significant albums of his art have been published numerous times including collections in 1972, 1979, 2005 and, most recently, in 2007. In 2000 the most sumptuous book of his seme-e and irezumi art, entitled "Tattooing," was brought out in a deluxe edition by Futami Shobo.

Despite his fame, Ozuma Kaname was a very humble man. In an autobiographical essay accompanying the art in his book "Tattooing," he commented that although he was pleased at the collection's publication he was, "a little ashamed that they (the pictures) aren't better." He concluded by saying, "As an Ukiyo-e artist, I hope that this book will find its way into the hands of tattoo fans the world over, and show them at least one aspect of Japanese culture and tradition, art and technique. Nothing could please me more than this." He need not worry on either count. He was a most renowned master.

Except for the most famous names (Kita Reiko, Muku Youji) most of these artists would labor in obscurity on their magazine assignments, turning in remarkable designs on short notice. In my discussions with the artist and former SM magazine editor Miyabi Kyodo he has told me of his early days in the magazine world when he acted as a "runner" and traveled to the artist's homes to collect their work just before deadline.

"It was more than a quarter of a century ago when I, as a beginning editor, worked with Kasuga Akira and Kobinata Ichimu sensei. At that time, they were already master illustrators and were extraordinarily quick in drawing. When I went to their places to get manuscripts, they would often ask me to wait a moment while they drew their assignments on a simple white piece of paper on the spot!"

In spite of the pressures of deadline, the five talented artists profiled so far, as well as many other "golden age" illustrators, brought a unique style and sensibility to their magazine work that certainly lifted their best efforts into the realm of erotic art.

To round out this section of a half dozen talented kinbaku artists and illustrators I've decided to include one very modern artist whose career never touched the world of 1970s (or beyond) SM magazines. In truth, there are quite a few graphic artists working today who occasionally turn to kinbaku for subject matter and inspiration. However, it would be churlish not to choose one of Japan's most famous and celebrated illustrators, the remarkable **Sorayama Hajime**.

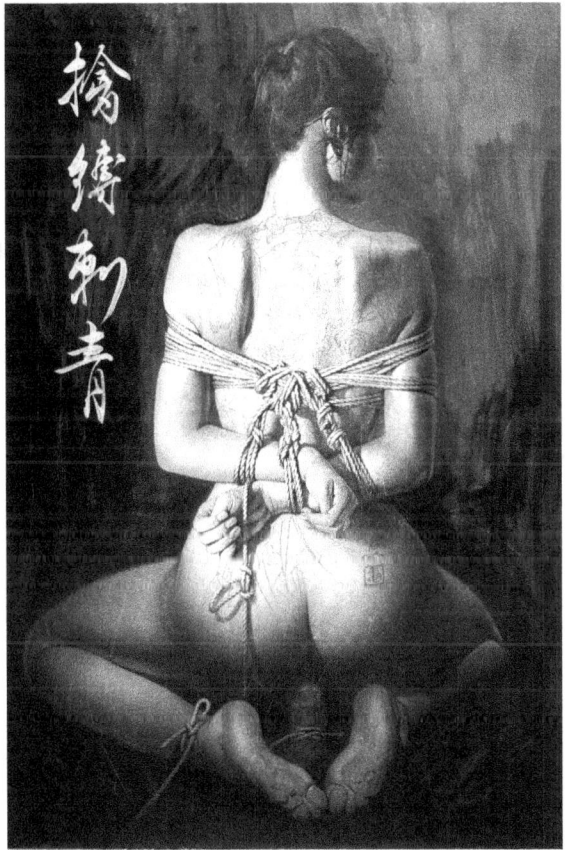

Sorayama was born in 1947 in Imabari, Ehime prefecture in southeast Japan. He entered Shikoku Gakuin University in 1965 but transferred to Tokyo's Chuo Art School in 1967. After graduation he began working as an all around illustrator in an advertising agency.

His breakthrough came in 1983 when he published an unusual book of his art that featured erotically posed female figures that were half human and half robot entitled, appropriately enough, "Sexy Robot." This was followed in 1993 by the even more famous "The Gynoids" on the same theme. Through these works he quickly became known as one of the most interesting and inventive "pin up" artists of his age which led him to work for Penthouse magazine as well as many other publications

However, unlike some of his more famous predecessors in the genre, like the renowned Playboy artist Alberto Vargas, the landscapes that many of Sorayama's unbelievably perfect and anatomically correct women inhabit are decidedly modern with more than a hint of danger amidst trappings from the worlds of science fiction and fantasy.

"Tightly Tied Tattoo" by Sorayama Hajime, circa 2013

All of this modernism makes it even more surprising that when Sorayama does include kinbaku in his art the results are so mesmerizing. Something startling happens when the ultra polished surface of Sorayama's work meets asanawa (kinbaku rope) and while it's long been noted that there's more than a hint of SM in many of this artist's compositions it's his remarkable and inventive juxtaposition of interesting ideas, soft bodies, shiny surfaces, unusual creatures, bizarre landscapes and hyper-realistic details that ultimately makes his work so unique.

An artist with wide ranging skills and talents, in 1999 Sorayama helped design the first interactive pet robot "AIBO" for the Sony Corporation which received a prestigious design award from the Japanese Government. He has also produced conceptual designs for famous filmmakers such as George Lucas and Dino De Laurentis.

In addition to the two famous books of his art mentioned earlier, a "Masterworks" edition was published in 2010 and the artist has enjoyed numerous gallery shows and exhibitions around the world over the years. However, for those interested in seeing some of his best illustrations involving kinbaku, the author highly recommends "Sorayama Vibrant Vixens" the decidedly adults only 2013 volume from the Swiss publisher Edition Skylight. One look at this brilliant artist's take on classical ukiyo-e prints and kinbaku clearly shows that the ultra modernist Sorayama also knows his rope!

A case in point, is the illustration included here. It was done to honor Sorayama's good friend Ozuma Kaname at the time of that great artist's passing. It's title is, fittingly, "Tightly tied Tattoo".

It's good to know that the art of kinbaku illustration is still alive and well and in such good hands.

Akechi Denki—a genius for rope

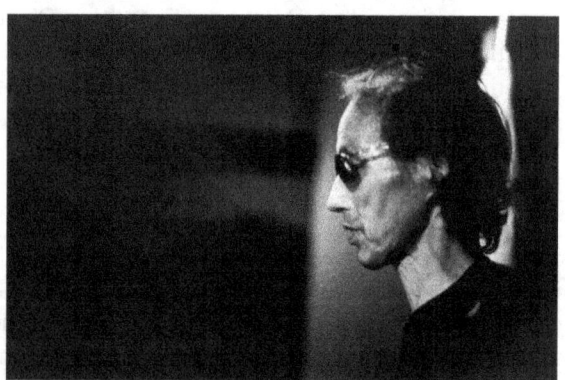

Akechi Denki (1940-2005) was one of Japan's greatest, most renowned, most admired and most accomplished professional rope artists. He was born in Tokyo on September 11, 1940 and often stated that his interest in shibari/kinbaku dated back to childhood when, in elementary school, he happened across a copy of Kitan Club magazine with illustrations of bound women. The beauty of these images fascinated him.

Akechi Denki (1940-2005), photo by Kanno

Unfortunately, in youth Akechi was diagnosed with a serious congenital heart ailment that afflicted him throughout his life. At age 20 he began working in the family interior decorating business but health issues continued to plague him. It's said he resigned himself to an early death. However, at age 30, thanks to an operation at the hands of a famous surgeon, he made a miraculous recovery. He then decided to use whatever time remained to him to pursue what fascinated him the most.

By the mid 1970s Akechi Denki had begun to participate in "avant-garde" SM shows in Tokyo put on by the GSC project. He took responsibility for all scenes involving shibari. At the end of these shows he also presented a brief performance of his own creation. These short "curtain closers" were to evolve into the accomplished SM shows he later launched under his own auspices at his Studio Phantom. It was also at about this time that he became friends with Tsujimura Takashi and would sometimes practice with the renowned older bakushi.

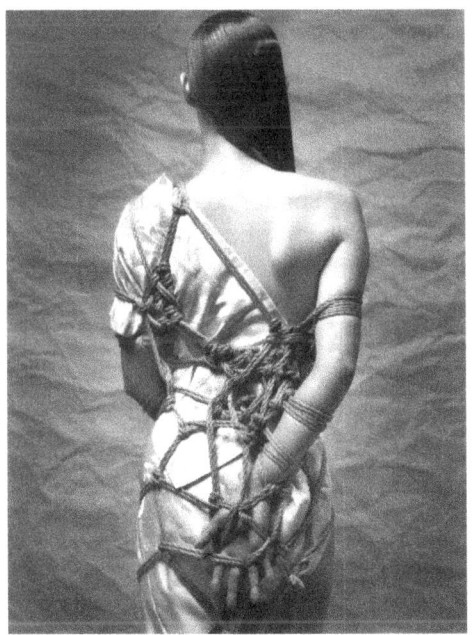

Akechi Denki rope design, photo by Kanno

In the 1980s, as the audio visual market boomed, Akechi Denki, in addition to his own stage shows, appeared in numerous videos, books of photographs and even on variety television programs gaining a wide and appreciative audience. Wearing his trademark dark sunglasses he also became the face of Japanese kinbaku internationally with several appearances overseas. With his tremendous skill, showmanship and entrepreneurial vigor, he helped legitimize the mania for SM and shibari/kinbaku.

Akechi Denki was always interested in hojojutsu, the traditional Japanese martial art of rope restraint that developed during Japan's feudal period, and incorporated several classic hojojutsu techniques into his own kinbaku style. That style was remarkably intricate but always astonishingly beautiful to look at with its even bands and elegant geometric patterns ever reminiscent of the finest qualities of Japanese art and design.

Akechi Denki was much admired and loved in his time. His dark glasses, worn for anonymity, were also said to hide remarkably kind eyes and a gentle, thoughtful, soul. He once told an interviewer that as a young man he wept the first time a girl allowed him to bind her and when asked a few weeks before his death what shibari meant to him this great master replied, "Shibari is communication between two like minded people using rope . . . a connection between the hearts of two people. The rope should always embrace with love."

Luckily, many of his performances have been captured on tape and DVD and two of the most beautiful shibari/kinbaku photo books ever published, "Pleasure and a Little Pain" (1995) with photos by Tanaka Kinichi and "Akechi" (2007) with photos by Saitoh Yoshiki, celebrate his work. All of these can be studied by future aficionados and so his legacy and the inspiration of his incredible rope skills will remain. However, the mystery of his talent, of how he would "disappear" into his kinbaku and emerge with startling beauty is lost forever. It is not an exaggeration to say that if the best kinbaku can be compared to music then Akechi Denki sensei was its Mozart.

What must never be forgotten is his philosophy; that shibari is an art for two like-minded hearts and must always be a loving exchange.

Sugiura Norio—photographer

It is a commonplace that photography has been and is one of the key components in the appreciation of shibari/kinbaku art. Since the time of Itoh Seiu, photography has given the world ravishing erotic images of kinbaku's complexity and effect. Too often this art has been in the service of crude pornography but often the tipping point between pornography and erotica is a thin one, balanced only on the skill of the photographer and the intent of the image.

Over the years there have been many wonderfully talented artists

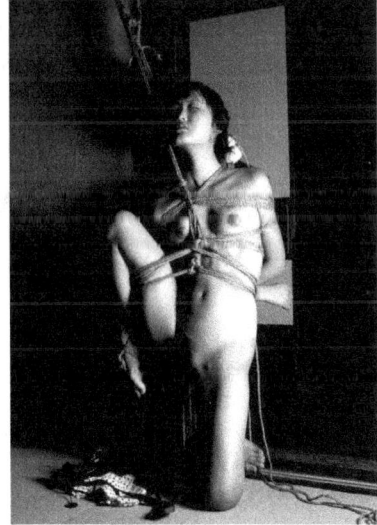

Photo by Sugiura Norio

who have made significant contributions to the art of shibari/kinbaku lensing. Tanaka Kanichi and Fuji Akio quickly come to mind but probably no photographer has created more exceptional images than the master Sugiura Norio.

Sugiura was born April 9, 1942 in Nagoya, Japan's 4th largest city, located in the Aichi prefecture. As a student he attended design school but soon dropped out disillusioned by the experience and needing to make a living. A variety of vaguely art related jobs followed including being a scenic construction coordinator for a TV puppet show and working as a lighting technician at a striptease theater.

It was here in the 1970s that Sugiura met the famous SM author Dan Oniroku and began working for him, first as an assistant director for some of Dan's theatrical presentations and then on Dan's influential magazine, SM King. Starting in the editorial department he began to organize the photo sessions and, as he puts it, "learned how to handle the camera."

If this casual claim is actually fact it's one of the more remarkable instances of the successful "self taught" artist on record for Sugiura quickly became the consummate professional with a uniquely expressive style. This style consists of the dramatic use of single source lighting that envelopes his bound subjects in a soft glow in order to accentuate their forms with shadows and highlights and an unerring instinct for the dramatic which always seems to find the remarkable expression or pose.

After SM King folded Sugiura spent several years in the SM pinku eiga film world before establishing himself as a freelance photographer. In the early 1980s he worked mainly for the magazines "SM Select" and "SM Fan", then the most popular SM publications of the time. By the end of the decade he had begun to do the covers for various journals, including "SM Mania" and "SM Secret Novel," and had become a much sought-after cover photographer, a key component to a magazine's financial success.

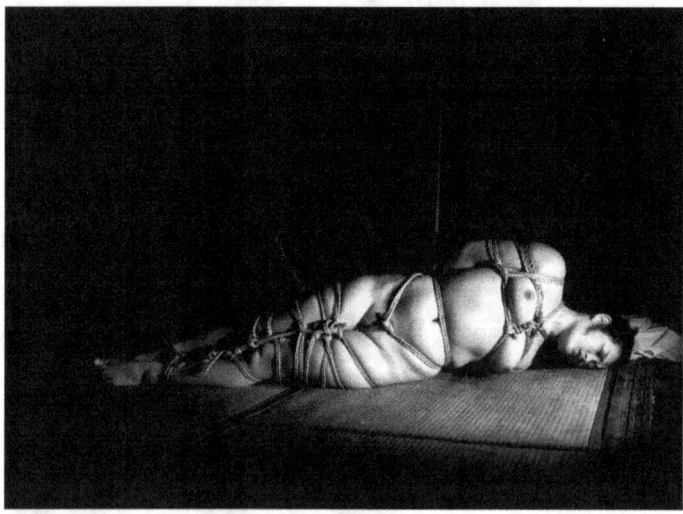

Photo by Suguira Norio

Since the 1990s, Sugiura Norio has been associated with Sanwa publishers and has produced numerous books of stunning glossy shibari/kinbaku photographs, including several on the history of Japanese bondage and the *Kinbakuzue* ("Kinbaku Collection") series. In these efforts Sugiura has worked with the finest bakushi, including Nureki Chimuo, Marai Masato, Nagaike Takeshi and many others. He continues to work for various publishers and has even joined the Internet age by opening a website dedicated to his work, *Kinbakusajiki* ("Kinbaku Box Seat") at www.sugiuranorio.jp/.

On set Sugiura is a sight to see. Something of a tyrant to his assistants and models, he yells his instructions and suffers fools badly. Nureki once said that Sugiura, "dominates with his voice" as much as Nureki does with his ropes! Regardless of the method, the results are often spectacular. And although Sugiura has done his share of images that stray into the pornographic, his best work more often reaches the heights of art. He is an inspiration to anyone who has ever tried to take an erotic photograph.

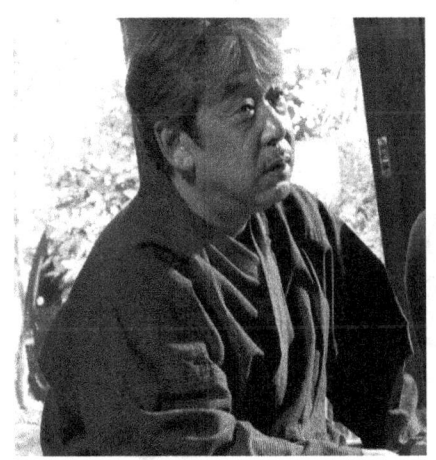

Yukimura Haruki

Yukimura Haruki—bakushi, publisher, producer

As with several of the preceding rope masters, Yukimura Haruki (born 1948) holds an honored place as one of the most active and accomplished bakushi at work today and the last surviving member of the great triumvirate of Nureki Chimuo, Akechi Denki and himself that dominated the Kinbaku publishing and video scene from the 1980s to the early 2000s.

He is also an astute businessman and producer with an astounding 2,500 shibari/kinbaku videos and DVDs to his credit! That might seem to indicate a mass production mentality but this isn't the case as Yukimura is also one of the truly elegant craftsmen in the world of professional shibari/kinbaku.

Although interested in shibari since childhood, Yukimura was a working photographer when he began using rope for erotic photo sessions. Gradually he discovered that he was spending more time doing the tying than the photos and by his early 40s he'd become a professional. This dual discipline (of bakushi and photographer) helps explain the combination of lovely intricate ties always caught at the right photographic angle and in the most attractive lighting that distinguishes his best work. Yukimura is also a classicist and often prefers authentic Japanese settings and beautiful kimonos for his books and videos which add to their artistry.

After working for Cinemagic and the Taiyo group, among others, producing and appearing in numerous kinbaku videos, Yukimura started his own company, Sunset Color Video, to handle the twenty or so titles he produces each year. His "Y's Play Bondage" series is particularly highly regarded. He is also sought after to tie for photo collections and has himself produced two high quality shibari/kinbaku photo art books, "Trans Body Bondage" (photos by Takahashi Junko) and "Shibari 1, 2, 3," (photos by: Oka Katsumi, Higure Keisuke and Watanabe Tatsumi), that rival in quality anything in the field.

Influenced by Nureki, whom he met early in his career, his style of kinbaku is unique and all his own. Dubbed the "caressing style" or **newaza** (taken from judo) by himself and his admirers, he dislikes suspensions and usually keeps his partners on the tatami mat where he always strives for beauty in the tie and in the expression and pose of his models. It's said his motto is, "Tying is serving the woman" and when recently asked what shibari meant to him he replied, "*To me, shibari is an emotional exchange between a man and a woman. That's unique to Japan—to express love and emotion entirely through the medium of rope. So shibari is not how you do this tie or that tie, it's how you use the rope to exchange emotions with another.*"

In 2000 he did the kinbaku for the most entertaining fiction film "I am an SM writer," based on a novel by Dan Oniroku, and in 2007 he was profiled in the documentary "Bakushi" along with Nureki Chimuo and Arisue Go. Shortly thereafter he began to give private lessons on visits to both Europe and North America. In late 2012 he travelled to Los Angeles under the auspices of the LA Rope Dojo to give a series of sold out tutorials, thus becoming the first Japanese grandmaster of kinbaku to teach classes in the United States.

His position as one of Japan's greatest rope masters is secure.

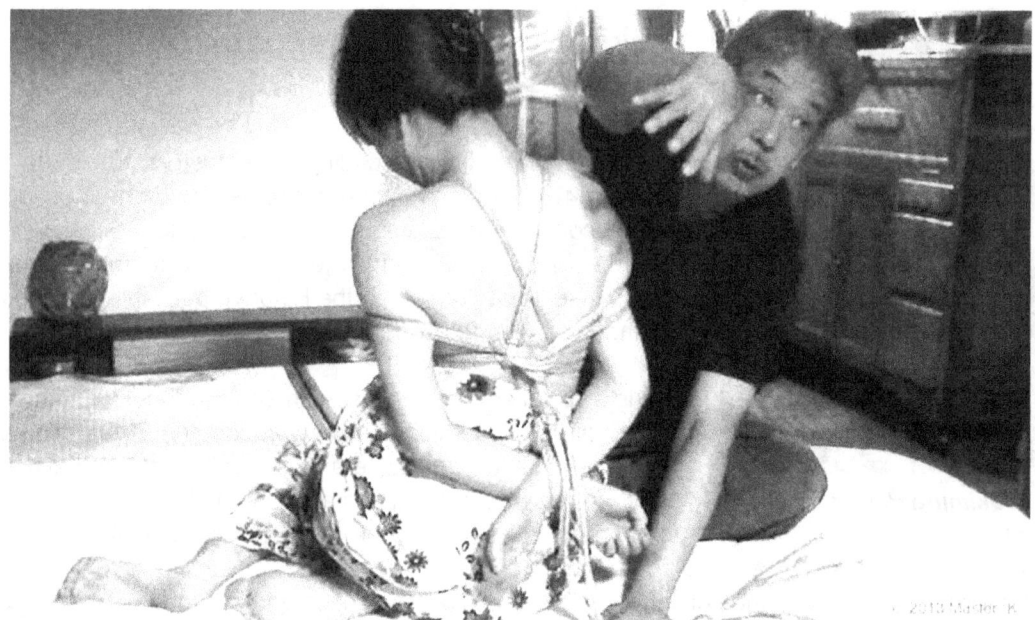

Yukimura Haruki during class in 2013

(Authors note: In 2010 I had the great honor of beginning lessons with Yukimura sensei in Japan and in late 2013 was awarded a first class teaching certificate allowing me to instruct others in his unique, beautiful and brilliant form of newaza kinbaku.)

Arisue Go—talented bakushi for "model books," major films and TV

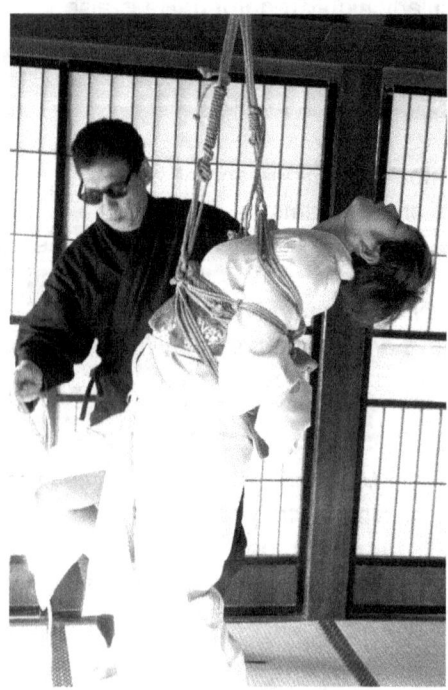

Arisue Go

Arisue Go is one of Japan's most well known and prolific bakushi, with a distinguished career that already spans decades. Born in 1954, Arisue's interest in shibari/kinbaku dates back to childhood when at an early age he "sensed the eroticism of traditional Japanese bondage." Inspired by the seme-e paintings of Itoh Seiu and the works of Minomura Kou, editor of the legendary Kitan Club and Uramado SM magazines, he began to teach himself the traditional techniques of shibari/kinbaku.

Arisue began his career as a bakushi in the 1970s after graduating from a distinguished Tokyo University where he majored in literature. This was a golden age for SM publications in Japan and he did extensive work for several well-known magazines including SM Select and SM Fan. In the 1980s, as the "adult" video market boomed, Arisue was employed as a bakushi on numerous AV productions for Cinemagic, Toho, Taiyo Tosho, Hoyusha and Sanwa Shuppan. He also created his own bondage video label, Azabu Eiga. It was also around this time that he began "rigging" for movies when he did the kinbaku for the erotic romance *Akai Nawa Hateru Made* ("Until the Red Rope Runs Out"), directed by Suzuki Junichi.

In Japan, light, decorative bondage often makes an appearance in collections of photographs of beautiful celebrities and Arisue has done the bondage for soft-core photos of such famous actresses as Toyota Maho, Akiyoshi Kumiko and Oginome Keiko. He once even tied a female pro wrestler for a similar photo collection. Arisue's gentler flowing style of shibari makes him an ideal bakushi for this type of work and he is much in demand by publishers. His best effort in this field is probably "Pleasure in the Fall," a 1998 large format album produced by Japan Mix and featuring the former Nikkatsu actress, Ogawa Minako. Both the photos by Kawai Takao and Arisue's shibari/kinbaku are exemplary.

Arisue also does SM/shibari/kinbaku club shows and has a special interest in multimedia performances in cooperation with other artists. He has collaborated on performances with manga artist Uzuki Taeko and bondage star Saotome Hiromi and appeared at SM performance festivals and with jazz musicians. As his fame has grown he's become a popular guest for various media outlets including a 2007 comedy guest spot on a Japanese live talk radio program where he suspended a guest!

Arisue celebrity really began to rise when he did the rope work for and performed in the successful mainstream feature films *Hana to Hebi 1 & 2* ("Flower and Snake 1 and 2") in 2004 and 2005, directed by Ishii Takashi and based on the SM novel by Dan Oniroku. These films helped make Arisue Go a name recognized outside of Japanese SM circles and brought his work to a wider international audience. He has continued to do the Kinbaku for additional versions of Dan's venerable SM classic, including "Flower and Snake Zero" in 2014.

In that same year he scored another hit by doing the kinbaku for the delightful "Tokubou" a 1 hour, 13 episode TV co-production of Yomiuri Telecasting in Osaka and Nippon Television in Tokyo and based on an eight volume series of manga (comic) books by female author/artist Takahashi Hidebu.

"Tokubou" can best be described as a dramatic police procedural with a great deal of wit. It's the story of Asakura Sohei (played by the fine actor Tsuyoshi Ihara), an inspector in the elite "Moral Influence National Police Agency Special Crime Prevention Section" (or "Tokubou" for short) whose job it is to investigate crimes and criminals that are difficult to prosecute and even trickier to get standard convictions for. The gimmick here is that, since these criminals can't easily be prosecuted, Asukura is both investigator and judge and when he finds the guilty party he ALSO becomes the agent of punishment and, after opening his briefcase full of rope, administers "corrective enforcement" by tightly

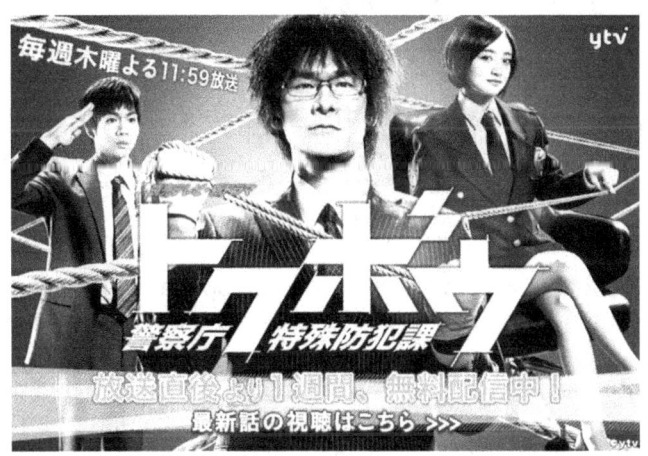

Adverstising for the Yomomuri Telecasting/Nippon Television series "Tokubou"

binding and then humiliating these malefactors and forcing them to admit and mend their evil ways. Arisue's kinbaku is most impressive here since it's often done for comic effect.

Over the years Arisue has been profiled in mainstream Japanese men's magazines and, through one of Japan's top publishers, even released a humorous book of short stories about the event filled and thinly fictionalized life of a famous bakushi. Other publishing ventures have included several "how to tie" books including a notable volume, *Jissen Kinbaku: Shibari kata Kyoshitsu*, published in 1997 by Hokuou Shobo and "The Basic(s) of Japanese Bondage Theory" (published by Sanwa in 2008) as well as several "how to" books in English.

Amid such varied bondage work, Arisue Go has one basic aim which is, "to learn traditional techniques and apply them to expand the boundaries of his own unique form of kinbaku." To date he has performed as a bakushi more than 3,500 times.

As important as his shibari/kinbaku skills, Arisue Go is also a wise and deeply thoughtful commentator on the history, traditions and philosophy behind kinbaku. The major essay in his 1997 book *Jissen Kinbaku: Shibari kata Kyoshitsu* is a wonderful and concise meditation on the many aspects of his art. Like Nureki Chimuo and Yukimura Haruki, Arisue Go was profiled in the 2007 documentary "Bakushi" and joins these two other distinguished rope masters as among the most proficient and well known professionals working today.

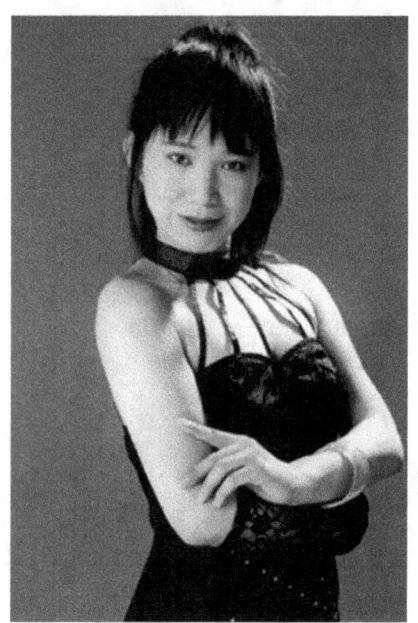

Saotome Hiromi

Saotome Hiromi—kinbaku model, author

Where would the lover of shibari/kinbaku art be without the models? A foolish question perhaps but all too often as we discuss the finer points of art, theater, photography and their relationship to kinbaku, the models are conspicuously absent from the dialogue. Why is this? Is it perhaps because, to the uninitiated, the models appear as figures that something is "done to" and not as "active" participants? Or is it because we're too easily dazzled by the crafts of the rope master, artist and photographer? In either case, this is a gross injustice since without the model there is usually no art. As someone who has attempted to take kinbaku photographs over the years, I know firsthand how dependent I am on the grace, beauty, and expressiveness of the courageous people in front of my camera.

Naturally, there are "models" and there are models. That is, there are people who try to make a living modeling in a variety of venues and then there are those who truly love the experience of shibari/kinbaku and happen also to be photographed. It is from the honest emotions of this second group that, in my opinion, the best shibari/kinbaku art usually springs. One of these exceptional people is the lovely and talented Saotome Hiromi.

Born in Tokyo in 1963, Saotome seems to have had an interest in SM from a very early age. She began her professional career as a model in 1983 and as an actress in 1984 with a small part in the Nikkatsu film *Nawa Shimai: Kimyona Kajitsu* ("Rope Sisters: Strange Fruit"). This led to numerous appearances in films for a variety of companies including Tokkatsu and, in a leading role in the successful *Jigoku no Roper* series of films, for the Shintoho studios. To date Saotome Hiromi has starred or appeared in over 80 adult videos and films.

In 1986 she began appearing with Osada Eikichi during the last years of that ground-breaking artist's long career and added live stage performance to her credits. At the same time, she continued to be a frequent partner in still shoots for Sugiura Norio with kinbaku by Nureki Chimuo. In 1988 she began doing one woman performances featuring self bondage and suspension.

Although this type of performance art has become more common recently and several gifted female artists have been drawn to the form, when Saotome Hiromi began her shows in the late 1980s she was almost alone. In these performances her goal was always to dramatize, "the emotional side of sadomasochism" and her combination of erotic dance, symbolism and shibari/kinbaku is both a fascinating mixture and quite unforgettable.

If this weren't enough to demonstrate that Ms Saotome is no ordinary "model," she also writes. Beginning in 1985, her intelligent, thoughtful, and knowledgeable articles on SM began appearing in such magazines as SM Sniper and SM Mania. In addition, she is responsible for some of the best historical writing tracing the history of SM in Japan. Her books include:

1998-*Sei no Shigoto shitachi* ("Masters of the Underground Erotic/Sex Trade")

2000-*Hiromi no Korega SM da* ("Hiromi's SM")

2003-*Kitan Club no Hitobito* ("The People of Kitan Club")

In 2006, Kawade Bunkou published her *Roman Porno no Joyuu* ("The Actresses of Roman Porno"); a fitting tribute to the beautiful and talented actresses (and models) who have fired so many imaginations.

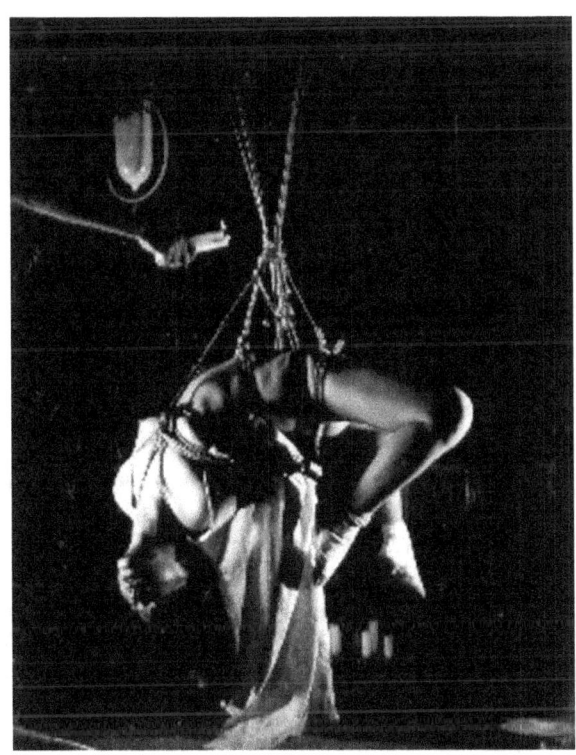
Saotome Hiromi in performance

Marai Masato, Randa Mai and Naka Akira—a post 1980 generation of bakushi, stage performers, producers

While Nureki Chimuo and Yukimura Haruki, among others, were the most famous veteran bakushi working in Japan post 1980, a younger generation of skilled rope masters also began to move into the limelight beginning around the same time and impressed in a variety of kinbaku related activities. That said, the histories of these individuals provide interesting lessons in the vagaries of kinbaku careers in the modern era.

Marai Masato is perhaps the least well known of these three in the West but his work has been seen in many books and magazines that have been distributed here. In fact, one could call him a specialist in creating artful kinbaku for publishing and the photographic image.

Born in 1957 in Tokyo, Marai Masato majored in architecture at University. While there he indulged his interest in SM by writing both fiction and nonfiction articles for the popular SM Fan magazine. He also got the chance to assist on several photo sessions for the same magazine and in so doing met two people that were to be very influential to his future endeavors, Sugiura Norio and Nureki Chimuo.

After graduating with his degree he took a job at an architectural design firm but found the work uninteresting. Within a year he quit this job and joined Sanwa Publishing as part of their SM editorial staff. As a major publisher of SM material, Sanwa offered Marai the unique chance to develop his own skills as both a photographer and bakushi and after six years at the company he got the remarkable opportunity to work closely with Nureki Chimuo on several projects. In time honored Japanese fashion, the pupil began watching the master and "stealing" as much as he could and within a few years the neophyte bakushi began creating his own style of kinbaku.

Marai Masato is a most creative rope master whose designs and constructions are both safe and attractive. Like most bakushi that work principally for magazines and photographs, he seems to prefer thin, 4 mm asanawa (hemp/jute rope) which allows him to do very intricate and detailed patterns.

For many years Marai has worked as a freelance bakushi and did the kinbaku for numerous magazines, including SM Secret Novel and SM Maniac, and also glossy photo books featuring famous AV stars. He collaborated with Sugiura Norio and became one of that master photographer's principal collaborators on his Sanwa publications, especially the Kinbakuzue series of books. His work was also conspicuously represented on Sugiura's art photo website, *Kinbakusajiki.*

Unfortunately, with the demise of so many SM magazines, the soft DVD market and publishing's struggles with the Internet, Marai has found it harder and harder to practice his art and earn a living. This is a shame for he is a truly gifted bakushi

Fortunately, in the last several years Marai Masato has been able to produce several excellent "how to tie" instructional books through his association with Sanwa Publishing. Geared toward the more advanced student and beautifully photographed these books both demonstrate and preserve Marai's skilled and unique Kinbaku style.

Of all the younger bakushi of the post 1980 generation in Japan, the best known in the west for many years was undoubtedly the charismatic **Randa Mai**. With his trademark dark glasses and five o'clock shadow, Randa (born 1959 in Tokyo) was something of a rock star in the modern world of shibari/kinbaku. Even his name exuded charisma and poetry, translating loosely as "wild field dancer."

An interest in tying a girlfriend in high school led the young Randa to form an SM club for aficionados in college and soon this energetic and ambitious bakushi was making AV videos, performing in clubs, writing articles and appearing as an SM expert on such mainstream Japanese television shows as "Tonight" and "Gilgamesh Tonight." In addition and as several other notable bakushi have done, Randa early on formed his own video production/distribution company to produce his own SM videos. These appeared frequently over the years (along with projects for other AV companies such as Cinemagic and Art Video) with programs under the "Black Shower" and "RD" and "RE" labels perhaps being the most representative.

As a performer Randa Mai did an SM club act that in slickness and flash would rival Las Vegas. On stage he was remarkable to behold as he danced around his beautiful, skilled and acrobatic partners combining his tremendous energy and pure showmanship with color, lights, whips, ropes and razzle dazzle effects to create a true SM extravaganza.

As notable as all these efforts were, it is Randa Mai's quieter role as a kinbaku teacher that just might be his most impressive accomplishment. Although he claimed to be self taught, influences from earlier shibari/kinbaku masters are clearly evident in his "system" which features simplified techniques but great sophistication. For instance, watching him create a tsuri (suspension) is a lesson in the mastery of balance and would be of value to any rope lover no matter what their experience level. From the late 1990s to the early 2000s there has appeared a steady stream of expert and quite useful Randa Mai instructional books (the first from Tukasa publishers appeared in 1997), Internet tutorials and video/DVDs, including a most impressive three-DVD set that clearly outlines the main principals of his skillful technique.

Unfortunately, this all came to an end around 2011 when illness suddenly caused this most charismatic and skillful "bad boy" of kinbaku to retire from most of his rope related activities. One can only hope that he recovers soon and this "wild field dancer" returns to the Kinbaku scene..

As the reader may have noticed, many of the most talented shibari/kinbaku artists have admitted to a fascination for this type of material since early childhood. Whether these are cases of early imprinting, societal influence or simply "hard wiring" is open to debate. However, in the case of the very talented **Naka Akira** there is no question of this. He had no interest in SM or shibari/kinbaku until he was thirty!

At that time, Naka Akira (born 1959) was working for a modeling agency placing models and actresses for AV work. One day, the Cinemagic Company called to engage an actress for an SM video and he accompanied her to the shoot. According to Naka, to his amazement and in spite of consciously having "no interest" in SM, he was very "stimulated" by what he saw.

This may in part be explained by the fact that the bakushi working that day was Nureki Chimuo and

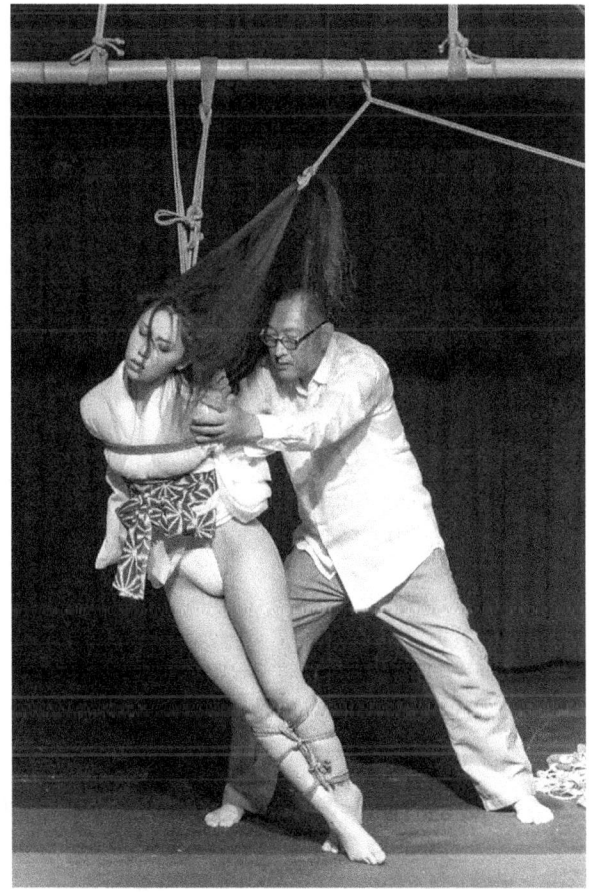

Naka Akira in performance in Los Angeles, 2014

Naka was very impressed by the master's stunning rope work. Nureki, for his part, realized Naka's keen interest and graciously invited the young man to attend one of his famous Kinbiken (rope study) sessions. According to Naka, he was a regular participant for the next five years.

Looking at his powerful style, it's easy to see Nureki's influence. In fact, it's remarkable how close the disciple's technique is to the master's. It is no exaggeration to say that when one sees Naka Akira's Kinbaku it is Nureki's style. When asked in a recent interview if he ever received formal lesson's from Nureki, Naka replied,

"No. It was very much a traditional Japanese master-disciple relationship in that he never actively taught me anything. Everything I learned from him I had to learn on my own, by watching. I attended the Kinbiken meetings for over a year before he even allowed me to untie one of the models he had tied, which is of course a great way to learn how the tie is done. If the disciple wants knowledge, he has to 'steal' it. The teacher doesn't just hand it over. This is the way master-disciple relationships are conducted in all the Japanese artisan fields, whether it's a traditional craft or fine cooking."

Eventually, Naka Akira's attendance at Nureki's Kinbiken meetings proved invaluable and provided him with a career breakthrough. At one of the meetings he met the president of Cinemagic, Yokobatake Kunihiko. The president had been observing Naka and offered him the opportunity to do the rope work for a Cinemagic video, but on one condition—that he also appear on camera. It wasn't just Naka's skill with rope that impressed Mr. Yokobatake, it was also the extensive tattoos that covered the young bakushi's torso! The president wanted them on film!

These tattoos represent a second passion for Naka Akira which does date from an early age. As a child he was fascinated with *irezumi* (tattoos). However, strict parental disapproval kept the young man from realizing this interest until he was thirty, exactly as with SM and shibari/kinbaku. Once committed, a year's worth of visits to the master tattoo artist Horitoku resulted in Naka's entire back being decorated with a famous scene from Japanese mythology, *Oniwakamaru no Koi Taiji*, the tale of a legendary hero's battle with a giant carp. This beautiful piece of body art has made Naka one of the most recognizable bakushi in Japan today.

Apparently, Nureki helped his young protégé get the first Cinemagic job with both a professional recommendation and by coining his stage name for him, resulting in Naka Akira; a moniker that has caused the young bakushi some embarrassment since it "sounds like an Enka singer's name." The closest thing to this in the US would be a colorful stage name that is most appropriate for a country western singer.

Regardless of the name, his first Cinemagic video was successful and this started Naka out on a busy career as a bakushi specializing in AV films and videos, many for Cinemagic and even more for the Art Video company. At one time, Naka wrote, produced, directed and/or appeared in up to 200 to 300 videos and DVDs a year, a remarkable number. Many would qualify as pornography but some, such as his beautifully executed *Nawa-etsu* ("Rope Joy") series from Art Video, are devoted completely to rope bondage without the "distractions" of SM play and hard core sex and, at their best, are truly fine examples of *kinbaku-bi*, "the beauty of traditional shibari art."

Of all the three bakushi profiled in this section, Naka Akira has perhaps been the most fortunate. Despite the downturn in the economics of kinbaku with fewer magazines, books, stage venues and DVDs being produced, Naka continues to be in demand for commercial projects. In recent times he's become master photographer Sugiura Norio's go to bakushi for many of his striking volumes of kinbaku photo art and he still does the occasional magazine and DVD.

More recently, Naka Akira has even branched out into doing shibari/kinbaku stage performances and has had tours to Russia, Spain and to the US. In 2014 he travelled to Los Angeles under the auspices of the LA Rope Dojo to give a series of sold out tutorials as well as give a sold out, standing room only performance at a mainstream club on LA's famed Sunset Boulevard.

To the question of why he was venturing into performing he replied:

"Part of it was that I wanted to reach a new audience, and part of it was to challenge myself by doing a different kind of work. From the beginning, I had very specific ideas about what kind of show I wanted to do. I knew I didn't want to do the sort of tough-guy posturing where the guy pulls the woman out on stage on a leash. When I bring my model out, I escort her, like a gentleman. And I knew I didn't want to do fast, acrobatic rope work. Instead, I work slowly and with feeling, and try to convey all the love and emotion that passes between a man and a woman when he's tying her up. I generally don't do any other kind of SM play in my shows, like whips or candles, because I want to use the time showing what can be done with just rope."

In his shows and videos Naka displays a classicist's sensibility and only uses the authentic traditional materials of hemp/jute rope, bamboo, and cloth for his kinbaku, eschewing even the metal carabineers that many bakushi use to facilitate suspensions. Despite this precocious ability and his obvious success, Naka Akira remains a humble man. In response to the question of whether he felt he might ever achieve his mentor Nureki Chimuo's level of skill, he's said,

"I don't yet have that kind of command of the rope. Learning to do that will probably take me my entire life."

Although Marai, Randa and Naka might be the most notable of the post 1980 shibari/kinbaku talents working in Japan today due to their numerous performances, books, magazines and video releases over the years, they are by no means the whole story. Every few years finds even younger names appearing or other talents coming into view. Performers as diverse as Mira Kurumi, Dirty Kudo, Kazami Ranki, Kanna, Hajime Kinoko, Miura Takumi, the female bakushi Kanou Chiaki, the mysterious Kitagawa-san, etc., etc. have suddenly come on the scene, several to fade just as quickly away. However, to this list must also be added the asterisk that these are just the bakushi who have appeared in the very public worlds of club performance, pornography, touring and, occasionally, true artistic endeavor and it is wise to remember that in Japan it has long been acknowledged that the best rope masters sometimes keep the lowest profiles.

Hiroki Ryuichi and Ishii Takashi—film directors

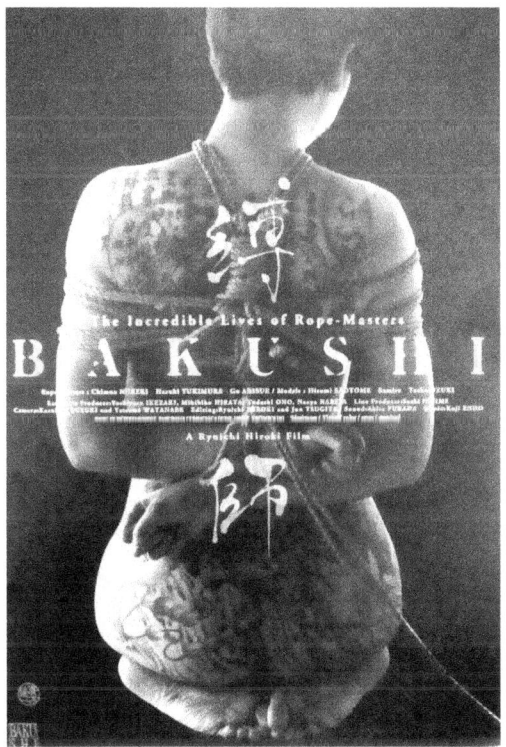

Poster for the film "Bakushi" directed by Hiroki Ryuichi

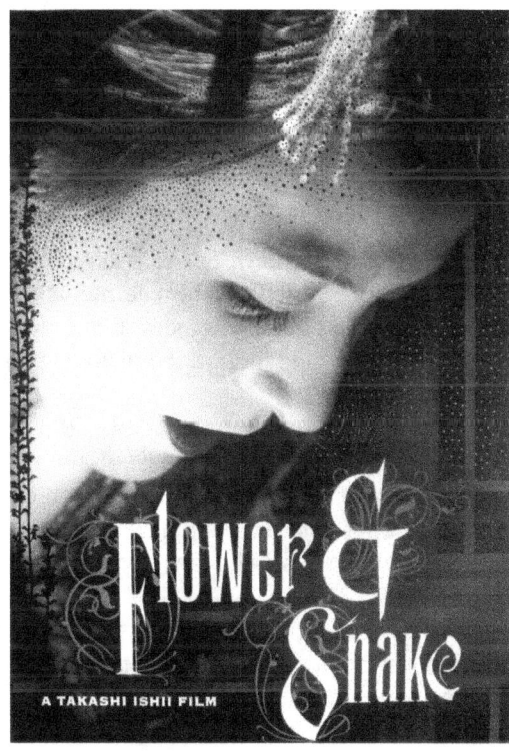

Poster for the film "Flower & Snake" directed by Ishii Takashi

From the beginning of the Nikkatsu era Japanese films have been made using SM and shibari/kinbaku as elements of plot or to provide erotic content and action. On occasion, these films have been interesting for elements beyond their eroticism but more often than not they have been strictly pinku eiga (soft core erotica) at best or true hard core pornography. However, recently, several Japanese directors have disdained the old filmic stereotypes and created works that in their sophistication, humor and visual style have brought SM material into a new era of modernity, maturity and psychological depth. In short, truly "adult" films in the best sense.

Like several of Japan's more famous filmmakers (Morita Yoshimitsu, director of "Lost Paradise" and Suo

Masayuki, director of "Shall We Dance," to name two), **Hiroki Ryuichi**, born January 1, 1954, began working in the pinku eiga/AV industry in order to learn his craft. Beginning in 1982 with *Seigyaku!-Onna o Abaku*, he worked steadily turning out a variety of fairly typical erotic films and videos for Nikkatsu and other studios until the early 1990s.

Then, like some of his colleagues, his ambitions led him to try to create something more "mainstream." This resulted in "800 Two Lap Runners," from the novel by Kawashima Makoto, which was voted seventh best film in Japan in 1994 by the Kinema Jumpo critics. Capitalizing on this success, Hiroki continued to develop general audience material but with a difference. His projects often concentrate on the psycho-sexual aspects of his character's lives and do so with remarkable understanding and compassion. Films such as "Midori" (1996), "Vibrator" (2003), "It's Only Talk" (2005), winner of the GRANDPRIX at the Singapore International Film Festival, and "M" (2006) all deal with characters (usually women) struggling with their sexual natures (often with hints of SM) and with the difficulties of communicating honestly and meaningfully with those around them.

In 2000 came the remarkably funny and wise "I am an SM writer" (discussed at length earlier) which best combines Hiroki's talents as a filmmaker with his fascinating take on SM psychology and his genuine interest in the subjects of SM and shibari/kinbaku. This interest is further explored in his fine 2007 documentary "Bakushi" (also discussed at length earlier) about the lives and working practices of three of Japan's most famous and accomplished rope masters.

Since then Hiroki Ryuchi has continued to turn out unusual, edgy films and one watches his evolving career with interest.

The career of director **Ishii Takashi** is even more varied. Born in 1946 in Sendai, the capital city of Miyagi Prefecture in northeastern Japan, Ishii attended Waseda University where he graduated with a degree in commercial art. He married immediately and, in order to support his family, went to work in several fields including manga (comics) and SM magazine illustration.

During the 1970s he produced dark and moody illustrations for such "golden age" magazines as SM Spirit, SM Select, SM Sniper and SM King. He also created the adult manga comic *Tenshi No Harawata* ("Angel Guts") which attracted the attention of Nikkatsu Studios. In short order they hired the young Ishii to turn his manga into a screenplay. It's easy to see why. As Matsushima Toshiyuki put it in his history of Nikkatsu studios, "Basically, Ishii's mangas were movies."

"Angel Guts: High School Coed" was released in 1978 and became a surprise hit for Nikkatsu spawning a series of seven films. Called effective, "darkly sinister works of exploitative art" by the authors of the Japanese Cinema Encyclopedia, the Angel Guts series gave Ishii his commercial foothold in the movie industry. He also continued drawing and a portfolio of his art was published in 1983. Finally, in 1988, he was allowed to step behind the camera and direct one of his "Angel" scripts.

In the years since, Ishii Takashi has enjoyed considerable success as a director with such films as *Shinde mo ii* ("Original Sin"), winner of the Kinema Jumpo award for best film in 1992, and the 1995 film *Gonin* ("The Five"), which won the Golden Leopard at the prestigious Locarno International Film Festival in Switzerland. However, it is the writing and direction of the two commercially successful *Hana to Hebi* ("Flower and Snake") remakes in 2004 and 2005, based on the famous novel by Dan Oniroku, that have made him known outside of Japan.

In these films Ishii's remarkable visual sense is taken to almost operatic extremes as he creatively dramatizes Dan's steamy novel of sadomasochistic obsession. Featuring a remarkable and courageous performance by the lovely Aya Sugimoto and boasting state of the art production values and fine kinbaku by Arisue Go, Hana to Hebi I and II show what can be done with SM and shibari/kinbaku material if placed in the hands of a true film artist. In 2013 came the similarly themed Amai Muchi ("Sweet Whips").

Hiroki Ryuichi and Ishii Takashi: two talented directors creating modern films of merit to further the understanding of SM and shibari/kinbaku for a new age.

Osada Steve—Western-born bakushi, stage performer

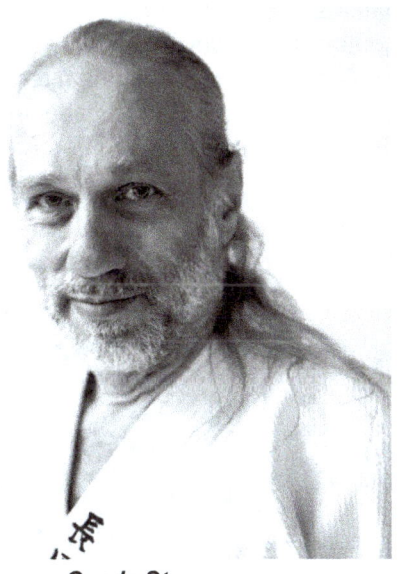

Osada Steve

Osada Steve is the only non-Japanese on this list. This unique distinction is key to his importance but before profiling Steve this author must, in the spirit of fair disclosure, state that Osada Steve has been a good friend for many years. That said, this friendship has in no way that I can discern either affected my critical judgment of his work or my conviction that he deserves his place on this list of thirty influential individuals in the history of shibari/kinbaku. Of course, the reader must be the ultimate judge.

Of German extraction, Osada Steve has lived in Japan for many years after sojourns in India, Thailand, and Hong Kong and extensive traveling throughout much of the rest of Asia. He is something of a martial artist having trained in the disciplines of karate, aikido and taekwondo, reportedly gaining such proficiency in the latter that he was engaged to teach it to the Thai Air Force in the early 1970s.

After coming to Japan in the late 1970s, Steve worked at several occupations before gaining some success in the publishing world. In 1998 he had a fateful encounter when he first met the late Osada Eikichi (the father of the SM club show) at a photo shoot for Tokyo Journal magazine. Fascinated by Eikichi's art and energy, he returned to watch the act several times before eventually beginning to assist the maestro with bookings and behind-the-scenes help, much in the same way that Osada Eikichi himself had done with *his* first mentor, Kazuya Mukai.

Steve proved a dedicated student of Eikichi's, observing his every move and studying his style of kinbaku for several years until Eikichi sensei's death in 2001. After formally assuming the name of his mentor, Steve started to perform in his own SM club shows, at one time giving up to 400 performances a year throughout Japan.

Steve's sincere interest in the art of shibari/kinbaku has also caused him to train under the late Akechi Denki sensei to gain a greater understanding of suspensions and also under Yukimura Haruki to master newaza style techniques. This combination of intense study and sincere dedication has led to an all-encompassing style and Steve is comfortable performing in large theaters and for smaller gatherings where he displays an almost meditative but intense technique.

On stage Osada Steve achieved a high level of performance excellence with his beautifully crafted kinbaku and elegantly choreographed musical presentations. In this he was helped in no small measure by his lovely and skilled aerialist partner, Asagi Ageha. Their suspension dominated act combined grace and speed as Asagi was lifted high in the air to quite literally dance above their audiences. The team richly deserved their reputation as one of the best SM club acts in Japan when they were active.

In addition to performing on stage, Steve also teaches, appears in videos and ties for magazines and books. In addition, he is the founder of the Osada dojo and ryu (school) of kinbaku which has branches in Japan, Europe and Australia.

While he is not the only accomplished Western "bakushi" pursuing the art of kinbaku, he is the only one living and working professionally in Japan. These are truly remarkable accomplishments for a *gaijin* ("foreigner") in a country notorious for its studied skepticism of outsiders. However, it is not just these accomplishments, impressive as they are, that cause me to hold Osada Steve in such high regard. It is also because of his constant willingness to share his information on kinbaku, that most Japanese of erotic arts, with the West. For years he has been tireless and generous with his time and advice and it is for this groundbreaking position as a learned conduit of information on shibari/kinbaku to the rest of the world that he deserves our sincerest thanks.

Miyabi Kyodo—modern seme-e master

Without question, one of the finest modern shibari/kinbaku graphic artists working in Japan today is the astonishing Miyabi Kyodo whose hyper-realist, computer generated, erotic art works have taken the styles of classical ukiyo-e and seme-e into the 21st century.

Miyabi Kyodo, an artistic nom de plume that translates as "Elegant person/man of Kyodo," was born in 1957 in Sapporo, the major city of Hokkaido, Japan's northernmost and second largest island. After a childhood and youth that included interests in martial arts and music, he graduated from Doshisha University with a degree in literature. However, shortly after graduation, his interest in SM lead him to start working for SM Club magazine where he eventually rose to the position of senior editor. At the magazine his varied duties included being a fiction editor, bakushi and cartoonist. At the same time, he also worked outside of the SM world as a commercial designer.

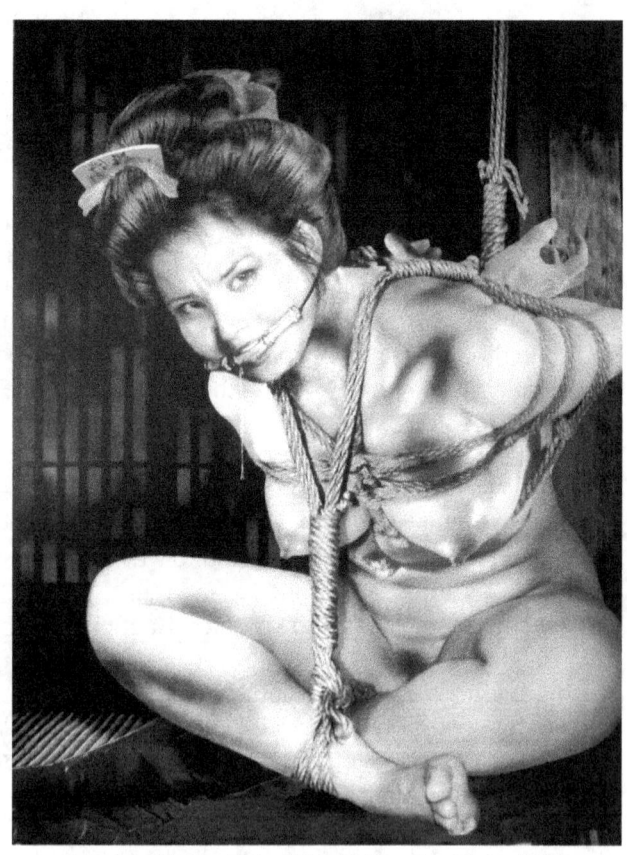

"Agura Shibari" by Miyabi Kyodo, circa 1999

It was during his time at the magazine that he met the legendary Minomura Kou (AKA the artist Kita Reiko) who became his most important artistic influence. As a junior employee, one of Miyabi's first jobs was to collect magazine copy and artwork from the various contributors by going to their homes. Minomura was recovering from a stroke at this time and Miyabi spent many hours talking and learning from this remarkable master. Because of this it can truly be said that Miyabi Kyodo was the last student of the great Kita Reiko. Miyabi left SM Club in 1985 to pursue his own career as an independent artist.

Miyabi's SM art is virtually like no others in Japan. Intensely erotic, its precise hyper-realism (created on computer with hundreds of hours devoted to each piece) allows the clear depiction of every knot, bead of sweat and elegant expression in almost photographic clarity. The artist's expert knowledge of kinbaku and body mechanics, learned from firsthand experience, also lends his work a vivid and astonishing reality.

Like the great shunga artists of the past, Miyabi concentrated on private commissions for many years. However, that all changed when film director Ishii Takashi was inspired by Miyabi's art and included many of his finest compositions as part of the plot in his second successful "Flower and Snake" remake ("Flower and Snake II-Paris") in 2005. This introduced Miyabi's works to a much wider public. In 2006 a showing of his work was held at the Vanilla Gallery in Tokyo.

Luckily for his fans, publishers have also taken note of Miyabi's remarkable skills. In 2002 Sanwa published a deluxe edition of some of Miyabi Kyodo's most powerful compositions. This was followed up with a second volume in 2013. Both have become prized collector's items.

In creating such art, Miyabi Kyodo continues the traditions of evocative seme-e begun in the early Edo era that inspired the SM pioneer Itoh Seiu, encompassed the mid-twentieth century genius of Kita Reiko, and still resonate with us today in the intriguing and artistic world of modern shibari/kinbaku.

Introduction to the Photo Gallery of the Second Edition

The photo gallery for this second edition of "The Beauty of Kinbaku" has been, decidedly, a "work in progress." In fact, if you're reading this version of the introduction you will soon be viewing the fifth and final version of the gallery!

The reason for this is that once the decision was taken to publish a more affordable edition of the book the photo gallery had to be completely rethought in terms of black and white imagery, paper quality and number of pages to be included.

My desire to preserve the quality and usefulness of the gallery that so many readers responded to in the first, hardcover edition of this book was another factor and this lead to several earlier second edition versions of the gallery that ultimately, through trial and error, have finally resulted in this definitive version. I would like to thank my publishers for their patience and perseverance as their all too demanding author tried to "get it right."

Most of the images presented here have been drawn from the first, hardcover edition and are those which could best be termed "audience favorites." These have been carefully redesigned and reconceived in black and white for the clearest definition possible in a paperback format.

In addition, brand new images have been especially created for this paperback edition which represent the styles of shibari/kinbaku that the author enjoys doing in the course of his own work as a bakushi.

That this was possible and, in the author's opinion, successful, is due in large measure to the great generosity of LA celebrity photographer Michael Helms (www.michaelhelms.com) who allowed us to include some of his beautiful images of the author's work in this volume.

A smaller number of pictures unique to this edition come from a photography show that was presented in Tokyo at the Shinzuku-za gallery in 2013 to coincide with the launch of the Japanese edition of "The Beauty of Kinbaku" by Suirensha publishers. These pictures were taken by my student Zetsu and the author and publisher would like to express their thanks to him for permission to reprint them.

Finally, the author and publisher would like to express their sincere gratitude to the talented Liquid-erotica, Erotic Exposures and DNE Photography for permission to reprint their striking images. All other images were photographed by the author.

In this gallery the reader will see many different types and styles of shibari/kinbaku from the simple to the complex. For this reason each photograph has been given a title which usually includes the Japanese name of the tie. This feature is for those readers who would like to learn more about each shibari/kinbaku pattern shown by cross referencing any photograph in the gallery with the names and definitions to be found in the glossary.

Finally, for their grace, beauty, understanding, patience, for the just plain fun experienced during the creation of these photographs and for their genuine desire to find the artistic in the erotic, I wish to express my profound thanks to each and every one of the 21 models that grace these pages.

All shibari/kinbaku in the following gallery is by Master "K."

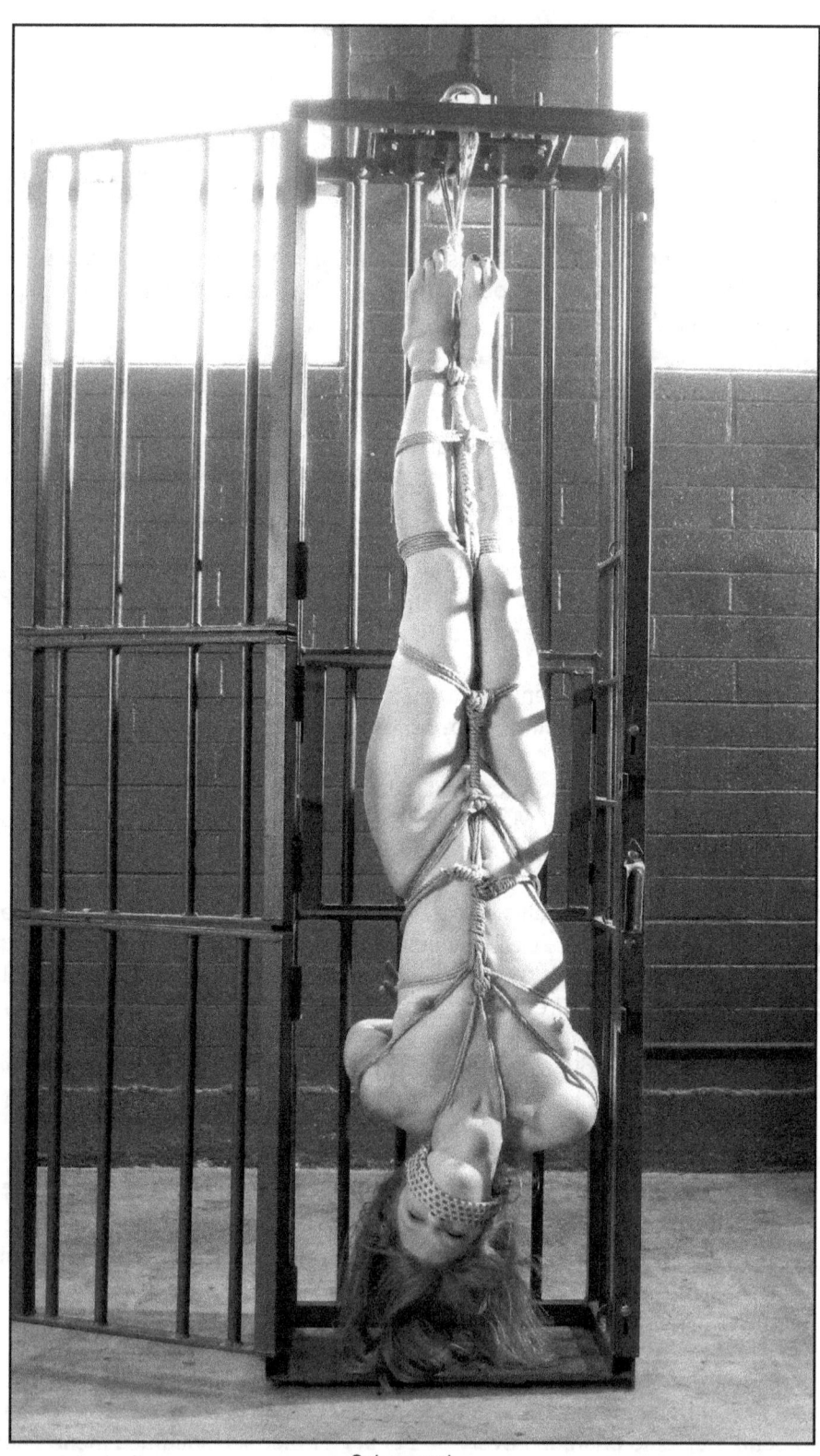

Sakasa zuri
(photo by Master "K")

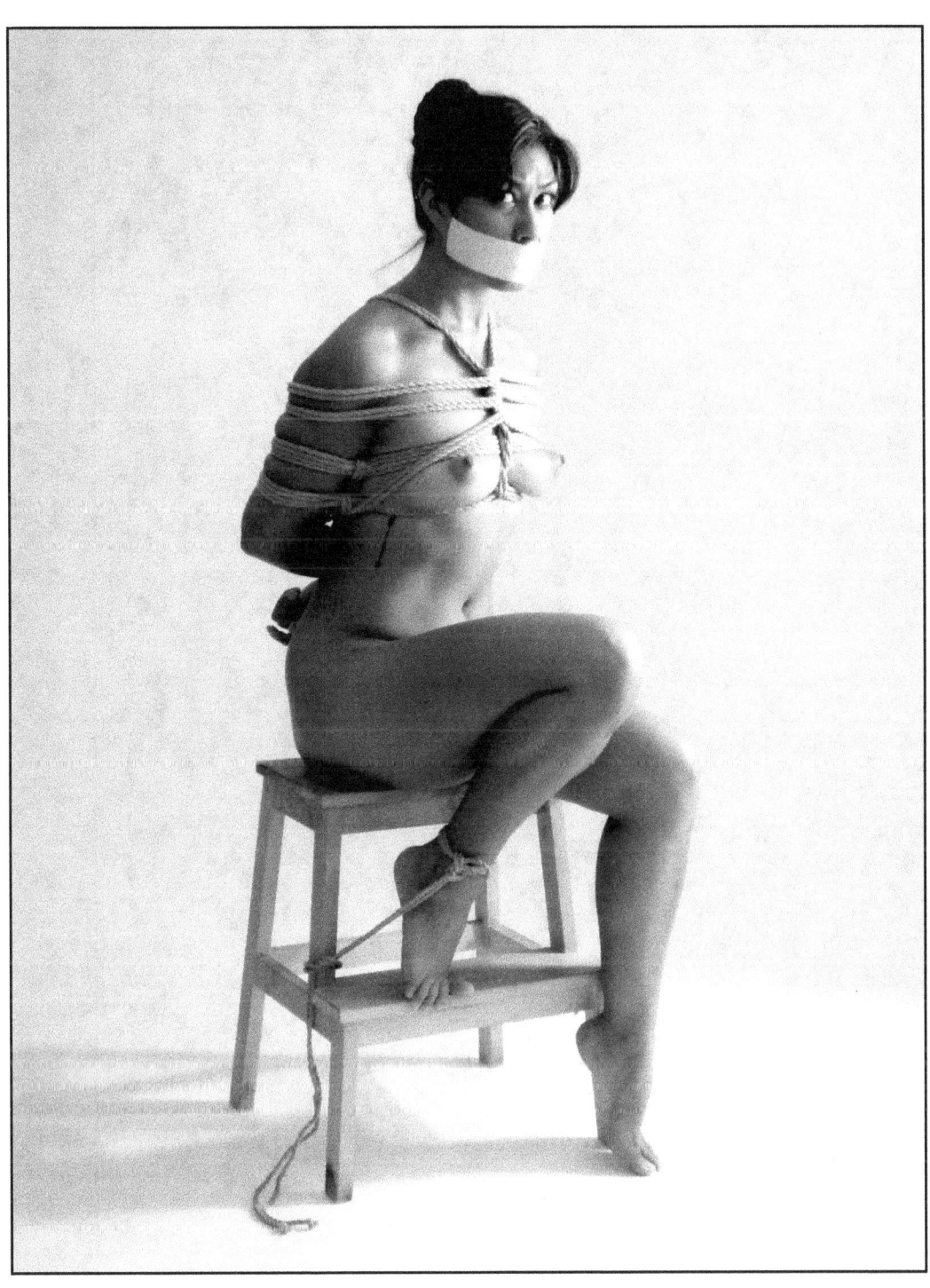

Decorative gote in the style of Yukimura Haruki
(photo by Master "K")

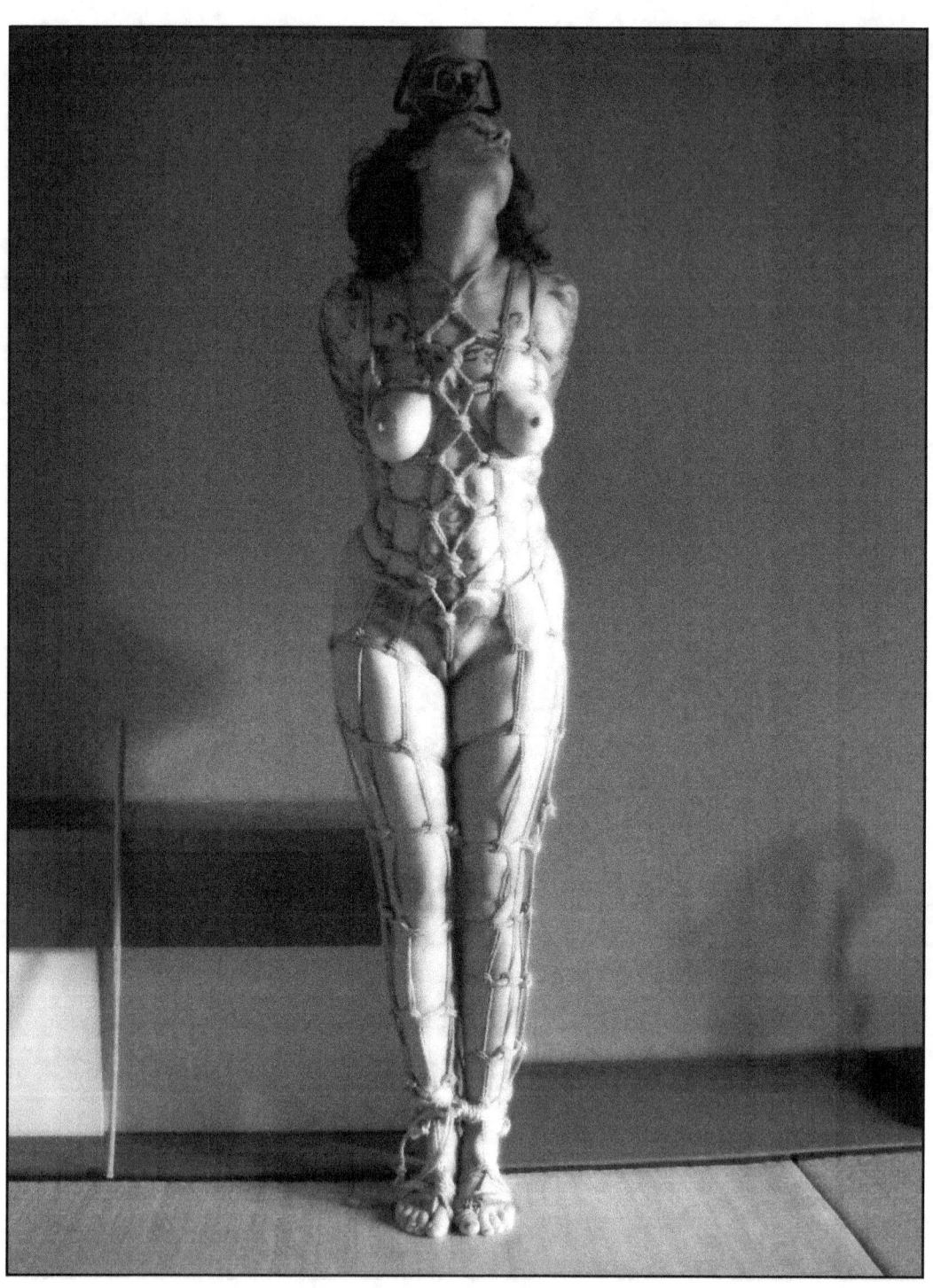

Ganji garame #1
(photo by Master "K")

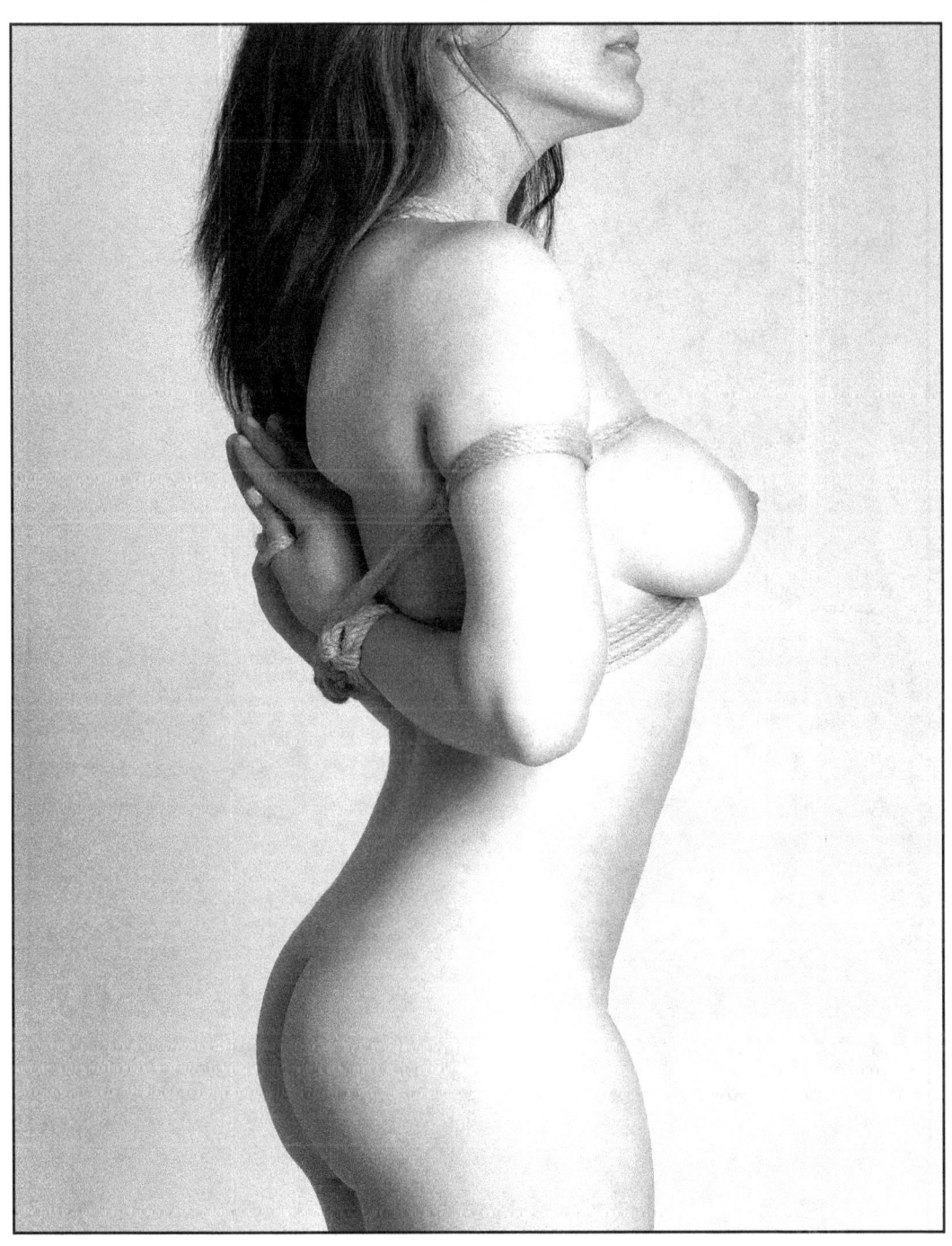

Ushirode-gassho shibari—Christian version
(photo by Zetsu)

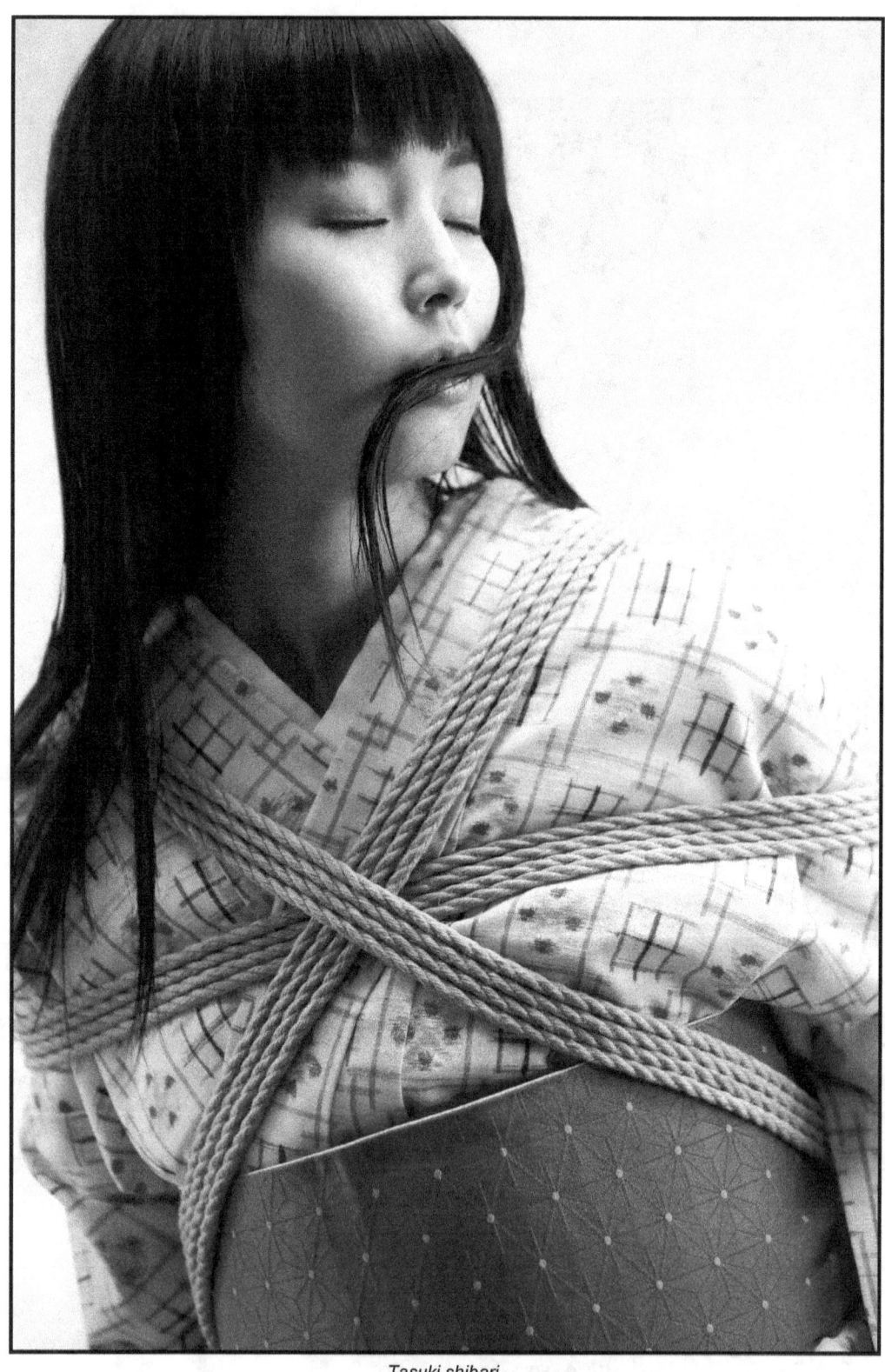

Tasuki shibari
(photo by Michael Helms)

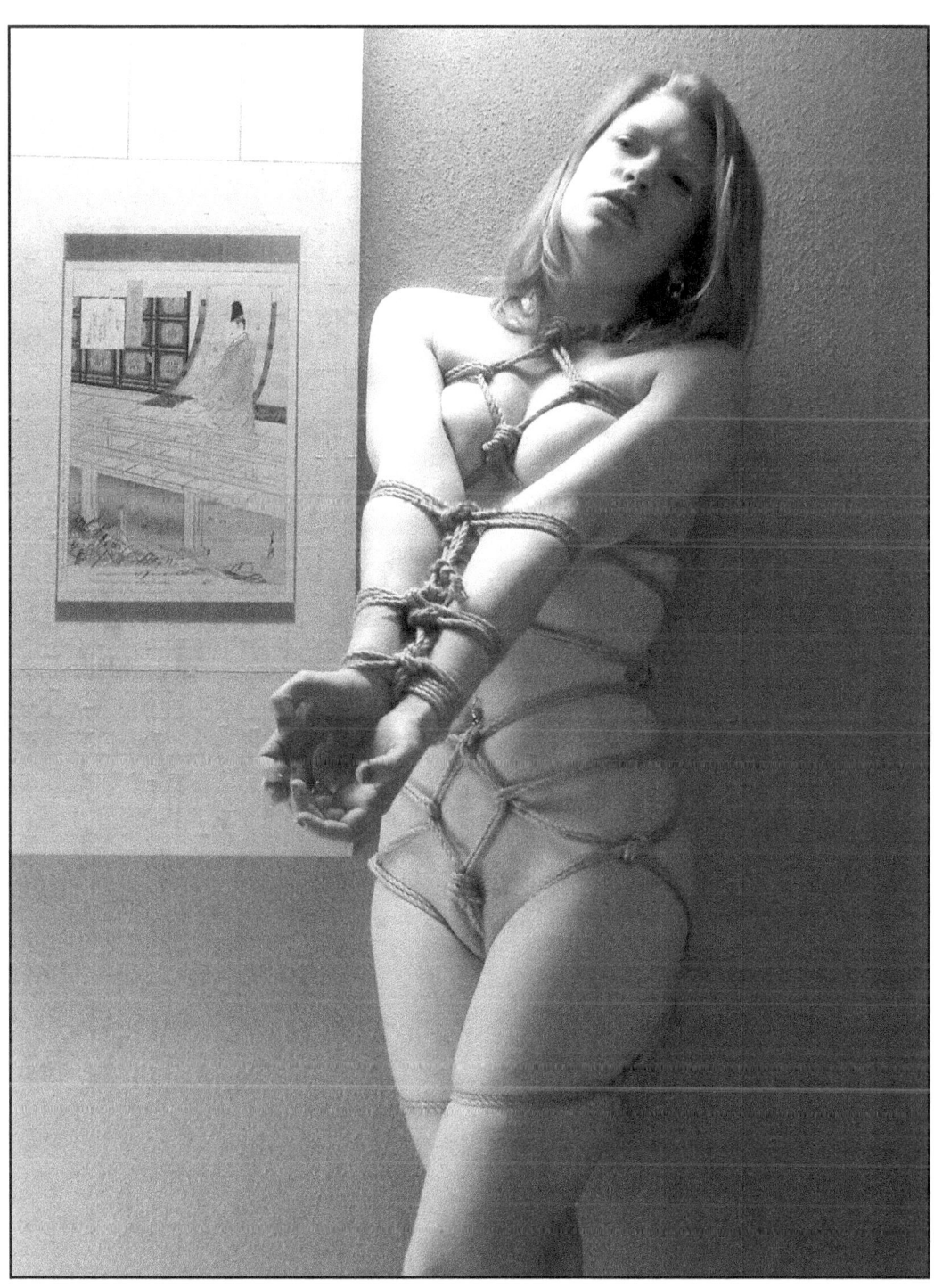

Mae te nawa shibari with hishi karada
(photo by Master "K")

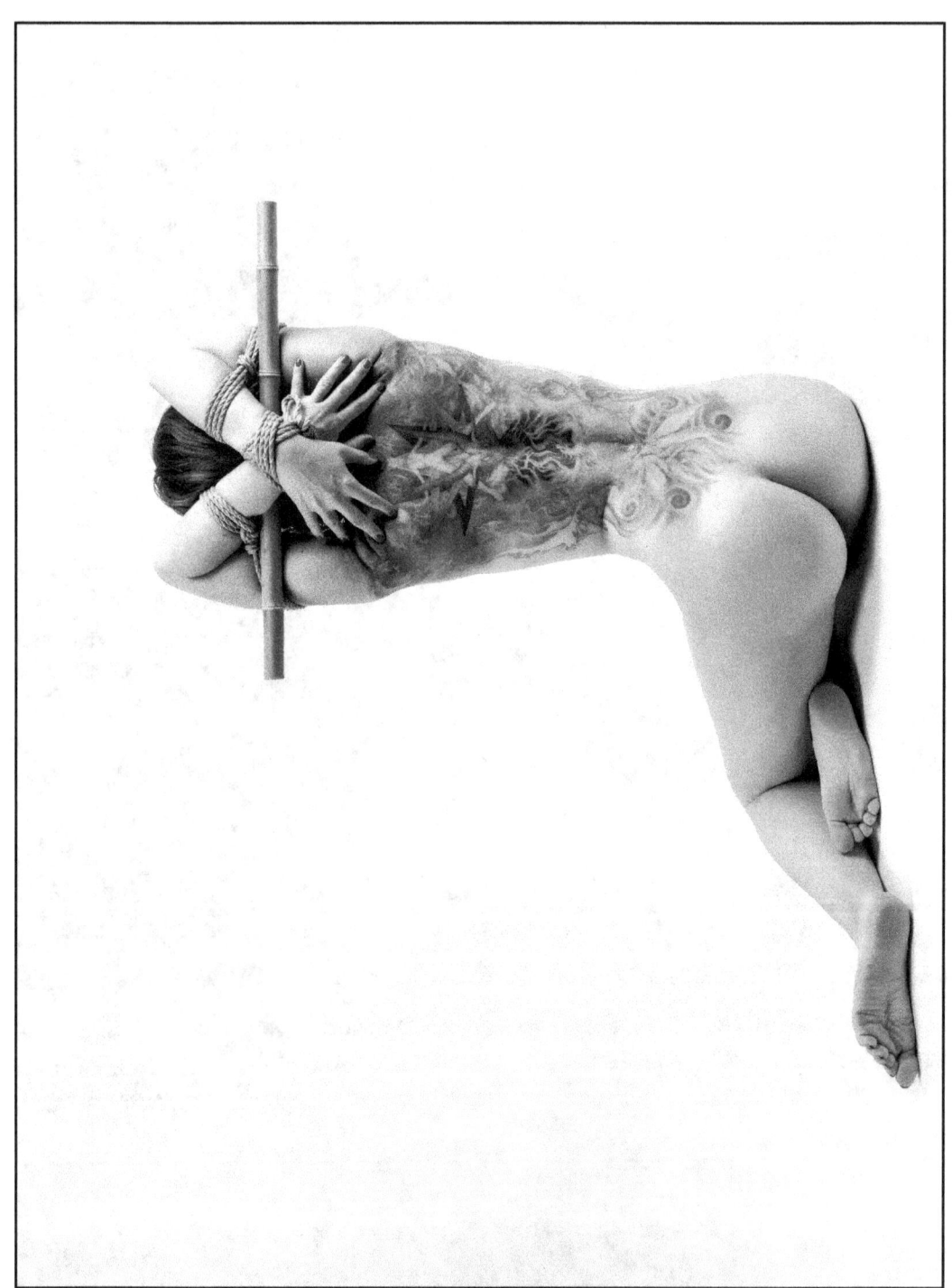

Takenotsue (bamboo) shibari #1
(photo by Zetsu)

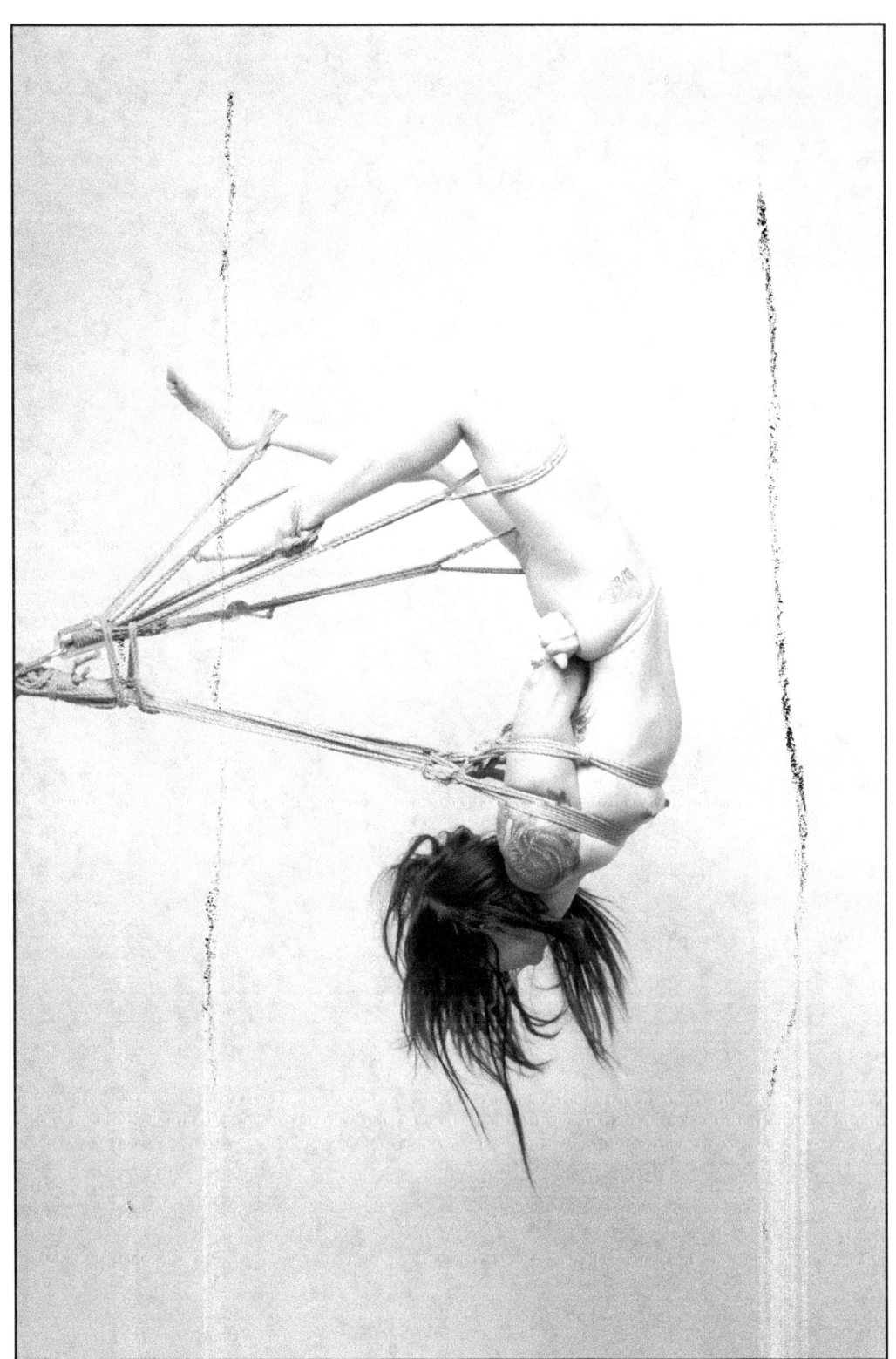

Gyaku-ebi zuri
(photo by Zetsu)

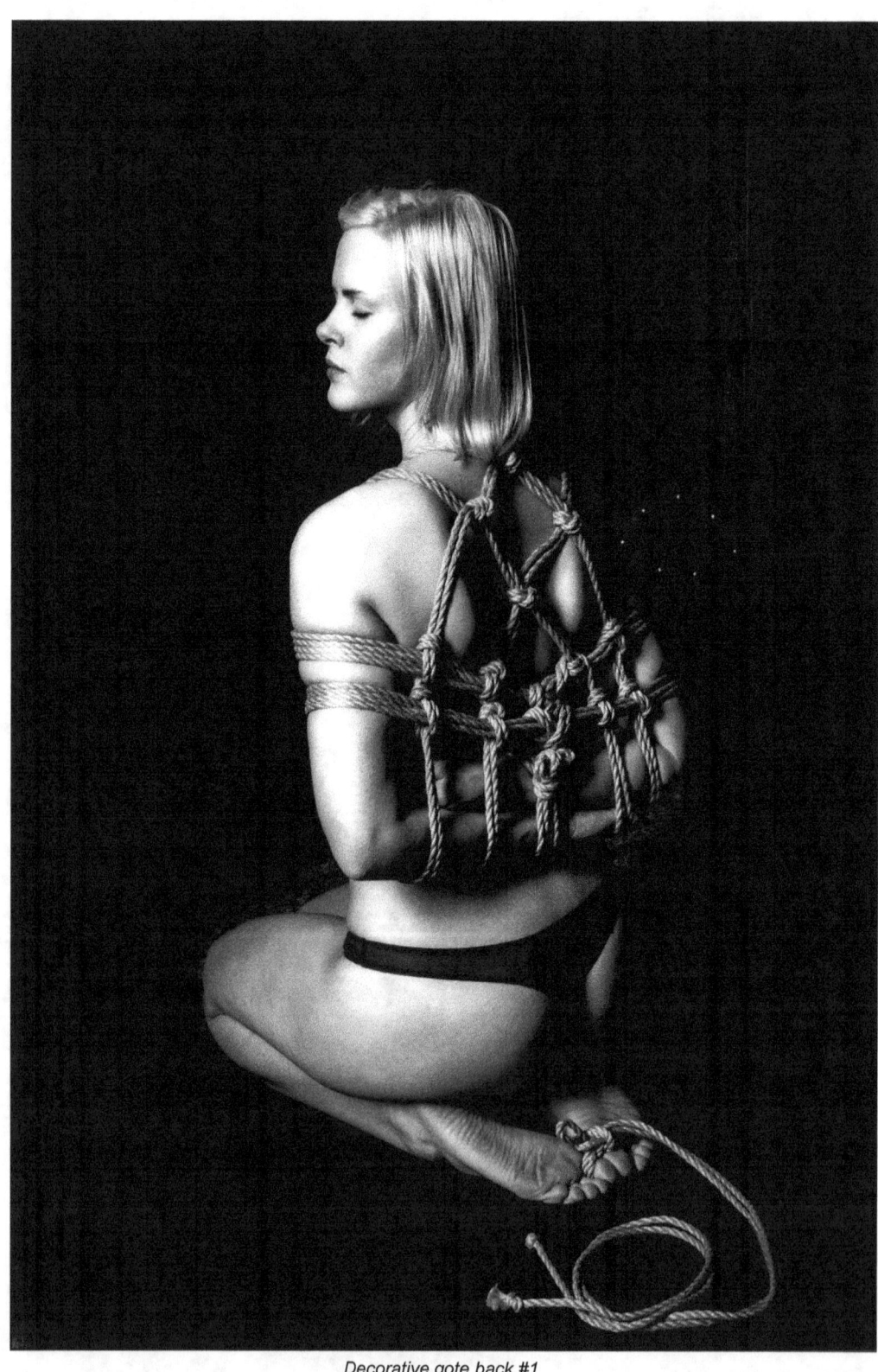

Decorative gote back #1
(photo by Erotic Exposures)

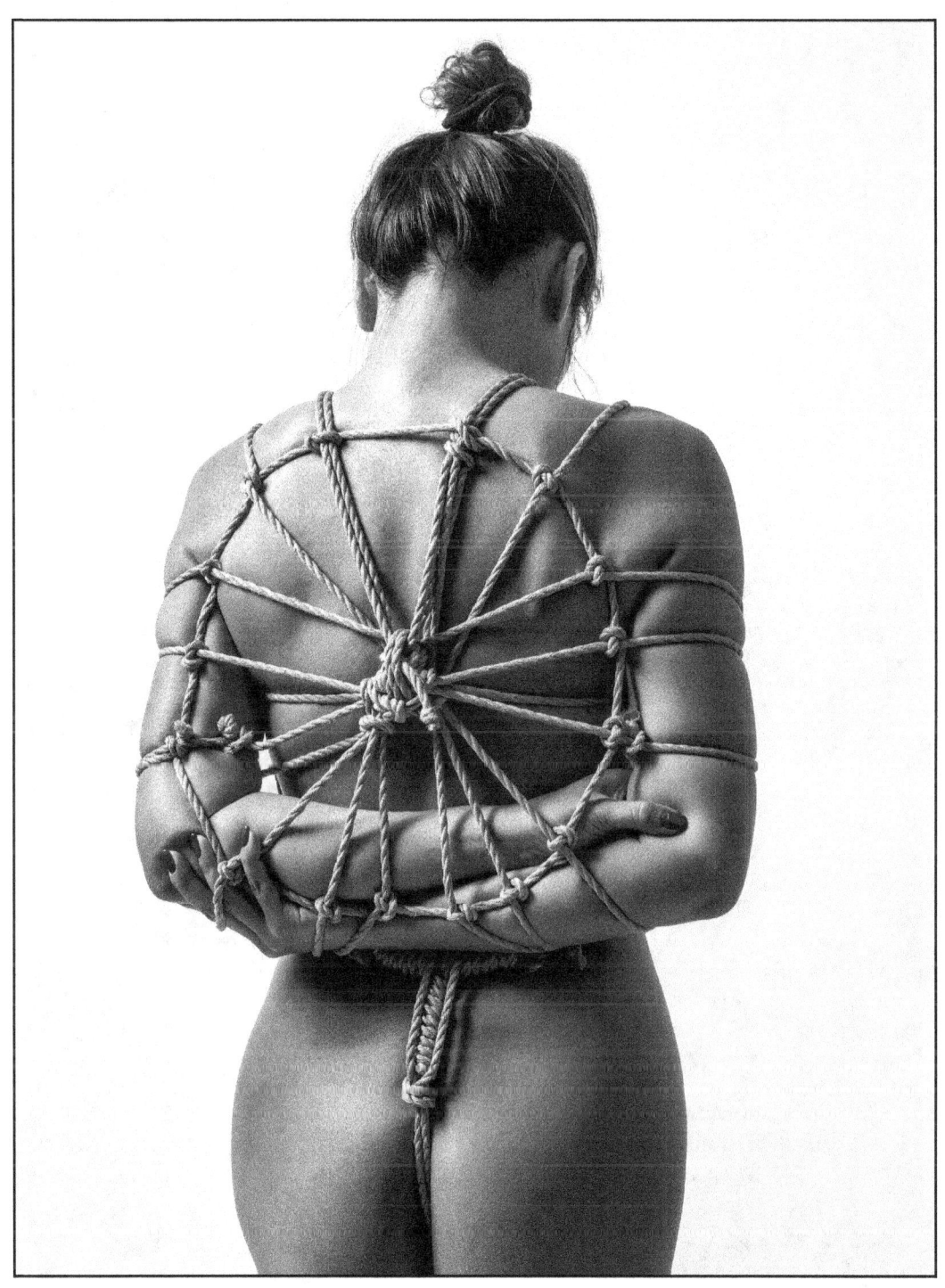

"The Wheel"—Shibari design by Master "K" after a hojojutsu pattern
(photo by Zetsu)

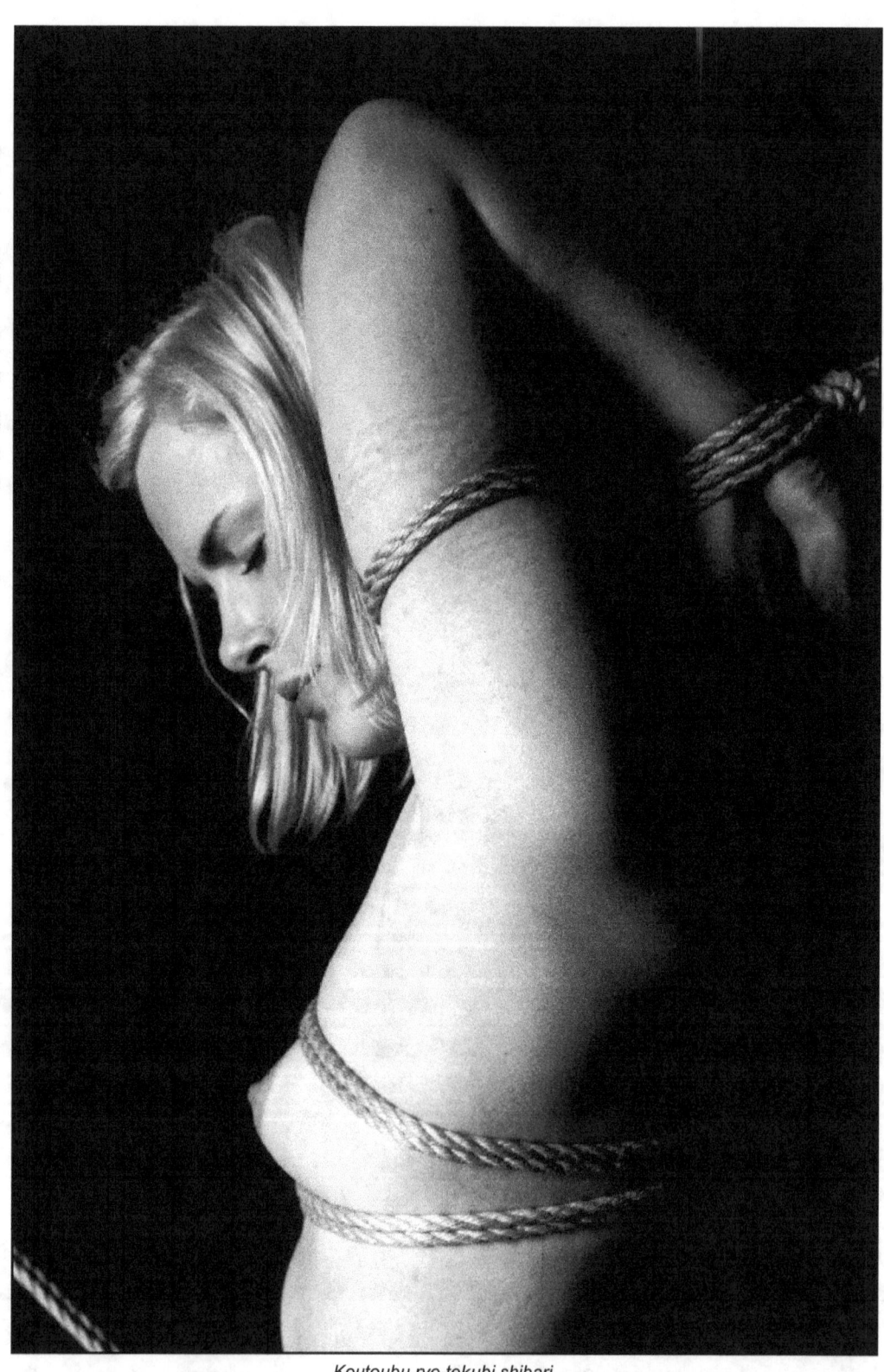

Koutoubu ryo-tekubi shibari
(photo by Erotic Exposures)

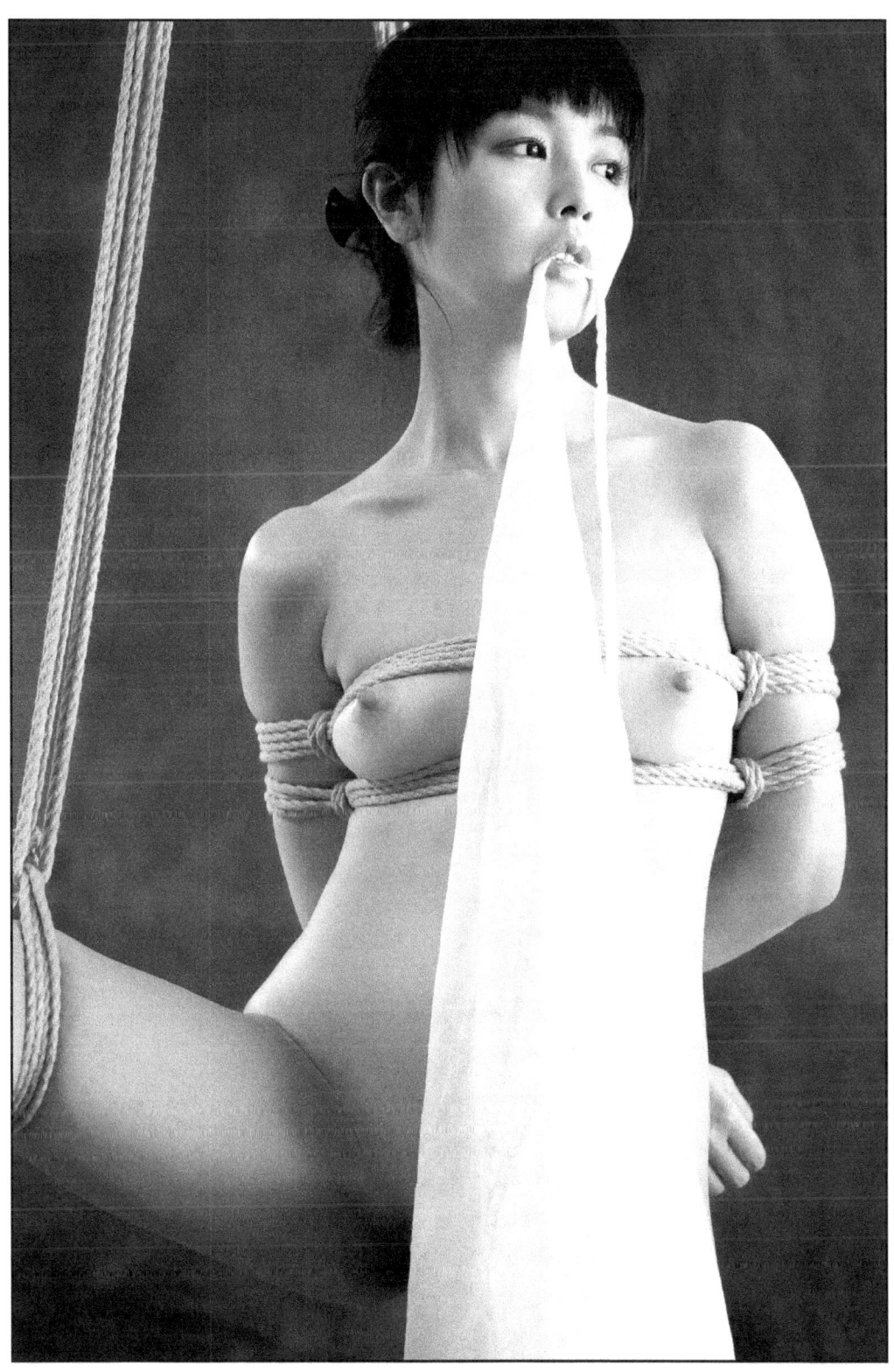

Kata-ashi zuri shibari #1
(photo by DNE)

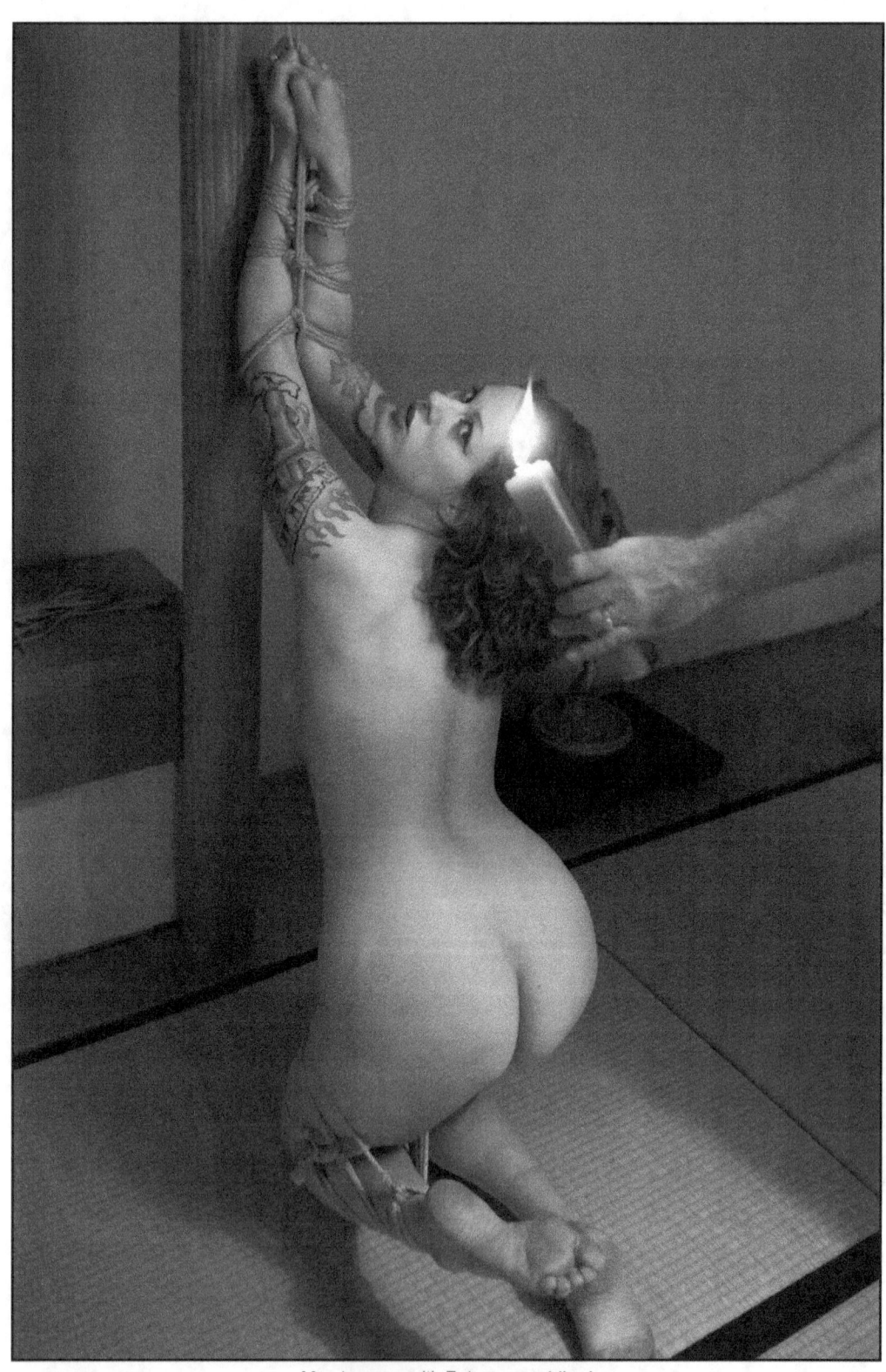

Mae te nawa with Futomomo shibari
(photo by Master "K")

Asanawa as sarugutsuwa
(photo by Erotic Exposures)

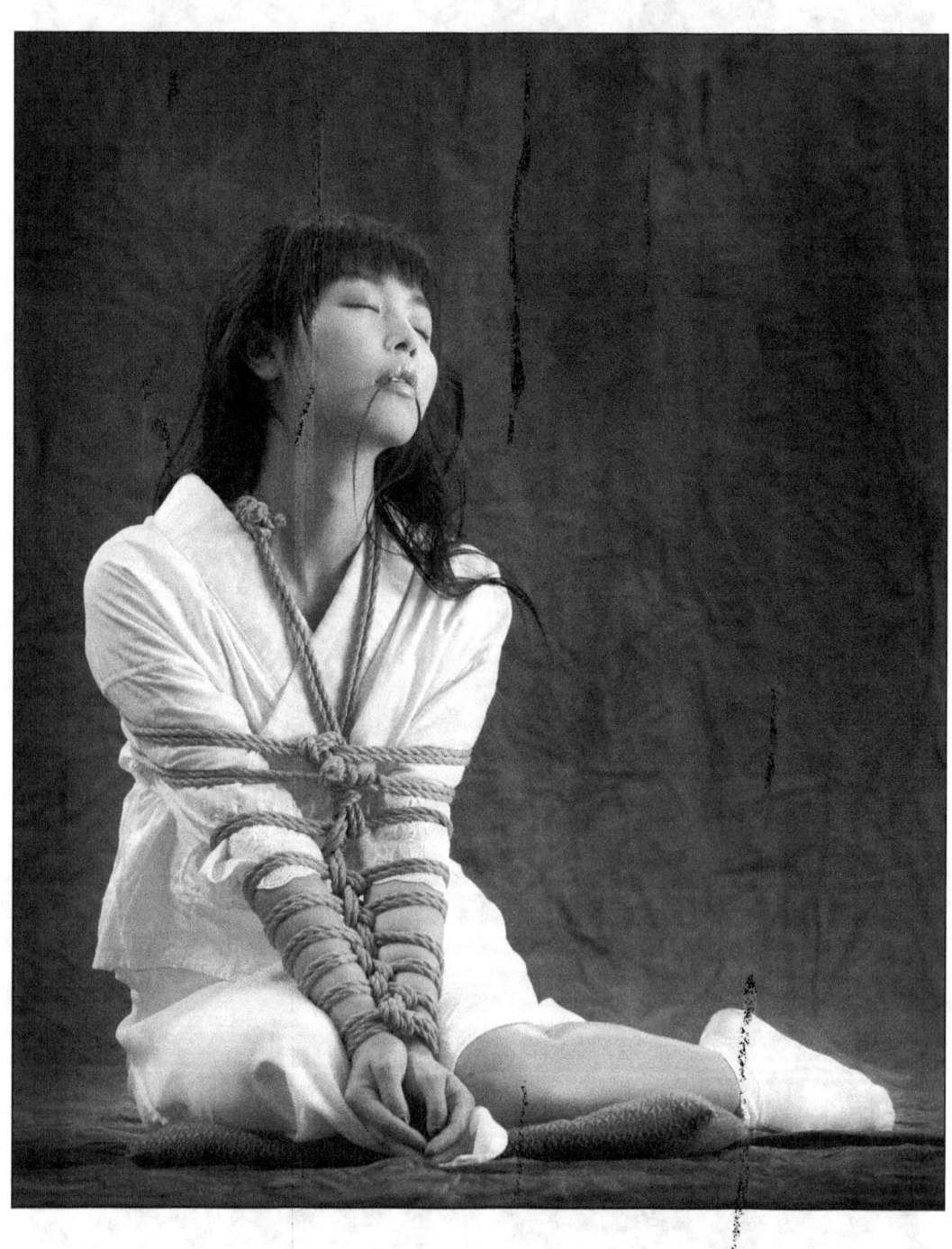

Decorative mae te nawa shibari
(photo by Michael Helms)

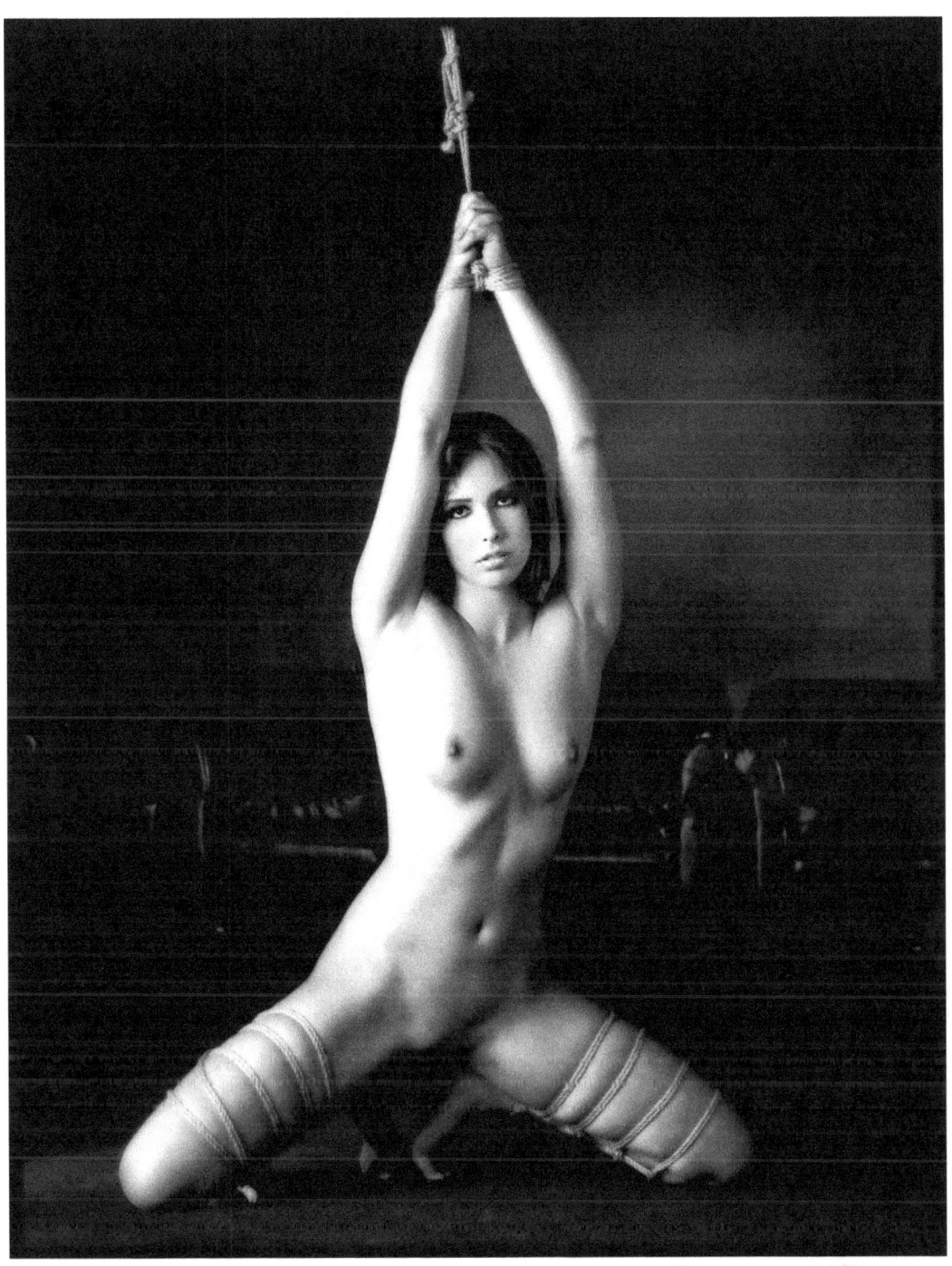

Newaza style pose—Tejou shibari with Futomomo shibari
(photo by Liquiderotica)

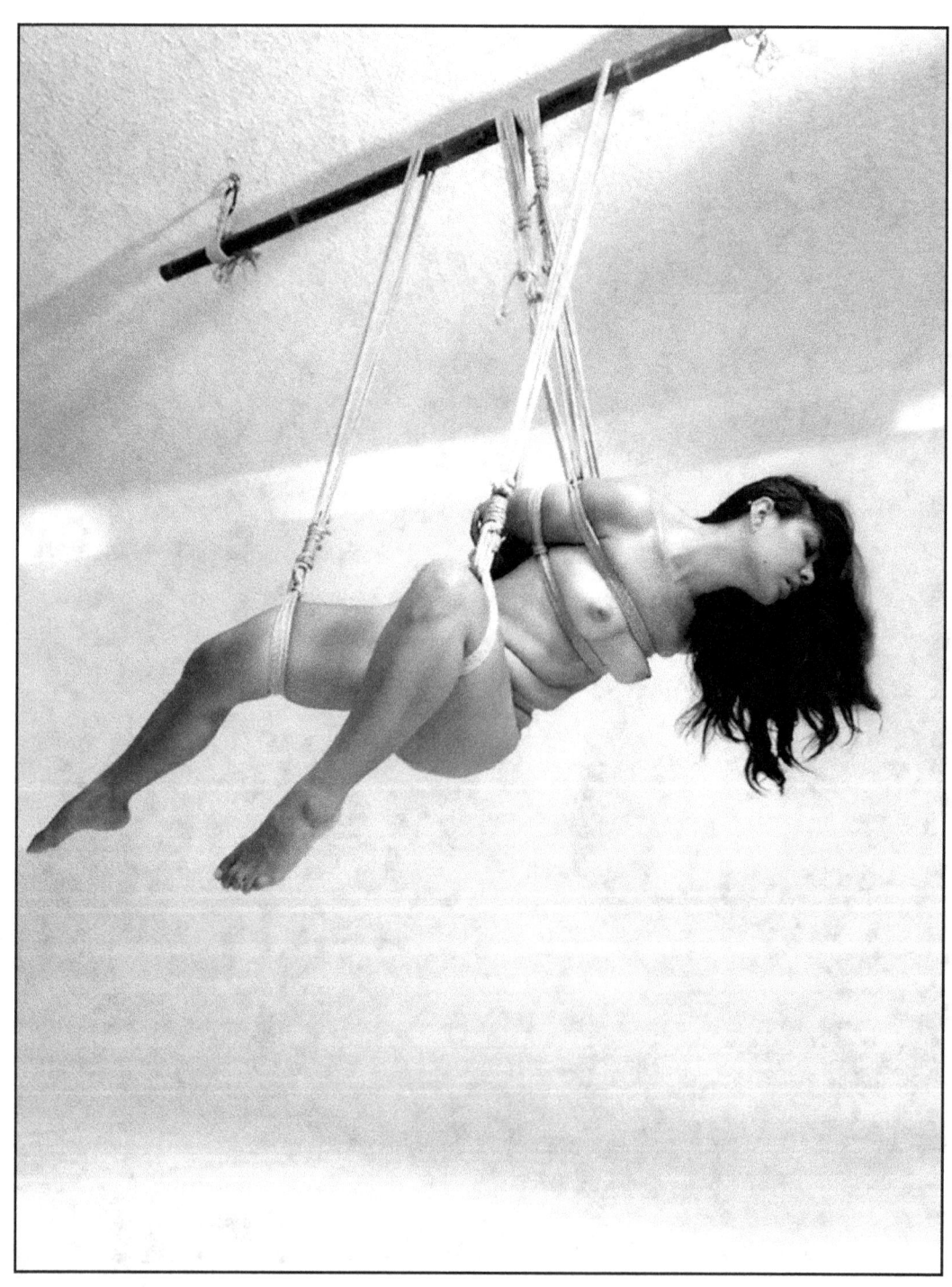

Yoko zuri transition from M-ji-kaikyaku zuri
(photo by Master "K")

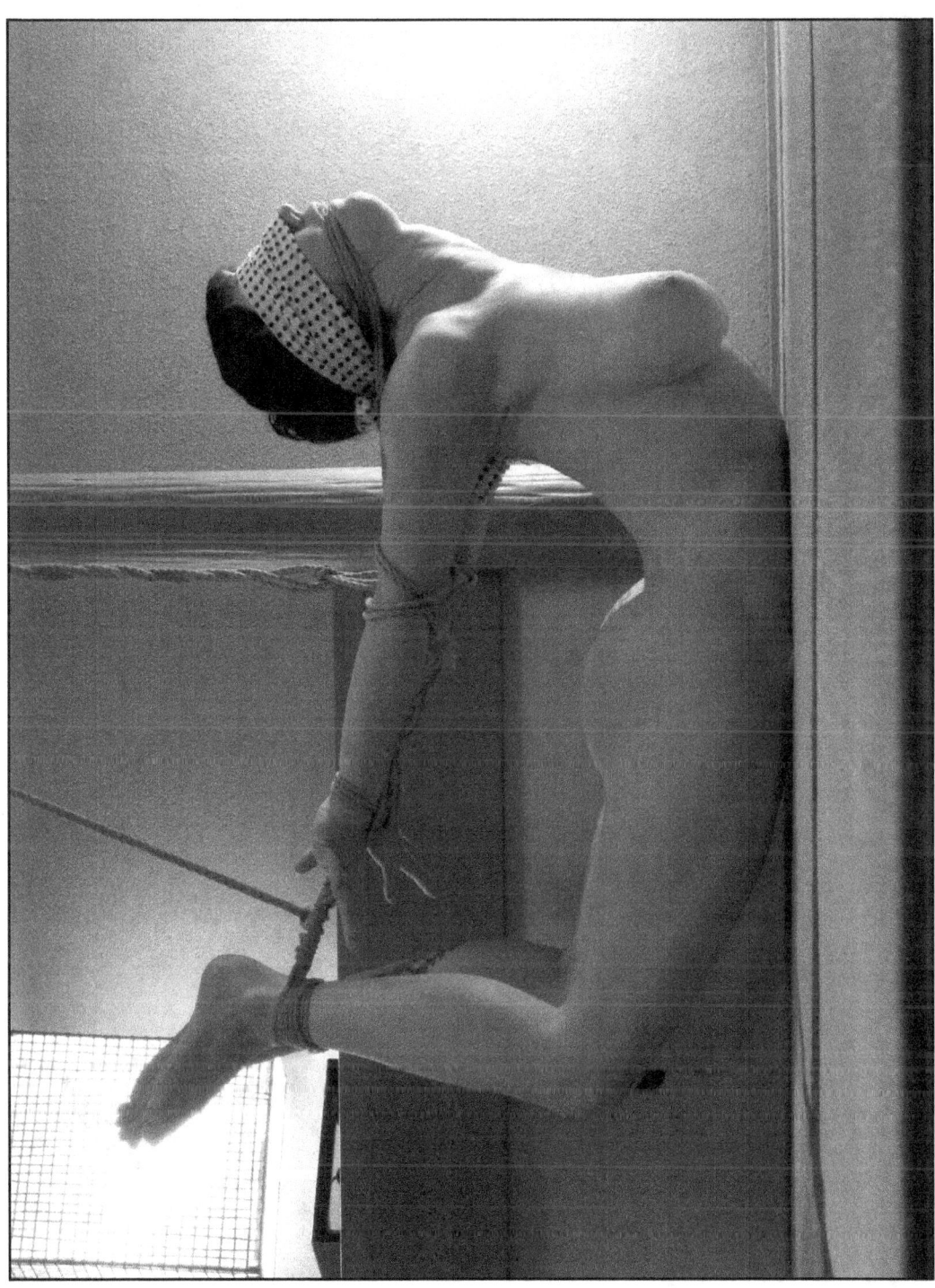

Suruga-doi shibari
(photo by Master "K")

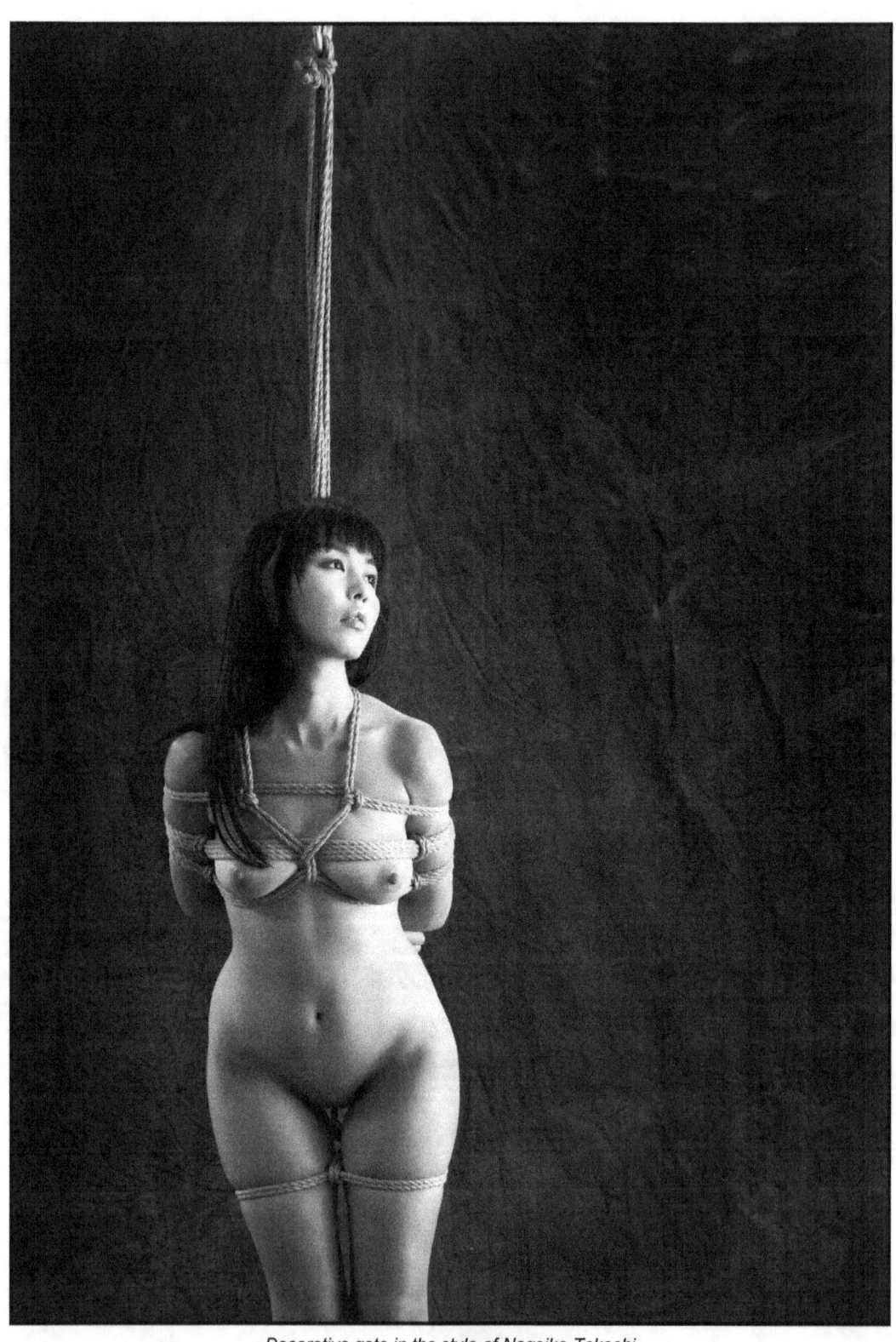

Decorative gote in the style of Nagaike Takeshi
(photo by Michale Helms)

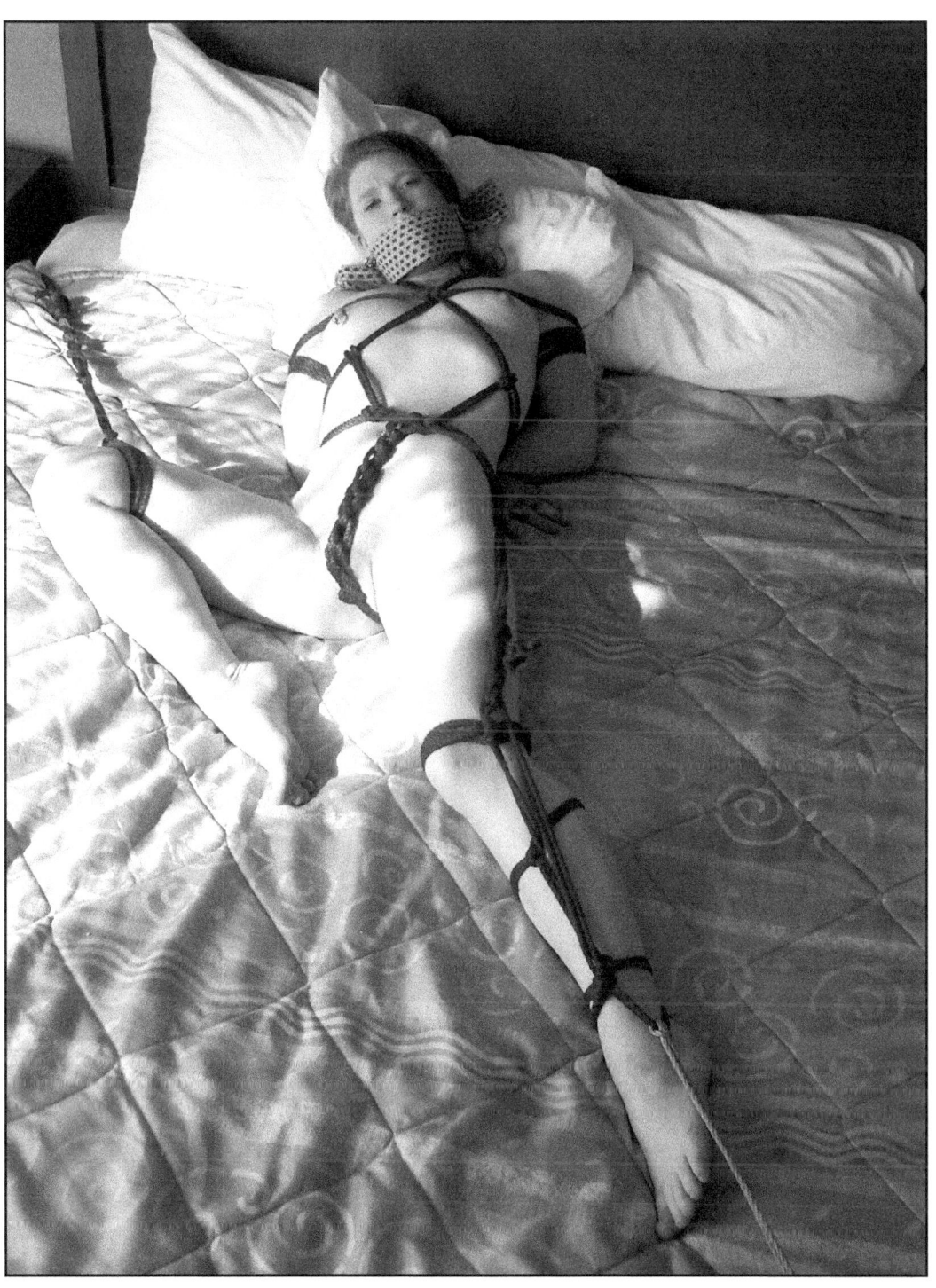

Large hishi hojojutsu pattern
(photo by Master "K")

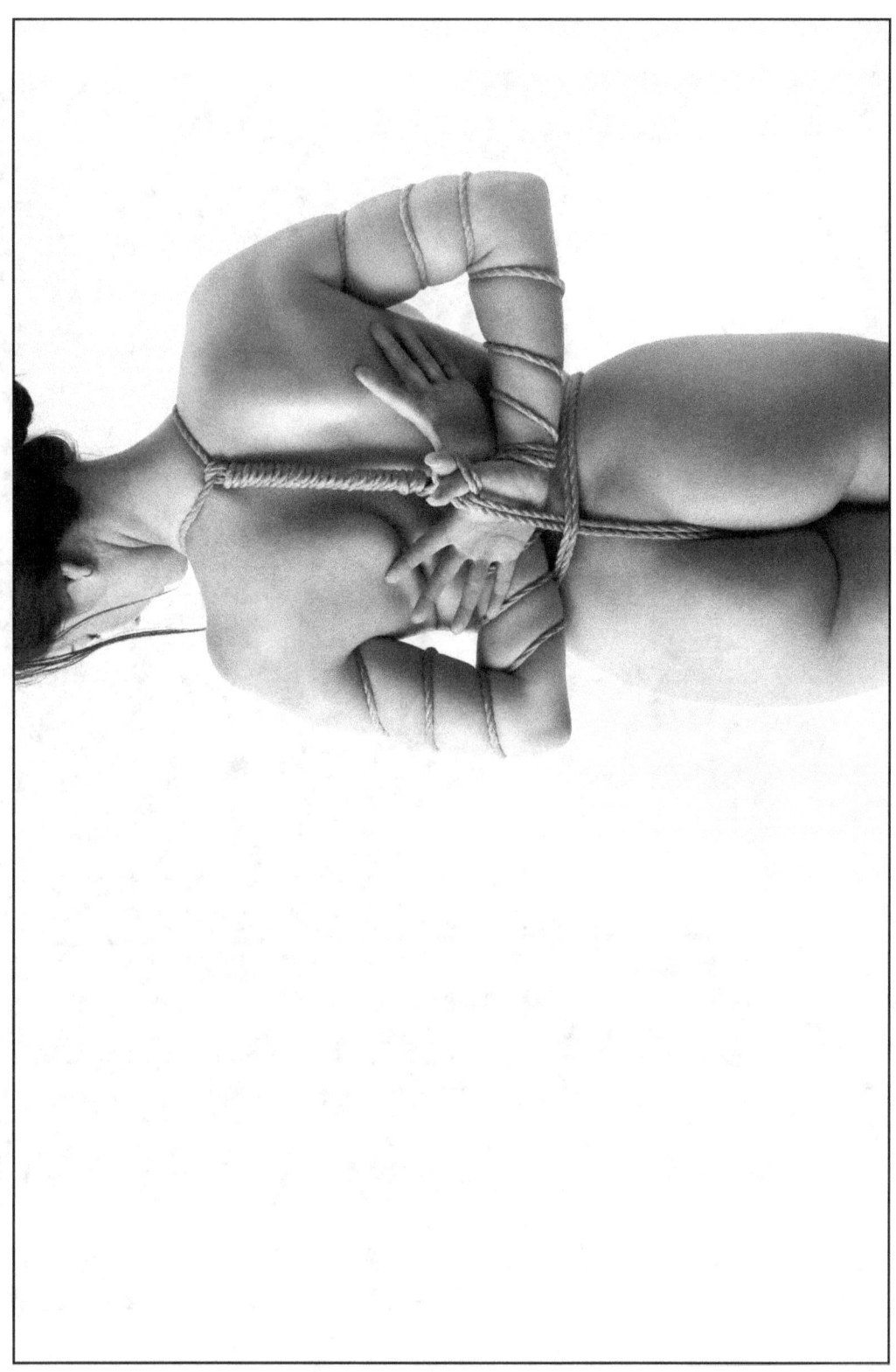

Decorative gote back #2—Chinese "Five Flower" pattern
(photo by Michael Helms)

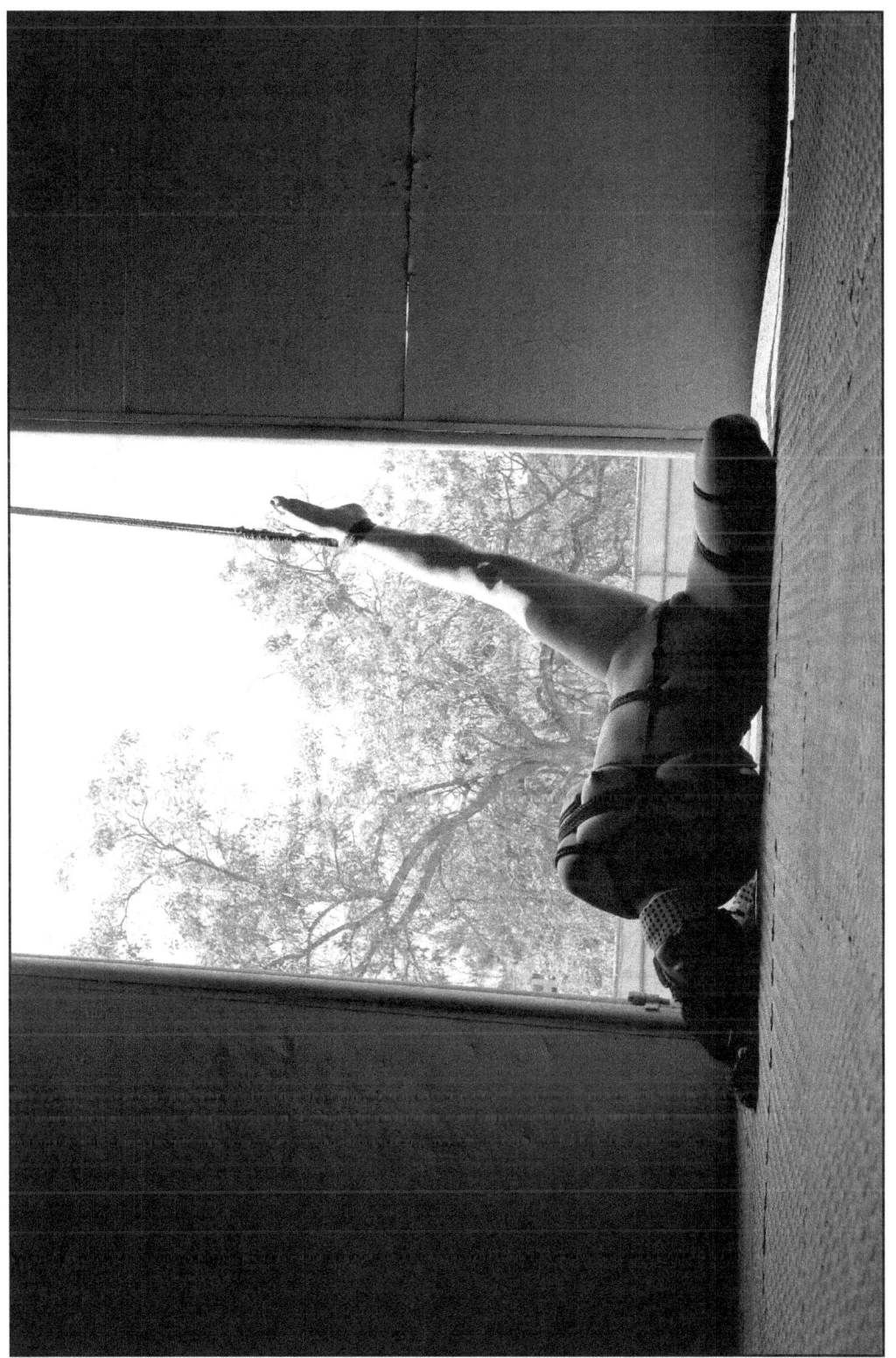

Kata-ashi zuri shibari #2
(photo by Master "K")

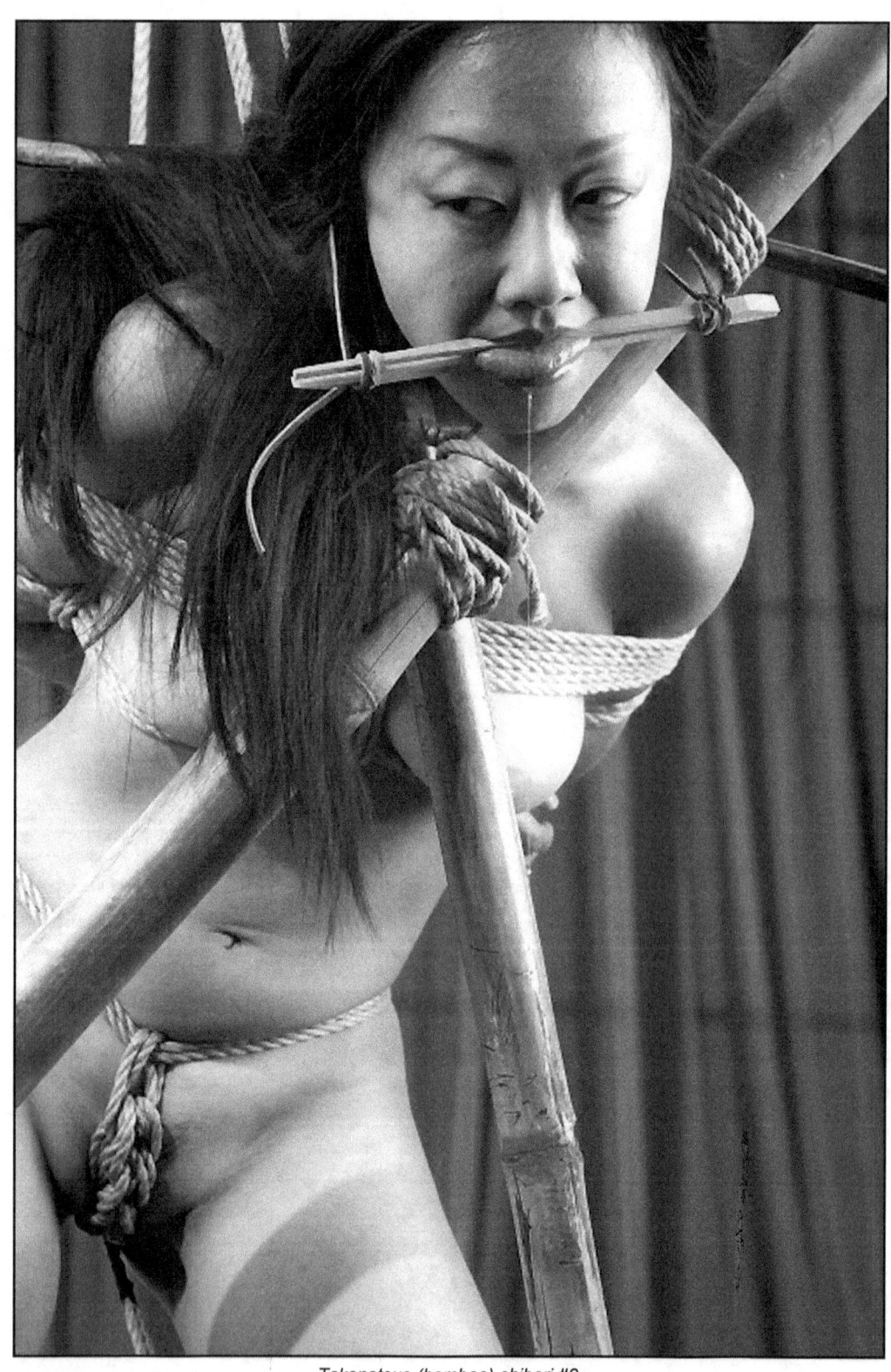

Takenotsue (bamboo) shibari #2
(photo by Master "K")

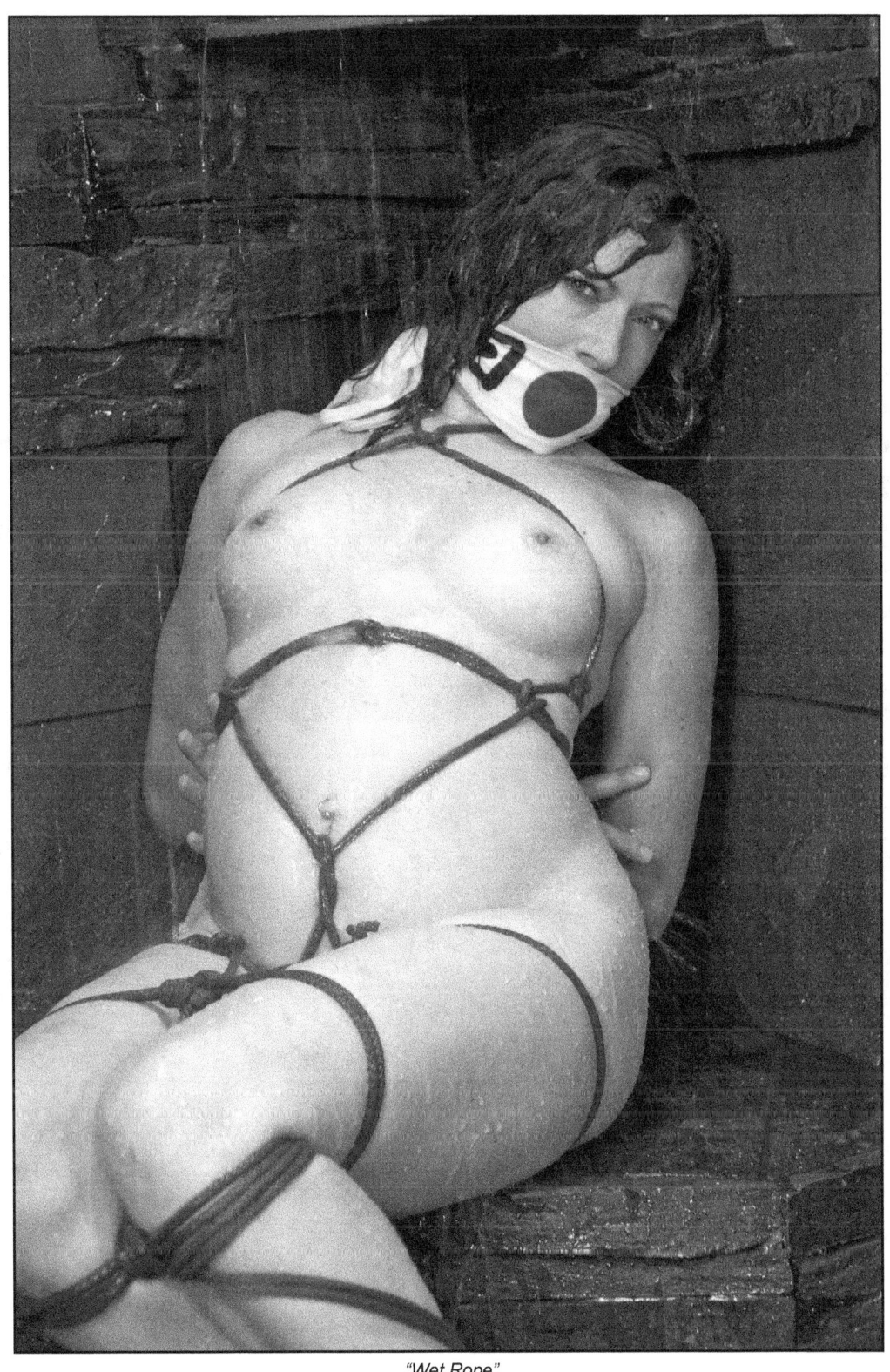

"Wet Rope"
(photo by Master "K")

134

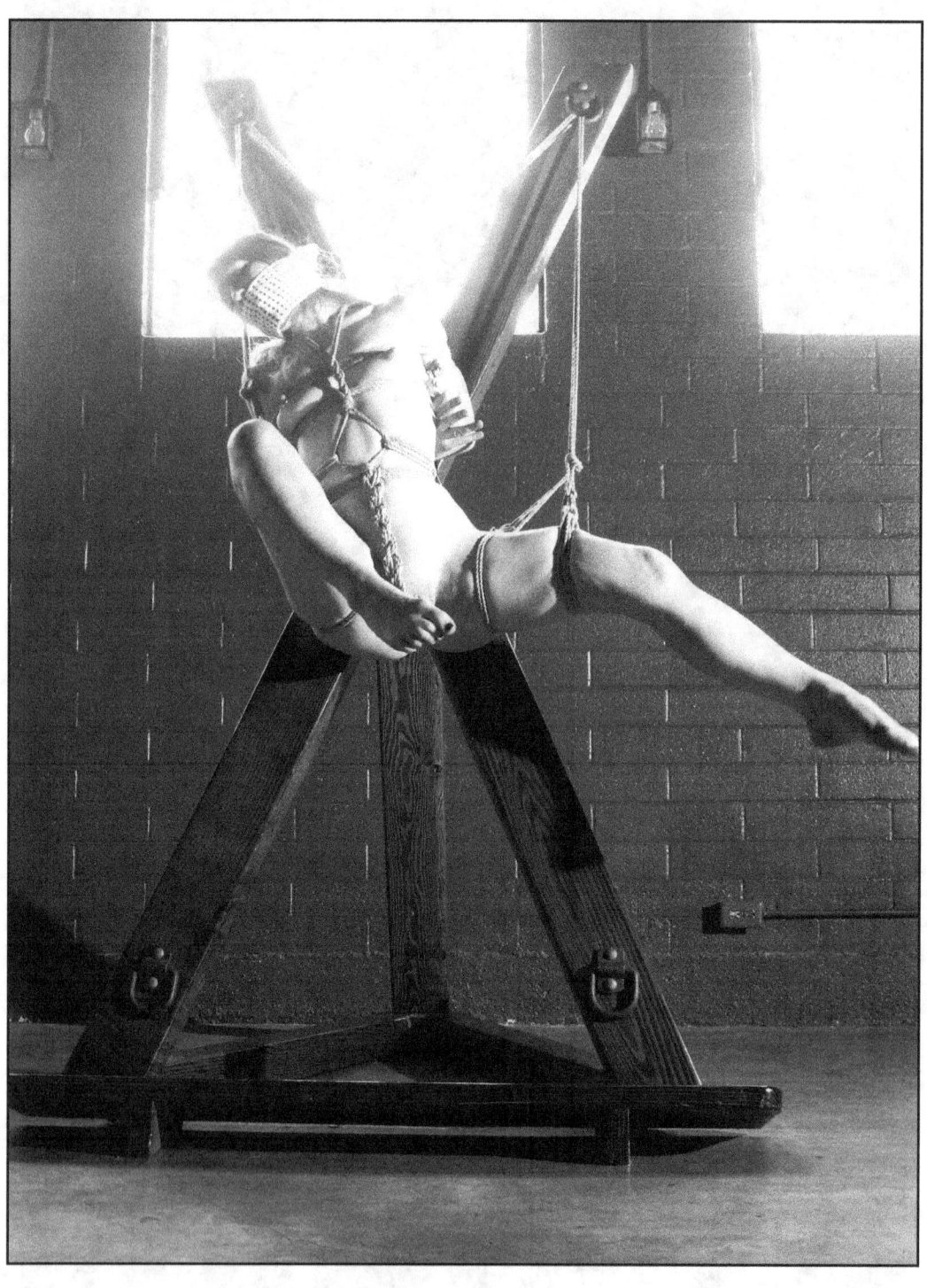

M-ji-kaikyaku zuri
(photo by Master "K")

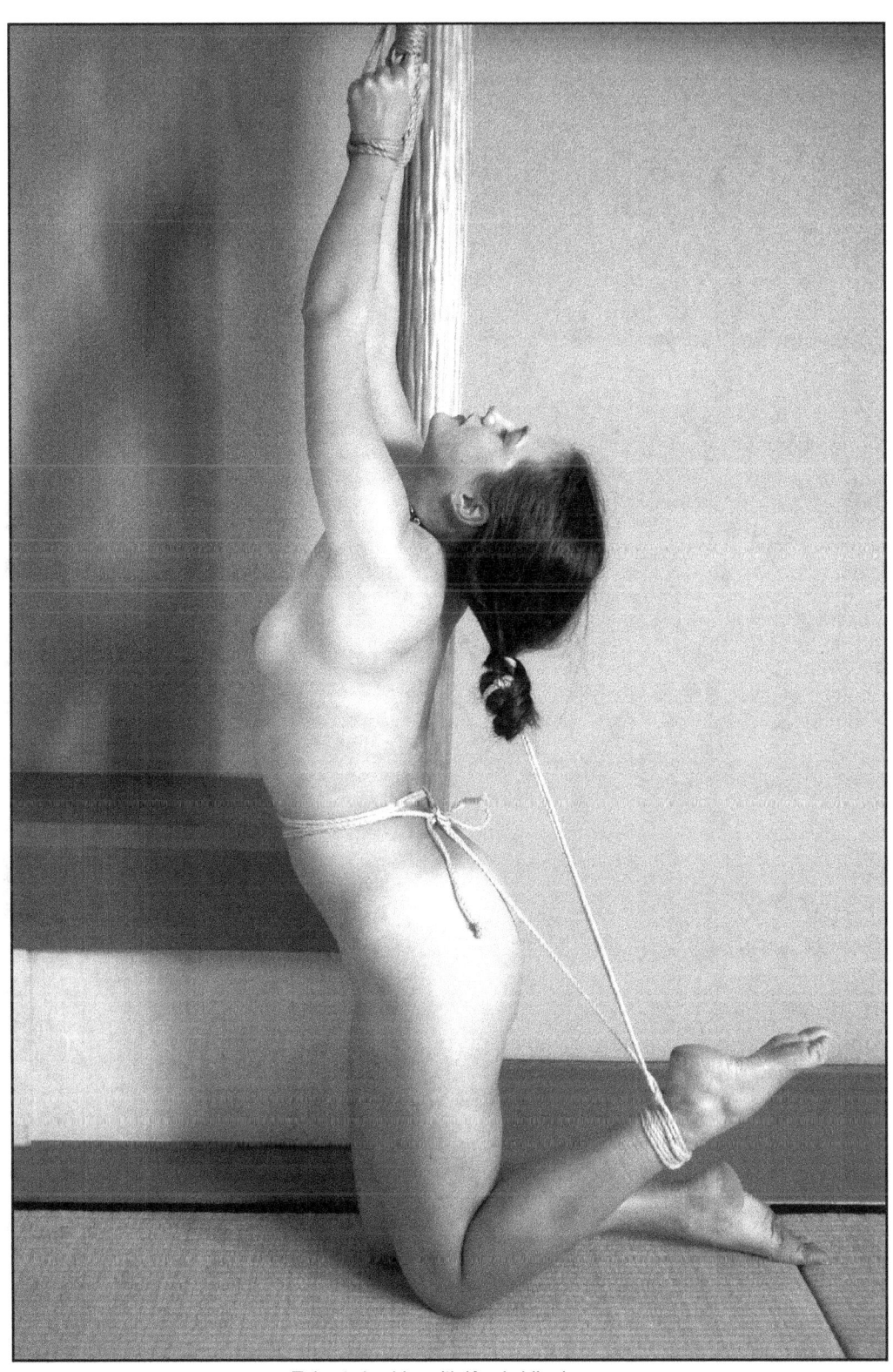

Tejou to hashira with Kami shibari seme
(photo by Master "K")

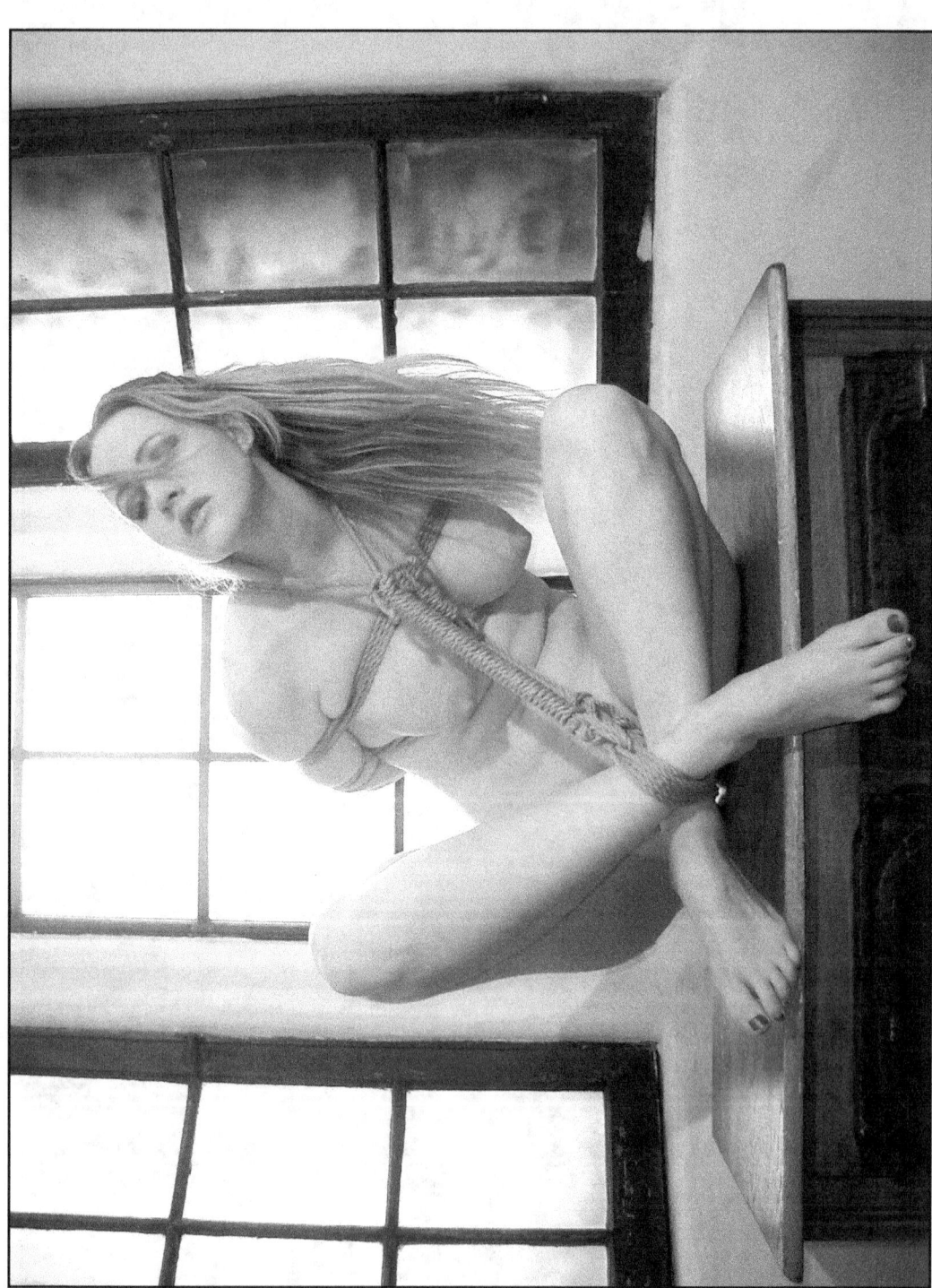

Agura shibari
(photo by Master "K")

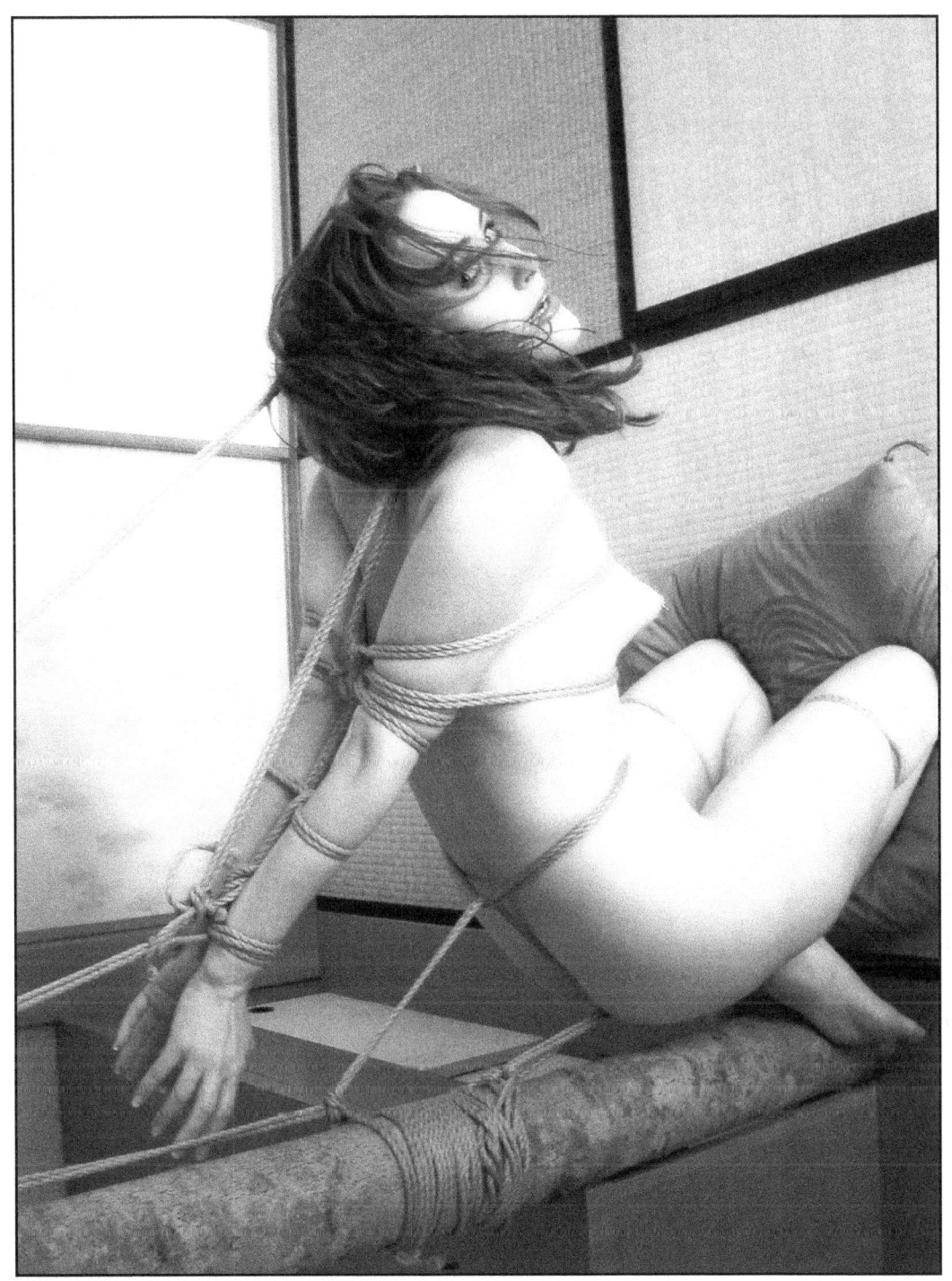

Ganzi garame #2 using hasira with Ushirode-gassho shibari
(photo by Master"K")

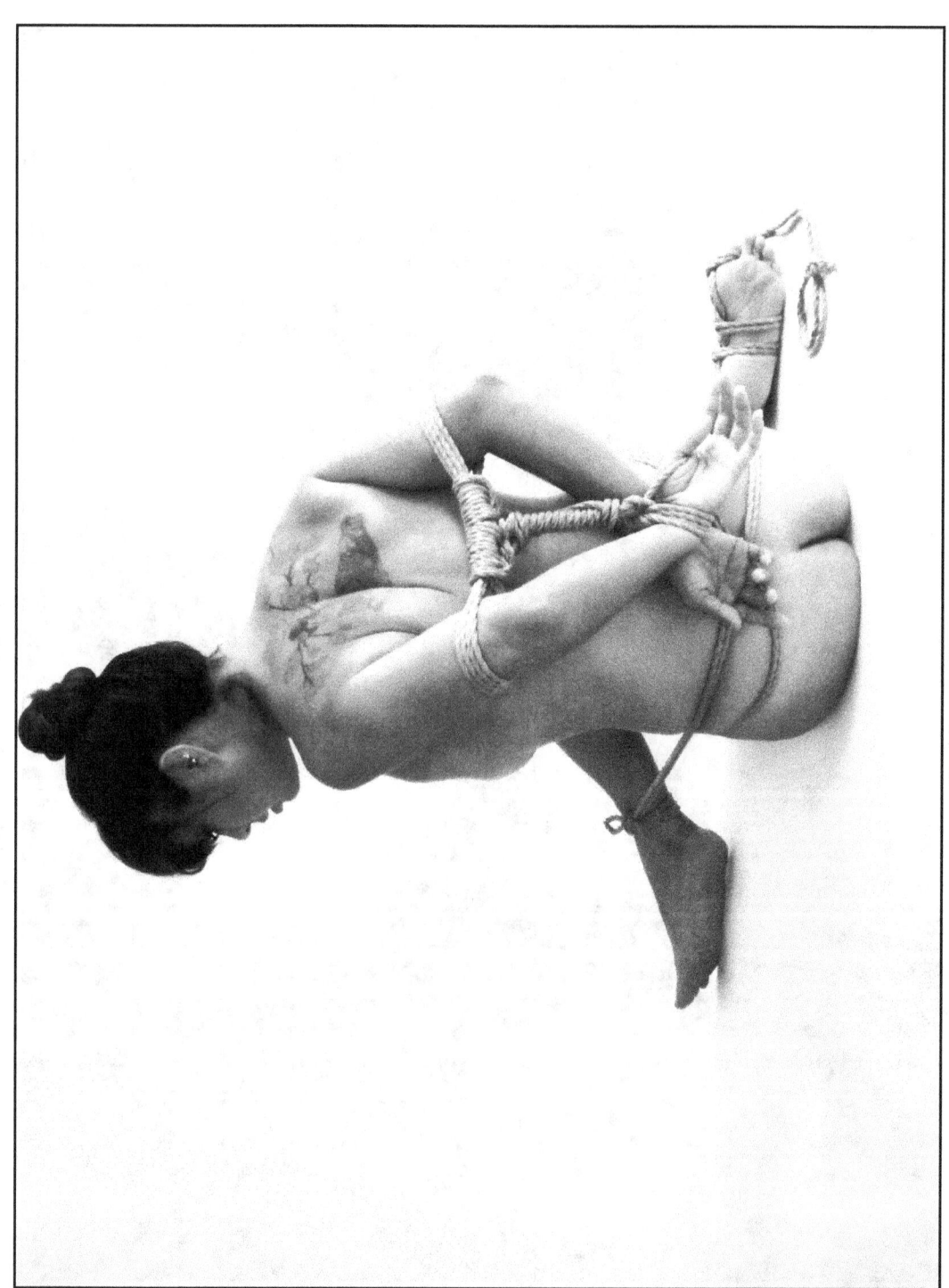

"Swan" pose—Ninoude shibari
(photo by Master "K")

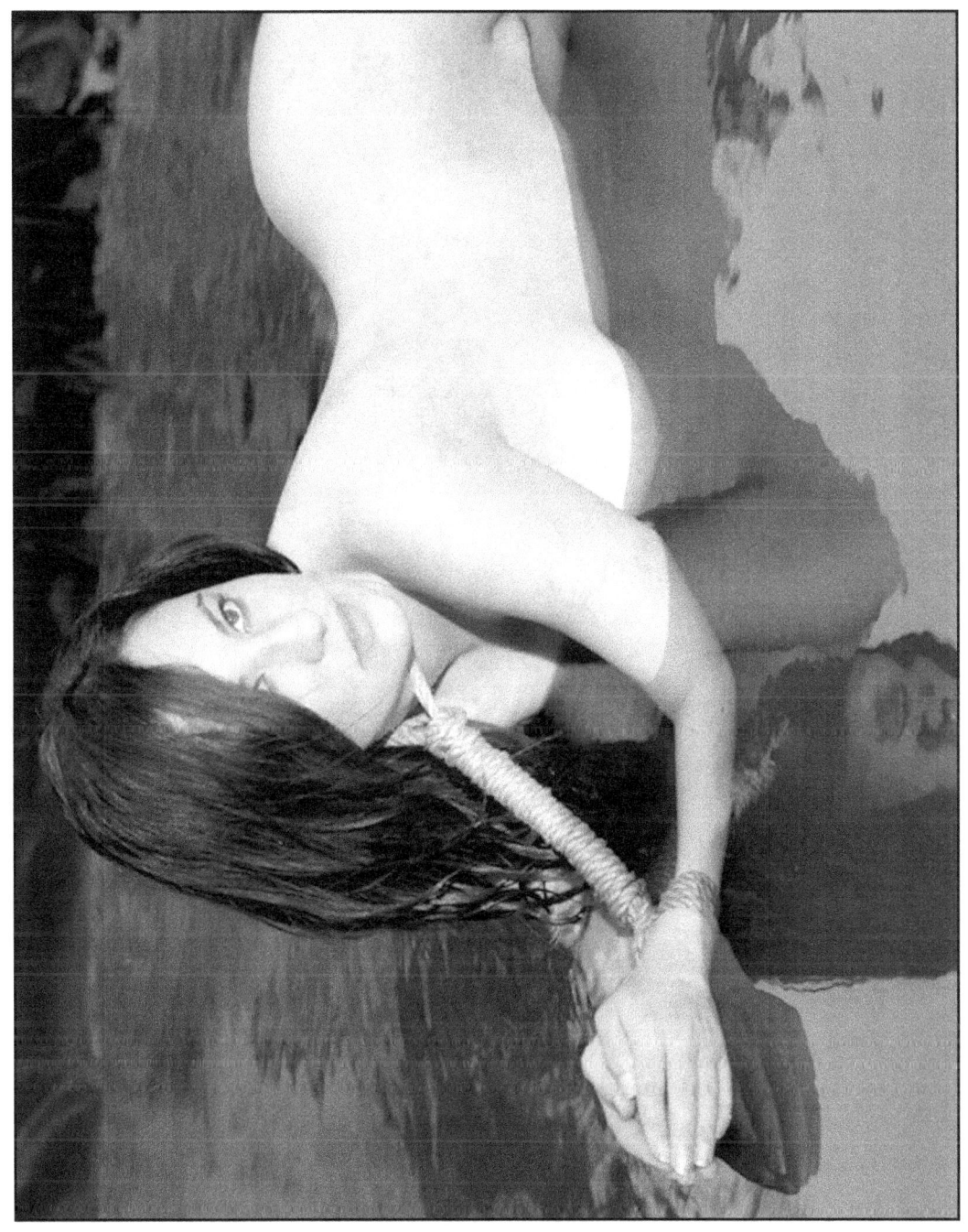

Hojojutsu wrist to neck tie—Tsuka maki pattern
(photo by DNE)

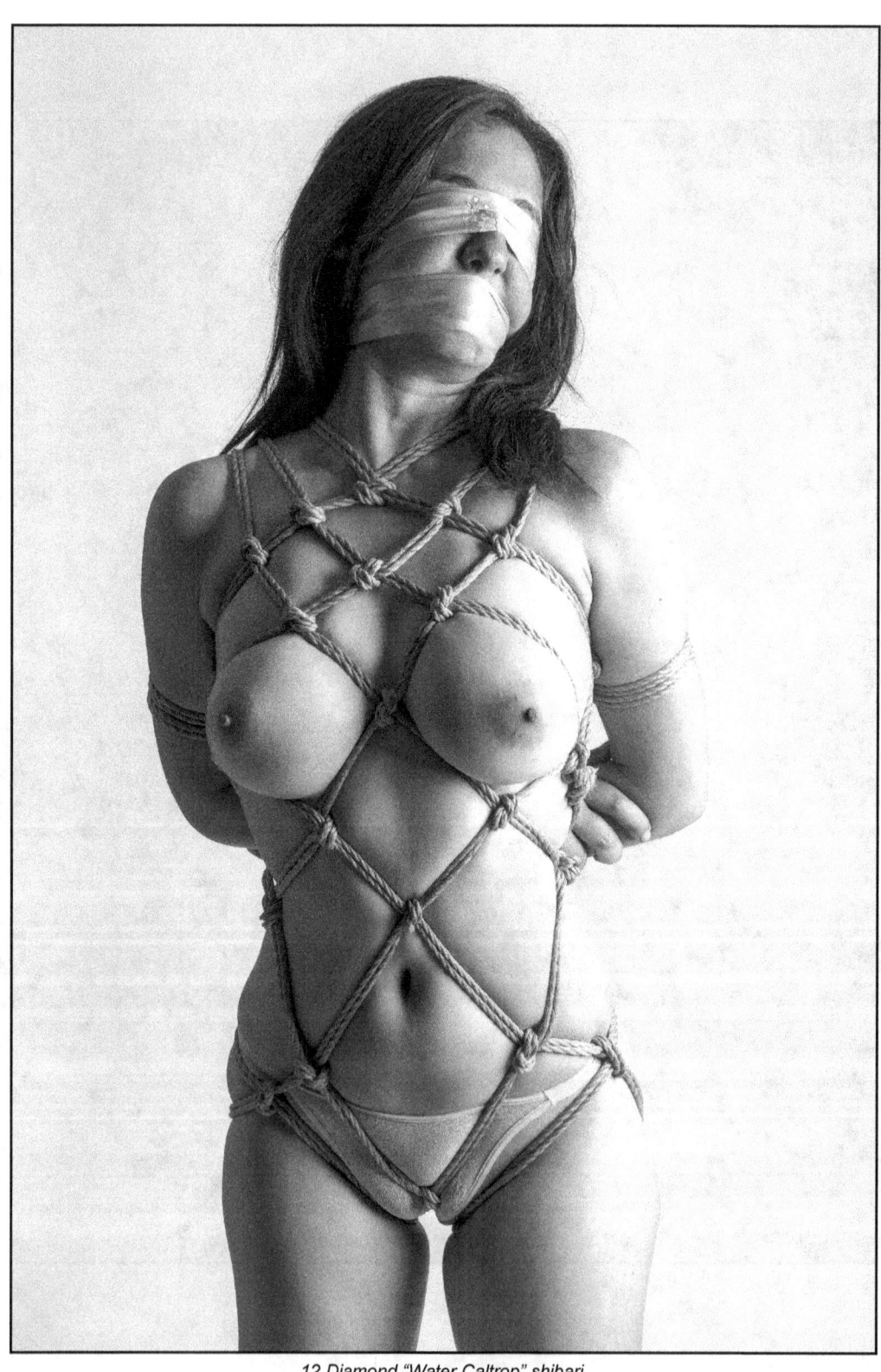

12 Diamond "Water Caltrop" shibari
(photo by Zetsu)

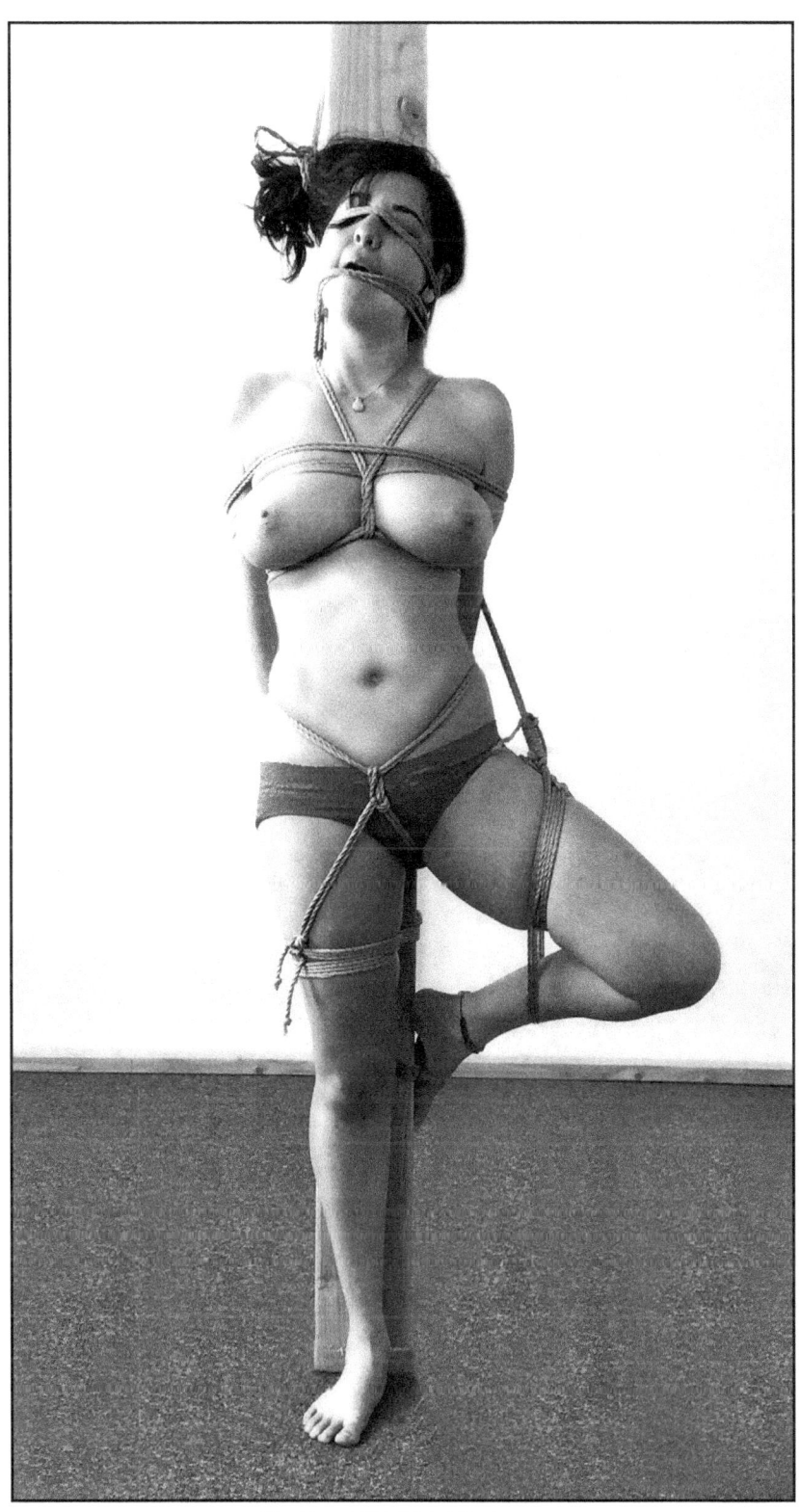

Hashira ushirodaki shibari seme
(photo by Master "K")

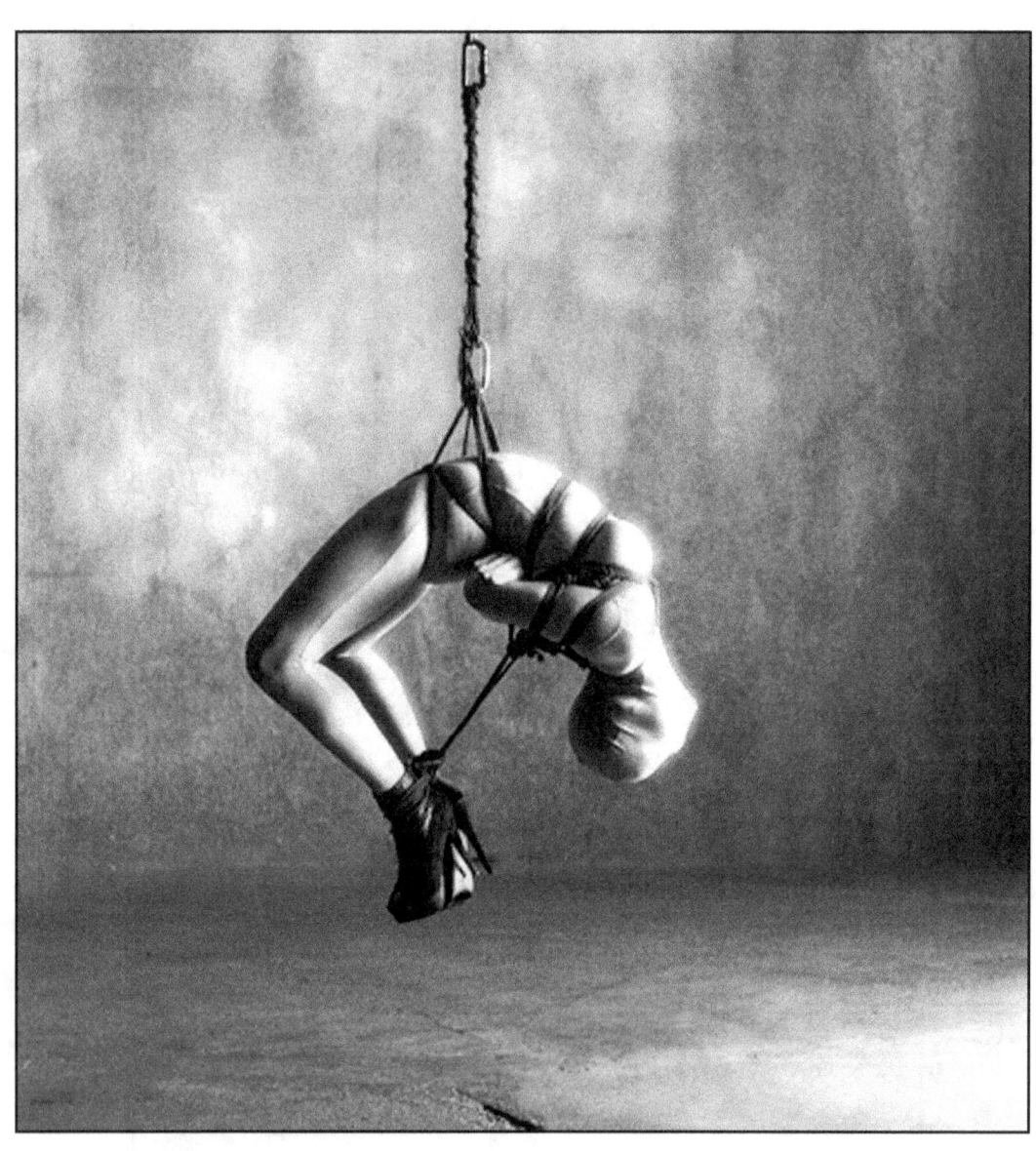

Aomuke zuri seme
(photo by Master "K")

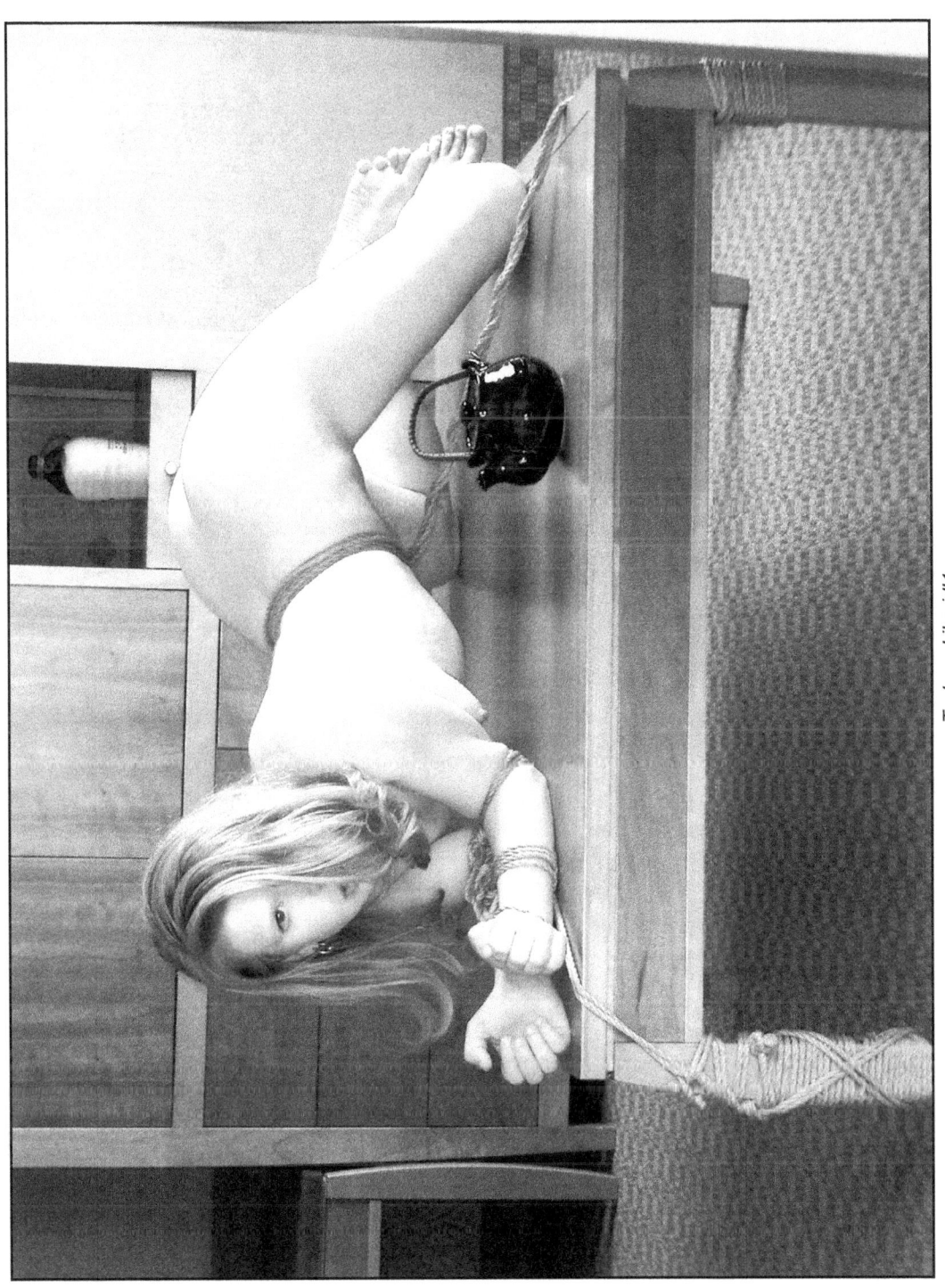

Tsukue shibari #1
(photo by Master "K")

144

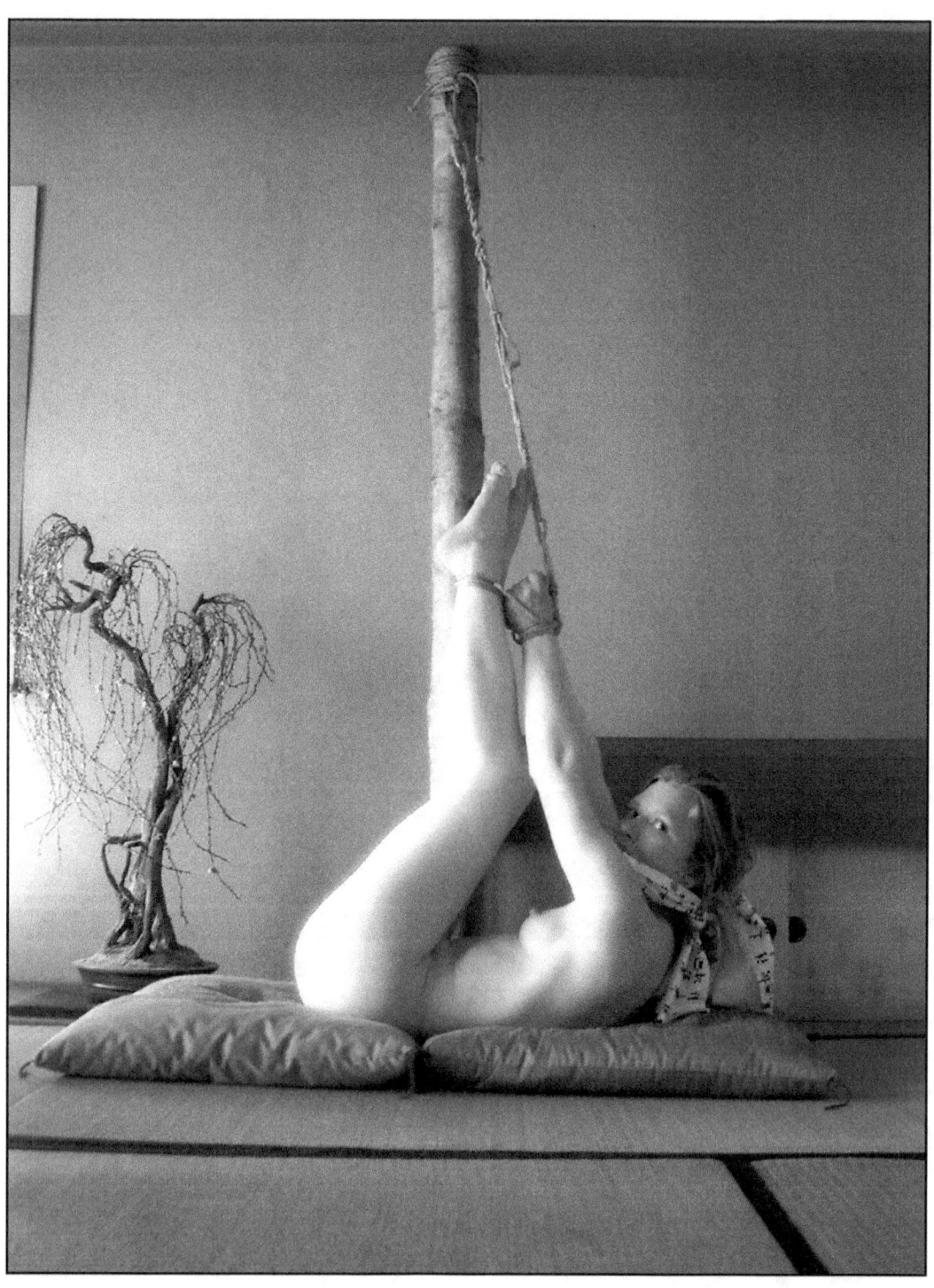

Tanuki shibari
(photo by Master "K")

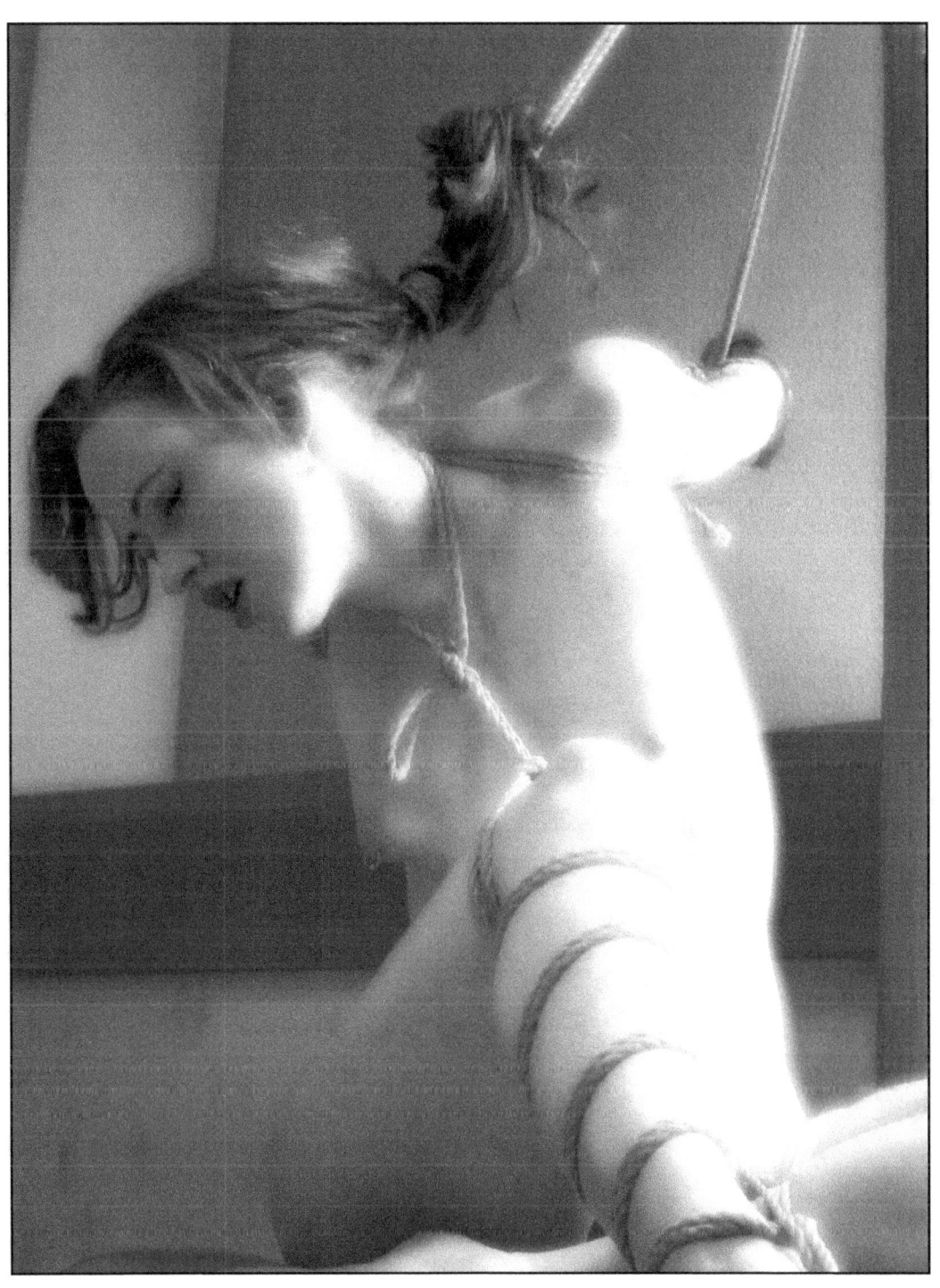

Kami shibari
(photo by Master "K")

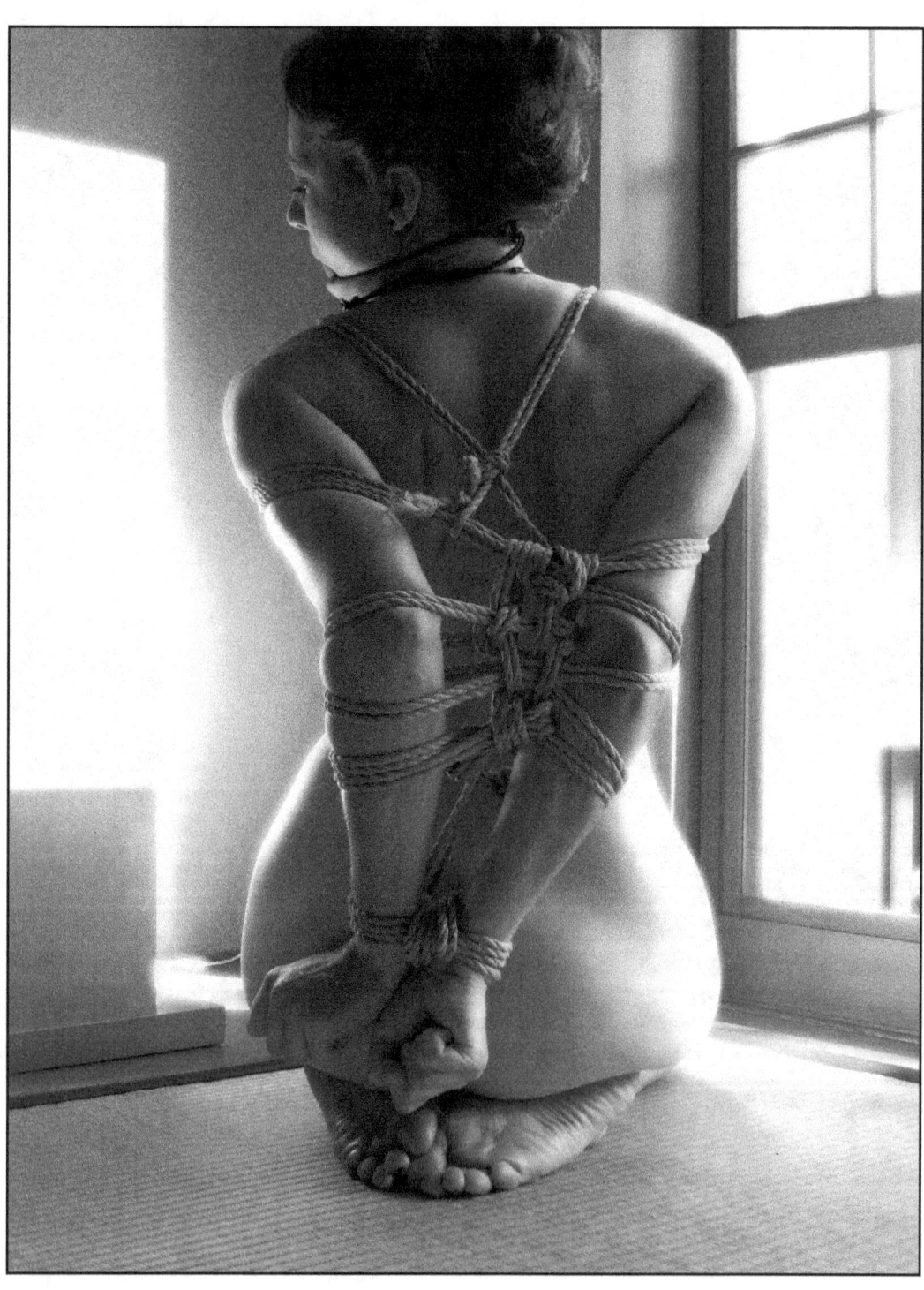

Ushirode-gasso shibari—Buddhist version
(photo by Master "K")

147

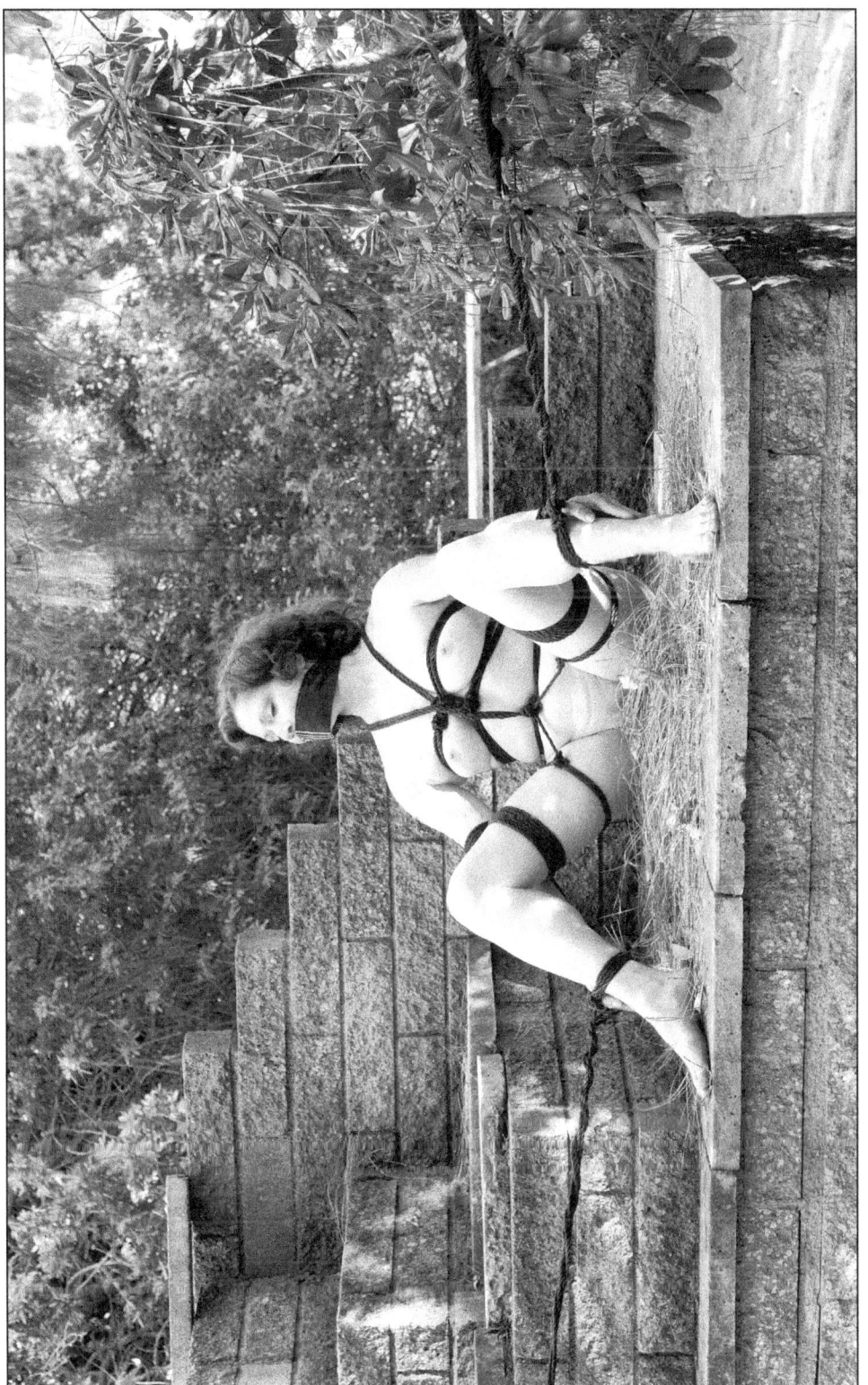

Kaikyaku kani shibari
(photo by Master "K")

148

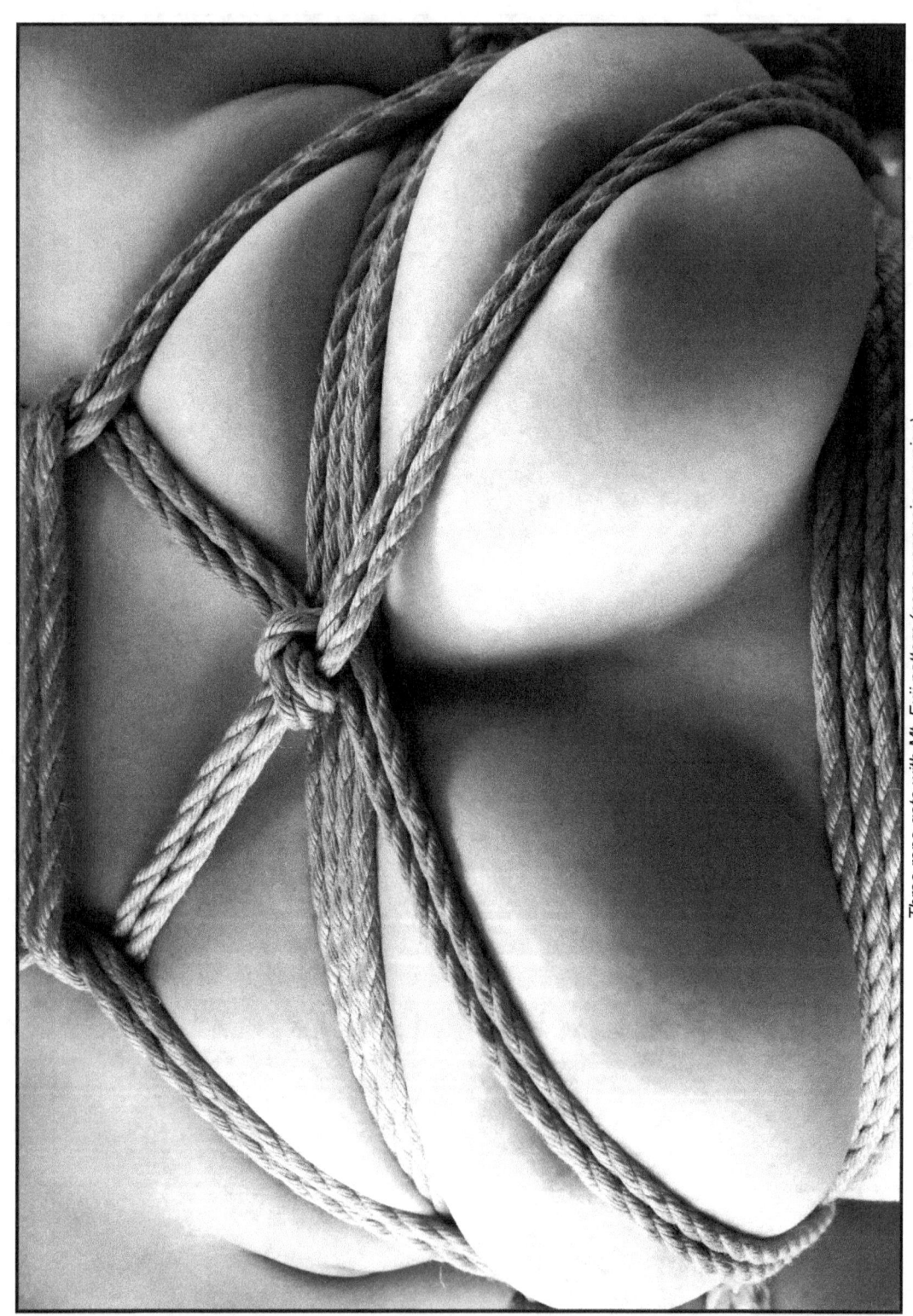

Three rope gote with Mt. Fuji pattern (non-suspension version)
(photo by Michael Helms)

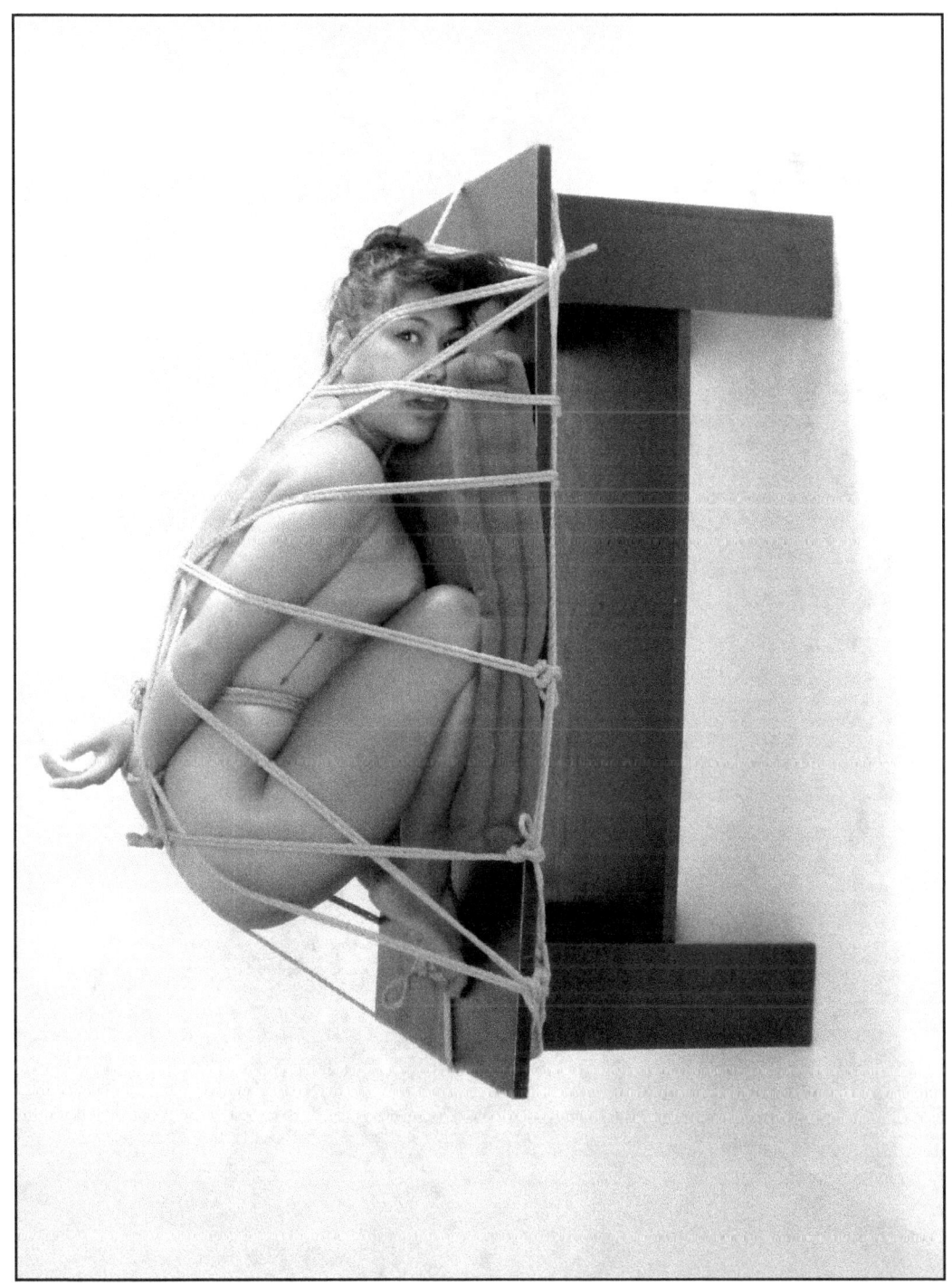

Tsukue shibari #2
(photo by Master "K")

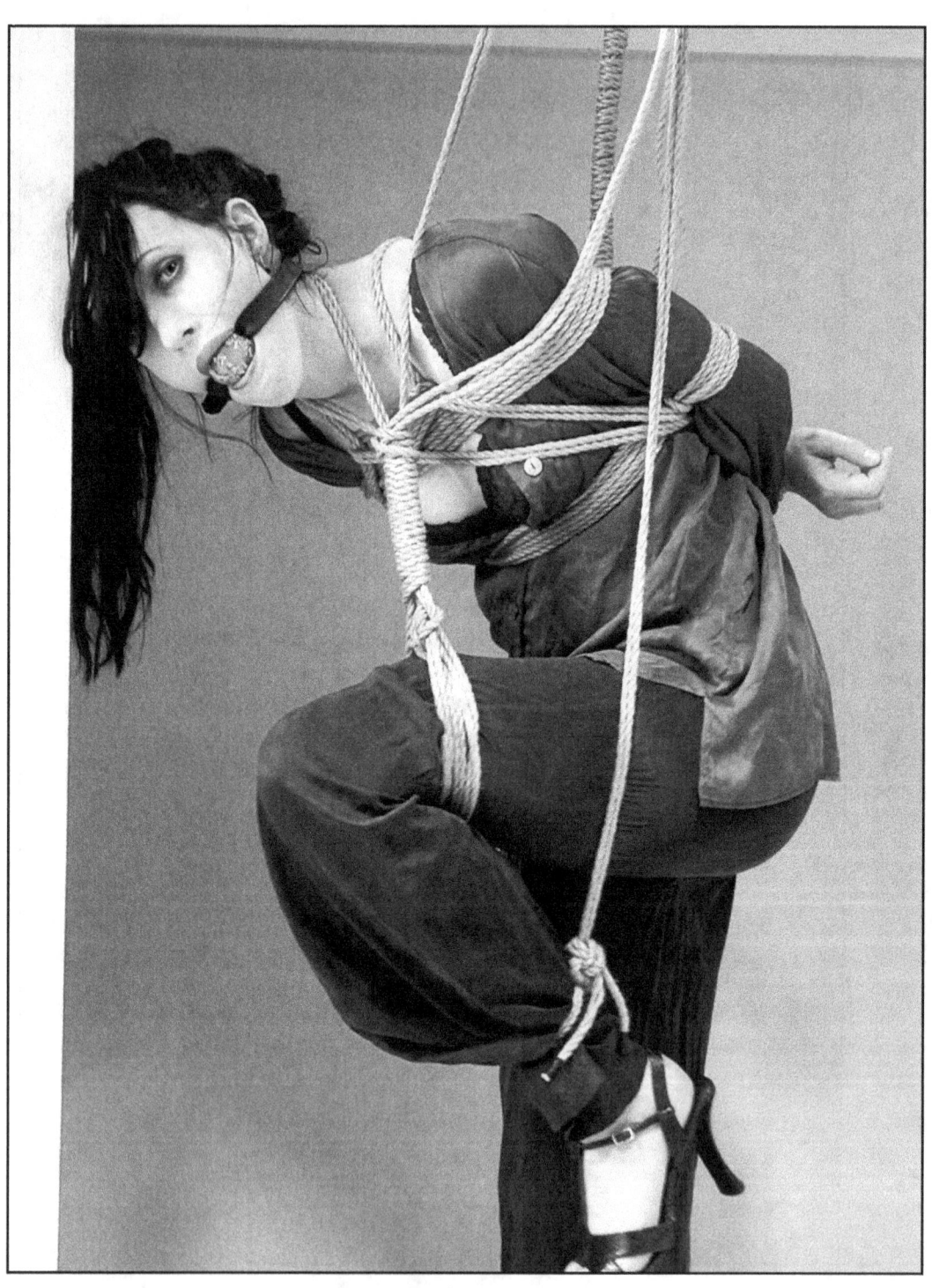

Kata-ashi zuri shibari #3
(photo by Master "K")

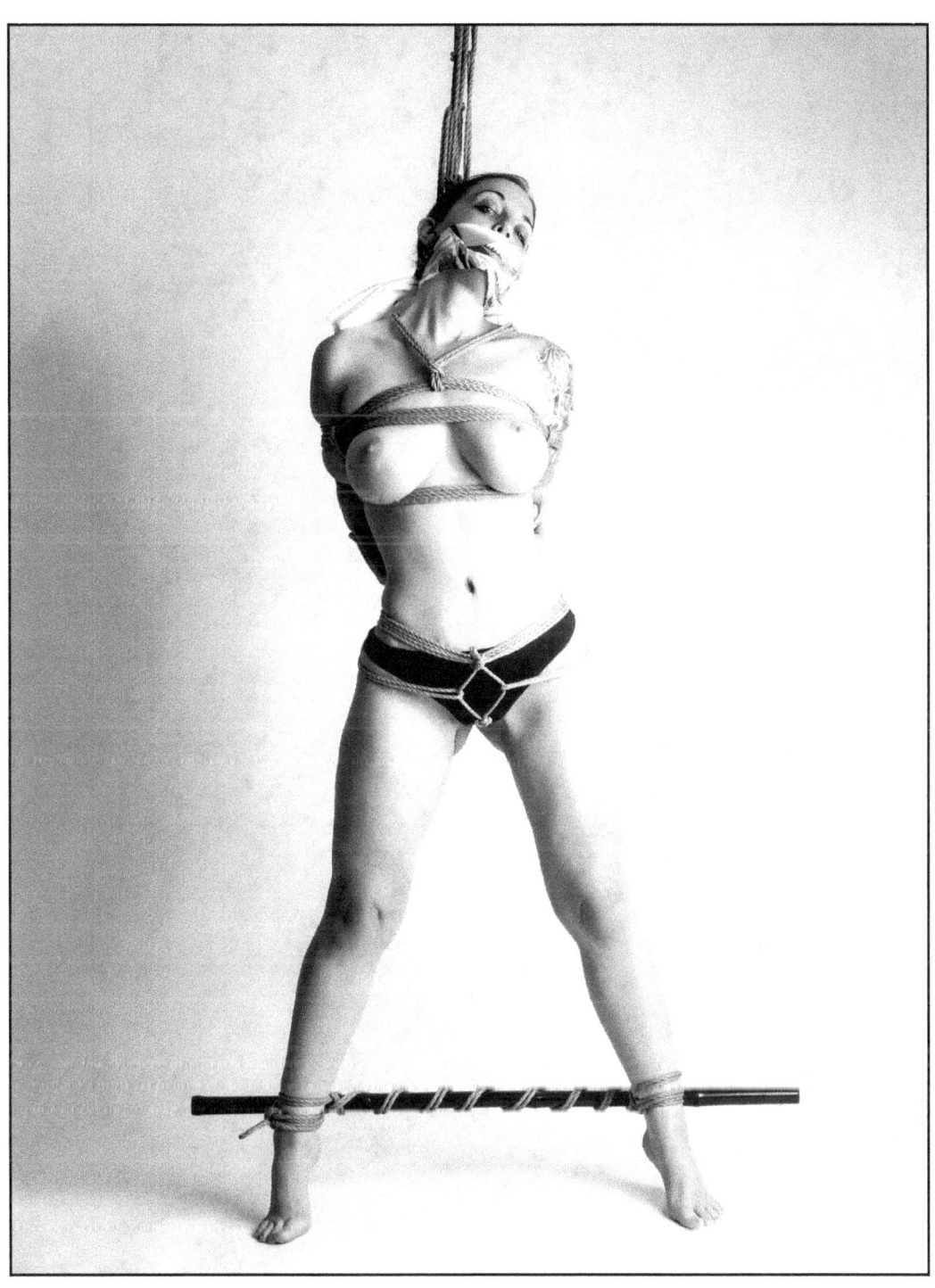

Takenotsue (bamboo) #3
(photo by Zetsu)

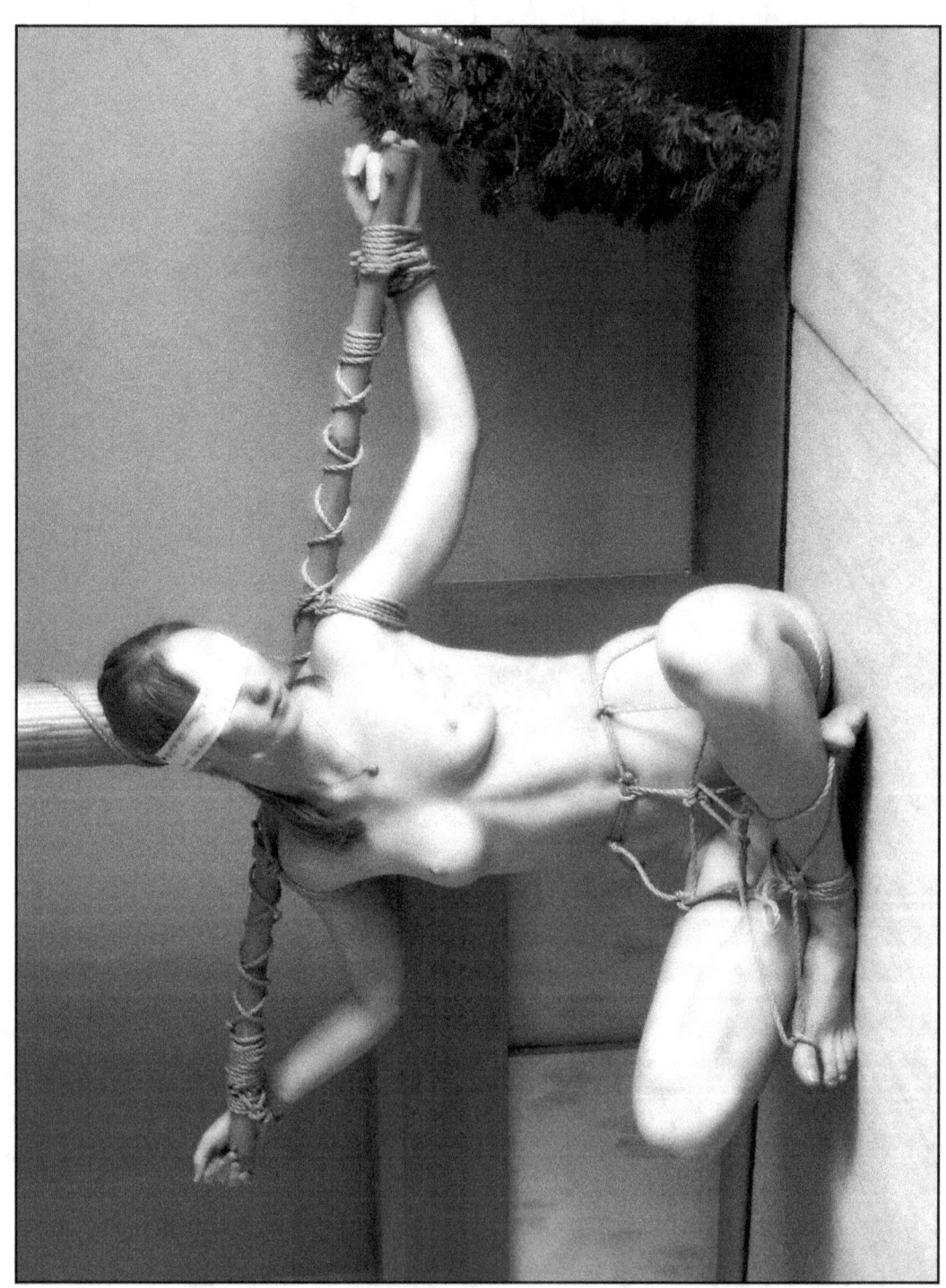

Takenotsue (bamboo) shibari #4
(photo by Master "K")

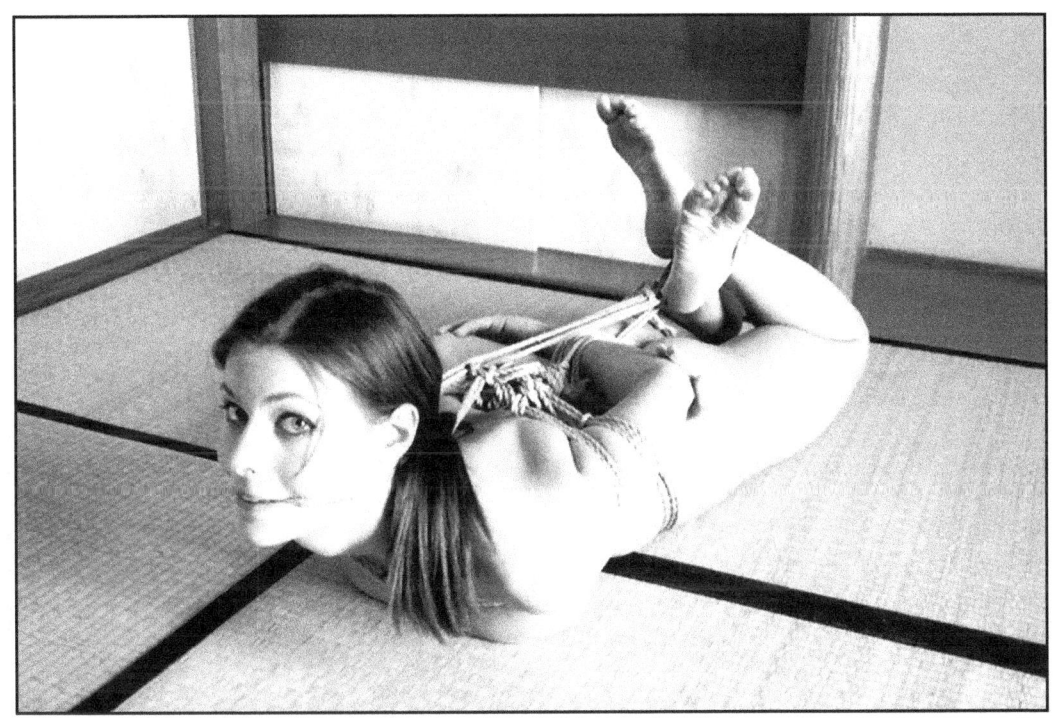

Gyaku-ebi shibari
(photo by Master "K")

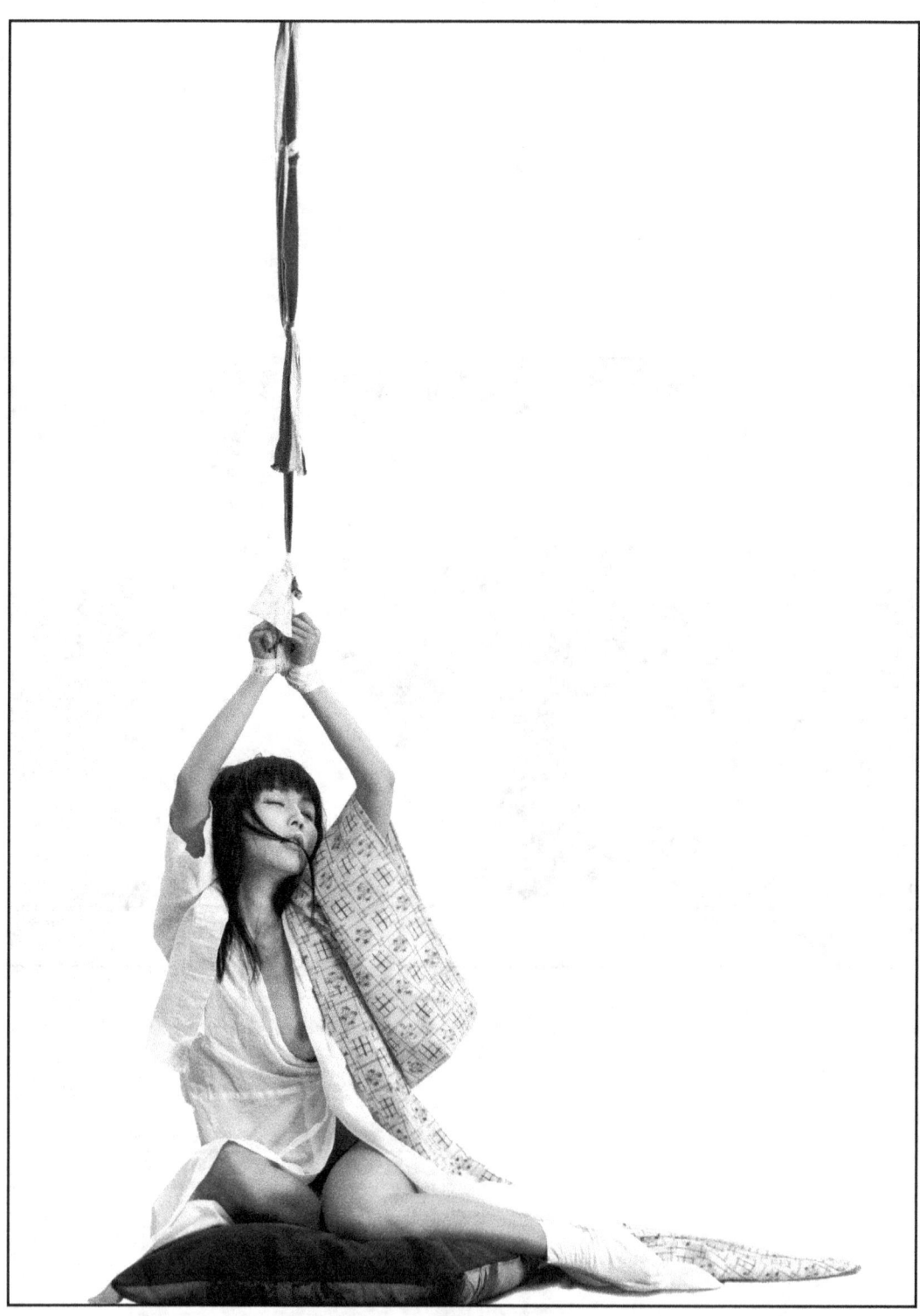

Tejou shibari using kimono cords—Tribute to Urado Hiroshi
(photo by Michael Helms)

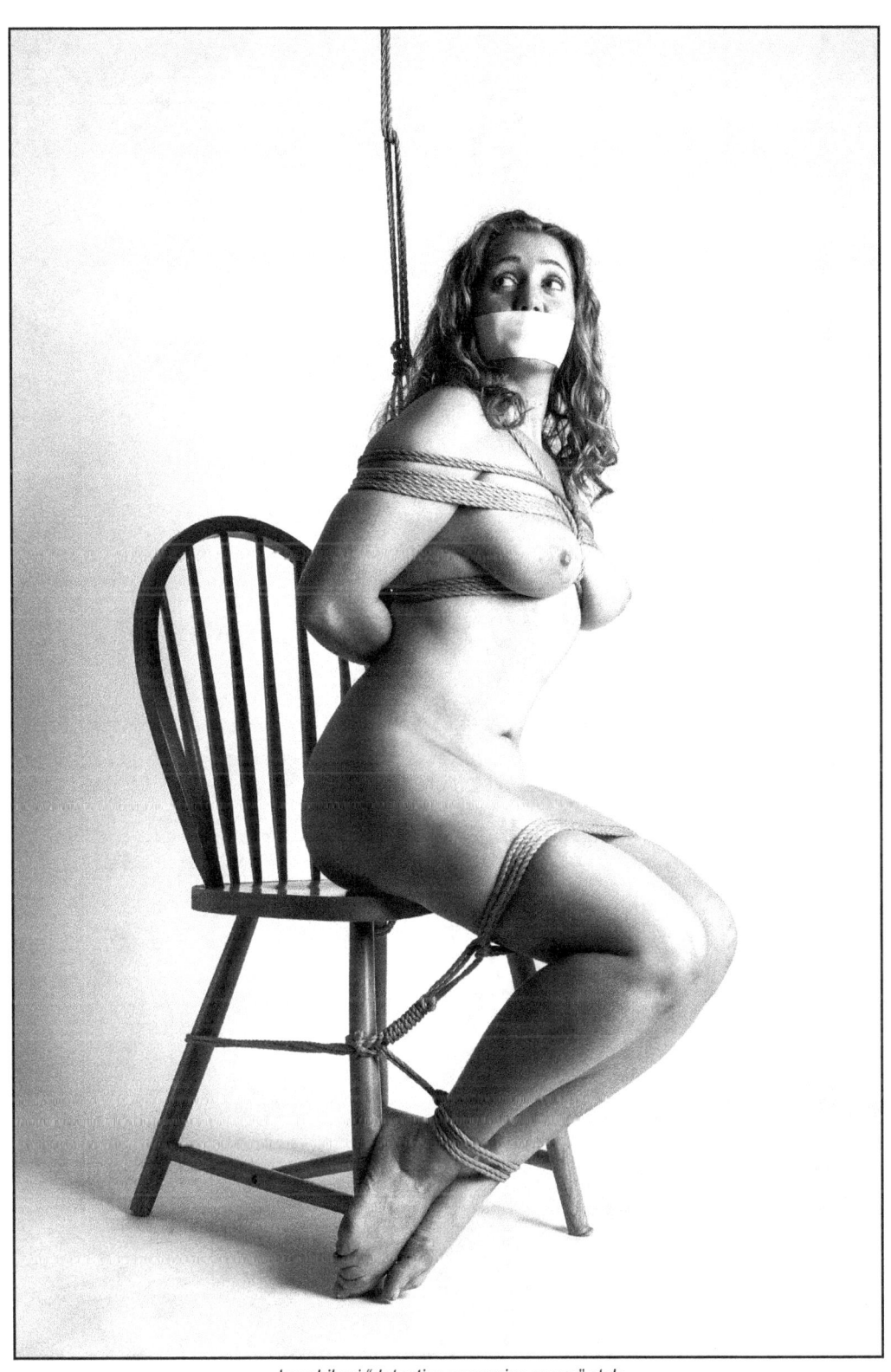

Isu shibari "detective magazine cover" style
(photo by Zetsu)

156

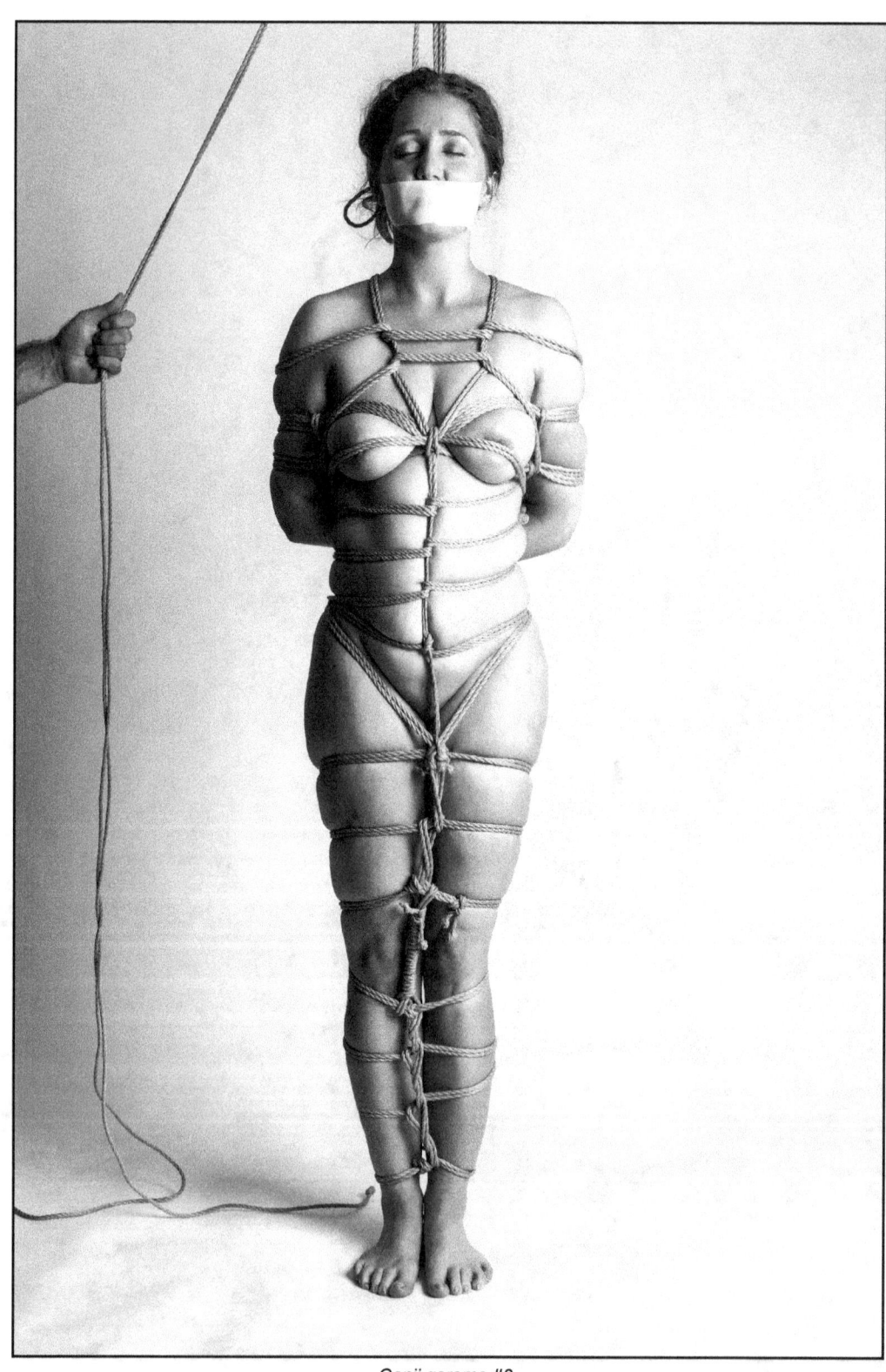

Ganji garame #3
(photo by Zetzu)

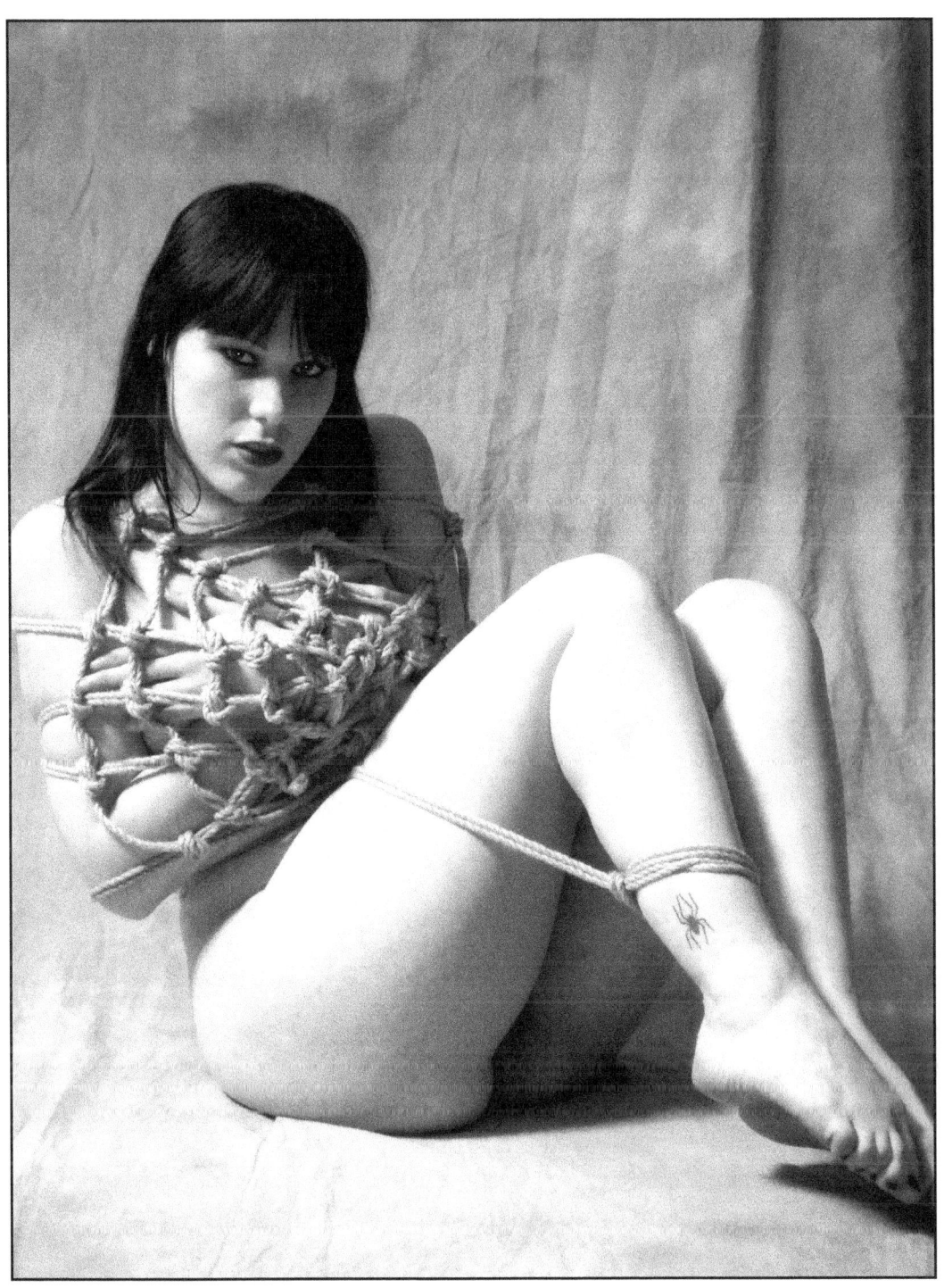

"Along Came a Spider"—Jiai shibari with spider's web overlay
(photo by Master "K")

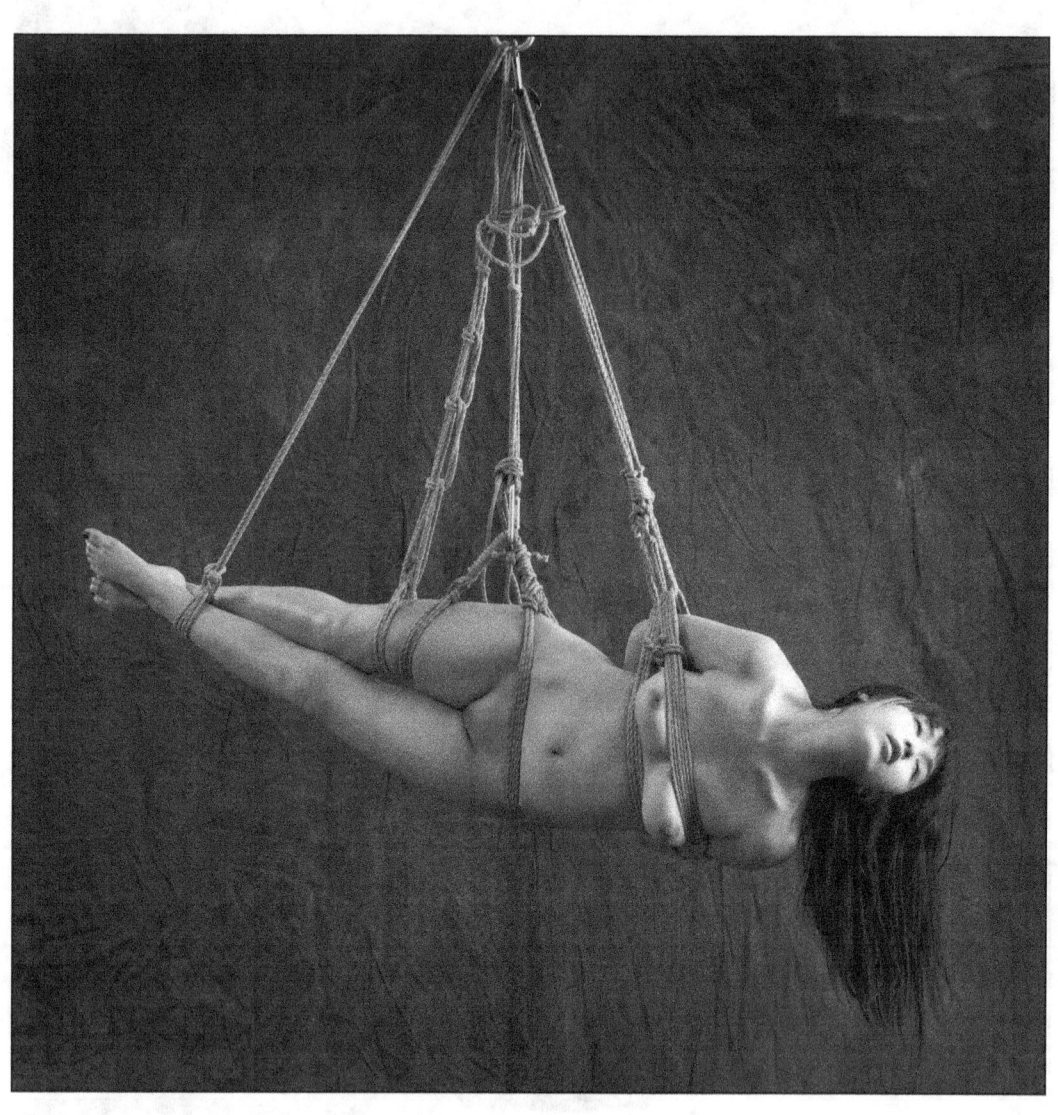

Yoko zuri
(photo by Michael Helms)

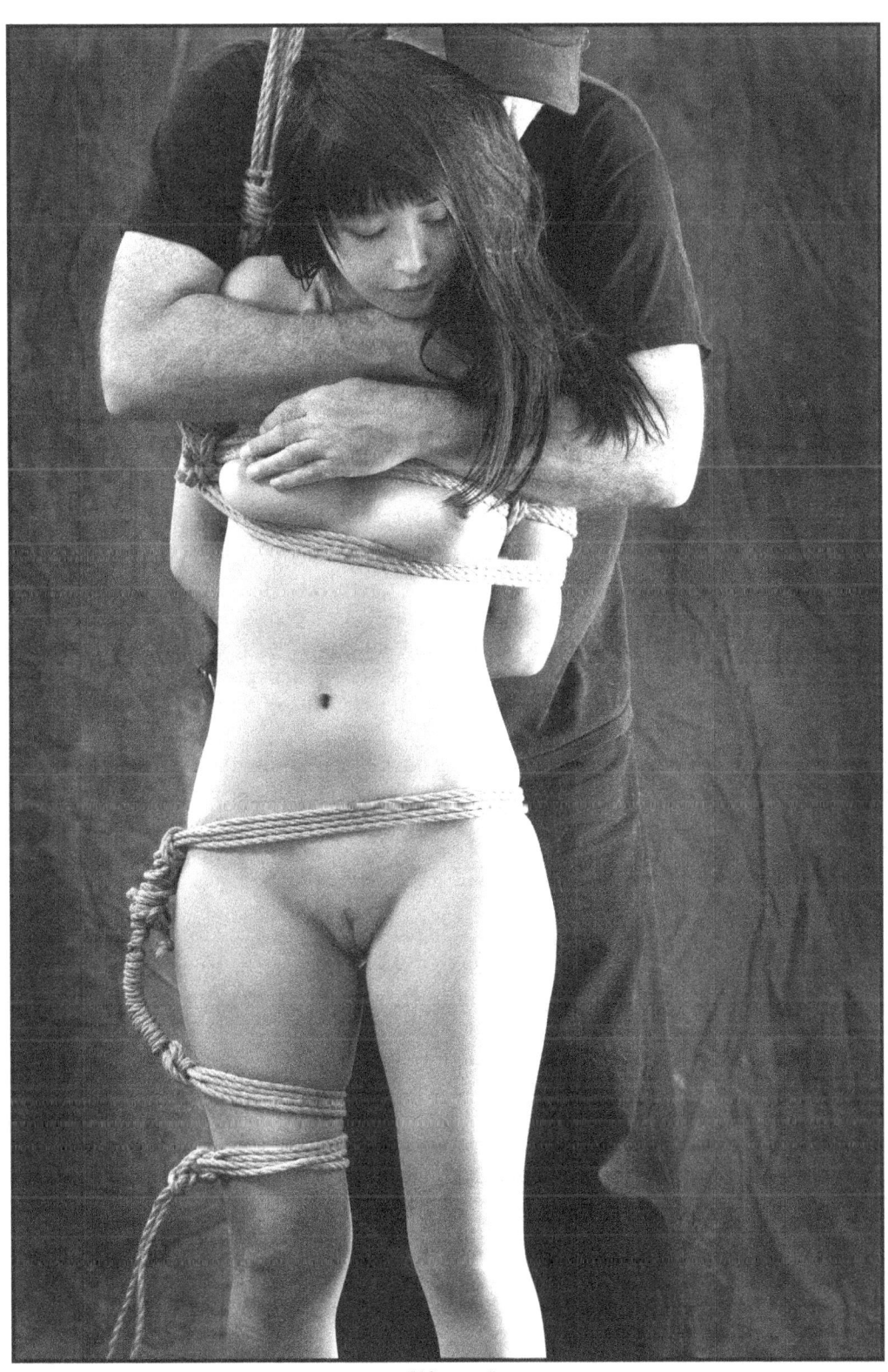

"Aftercare"
(photo by Michael Helms)

What's in a name?
Shibari/Kinbaku Glossary

Some of the most frequently asked questions from correspondents involve the names of various shibari/kinbaku ties. In addition to the understandable desire to put an authentic name to a particular tie, there is often annoyance expressed because certain ties seem to have several names or because the spelling of the name seems to vary widely from source to source. There is no doubt that this element of learning about shibari/kinbaku can be vexing but the reasons for the confusion, once understood, are fairly straightforward.

The first complication arises because the Westerner is usually reading the names of shibari/kinbaku ties in *romaji*, the 19th century system of translating and transcribing the sounds corresponding to the pictographs of Japanese kanji (the Japanese writing system imported from China) into the Latin alphabet. This system, though useful and updated intelligently over the years, still has its imperfections and the attempt to create speak-able words sometimes creates vagaries in spelling. Consequently, different sources will sometimes . . . differ.

The second complication arises because of the way different shibari/kinbaku names have come into use. Some historical names were inherited from the feudal world of the shogun and hojojutsu. Such terms as *hishi, kikkou, ebi* and *tsuri* have long histories dating back hundreds of years. Others, like *imo mushi, kaikyaku kani* and *teppo* are more recent and come from a time when prominent bakushi, like Itoh Seiu and Minomura Kou, were expected to name their own ties just as artists named their paintings or sculptures. As in any language, the names that stuck were accepted and those that weren't faded away and sometimes there were duplications, corruptions and changes over time.

To add to the confusion, certain Western practitioners have made up names that "sound" exotic and slightly Japanese and foisted them on a gullible public. One of the more notorious examples is the use of the word "shinju" or "sinju," usually translated with much pomp and circumstance as "the pearls" and said to mean ties for the female breast. This name was actually coined by a European trying to sound knowledgeable and has never been used in real shibari/kinbaku terminology.

The following list represents 40 years of collecting authentic shibari/kinbaku names and phrases. It is quite detailed and notes most of the approximately 40 basic ties and many of the numerous variations and other terms that make up the shibari/kinbaku lexicon. In short, it isn't perfect but it is fairly complete. As regards spellings, please note that the author uses those spellings that he has been taught or has seen most often in reliable Japanese documents and books. However, each listing usually includes name and spelling variations that appear in the literature from time to time.

Does learning the correct name for all the shibari/kinbaku ties make you an expert? No. However, it is hoped that this list will increase the reader's enjoyment in much the same way that learning the correct names for Italian and French dishes, or any other sophisticated cuisine, increases the pleasure of dining out.

The Glossary:

Agura shibari—Generalized term for any tie where the submissive partner is bound and sits in a crossed legged ("Indian style") position. Sometimes referred to in historical sources as the *Zazen shibari*; taken from the cross legged Zen Buddhist prayer position. Although somewhat similar in appearance, this tie should not be confused with the far more restrictive *Ebi shibari*.

Aomuke zuri (*tsuri*)—Generalized term for any suspension (*tsuri*, see below) where the subject is suspended face up.

Asanawa—Traditional Japanese style bondage rope made of hemp (jute).

Bari—Sometimes the word *shibari* is abbreviated to *"bari"* when describing various ties, as in *Ebi-bari* (see below).

Donawa—The rope (*nawa*) used to support the waist during a *tsuri* (suspension); a waist rope. Because of the danger of injury, this rope is often tied over an *obi* (the stiffened cloth decoratively tied around the kimono wearer's waist) to protect the soft tissue of the abdomen. Without an obi this rope is placed over the upper hips (see *Koshinawa*, below) or only used to support the back with the subject positioned face up, as in the *Aomuke zuri*.

Dorei—A slave. In SM play a term occasionally used to denote a rope captive or partner.

Ebi shibari (or *Ebi-bari*)—The "shrimp" or "prawn" tie where the subject sits cross legged (Indian style) and the upper body is tied close to the ankles in a submissive bow. Originating in the 1500s, it is one of the oldest shibari ties. It was used as a torture technique (*ebizeme*) for hundreds of years and was mandated as an official torture technique/punishment for crimes in 1742 by the rulers of Tokugawa Japan. It is referenced in many historical manuals and art works.

Enchou ude mae te shibari—The "reach forward binding" where the wrists and arms are bound together with one interwoven *nawa* (rope) and extended in front of the body. Commonly abbreviated to *Mae te shibari or Mae te nawa shibari* or *Mae te gassho shibari* (forward prayer tie—Buddhist version).

Futomomo shibari—The classic ankle tied to thigh shibari (often combined with any version of an upper body arm/wrist tie, i.e. *Takate-kote shibari, Tasuki shibari*, etc.). This leg/ankle tie is very old being referenced in some versions of the Shijuhatte, the Japanese version of the Kama Sutra containing 48 sexual positions which arrived in Japan, probably from China, after 550 AD. There are several variations of this tie.

Futomomo zuri—A suspension (*tsuri*) done with the primary attachment being a leg bound in a *futomomo shibari* (see above).

Ganji garame—Generalized term meaning to be completely bound hand and foot; to be immobilized. In shibari/kinbaku various techniques are usually used to create this predicament.

Gōmon shibari—A generalized and somewhat archaic term from Japanese history used to describe shibari/kinbaku ties intended to torment or punish (erotically or otherwise) the bound subject; an aspect of shibari/SM "predicament" play.

Gote shibari—The most common abbreviation for the *Ushirode takate-kote shibari* (see below); the basic box arm tie, the building block of most shibari/kinbaku ties. The arms are tied behind the back and parallel to the ground with the elbows bent at right angles and the hands at mid-back or lower and held in place by ropes that circle above and usually also below the breasts. There are many variations of this tie from the simple to the complex.

Gyaku-ebi shibari—A reverse *ebi*, very similar to the Western hog-tie, where the hands and feet of the submissive are tied together behind the back. There are numerous versions both simple and complex. A very strict position for the very limber!

Gyaku-ebi zuri (tsuri)—The suspension version of the *Gyaku-ebi* (see above) with the subject tied and suspended in mid-air, face to the ground, with the hands/feet/legs tied up and behind as in the conventional hog-tie. One of the more common suspension positions in shibari/kinbaku. Please note: this suspension can be quite dangerous because the bound subject's own weight pressing down against the ropes can sometimes cause nerve compression and loss of sensation in the arms or hands.

Hashira ushirodaki shibari—Literally to "embrace" (*daki*) the pole with the hands tied behind; an abbreviated term for tying someone to an upright wooden post or pole (*hashira*) such as often exits in the traditional Japanese tatami style room. An alternate term would be *Hashira Kousoku* or wooden post/pole "restraint." There are various styles.

Hayanawa—A style of *hojojutsu* (see below) martial arts binding used during Japan's Edo era (1603 -1868). Done with a strong, thin cord also called a hayanawa ("fast rope") or torinawa ("capture rope") and performed at speed, this energetic tying technique was usually accomplished by one police constable in the course of an arrest and while the prisoner was actively resisting.

Hikyaku zuri (tsuri)—The so called "messenger" or "postman's" suspension where the subject is supported by the *takate-kote* or *gote* and the legs are lifted and fixed into a position resembling a runner's stride.

Hishi shibari (sometimes called the Hishigata or Hishi nawa shibari)—The "diamond" (*hishi*) pattern or "water caltrop" tie. Taken from early *hojojutsu* (see below) techniques, this historical and very attractive shibari has several distinct variations but basically creates diamond (*hishi*) shapes (sometimes referred to as "rhombus" or "lozenge" shapes), sometimes with small knots at each of the 4 points, in quite complex patterns of linked quadrangles.

Somewhat similar to the *Kikkou shibari (see below)* and occasionally confused with it, this tie is said to be based on the 4 sided sharp pointed device used by feudal armies to impede mounted pursuers. This, in turn, was based on certain water plants whose pointed structures, fruits or seeds contain spiny burrs. The *hishi* tie pattern is generally done as a restrictive tie with the hands bound behind the back but it can also be done without hand involvement. This tie is one of the loveliest and most distinctive of shibari patterns.

Hojojutsu—The ancient martial art of capturing/arresting with rope; also sometimes referred to as *Nawajutsu*.

Honnawa—A style of hojojutsu binding used to provide secure long-term binding of prisoners in Edo era Japan (1603-1868). This method of tying was used for transportation of prisoners to a place of incarceration and examination, restraint at legal proceedings and, in the case of particularly severe crimes, for the public display of the prisoner prior to execution. During the Edo era the complex honnawa rope patterns created on prisoner's backs were often used to define the prisoner's social status, crime and punishment. This style of tying is an ancestor to modern shibari/kinbaku.

houchi—verb; to leave as is, leave to chance, leave alone, neglect. In Japanese shibari/SM play this term is used to describe leaving the bound submissive well tied to appreciate the tie and/or his/her predicament; a type of psychological SM play requiring great caution and constant discreet surveillance for safety.

Imo Mushi shibari—The "green caterpillar" tie. An asymmetrical shibari, probably from the Showa era (1926-1989) of Japan, where the subject is bound with the hands tied behind the back and the legs entwined around each other and tied so that the ankle of one leg is tied to the thigh of the other and the ankle of the second leg is (usually) pulled up and behind the back, as in the *Gyaku-ebi* (hog-tie) and bound to the hands. Another position for the very limber!

Ippon nawa—Literally, one piece of rope. In shibari/kinbaku this term means a tie done using one rope only. Note: in Japanese you have a multitude of "counters." "Pon" is used to count round shaped objects like bottles, trees and also pieces of rope. Two ropes would be "nihon nawa."

Isu shibari—A generalized term for any shibari/kinbaku tie where the subject is bound to a chair.

Iwato-nawa shibari—One of the most interesting archaic shibari/kinbaku terms in that it references the Japanese creation myth of the sun goddess Amaterasu who once went into hiding in a cave near a place called Iwato, throwing Japan (and the world) into darkness. In order to tempt her out again, a young girl was compelled to dance naked at the entrance to the cave. When Amaterasu stepped out to look, the cave entrance was blocked behind her and sunlight returned to the world. In shibari/kinbaku this term refers to any tie where the subject's legs are pulled wide apart with ropes at the ankles and/or thighs, exposing the groin/genital area, while the upper torso is also bound. The author leaves the symbolism to the reader's imagination.

Jiai shibari—The "self-embracing" tie; so called because the arms of the subject are crossed in front of the body then bent up at the elbow and secured with each hand placed on top or close to the opposing shoulder so that the bound subject appears to be embracing themselves.

Jōshiki—The Japanese term for the "universal common sense" that all intelligent people are supposed to possess; a useful word to remember when practicing any type of shibari/kinbaku.

Kaikyaku kani shibari—The "spread-legged crab" tie; an erotic position where the subject's wrists and upper arms are bound to the upper ankles and thighs of their respective spread legs. In a well constructed version of this tie the legs are then secured to separate support points to further spread the legs and immobilize the subject.

Kami shibari—Generalized term for a hair tie. That is, a tie where the (preferably long) hair of the submissive is bound with rope. Sometimes this tie is incorporated into other shibari positions.

Kannuki—noun; a "gate bar," that piece of metal or wood put across a gate to keep it from being opened. In shibari/kinbaku it is a generalized term for the various cinching ropes used to tighten the wrapped nawa at the breasts, legs, ankles, wrists, etc. Also known as the *shibori-nawa* ("squeezing rope") or *tome nawa* ("stop rope").

Kariudo shibari – The "hunter's" tie; so called because the arms when bound resemble a rifle (or bow, spear) put over the subject's back. This is an asymmetrical tie with one arm bent over the shoulder and bound to the second arm which is tied behind the back and bent up from the waist. This historical shibari is also referred to as the *Teppo shibari* or "gun tie."

Kata-ashi Sakasa zuri (tsuri)—The single legged version of the classic, dramatic and dangerous, head down inverted suspension (see *Sakasa zuri*).

Kata-ashi zuri (tsuri) shibari—Any of a number of styles of one leg up lift ties with, traditionally, the subject balanced gracefully on one leg while the other is pulled up to a support point. Alternatively, the bound subject can be positioned lying down with one leg lifted.

Kata karada bagu—A generalized term (sometimes abbreviated to *Kata* or *Karada*) for any of a variety of rope body harnesses both decorative and restrictive. The term *kata* is used in kabuki theater and refers to the "form" or "pattern" of acting, make-up, scenery, music, etc., handed down over generations but changeable according to a skilled performers taste. Please note: the origins of this useful term as applied to shibari/kinbaku are obscure and it is seldom encountered in Japanese kinbaku literature.

Kikkou shibari—The famous "tortoise shell" tie, so called because the pattern created resembles that found on the Japanese tortoise. This can be a full body tie or used only on the torso. There are two styles of *Kikkou shibari* taught, each descended from different hojojutsu schools.

The more traditional style creates one or more *hexagonal* (six sided) shapes on the bound subject. An alternative and archaic name for this famous six sided style is *Nyugarame*, supposedly taken from the Rokugi ryu (school) of hojojutsu dating from the Tenmei years in Japan (1781-1788).

A second style of *Kikkou shibari*, also valid, appears to originate from a *honnawa* (see above) tie done by the Taisho ryu of feudal hojojutsu. It has been popularized in manga illustrations and taught by some *bakushi*. This version creates at least two or three diamond (*hishi*) shapes running from the neck to the pubic area. However, in modern practice this style is more properly called the *Hishi shibari* (see above).

Kinbaku—the art of traditional Japanese erotic bondage.

Kinbaku-bi—Usually translated as "the beauty of traditional shibari art." That is, shibari done in the traditional manner for an aesthetic/erotic effect.

Kinbakushi—A term meaning "rope artist," the one who ties; often abbreviated to *Bakushi*. See also *Nawashi* (below).

Koshinawa—The rope (*nawa*) used to support the hips during any suspension (*tsuri*), i.e., a hip rope. This term was/is also used in the martial art hojojutsu to describe the leash/rope tied around a prisoner's waist to control movement and discourage flight.

Koutoubu ryo-tekubi shibari—Upper body tie where the hands are bound together *(ryo-tekubi)* behind the head *(koutoubu)* and then affixed to the chest harness created from the same length of rope. Note: this tie is also sometimes known as the *Koutouryoute shibari* or *Hiji-takate shibari*.

Kuzushi nawa—A term used to describe a kinbaku tie whose design is "calculatedly unstudied," that is, deliberately and artfully unsymmetrical. This term is taken from Japanese calligraphy and art and used to describe, for instance, the deliberately misshapen but exquisitely beautiful pottery sometimes used in the "tea ceremony."

Maai—Distance or distance between opponents. This is the Sino-Japanese concept of "distance to the other" which is primarily encountered in martial arts like Kendo or Judo. In the Newaza style of shibari/kinbaku (see below) it is used to refer to the closeness or distance between the one tying and the one being tied in both a psychological and a physical sense.

Mae te nawa shibari—Common abbreviation of *Enchou Ude Mae te shibari* (see above); the "reach forward binding" where the wrists and arms are bound together with one interwoven *nawa* (rope) and extended in front of the body.

M-ji-kaikyaku shibari—An ankle tied to thigh shibari connected to any version of an upper body arm/wrist tie (i.e. *Gote shibari*, *Tasuki shibari*) etc. which causes leg immobility and the seated, bound subject to resemble the letter "M." There are several versions of this tie.

M-ji-kaikyaku zuri (tsuri)—A suspension where the subject is supported by the *Takate-kote or Gote* and the thighs, with the thighs individually pulled up and spread out *in front* of the body causing it to resemble the letter "M"; sometimes simply called the *Ryo-ashi zuri* or the *Kaikyaku zuri*.

m-jo—This is the most widely accepted term in Japan for the one captured in rope, the "rope submissive." However, most rope captives/submissives (especially those who pose for photographs) think of themselves simply as "models."

m-o—Male version of a m-jo.

Matanawa—Generalized term for any pubic area tie or "crotch rope"; sometimes referred to in older shibari/kinbaku literature as the *tatenawa*.

Momo shibari—The "peach" tie; a distinctly sexual tie which balances the subject on their knees and upper torso, causing the posterior to be lifted. The hands are bound in front then drawn underneath the body between the spread legs and attached to the ankles. When completed this tie is quite similar in effect to several of the classic erotic positions of the Shijuhatte, the Japanese version of the Kama Sutra.

Mudanawa—A term meaning "useless rope" and used by shibari artists/masters to describe any *nawa* (rope) used for purely ornamental or aesthetic, as opposed to functional, effect.

Mune hishi gote shibari—An inventive upper body pattern that begins as a *Tasuki shibari* (see below) but then elegantly transforms into a *Takate-gote or gote shibari* with a diamond (*hishi*) decorative element.

Nawashi—Actually this means "a maker of rope" but in SM circles it can mean a "rope artist"; a more modern term (late twentieth century) for the shibari master. See also *Kinbakushi* (above).

Newaza—Floor techniques. Taken from martial arts such as *judo*, this useful term is used to describe shibari/kinbaku ties done principally on the tatami mat, as opposed to techniques used for suspensions (*tsuri*). This style of shibari/kinbaku was made famous by the renowned bakushi Yukimura Haruki and, in the right hands, can be very sensuous and erotic.

Ninoude shibari—An archaic name for the shibari/kinbaku tie where the hands and upper arms are bound behind the back with the rope intertwined *only* between the wrists and upper arms. All cords remain behind the back *without* passing fully around the body; also known in modern practice as the *Jouwan gote shibari* and the *Ude kake gote shibari*.

Oujou shibari—A classic example of *shuuchi* (embarrassment) style shibari/kinbaku where the bound subject is tied to the *hashira* (wooden support pole) of the tatami room *while kneeling* and with the ankles crossed and bound, causing the legs to be spread.

Ryo-ashi zuri (tsuri)—Any suspension where both (*ryo*) legs (*ashi*) are tied and suspended together. Depending on the *kinbaku* source referenced, there are several styles of *tsuri* (suspension) where this technique is used.

Ryo-tekubi shibari—This is the simple wrists (*tekubi*) together (*ryo*), in front of the body, tie. Depending on the complexity of the binding technique used, this tie is sometimes called the *Tejou shibari* (or handcuff tie) and has it's origins in the martial art *hojojutsu* (see above).

Sabaki—from the verb, *sabaku* (to handle). Generalized term for the different techniques used by various rope masters (*nawashi, bakushi*) to wind, coil or handle their ropes prior to or during use or storage.

Sakasa zuri (tsuri)—Inverted suspension. The subject is hung upside down by the legs/feet only—very dangerous.

Santen zuri (tsuri)—The subject is suspended by the *takate-kote* or *gote* upper body tie and the ankles, with the ankles and/or legs pulled up *in front* of the body. The word "*santen*" means mountain top or summit and in this *tsuri* the bound subject supposedly resembles the shape of a mountain range's peaks.

Sarugutsuwa—The traditional word for "gag" used in *kinbaku*. The English word "gag" is also used in Japan and translated/pronounced as "*gyaggu*" but this is a recent introduction. The standard *sarugutsuwa* is a cloth tied through/across the mouth with the material being a woven cotton trade cloth or *tenugui,* which has many purposes from cleaning to cooking to bathing to dress.

Seme—(n.) to persecute, blame or torment.

Seme-e—Art depicting torment or torture.

Shibari—(v.) to tie up, the action of tying; (n.) Japanese style bondage.

Shikominawa—A term used to describe the secure support rope that is often used when doing suspensions (*tsuri*) in shibari/kinbaku play or performance. To this "preparatory" rope (or ropes) metal carabineers are sometimes attached to which the suspension ropes themselves are then strung or the suspension ropes (*tsuri nawa*) are attached directly. The construction of the *shikominawa* must be carefully and precisely executed in order to provide strong and stable support. There are several standard design patterns for this construction. This support rope is also sometimes known as the *tsuri shiro*, which literally translates as "suspension castle" or "fort."

Shuuchi shibari—A generalized and somewhat archaic term used to describe shibari/kinbaku ties intended to "make shy" or embarrass the bound subject, an aspect of shibari/SM psychological play; sometimes written as *shuuchinawa*.

Suruga-doi shibari—As much 16th-century Tokugawa torture technique as straightforward shibari, this tie causes the wrists and ankles to be bound very closely together behind the subject's back and then pulled up to a support thus causing the submissive to rest on his/her pelvis. This tie differs from the *gyaku-ebi* (see above) in that it is much more stringent. It is said that in feudal Japan prisoners were sometimes suspended using this tie and even had weights applied to their backs for further discomfort. It is named after the ancient Suruga province, now an area that is part of the Shizuoka prefecture which is located in the center of Japan, near the Pacific Ocean and home to Mt. Fuji. A tie *exclusively* for the fit and very limber who enjoy a serious challenge.

Takate-kote shibari—See *Ushirode takate-kote* (gote) *shibari* (below).

Takenotsue or Takezao shibari—Tying someone using a bamboo rod, stick or pole. There are many different versions of this style of shibari which has a long history dating from feudal Japan.

Tanuki shibari—Named after the "raccoon dog" or badger-like animal of Japan and source of many Japanese legends and folk tales. This tie is so called because the hands and feet are tied close together in front of the subject and then the subject is sometimes suspended from a support point (either completely in the air or resting on their back with just the legs/feet pulled up) in the manner of a four legged game animal after the hunt. This tie has a history dating to at least the early 1600s when it was called the *Buri buri zeme* (torture) and reportedly was used to punish disobedient prostitutes in Edo's famed Yoshiwara pleasure district.

Tasuki shibari—Standard abbreviation for *Ushirode tasuki shibari* (see below); an upper body tie where the rope (*nawa*) binding the wrists/arms behind the back comes over each shoulder and crisscrosses *between* the breasts.

Tawara shibari -The "straw bag" binding. So called because it resembles the way sheaves of rice straw were/are bound by farmers in the field. The upper torso is looped horizontally with *nawa* several times above and below the breasts with the hands tied separately to the legs just below the buttocks. Often the legs are then tied together with more horizontal loops (after the upper torso is safely secured to an overhead support) and then all the loops are connected with several vertical strands to make the distinctive sheave pattern.

Teinei shibari – Literally, "courteous shibari/kinbaku"; a style of shibari/kinbaku where the person doing the tying is polite and careful when working with their submissive partner. Recommended at all times and especially so when tying someone for the first time.

Tejou shibari—Handcuff tie, see Ryo-tekubi shibari (above).

Tengu shibari -The "demon" tie; so called because the bound subject's arm position resembles classic Japanese illustrations depicting the wings of mythological demons. In this shibari each wrist is bound to the respective upper arm and then each arm is pulled slightly back and bound to a, usually, decorative upper body harness (*kata karada*) creating the look of "demon wings."

Teppo shibari – The "gun" or "hunter's" tie (see also *Kariudo shibari* above); so called because the arms when bound resemble a rifle (or bow, spear) put over the subject's back. This is an asymmetrical tie with one arm bent over the shoulder and bound to the second arm which is tied behind the back and bent up from the waist.

Tomoe-tome -The "comma" stop or twist, so called because the shape created resembles that of a comma. This very useful and attractive technique is employed by some *bakushi* to affect changes in the direction of a rope being used to create a shibari/kinbaku pattern without the use of knots, as in the days of Edo era *hojojutsu* (see above).

Tsugi nawa—Patched rope. The technique by which two lengths of *nawa* (rope) used for shibari/kinbaku are joined together to create one continuous double length cord. This is a useful technique when executing some of the more complicated shibari/kinbaku patterns and/or ties and is often used in shibari/kinbaku stage performances.

Tsuka maki—The "sword hilt" wrap or finish. The tightly twisted wrap used to complete several classic shibari/kinbaku ties. It uses up the end of the rope (*nawajiri*) and imparts added strength to that section of the tie.

Tsukue shibari—Generalized term for any shibari where the subject is tied to the (usually) low table found in the traditional tatami suite; especially one that utilizes the table's legs as a binding point.

Tsuri—Any rope suspension. The subject is bound and supported in mid-air from a secure suspension point. The second classic torture technique (*tsurizeme*) from Tokugawa Japan now evolved into a mainstay of shibari play and SM club performance. There are many different types of *tsuri* but all suspensions must be done with great care and skill; sometimes abbreviated to *zuri* (see below).

Tsuri nawa—The main rope *(nawa)* used to support a suspension *(tsuri)*.

Ushirode-gassho shibari—A tie usually referred to in English as the "reverse prayer tie" where the hands/arms are tied behind the back in a fixed position resembling that used during prayer. This tie is also only for the limber! There are Buddhist *and* Christian variations. Note: this tie is sometimes called the *Haimen gassho shibari* or, literally, "back-side prayer tie" or, for the Buddhist variation, the *Hiji-gatame shibari*.

Ushirode-kote zuri (tsuri) shibari—Generalized/abbreviated term for suspending a subject with his/her hands and arms immobilized *and* lifted by the *Takate-kote* or *Gote shibari*. This is one of the oldest suspension (*tsuri*) torture techniques from feudal Japan and mentioned in many histories.

Ushirode takate-kote (gote) *shibari*—The basic box arm tie; the building block of many shibari/kinbaku ties. The arms are tied behind the back and parallel to the ground with the elbows bent at right angles and held in place by ropes that circle above and below the breasts. There are many variations of this tie from the simple to the complex.

Because this tie has been referenced in so many historical sources over the years, it has been known by a variety of names and written using several romaji spellings. For instance, the name is sometimes simplified to *Takate-kote* or *Takate shibari* or, even more simply, to *Go-te*, *Kote* or, more commonly in the modern era, *Gote shibari* and sometimes written as *Ushirotakategote*.

The main reason for this variety is that, as with the *Kikkou shibari* (see above), there are two different schools of thought on this famous tie. One tradition is defined above but another insists that the term *Taka te kote* be used only for ties where the hands are crossed high (*taka*) up on the back; a difficult position for most rope submissives to achieve. For ties that utilize the basic box shape but with the arms bent and hands generally tied parallel to the ground or lower, this second school of thought favors the term *Go-te*, *Gote* or *Kote shibari*.

Ushirode tasuki shibari—An upper body tie or harness where the rope (*nawa*) binding the wrists/arms behind the back comes over each shoulder and crisscrosses *between* the breasts, as opposed to the usual *Ushirode takate-kote* or *Gote* shibari pattern (see above). This term is taken from the name of the cord used to tuck up the sleeves of a kimono and the binding pattern used to achieve this. Sometimes simplified to *Tasuki shibari*.

Ushirotakategote Isuyō-m-ji kaikyaku shibari—A long name to describe the traditional Japanese "chair tie" where the subject is seated upon a chair (*isu*) with their hands/arms bound in an *Ushirode takate-kote* or *Gote* (see above) and their legs/feet are pulled up, spread and tied to the two arms (or sides) of the chair so that the subject, sitting upright, resembles the letter "M."

Utsubuse zuri (tsuri)—Any face down suspension (*tsuri*) with the subject tied facing the ground.

Vincilagnia—erotic arousal from bondage; from the Latin *vincio* to bind or fetter and *lagneia*, lust. This is the only non Japanese word in this Glossary.

Yoko zuri (tsuri)—Any sideways suspension (*tsuri*) with the subject tied parallel to the ground.

Yukata shibari—Tying someone in any shibari style who is wearing the light, informal, summer kimono (*yukata*); a classic piece of wardrobe for traditional shibari/kinbaku art photography.

Zuri—Alternate spelling/abbreviation for *tsuri* (suspension). This spelling is used when the term *tsuri* is preceded by another word indicating the type of suspension being done, i.e., *Gyaku-ebi zuri*.

How to do Kinbaku—a brief guide for beginners

When my publisher asked that I include a short section of shibari/kinbaku tutorials in this book I was initially reluctant. Although an obvious request for a book that is trying to be a thorough guide on its subject, it gave me pause because my many years as a teacher have shown me how complex a subject shibari/kinbaku is to teach. The truth is I prefer to teach face to face, one on one, and generally avoid group lecture situations. The reason is simply that I want to look my students in their eyes and know they understand. When teaching an erotic art descended from a martial art, is anything less advisable?

Therefore, for the reader seriously interested in learning the techniques of shibari/kinbaku my first piece of advice is to try to find a competent teacher to guide you. Lessons are usually not that expensive and a good teacher will not only be able to give you good instruction on the basics *based on your specific needs and interests* but make it more enjoyable, too. My own tutorials offer technique, art and history and I know other instructors that offer similar lessons.

Failing that, the next best options are the DVD and video "how-to's" mentioned in this book. Several of the finest shibari/kinbaku masters (Yukimura Haruki, Osada Steve, Arisue Go, Randa Mai, Nureki Chimuo, etc.) have put out excellent programs over the years and many are fairly easy to find and most are relatively easy to follow.

If the video route isn't possible then books are the last best option and several good ones are available. In addition to Randa Mai's texts from the late 1990's, Arisue Go has recently released several useful "how to" books from Sanwa publishers. The problem with books that purport to teach specific rope or bondage techniques is that they require close attention to learn from and it's often easy to be confused. When using a book be prepared to go slowly and, if something doesn't seem to make sense, give it plenty of thought before proceeding.

In the spirit of completeness I must also add that the two WORST ways to try to learn the techniques of shibari/kinbaku are by trying to copy still pictures (in books or off the Internet) or by trying to copy pornographic video material. This should be obvious but I've been amazed by how many times I've been asked my opinion of these dubious resources. For the record, trying to copy Internet stills is foolish because one can see so little of the shibari/kinbaku pattern. After all, only one side of the model is usually shown! And aping pornography is even worse since many programs are faked, producers of such material sometimes care little or know little about safe, sophisticated, techniques and most scenes of "bondage" in these "adult" videos usually don't focus on the bondage long enough to learn from.

And then there are the "how to" web videos that pop up constantly on the Internet. While some of these ephemeral tutorials are nicely done by expert people, my advice here would be to go slowly. Research carefully who is offering the Internet content under consideration and look to see what other viewers have said about them, their skills and the tutorial in question. In short, approach streaming "how to's" with caution and, remember, always use **joshiki** ("common sense").

With all of the above as an introduction, in the following chapter I offer two relatively easy to do, "beginner" ties for the *novice*. There are many versions of these patterns but over the years the simple methods I demonstrate here are the easiest I've found for the person new to rope to understand and follow. They also help the student understand some important Kinbaku construction principles.

The Basics:

1. Safety.

It goes without saying that safety is of paramount importance when engaging in any tying or other sadomasochistic activity. Over the years many intelligent precautions and procedures have evolved to increase the safety and enjoyment of SM "scenes." Some important ones include:

Know your partner's physical/psychological limitations (injuries, ailments, psychological mind set) well before beginning any activity.

Establish good communication with your partner before you begin tying so any difficulties that arise during a scene can be quickly and efficiently dealt with.

Be sure any equipment you intend using is in top working order.

Throughout the scene, maintain constant checks on the subject being tied by monitoring breathing, circulation and comfort.

Never leave your tied partner alone.

Never indulge in alcohol or any other stimulants while engaging in a scene.

Establish a code word to end a scene immediately and without question.

Prepare appropriate and comforting aftercare upon conclusion of a scene.

There are numerous others and this author assumes the reader to be familiar with these important basic aspects of safe and responsible sadomasochistic play.

2. Common sense.

In addition to the above, it's also important to bear in mind **joshiki**. This is the Japanese concept of "universal common sense" or knowledge that all reasonable people are supposed to possess. In short, be aware of what you're doing whenever it comes to rope play and if something seems questionable don't do it until it has been thought out thoroughly.

Shibari/Kinbaku—Basic Philosophy, Practice, Materials and Eroticism:

1. Philosophy.

It must always be remembered that the general intent of shibari/kinbaku is to provide pleasant erotic restraint of/for a beloved partner in a safe, stimulating, and artistically attractive way.

That said, it also must never be forgotten that one of the chief ancestors of shibari/kinbaku was hojojutsu, the capturing and tying martial art of feudal Japan. This was/is a serious martial art intended to restrain dangerous opponents and was never intended as either a gentle or a safety conscious activity.

This transformation from the dangerous to the erotic was accomplished over many years by the careful re-working of ties and tie patterns. Therefore, a solid understanding of the underlying principals of each tie's construction is vital.

Question:

"If my tie basically looks right aren't I doing shibari?"

Unfortunately, no. What makes a tie authentic is the careful and safe construction of the basic tie and not the general "look" of the finished product. This is consistent with the Japanese martial art concept of the difference between **omote waza** ("overt techniques") and **ura waza** ("hidden techniques") when learning a martial art. In shibari/kinbaku, as in most Japanese martial arts, there is the surface that is obvious (the "look") and then there is the hidden technique (the "construction") of creating the tie or pattern. Although the basic "hidden techniques" are not necessarily complex or difficult to learn, these basics must be executed properly in order for a shibari/kinbaku tie to be considered both safe and "authentic."

2. Practice.

In hojojutsu, rope tied around the neck was/is used as a basic method in creating the various ties. In addition, the brachial nerve bundle running down the arms to the hands was often tightly bound with one thin cord in order to constrict the nerves, cause numbness and so incapacitate the opponent. Clearly, these are both very dangerous techniques that could cause serious injury or even death.

This is why in shibari/kinbaku other methods were devised to *eliminate* these dangerous hojojutsu techniques. Three of the most important are:

1. Avoidance of the neck. In shibari/kinbaku the neck is always carefully considered in the proper construction of the ties. Cord passes around the neck but is *never* tied to the neck.

2. Use of "wrapping" techniques. In shibari/kinbaku most ties that engage the arms are created using several side by side layers of evenly placed 6 mm in diameter (or larger) cords and then *comfortably tightened*. This wrapping or layering spreads the force of the pressure caused by the rope against the arms and helps avoid unwanted brachial nerve compression. This is why most shibari patterns are constructed using 7 to 8 meter (by 6 mm in diameter) cords that are first *folded in two at the middle* in order to increase the area where the rope touches the skin.

3. Use of the "safety release" knot. Shibari/kinbaku is not about fancy knots. This is a mistaken notion fostered by uninformed Western rope practitioners. In fact, most patterns are secured using a simple "over hand" knot. As will be seen in the following tutorials, when binding the wrists or tying the legs, either singularly or together, a "safety release" knot (sometimes called the "quick release" knot) is generally preferred.

This simple device is constructed by wrapping the doubled cord at least twice around the wrists (or leg, upper arm, ankle, etc.) and then collecting all strands in the over hand knot before tying it off. This allows the wraps to spread the force and prevent any single cord from increasing the pressure on the bound area if pulled. Please see the following five photographs:

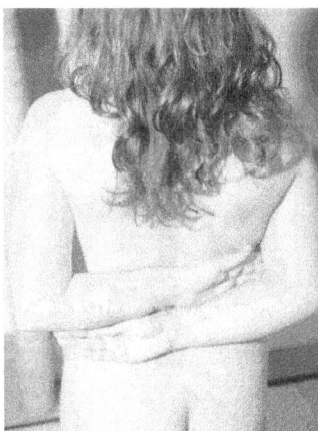

1. Hands held parallel to ground.

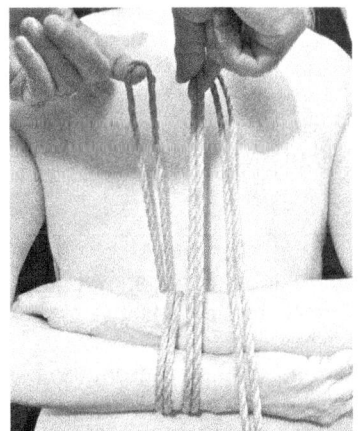

2. Two wraps of folded cord evenly placed.

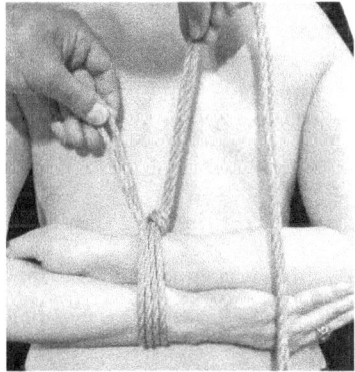

3. Start of over hand knot collecting both wraps.

172

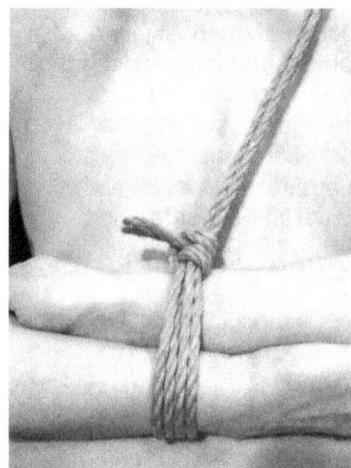

4. All cords collected by overhand knot.

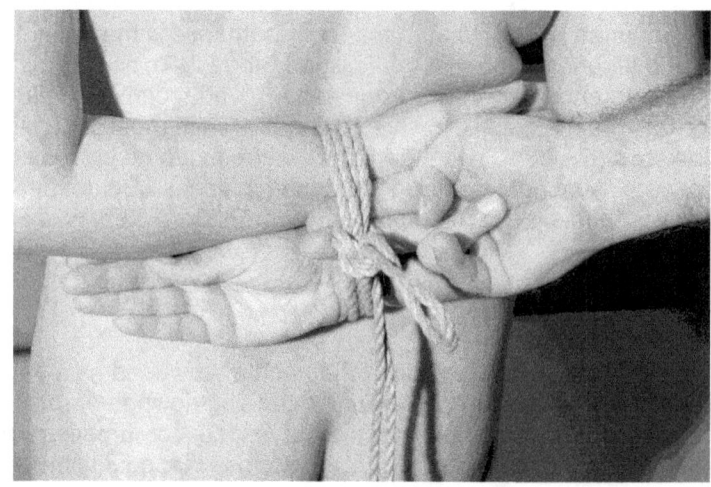

5. Note space between cords and wrists.

The advantages of the safety release knot are the ease of untying it in any emergency or interruption in a scene and the fact that the entire (often complex) shibari/kinbaku pattern need not be completely undone in order to release the hands of the bound partner. Remember, shibari/kinbaku ties are not about fancy knots or tight tying. Instead, they are all about artful construction.

Finally, in terms of basic practice, the principal of **joshiki** ("common sense") must be mentioned again. This time it's invoked to remind the reader that every shibari/kinbaku partner is different and a comfortable, enjoyable, tie or pattern for one person might not be comfortable or enjoyable for another. Likewise, something that worked well on one day might not be comfortable or enjoyable on another. Further, something that worked well on one day might not work at all on another, *even with the same partner*. In short, in practicing shibari/kinbaku it is wise and necessary to be thoughtful, considerate, and to always use common sense.

3. Materials.

Shibari/kinbaku ties are usually constructed using 7 to 8 meter (in length) by 6 to 8 mm (in diameter) rope called **asanawa** ("hemp/jute rope"). A single small knot, called a "button" is tied on the ends of each cord to facilitate wrapping and for ease in tucking the ends away.

This Japanese style cord is unlike any known in the West since most Western hemp is imported from Central Europe. True asanawa is strong, soft, and most importantly (and unlike most Western cotton or nylon rope), WILL NOT stretch. This is vital when creating shibari/kinbaku patterns for aesthetic and safety reasons.

Fortunately, it is becoming easier to find and purchase this beautiful type of rope worldwide. However, should nylon rope be the only option then similar length and diameter cords made in the "regatta braid" pattern will provide a generally suitable alternative.

4. Eroticism.

Happily for an erotic art, many of the shibari/kinbaku ties stimulate the **seikantai** ("erogenous zone") areas of the human body. In Japanese theory, these sensitive areas run through three basic locations:

1. Down the back about 2 cm on either side of the spine, from the neck to the tail bone.

2. Along the inner thighs from the genital area to the inside of the knee.

3. Down the front of the body in two vertical lines that form a long, extended "V" shape and proceed from the shoulders, cross the nipples, pass just to the right and left of the navel, and end in the genital area.

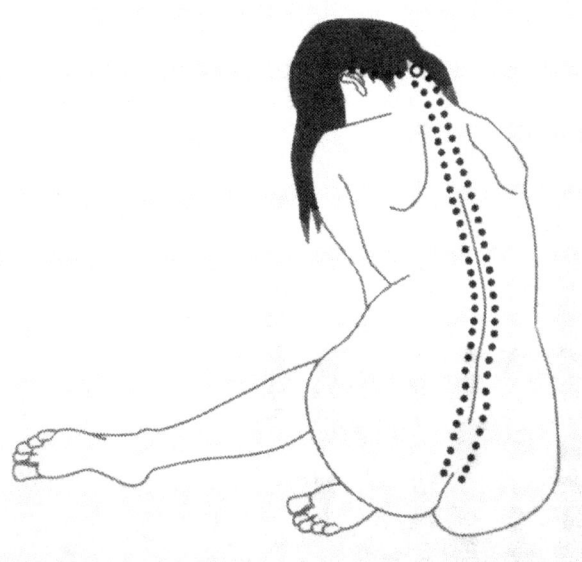 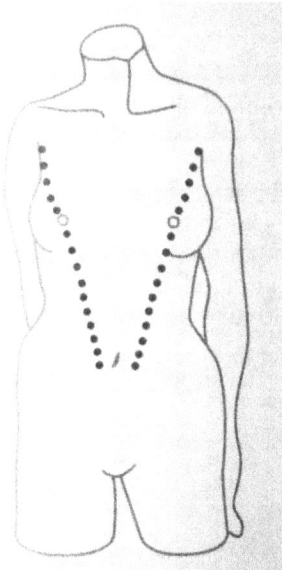

There are, of course, other erogenous zones but you'll notice in the following tutorials how many wraps, turns and knots of the shibari/kinbaku patterns being demonstrated are positioned to gently stimulate these three specific areas in order to create pleasant sensations in the body of the bound subject. In addition to the more typical sadomasochistic delights the receptive person feels in being restrained by a loving partner, this deliberate and consistent stimulation of the seikantai areas makes shibari/kinbaku unique among the tying arts.

For this reason the skilled shibari/kinbaku practitioner usually proceeds slowly in both the tying and untying of the bound partner to maximize and lengthen this loving and erotic experience.

Two classic Shibari/Kinbaku patterns

Three rope Takate-kote (or Gote) shibari

Perhaps one of the most fundamental ties in shibari is the classic takate-kote (also called gote) shibari or basic Japanese box arm tie. It is fundamental not only because it is one of the most recognizable of shibari patterns but also because so many other classic forms of shibari/kinbaku incorporate it. To name just a few, the ebi, agura, kata-ashi zuri and various styles of gyaku-ebi shibari all use some form of the takate-kote in their construction. It is also important because it is a perfect example of how a hojojutsu upper body tie once centered on the neck has been redesigned for safety and erotic pleasure. To learn it is to begin the serious exploration of basic shibari/kinbaku technique.

While the takate-kote can be used as a decorative kata karada bagu (body harness) without any application to restraint, it is one style of the restraining takate-kote that will be described here.

Taking the traditional shibari rope (or nawa) of 7 or 8 meters in length (6 to 8 mm in diameter) fold it in half leaving approx. 3.5 meters on each side. Position your partner (who for this description we'll assume is a woman) and have her stand with her back to you and her arms folded behind her parallel to the ground (**see picture 1, above**).

174

About 3 inches above each wrist bring the folded center of the cord twice around her lower arms leaving enough rope at the loop end to make a simple overhand "safety release" knot to secure her wrists (**see pictures 2, 3 and 4, above**).

While effective, this type of knot has the advantage of being a quick release should it be necessary. It is important to note that the wrists need not be tightly tied together because shibari/kinbaku is an art where the wrapping and positioning of the nawa is often, as here, used to prevent release and the apparent slack will be taken up momentarily (**see picture 5, above**).

With her wrists now secure, bring both ends of the rope to your left and up and firmly wrap the cords evenly over her upper left arm and across her chest just above her breasts. Continue to bring the ropes around her right arm and back down to where her wrists are held. Loop the cords behind the rope leading to the left and pull it back upon itself. This will cause the chest rope to tighten slightly and her wrists to raise.

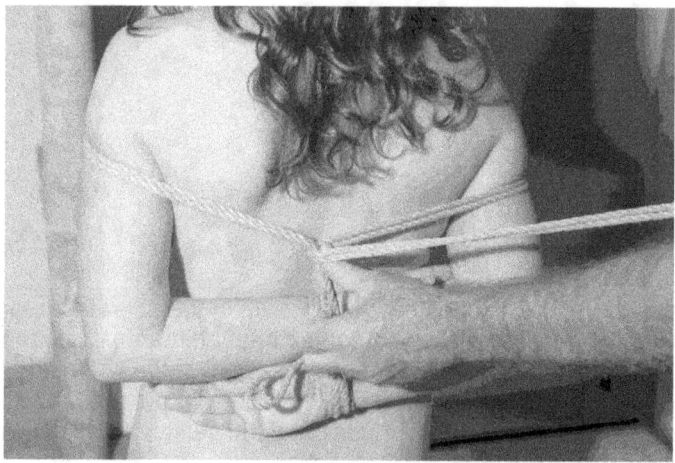

6. First rope continues around the chest and is doubled back upon itself.

Doubling back now in the opposite direction, reverse the path of the nawa and add a second row of 2 strands above the breasts being sure not to cross the first set.

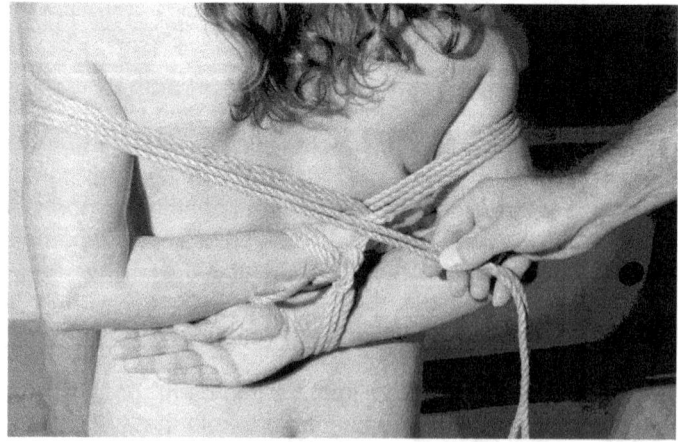

7. Completing first rope second wrap .

This time, when you bring the rope back down the left side and loop it back upon itself once again, you will notice that you've used up most of your 7 to 8 meters.

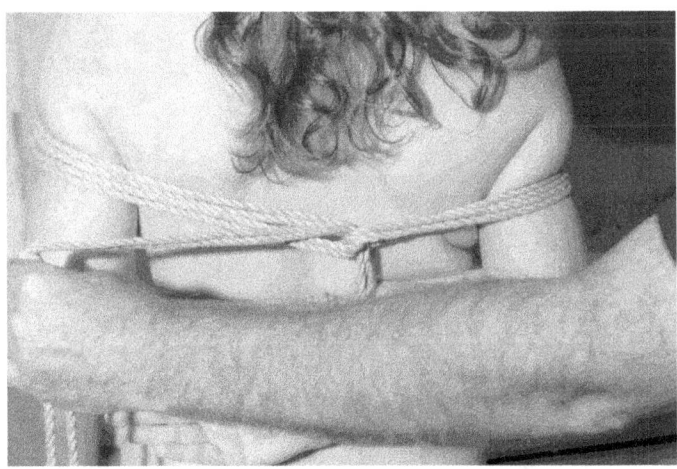

8. Second wrap of first rope doubling back on itself.

It's now time to knot your first rope.

This is most simply done by wrapping the end of your rope around all the wrapped horizontal cords above the tied wrists in a figure eight pattern and then tying it off with a simple overhand knot. Any remaining cord can be looped around the line leading up from the wrists creating a **tsuka maki** or the characteristic "sword hilt" wrap and then knotting the ends and/or tucking in the buttons to finish. The main knot should be positioned *just* to the right or left (your preference) of the spine but never right on it. This allows for the knot to gently and subtly stimulate a portion of the **seikantai** ("erogenous zone") area of the subject's back. It also allows the subject to be more comfortable if they should be placed on their back for play. If this is done, the use of a supporting and cushioning pillow for the upper back is advised.

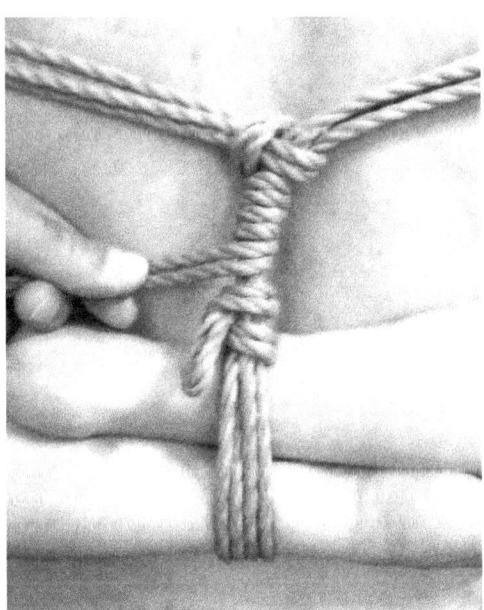

9. First rope complete with main knot positioned to left of spine and with ends finished in a "sword hilt" wrap.

At this point it is a good idea to run one finger under the cords along the entire length of this upper wrap, especially the area across the upper arms, in order to smooth and straighten the wrapped cords and make sure the force of the wrap is evenly spread.

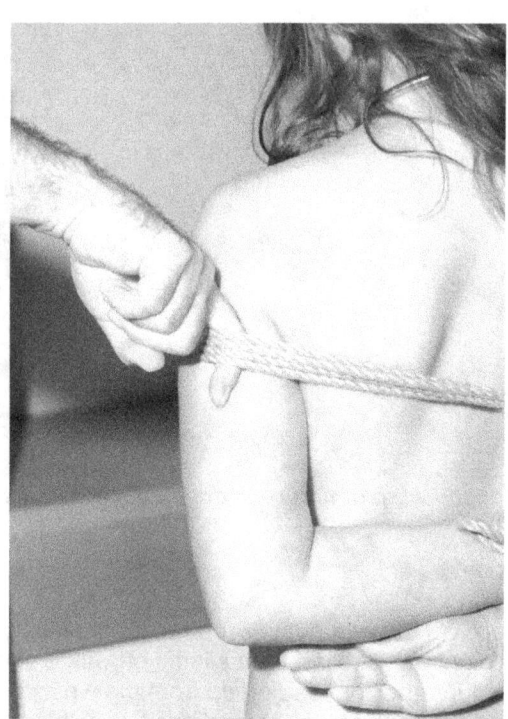

10. Run a finger under length of first wrap to straighten and smooth.

Now take a second 7 to 8 meter rope, find the center as before and attach that (by simple overhand knot) to the length of cord leading up from the wrists to the previously tied upper chest ropes. A good position for this attachment is right below the first knot.

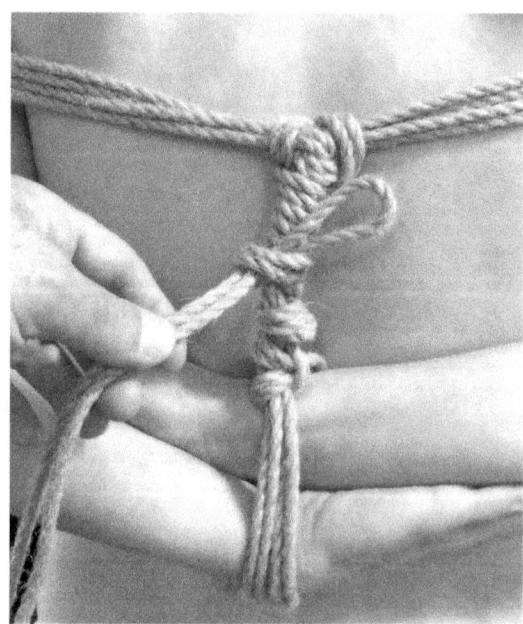

11. Second cord attached with an overhead knot to the "sword hilt."

As before, pull both ends to the left but this time position the double strand wrap *below* the breasts. Important! Be sure this wrap is positioned ON THE LOWER RIBCAGE and NOT below it which could restrict breathing. Continue the wrapping around and across the right arm and once again loop the cord upon itself, tightening the wrap. Be sure this wrap is not too tight.

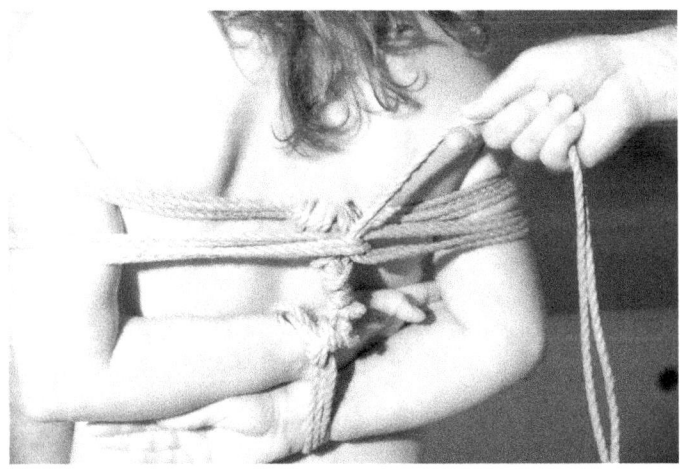

12. Second cord wrapped below the breasts and looped back upon itself.

After completing the second wrap in the opposite direction, begin another figure eight pattern to secure the horizontal wraps below the breasts. When you have 10 to 12 inches left finish the figure eight with a simple overhand knot.

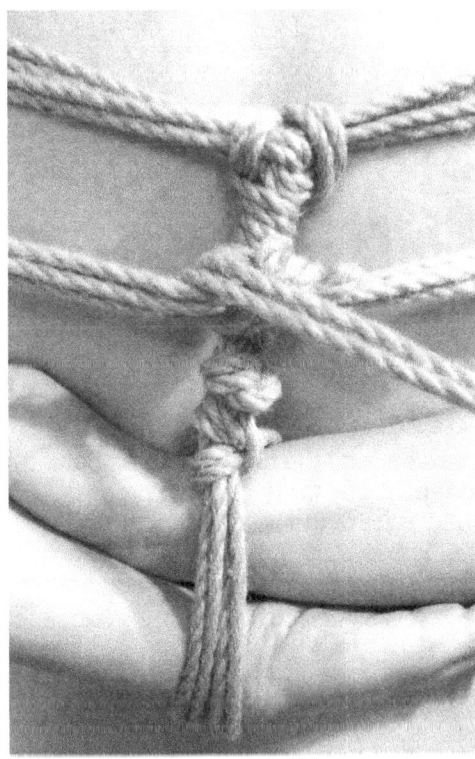

You will notice that you now have two rather long loose ends remaining.

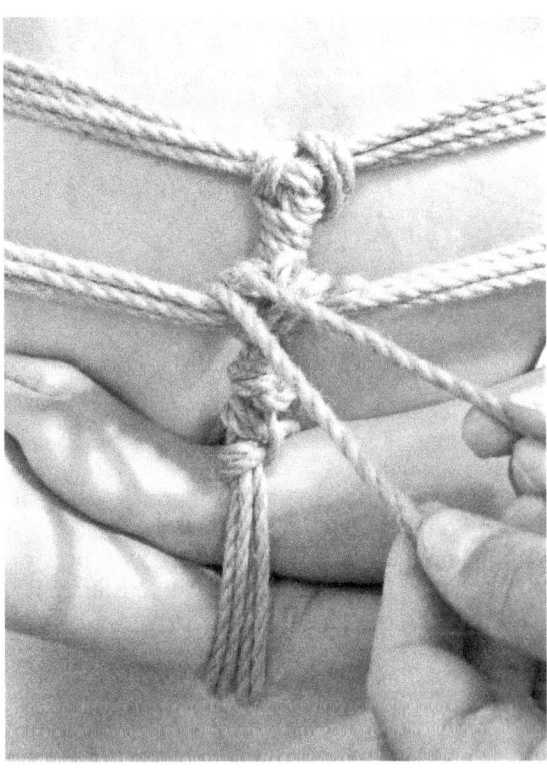

13. Beginning the figure eight pattern securing the lower wraps.

14. The two leftover lines of 10 to 12 inches will be used for lower wrap cinching.

These will now be used to gently cinch the wrapped ropes below the breasts, finishing and tightening the basic tie. Taking both lines, first pass them once around the post leading to the hands (thus stabilizing the tension,) then run them between the body and arm on one side of your partner. The lines should first go *over* the lower chest wrap ropes and then be pulled back *under* the lower chest wrap. Gently tighten the lower chest wrap as you do so. Be careful not to pull too quickly, too tightly or to pinch the sensitive flesh of the inner arms as you do this.

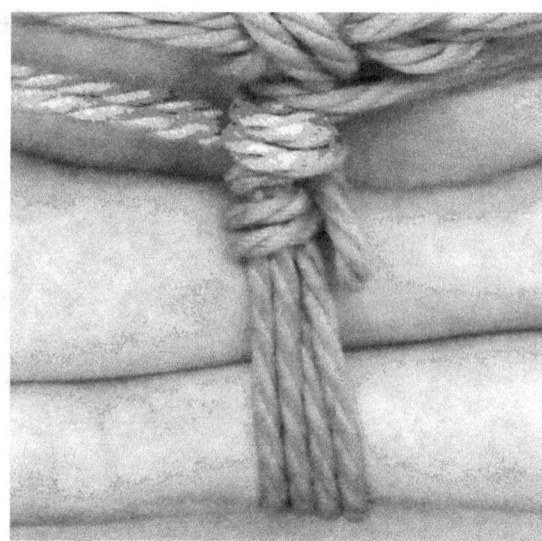

15. Rope ends loop around post to hold tension before cinching.

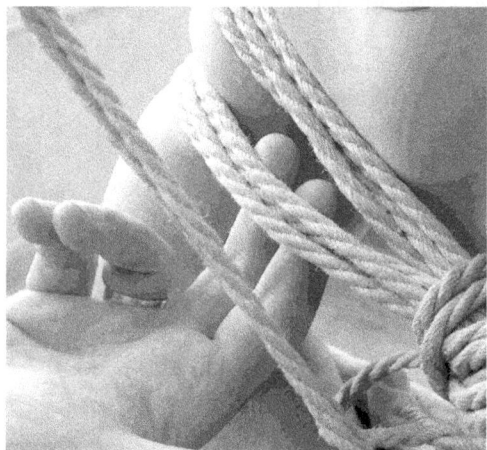

15. Cinching cord goes over lower wrap.

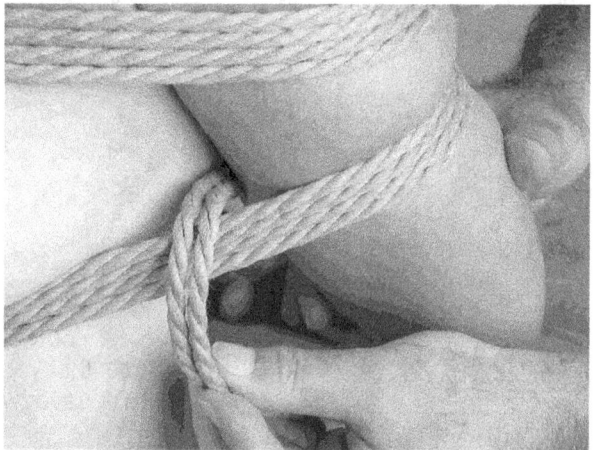

16. Then back under to cinch the lower wrap.

After the cinch has been pulled through and gently tightened on one side feed the cinching ropes behind the vertical "post" binding the hands to the partner's other side and repeat the same cinching process. Once both sides of the lower wraps have been cinched and tightened, secure the tie by wrapping the remaining short ends around the lower horizontal chest ropes at the post and then, if necessary, down the vertical post above the wrists (creating a "tsuka maki" or sword hilt wrap) and then finish with another simple overhand knot.

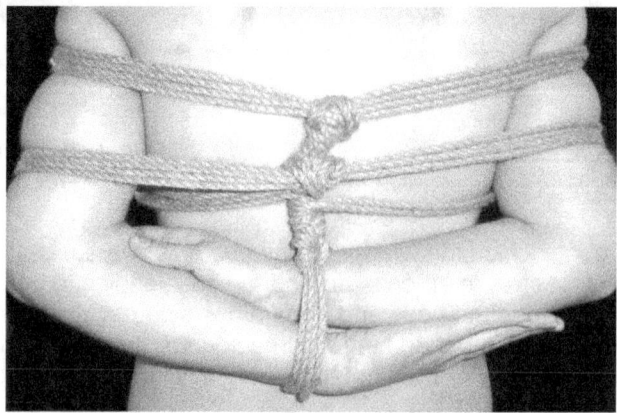

18. Cinches in place and single ends secured by overhand knot at the "sword hilt."

This completes this version of the basic, beginner's restraining takate-kote.

A third rope is now often added in the same manner as the second **(see picture 11, above)** and brought over the right (or left) shoulder and down between the breasts to loop around the lower chest wrap.

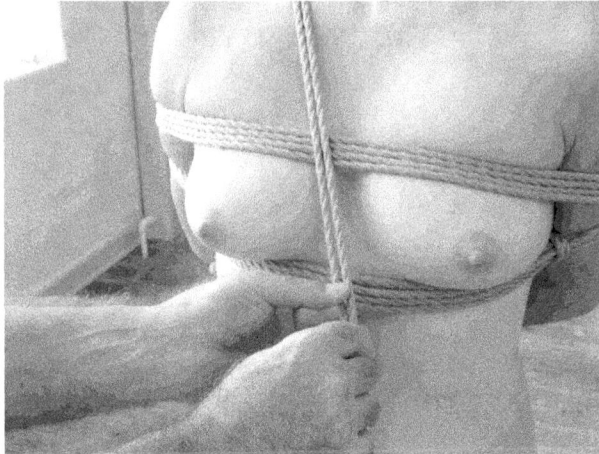

19. The third cord comes over the shoulder.

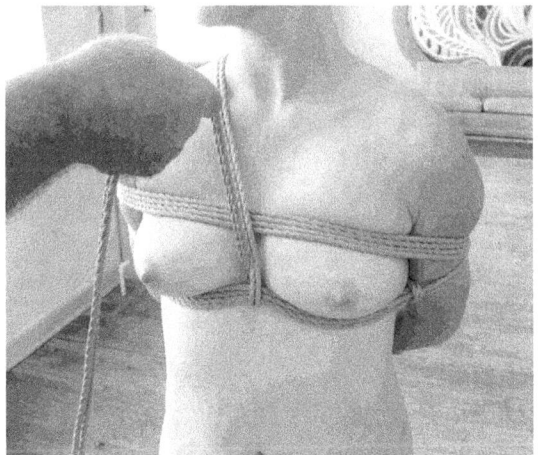

20. The third cord loops under the lower breast wrap and is gently pulled up.

Pulled gently but firmly back up and over the opposite shoulder using a variety of twist patterns and secured at the back with a final overhand knot, this technique causes a stimulating rush of blood to the area, increased erogenous sensitivity and an attractive "lift and separated" look for women.

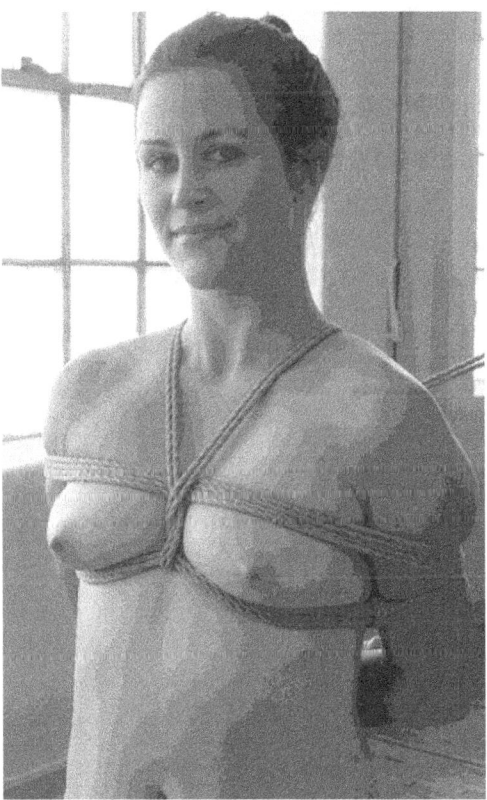

21. One simple version of the decorative chest wrap.

180

The remaining ends can then be used for creating more intricate patterns on the chest, back or upper torso, binding the legs or for securing the subject to another object (if this is done be sure your now helpless partner is in no danger of falling!). **Please note: this beginner's version of this classic tie should NOT be used for suspensions.**

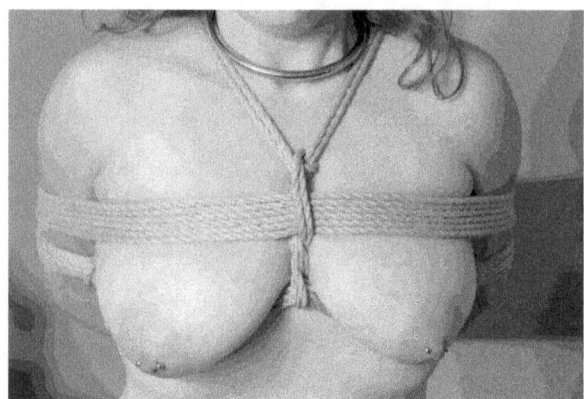

22. Second version of the wrap.

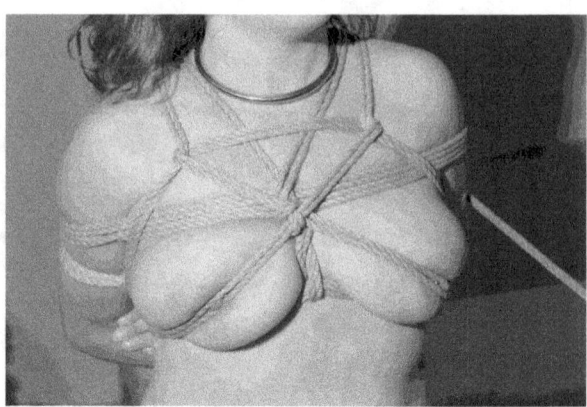

23. Third, complex, decorative version of the wrap.

As mentioned earlier, care should be taken not to tie either wrists, chest wraps or cinches too tightly. Tied *incorrectly or too tightly* this shibari might cause some difficulty in breathing as well as loss of circulation down the arms resulting in the hands "going to sleep." Making sure that breathing is normal and feeling the subject's hands frequently while tied for coldness is always recommended as is having your partner squeeze your hand from time to time to demonstrate strength and proper circulation. Of course, it is the bound subject's responsibility to inform his/her partner of any discomfort immediately. Remember, the wrists are tied with a quick release knot and a simple pull undoes the hands. Remember too, it is the combination of the various wraps and the positioning of the arms NOT THE TIGHTNESS OR FANCY KNOTS that causes this tie to be so effective a restraint, one that has been in use for many years.

It should be noted that the above version of this tie is only one of many possible variations. For instance, there are 1, 2, 3 and even 4 rope styles of takate-kote (gote). However, all use basically similar patterns to achieve their attractive and stimulating ends.

Finally, a note about the name of this shibari/kinbaku pattern. This tie is generally known in the West as the Ushirode Takete-kote shibari (often abbreviated to Takate-kote). However, many practitioners in Japan reserve that name only for ties where the hands are pulled high up on the back preferring to use the name Ushirode Gote shibari (or Gote) for ties where the arms are held parallel to the ground. Because of the strain on the arms and shoulders many Western submissives would find the "high hand" position difficult and uncomfortable to maintain. For this reason the use of both names for this "how to" seems an appropriate compromise.

Hishi shibari

The beautiful and distinctive hishi ("diamond") shibari is one of the most attractive and well known patterns in shibari/kinbaku. It's a wonderful example of a "decorative" shibari (a tie created to showcase a beautiful pattern) and also a good example of erotic shibari/kinbaku that subtly stimulates the various **seikantai** ("erogenous zones") of the receptive partner.

Hishi shibari is also an historically important tie in that it descends from early schools of hojojutsu. As previously noted, during the feudal years of Japan such patterns as the hishi were done on prisoner's backs and tied the neck area but today, for safety and in order to more beautifully accentuate the body and to create greater erotic stimulation, the distinctive part of the pattern is placed on the front of the body with the rope draped *around* the neck similar to a man's necktie. That said, it is still a surprisingly restrictive tie. Done properly, the receptive partner will feel the ropes and the complexity of the design throughout his/her body.

Hishi shibari is sometimes mistaken for the equally famous six-sided **kikkou** ("tortoise shell") shibari. This confusion is due to the fact that in the Edo Era the Taisho ryo (school) of hojojutsu called their diamond pattern tie a "kikkou" and some modern bakushi (Randa Mai, among others) have even taught the diamond (hishi) tie as the "kikkou." Confusion aside, this is one of the loveliest of shibari/kinbaku patterns.

As with the takate-kote, there are several styles of hishi shibari taught. The traditional style, popularized in manga illustrations, uses two 7 to 8 meter cords and creates at least 3 linked diamond (hishi) shapes running from the breasts to the pubic area. This is one of the most popular styles and will be the one described here.

Facing your partner, take your first cord, find the exact center and place that gently over the back of the subject's neck with the ends hanging down in front, 3.5 to 4 meters on each side. Starting three to five inches below the neck, begin to tie a series of four simple overhand knots being careful as you do so of your partner's face and eyes. The second knot should be between the breasts and the third and fourth above and below the navel.

Important! Be sure that that the loop around the back of neck is not tightened too much by creating the first overhand knot.

This shibari pattern is a good example of how the neck area is carefully considered in shibari/kinbaku to avoid the dangers of hojojutsu. It is also important to remember that everyone has their own sense of comfort regarding the neck area so always be sure to check with your partner as you proceed.

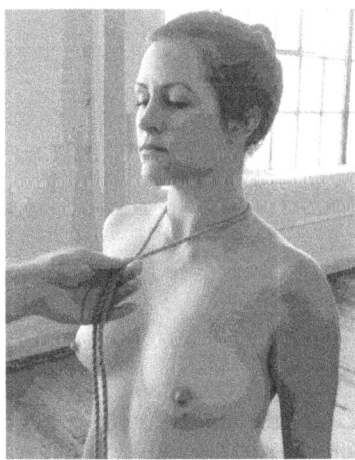

1. Facing the subject, place the middle of the first cord gently around the neck.

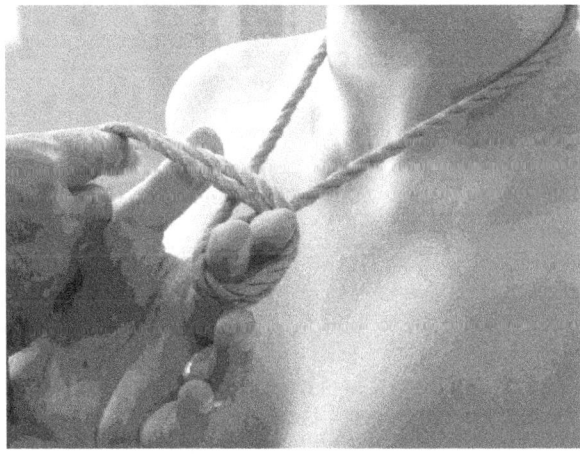

2. Begin making over hand knots. Be sure the cord around the neck is comfortable.

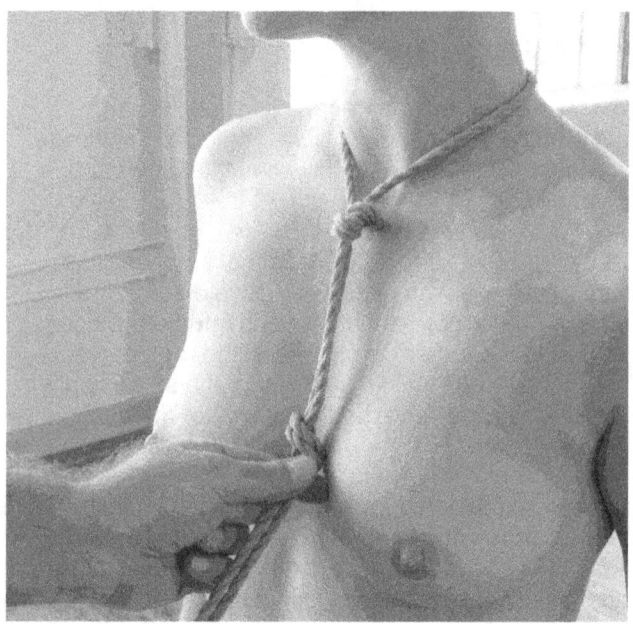

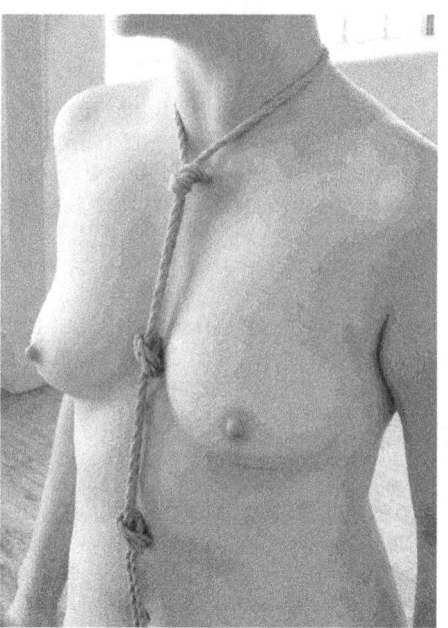

3. First and second knots, below chin and between breasts.

4. Place third and fourth (not shown) knots above and below navel.

Carefully run the strands through your partner's legs and gently pull up to the rope around the neck, then thread both strands *under* the loop at the back of the neck.

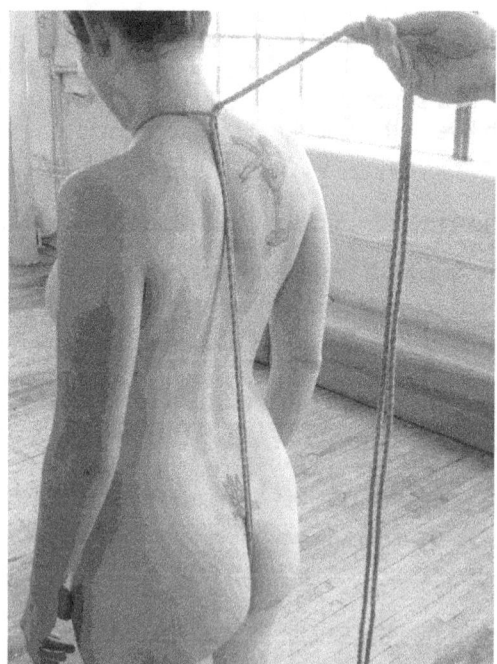

5. Gently thread cords between legs and through neck loop.

This next step is very important. With the loose end, tie another overhand knot at the neck rope. This will lock the neck loop in place and prevent further tightening. Be sure that the rope that is threaded up from the groin area is NOT pulled too tightly. The making of the kikkou design will do this shortly. A good measure of tension is three fingers of looseness between back and rope.

Be sure the neck rope is comfortable, does not impede breathing in any way and that the tension from the rope positioned between the legs is pleasant.

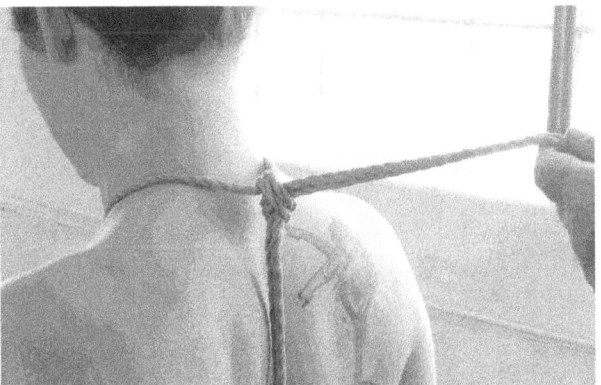

6. Overhand knot at back of neck. Three fingers of space between rope and back.

Now it's time to make the hishi pattern. Separate the two lines and have your partner raise his or her arms above the head. Begin threading first the left end of the nawa (rope) and then the right end from the back to the front as you create the hishi (diamonds).

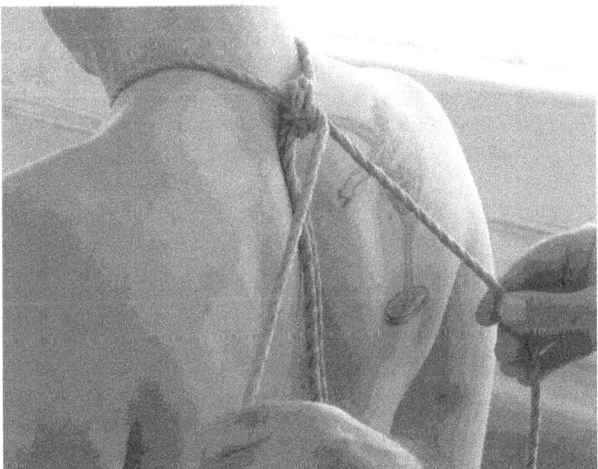

7. Separate left and right ends of the cord to begin making diamonds.

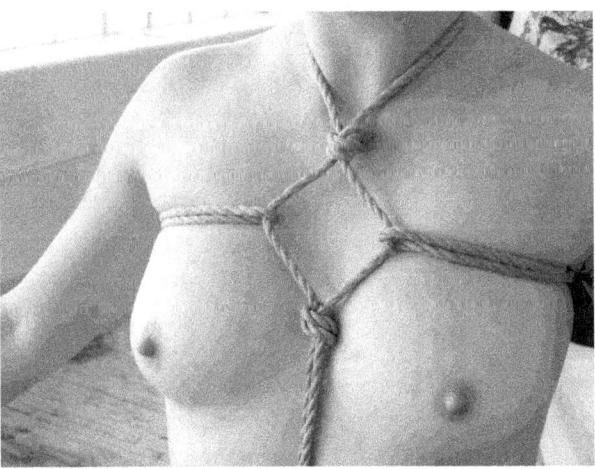

8. First diamond.

Obviously, the ropes cross at the back as you make the diamonds and when they do they should be twisted together one turn to keep the pattern secure. It is the twisting of the cord at the back that tightens up the pattern considerably which is why it's important to start with a fairly loose cord at the back.

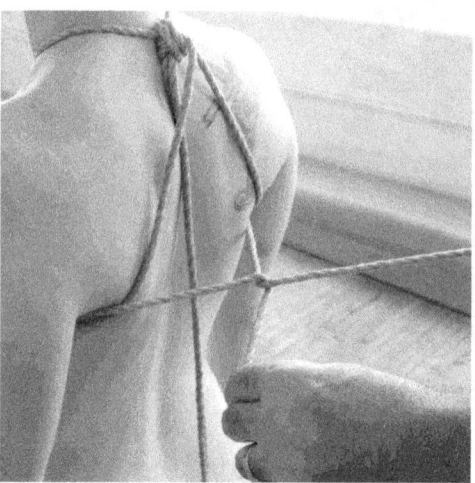

9. A simple twist keeps the pattern secure.

When you've run out of length on the first rope simply tie it off at the back of your subject with a twist and a simple overhand knot, being sure to maintain tension. Taking a second 7 to 8 meter cord, find it's center and attach it to the lines running vertically from the pubic area to the neck at the point that you finished with the first cord. As was the case with the takate-kote, using an over hand knot to attach the second rope is most efficient. Then continue as before until you finish creating the beautiful hishi pattern.

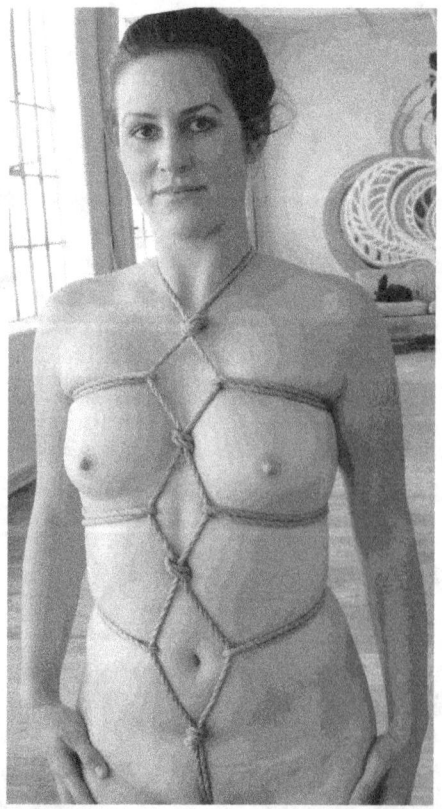

10. The completed single strand hishi ("diamond") shibari.

Once all the diamonds are created, the ends of the second cord should have a final overhand knot made in them at the waist to secure the design. The remaining cord length can then be used to bind the subject's arms behind the back or can be tied off.

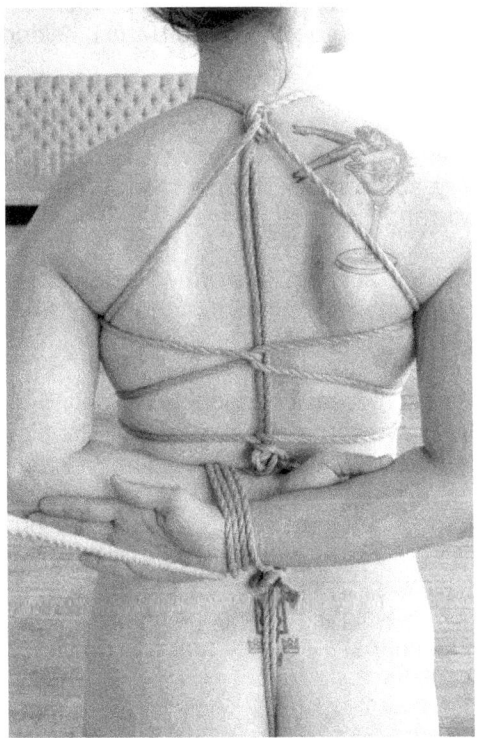

11. Completed hishi pattern back with hands bound.

Questions:

"Can I use any rope and get the same look and result as the shibari pictures I see on the Internet?"

Regrettably, no. Most "hemp" rope sold in the US and Europe comes from Central Europe, usually from Rumania, and is a different product from that which is used in Japan. True shibari/kinbaku nawa is made of jute and comes from two different plant species: the C. capsularis of China and the C. olitorius of India. The properties of this rope are quite different from Western style hemp. To have the best look and the correct feel when doing shibari/kinbaku bindings it's best to obtain authentic Japanese style asanawa.

"I've been told that shibari uses complicated knots with many names. Is this true?"

No. This is a confusion caused by ignorant rope practitioners unaware of actual shibari/kinbaku techniques. With the exception of one or two complicated, decorative patterns, almost all shibari/kinbaku ties utilize simple overhand knots -- if knots, as opposed to wrappings secured by the buttons at the ends of the cords, are used. Ornate knots were/are used in the decorative art of **Mizuhiki** (see the first chapter) but this type of small scale, macramé style tying would be inappropriate for hojojutsu, where ties had to be done quickly during arrests, and also for modern erotic shibari/kinbaku where the wrappings and overall patterns of the ties are used to bind and securely support as well as erotically stimulate larger areas of the body.

"I'd like to do a shibari suspension with my girlfriend. Could you send me written instructions?"

Due to the recent popularity of suspensions being done in clubs and at events and then broadcast on the Internet, I'm asked this kind of question quite often. The truth is, while they might give the person doing the tying (the "rigger") an ego boost, suspensions (**tsuri**) have little to do with most classic erotic shibari/kinbaku techniques. In fact, many of the most famous bakushi of the past (i.e., Minomura Kou) disliked them and several modern masters (i.e., Yukimura Haruki) seldom do them. The reasons are three-fold:

1. Suspensions usually remove the bound partner from many meaningful physical interactions once they're airborne.
2. They require quite a bit of finesse and some skill to do safely. There is no margin for error.
3. They usually require a fit, athletic and informed partner.

This is why most successful stage show suspensions are well orchestrated and rehearsed acts by two skilled performers with the suspended member of the team (usually a slight young woman of no more than 110 lbs) being something of an aerialist.

Still, they do look impressive and are, on occasion, capable of floating the receptive partner into a state of euphoria. For these reasons they have some place in modern SM play as well as on stage as the dramatic descendent of ancient torture techniques, … provided they're done safely.

Learning general principals from a book or by watching someone perform is usually not enough to successfully execute this complicated style of rope engineering. Ideally, the interested student needs to be taught by an experienced teacher who, using a variety of traditional methods, takes into account all of their partner's many variables, such as weight, height, age, injuries, comfort level (both physical and psychological), etc., in order to "custom make" a safe, comfortable and secure suspension that is appropriate to their needs.

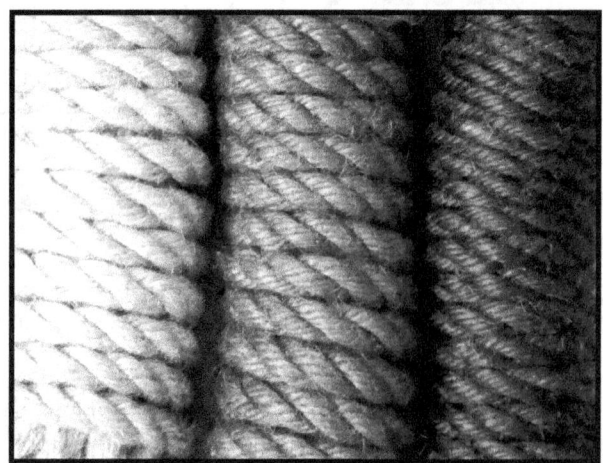

Afterword

Questions: "Is shibari/kinbaku an Art?", "What is the beauty of kinbaku?"

In the introduction these two questions were asked. It's now time to consider the answers.

I hope the reader will agree that, given the history of shibari/kinbaku and the different styles of creative expression that the practice has been used for, to say nothing of the remarkable artists that have taken it up to some degree as part of their creative lives over many years, the answer to the first question must be yes.

As for the second question, "What is the beauty of kinbaku?", that answer must be found in each reader's own perceptions. It is my hope that this book has been of some help in stimulating these perceptions, that it has been entertaining to the casual reader and useful to the experienced practitioner. If either goal has been met then the author will be more than satisfied.

As for my own answer, the true beauty of kinbaku has less to do with the history, the techniques or even the art that has come from it but rather resides in its ability to be an active and living, passionate and dramatic, affectionate and artful communication between two mature individuals. As the great Akechi Denki sensei once said, it is "An art for two like-minded hearts and must always be a loving exchange."

Please play safely.

Master "K" (Los Angeles, California—2015)

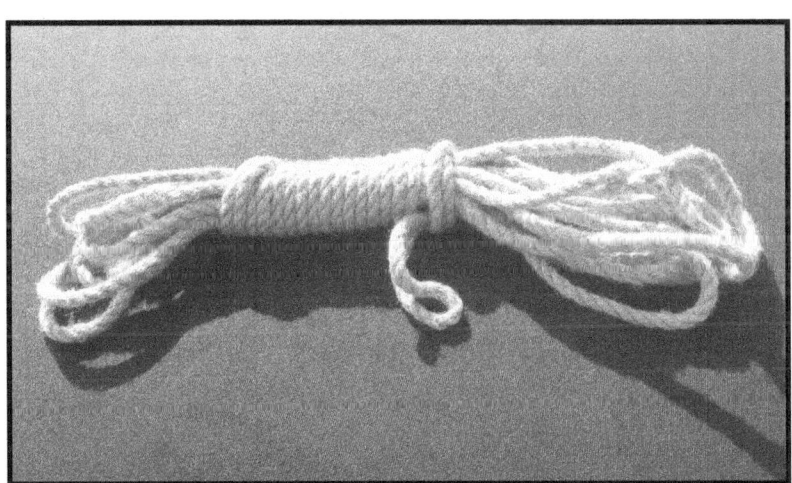

Bibliography

All books are in Japanese unless otherwise noted.

Akita, Masami (with Fuji, Akio and Nureki, Chimuo). *Nihon Kinbaku Shashin-shi (The History of Japanese Bondage Photography)*. Tokyo: Bibliotheca Nocturna,1996.

Araki, Nobuyuki. *Bondage/Kinbaku*. Koln, Germany: Taschen, 2012.

Arisue, Go. *Jissen Kinbaku: Shibari kata Kyoshitsu*. Tokyo: Hokuou Shobo Publishers, 1997.

Arisue, Go. *The Basic(s) of Japanese Bondage Theory*. Tokyo: Sanwa Publishing, 2008.

Arisue, Go. *The Book of Five Rings for Rope Arts, Vols. 1 and 2*. Tokyo: Sanwa Publishing, 2005.

Bennett, Terry. *Photography in Japan, 1853-1912* (In English). Tokyo: Tuttle Publishing, 2006.

Botsman, Daniel. *Punishment and Power in the Making of Modern Japan* (In English). Princeton: Princeton University Press, 2005.

Brandon, James and Leiter, Samuel (gen. eds.). *Kabuki Plays on Stage, Volumes 1—4* (In English). Honolulu: University of Hawaii Press, 2002.

Cortazzi, Hugh (ed.). *Mitford's Japan, Memories and Reflections 1866-1906* (In English). Great Britain: Japan Library, 2002.

Coutts, John Alexander Scott (AKA John Willie). *The Adventures of Sweet Gwendoline* (in English). New York: Belier Press Inc., 1999.

Coutts, John Alexander Scott (AKA John Willie). *Les Photographies de John Willie* (In French). Paris: Futuropolis, 1985.

Cunningham, Don. *Taiho-Jutsu, Law and Order in the Age of the Samurai* (In English). Boston: Tuttle Publishing, 2004.

Dan, Oniroku. *Hana to Hebi*. Osaka: Kitan Club,1962.

Dan, Oniroku. *Hana wa Kurenai (Flowers are Crimson), an autobiography*. Tokyo; Gentosha, 1999.

Dan, Oniroku. *Bishonen*. Tokyo: Shincho Bunko, 1999. Novel upon which the film, "I am an SM writer" is based.

Dan, Oniroku. *Perverse Pleasures*. Tokyo: Alligator magazine corporation, 1996.

Dan, Oniroku. *Seiyu Monogatari (A fictional work based on the life of Itoh Seiyu)*. Tokyo: Kitan-kai 1972.

Dan, Oniroku. *Tsujimura Takashi—Special Edition of SM King*. Tokyo: SM King magazine, 1973.

Fagioli, Marco. *Shunga, The Erotic Art of Japan* (In English). New York: Universe Publishing, 1998.

Fahr-Becker, Gabriele. *Japanese Prints* (In English). New York: Barnes and Noble Books, 2003.

Forbidden Images—Erotic art from Japan's Edo Period (in Finnish). Helsinki, Finland: Helsinki City Art Museum, 2002.

Fuji, Akio. *Bind*. Tokyo: Mole, 1992.

Fujisawa, Morihiko. *Nihon Keibatsu Fuzoku-shi (Japanese Punishment History and Customs)*. Tokyo: Fujimori Shoten, 1982.

Fujita, Seiko. *Zukai Hojojutsu*. Tokyo: Meicho Kankokai , 1992.

Fujita, Shintaro. *Tokugawa bakufu keiji zufu (an Illustrated Guide to the Punishments of the Tokugawa Shogunate)*. Tokyo: Kobe Naokichi, 1893.

Gorner, Veit and Moll, Frank-Thorston and Araki Nobuyoshi. *Araki meets Hokusai* (In German/English). Heidelberg: Kehrer Verlag, 2008.

Grimme, Matthias. *Das Bondage-Handbuch* (In German). Hamburg: Charon Verlag, 1999.

Habu, Junko. *Ancient Jomon of Japan—Case Studies in Early Societies* (In English). Cambridge, England: University of Cambridge Press, 2004.

Hanawa, K. and Maruo, S. *Bloody Ukiyo-e in 1866 and 1988*. Tokyo: Libro-port, 1988.

Hara, Taneaki and Osatake, Takeki (eds.). *Edo Jidai Hanzai Keibatsu Jireshu*. First published in 1930. Tokyo: Kashiwa Shobo, 1982 (reprint).

Henshall, Kenneth. *A History of Japan, Second Edition: From Stone Age to Superpower* (In English). London: Macmillan, 2004.

Hino, Kazeko. *Seme to Bigaku: Itoh Seiyu no Kinbaku Shidou (The Aesthetics of Domination: Itoh's Seiyu's Rope Bondage Teachings)*. Pamphlet. Tokyo: Edo Products (no date).

Inoue Kazuo. *Zankoku no Nihon-shi (Cruel Japanese History)*. Tokyo: Kappa Books/Kobunsha, 1979.

Inoue and Kiyoshi. *Shashin shu Zangyaku no Jokeishi: Gōmon to Keibatsu ni Miru Nihon no zankoku Hontai*. Tokyo: Sogo, 1971.

Ishigaki Akira. *Strange Fruit (a limited edition deluxe photo album)*. Tokyo: Doyou Shuppan Shinsha, 1982 (Reprinted in an edited version by Shinkosha, 1993).

Itatsu, Yasuhiko. *Yoryoku/Doshin Jutte Hojo*. Tokyo: Shinjinbutsu Jurai-sha, 1992.

Itoh, Kiku. *Itoh Seiyu Gashu (Collected Pictures of Itoh Seiyu) Genteiban (Limited Edition Deluxe Album)*. Tokyo: Shinchosha, 1997.

Itoh, Seiyu. *Binjin Ranmai*. Tokyo: Suikodo, 1933.

Itoh, Seiyu. *Edo no Sakariba*. Tokyo: Suikodo, 1947.

Itoh, Seiyu. *Gaka Seikatsu Uchimaku-Hanashi (an artist talks about his life)*. Tokyo: privately published, 1930.

Itoh, Seiyu. *Kuronawa-ki zen*. Tokyo: Suikodo, 1951.

Itoh, Seiyu. *Makura*. Tokyo: Suikodo, 1948.

Itoh, Seiyu. *Onna Sanjyu-roku Kii*. Tokyo: privately published, 1930.

Itoh, Seiyu. *Rongo Tsukai (Itoh's first seme-e art collection)*. Tokyo: privately published—banned by the censors, 1930.

Itoh, Seiyu. *Seme no Hanashi*. Tokyo: privately published, 1929.

Itoh, Seiyu. *Seme no Kenkyu (the first bondage photography collection in Japan)*. Tokyo: privately published—banned by the censors, 1929 (reprinted by Suikodo in 1939).

Itoh, Seiyu. *Six volumes on the history and customs of feudal Edo/Tokyo*. Tokyo: Castle North Studies, 1927-1932.

Itoh, Seiyu. *The Twelve Months of Strange Punishments (an art portfolio)*.Tokyo: Akebono, 1953.

Kanamori, Atsuko. *Oyo*. Tokyo: Rhinoceros Press, 1996.

Kasuga Akira. *SM Art of Kasuga Akira (album)*. Tokyo: Green Door Publishing, 1993.

Kawai Takao. *Pleasure in the Fall (photo album)*. Tokyo: The Japan Mix, 1998.

Kawaguchi, Hiroshi. *Itoh Seiyu Shashin-cho/Seme-e no Onno (Itoh Seiyu's photographic work)*. Tokyo: Photo Musee, 1996.

Kenrick, Douglas Moore. *Jomon of Japan: The World's Oldest Pottery* (In English). New York: Kegan Paul International Ltd.,1995.

Kern, Adam. *Manga From the Floating World* (In English). Cambridge (Massachusetts): Harvard University Press, 2006.

Keyes, Roger. *The Bizarre Imagery of Yoshitoshi*. (In English). Los Angeles: Los Angeles County Museum of Art, 1980.

Lamont-Brown, Raymond. *Kempeitai: Japan's Dreaded Military Police* (In English). Great Britain: Sutton Publishing, 1998.

Lesoualc'h Theo. *Erotique du Japon* (In French). Paris: Edition Henri Veyrier,1987.

Lopez, Donald S. *The Story of Buddhism: A Concise Guide to its History & Teachings* New York: HarperOno, 2001.

Maeda, Juan. *Juan Maeda Art Works (an art portfolio)*. Tokyo: Ioz Japan, 2000.

Master "K". *Shibari, The Art of Japanese Bondage* (In English/German), Glitter/Secret Press, Brussels, 2004.

Matsushita and Nakashiro (eds.). *Hentai-san ga Iku (interviews/profiles)*. Tokyo: Takarajima, 1997.

Midori. *The Seductive Art of Japanese Bondage* (In English). Emeryville: Greenery Press, 2001.

Mitchell, John D. and Watanabe, Miyoko. *Noh and Kabuki, Staging Japanese Theatre* (In English). Key West, Florida: Institute for Advanced Studies in the Theatre Arts Press, 1994.

Mitford, A. B. *Tales of Old Japan* (In English). Tokyo: Charles E. Tuttle Company, 1966.

Miyabi, Kyodo. *The Art of Miyabi (a deluxe Art portfolio)*. Tokyo: Sanwa, 2002.

Mizukoshi, Hiro. *Torinawajutsu* (reprint). Tokyo: Airyudo, 2000.

Muku, Youji. *Autobiography—Parts I and II (in SM Graffiti magazine)*. Tokyo: Koyushya Shuppan, December, 1980 and February, 1981.

Muku, Youji. *"Harem Mirage"—Muku Youji testimonial*. Tokyo: Softmagic, 2001.

Murdoch, James. *A History of Japan—Parts 1 & 2* (In English). New York: Frederick Ungar Publishing Co., 1964.

Musashi, Miyamoto (Translation by William Wilson). *The Book of Five Rings* (In English). Tokyo: Kodansha International, 2001.

Nakagawa, Ayako (et ala). *Nawa to Onna (an SM illustrator's album)*. Tokyo: Kitan-kai, 1970.

Nawa, Yumio. *Eleven articles on hojojutsu and traditional Japanese punishments in the Edo Era*. Tokyo: Uramado magazine, 1962 to 1965.

Nawa, Yumio. *Gōmon Keibatsu shi (The History of Torture and Punishment)*. Tokyo: Yuzankaku Shuppan, 1987.

Nawa, Yumio. *Jitte Hojou Jitten: Edo Machi Bugyou no Soubi to Taihou-jutsu (The Encyclopedia of Rope and Truncheon Capture: the Art and Equipment of the Edo era Constabulary)*. Tokyo: Yuzan Kaku Shuppan, 1996.

Nawa, Yumio. *Machigai Darake no Jikaigeki (Historical Shows are Full of Errors)*. Tokyo: Kawade Bunko, 1989.

Nawa, Yumio. *Ninjutsu no Kenyuu (The Study of Ninja Arts)*. Tokyo: Nishibo Shuppan sha, 1985.

Newland Amy (general editor). *The Hotei Encyclopedia of Japanese Woodblock Prints* (In English). Amsterdam: Hotei Publishing, 2005.

Newland, Amy and Uhlenbeck, Chris. *Ukiyo-e, The Art of Japanese Woodblock Prints* (In English). London: Grange Books, 1999.

Nureki, Chimuo. *Jitsuroku: Shibari to Seme (True Account: Shibari to Seme)*. Tokyo: Kawade Shobo Shinsha, 2001.

Nureki, Chimuo. *Kinbaku: Inochi aru kagiri (Kinbaku: For as Long as I Live)*. Tokyo: Kawade Shobo Shinsha, 2008.

Nureki, Chimuo. *Kinbaku no Bi, Kinbaku no Etsuraku (The Pleasure of Kinbaku)*. Tokyo: Kawade Shobo Shinsha, 1999.

Nureki, Chimuo. *Kitan Kurabu no Eishitachi, (The Artists of Kitan Club)*. Tokyo: Kawade Shobo Shinsha, 2004.

Nureki, Chimuo. *Kitan Kurabu to Sono Shuhen (Kitan Club and its Milieu)*.Tokyo: Kawade Shobo Shinsha, 2006.

Ono, Sokyo. *Shinto: The Kami Way*. Tokyo: Charles E. Tuttle Company, 2004.

Ono, Takeo. *Edo no Keibatsu Fuzoku-shi (revised)*. Tokyo: Tenbou-sha, 1998. NB: revised edition contains Sakuma, Osahiro's text, *Gōmon Jikki (Actual Record of Torture)*, 1893.

Ozuma, Kaname. *Tattooing*. Tokyo: Art Press, 2000.

Polizzotti, Mark (ed.). *Art and Artifice, Japanese Photographs of the Meiji Era* (In English). Boston: Museum of Fine Arts, Boston, 2004.

Randa, Mai. *DX: Professional Bondage Handbook*. Tokyo: Tukasa Co., 2006.

Randa, Mai. *Pro: Professional Bondage Handbook*. Tokyo: Tukasa Co., 2002.

Reiko, Kita (AKA Minomura Kou). *The Kita Reiko Picture Book (an art album)*. Osaka: Akebono Shobou, 1952.

Saotome, Hiromi. *Hiromi no Korega SM da. (Hiromi's SM)*. Tokyo: Kawade Shobo Shinsha, 2000.

Saotome, Hiromi. *Kitan Club no Hitobito (The People of Kitan Club)*. Tokyo: Kawade Shobo Shinsha, 2003.

Saotome, Hiromi. *Roman Porno no Joyuu (The Actresses of Roman Porno)*. Tokyo: Kawade Shobo Shinsha, 2006.

Saotome, Hiromi. *Sei no Shigoto shitachi (Masters of the Underground Erotic/Sex Trade)*. Tokyo: Kawade Shobo Shinsha, 1998.

Sasama, Yoshihiko. *Zusetsu: Nihon no Gomumon Keibatsu-shi (The Illustrated Guide to Torture and Punishment in Japan)*. Tokyo: Kashiwa Shobo, 1996.

Schmidt, Tom. *Bondage-Ausstieg aus der Selbstkontrolle* (In German). Hamburg: Mannerschwarm Scipt Verlag, 1999.

Schreiber, Mark. *The Dark Side: Infamous Japanese Crimes and Criminals* (In English). Tokyo: Kodansha International, 2001.

Screech, Timon. *Sex and the Floating World* (In English). London: Reaktion Books, 1999.

Segi, Shinichi. *Yoshitoshi, The Splendid Decadent* (In English). Tokyo: Kodansha International, 1985.

Shibatani, Saijiro (AKA Taki Reiko). *Historical seme-e (an art album)*. Osaka: Akebono Shobo, 1952.

Shigeru, Kayama and Minomura, Kou. *Beautifully Bound—The Only Album of Bound Women*. Osaka: Akebono Shobou, 1953.

Shimokawa, Koushi. *Nihon ero shashin-shi (The History of Japanese Erotic Photography)*. Tokyo: Seikyusha, 1996.

Slocombe, Romain. *L'Empire Erotique* (In French). Sevres, France: Editions La Sirene, 1993.

Sorayama, Hajime. *Sorayama Vibrant Vixens*. Zurich: Edition Skylight, 2013.

Sugiura, Norio. *Kinbakuzue 1-7 (Kinbaku Photograph Collection)*. Tokyo: Sanwa publishers, 2002—2006.

Takeo, Ono. *Edo no Keibatsu Fuzoku-shi (Edo Era Punishments)—revised*. Tokyo: Tenbou-sha, 1998.

Tanaka, Kinichi and Akechi, Denki. *Pleasure and a Little Pain (a photo album)*. Tokyo: The Japan Mix, 1995.

Tokitsu, Kenji. *Miyamoto Musashi, His Life and Writings* (In English). Boston: Shambhala Publications, 2004.

Toshiyuki, Matsushima. *Nikkatsu Roman Porno Zenshu (The History of Nikkatsu Roman Porno)*. Tokyo: Kodansha, 2000.

Turnbull, Stephen. *The Samurai Sourcebook* (In English). Great Britain: Arms and Armour Press, 1998.

Underwood, A.C. *Shintoism: The Indigenous Religion Of Japan* (In English). Pomona: Pomona Press, 2007.

Urado, Hiroshi. *SM Tanbi Bungaku Betsu-maki (You Can Play SM)*. Tokyo: SM Shinjinkai, 1972.

Van den Ing, Eric and Schaap, Robert. *Beauty and Violence, Japanese prints by Yoshitoshi* (In English). The Netherlands: Society for Japanese Arts, 1992.

Watanabe Yasuji. *Akai Hana—Haruki Yukimura sessions* (In French/English/Japanese). France: Le Lezard Noir, 2008.

Weisser, Thomas and Yuko. *Japanese Cinema Encyclopedia, The Sex Films* (In English). Miami: Vital Books, 1998.

Wiseman, Jay. *Erotic Bondage Handbook* (In English). Emeryville: Greenery Press, 2000.

Yamaguchi, Hiro (ed.), Itoh Seiyu. *Itoh Seiyu's Secret Notebook*. Tokyo: Futami Books, 2002.

Yamamoto, Takato. *Allure of Pharmakon*. Tokyo: Kawade Shobo Shinsha/Editions Treville, 2004.

Yamamoto, Takato. *Altar of Narcissus*. Tokyo: Kawade Shobo Shinsha/Editions Trovillo, 2002.

Yamamoto, Takato. *Divertimento for a Martyr*. Tokyo: Kawade Shobo Shinsha/Editions Treville, 2006.

Yamamoto, Takato. *Hiiro no Maniera (Scarlet Maniera)*. Tokyo: Kawade Shobo Shinsha/Editions Treville, 1998.

Yang, Jwing-Ming. *Ancient Chinese Weapons: A Martial Artist's Guide* (In English). Boston: YMAA Publication Center, 1999.

Yukimura, Haruki. *Shibari—1, 2, 3 (photos by: Oka Katumi, Higure Keisuke and Watanabe Tatsumi)*. Tokyo: Sunset Publishing, 1998.

Yukimura, Haruki. *Trans Body Bondage (photos by Takahashi Junko)*. Tokyo: Wailea Publishing, 1998.

In addition to the above volumes the author owns either complete runs or numerous issues of the following historical periodicals which have been exhaustively consulted in the writing of this book: Abu Hunter, Fuzoku Kitan , Kitan Club, Mania Club, Nureki/Kinbiken magazine, SM Club, SM Collector, SM Fan, SM Graffiti, SM King, SM Kitan, SM Maniac, SM Secret Novel, SM Select, SM Sniper, SM Spirit, Uramado, Yomikiri Romance Nude Fuzoku.

Index

194